AF478140

European Union Lobbying

European Union Lobbying

Changes in the Arena

Edited by
Robin Pedler

palgrave in association with the European
Centre for Public Affairs

First published 2002 by
PALGRAVE
Houndmills, Basingstoke, Hampshire RG21 6XS and
175 Fifth Avenue, New York, N.Y. 10010
Companies and representatives throughout the world

PALGRAVE is the new global academic imprint of
St. Martin's Press LLC Scholarly and Reference Division and
Palgrave Publishers Ltd (formerly Macmillan Press Ltd).

ISBN 0–333–97152–3

This book is printed on paper suitable for recycling and
made from fully managed and sustained forest sources.

Cataloguing in Publication Data

A catalogue record for this book is available
from the British Library.

A catalogue record for this book is available
from the Library of Congress.

10   9   8   7   6   5   4   3   2   1
11   10   09   08   07   06   05   04   03   02

Printed and bound in Great Britain by
Antony Rowe Ltd, Chippenham, Wiltshire

Contents

List of Tables

List of Figures

Notes on the Contributors

Chris Boyd is Senior Vice-President, Environment and Public Affairs at Lafarge. He is an economist. Before moving to his present role, he was a senior official in the European Commission, both in commissioners' cabinets and in several DGs, including the Environment Directorate General. He teaches Public Affairs at the European Centre for Public Affairs, Brussels (ECPAB).

Asunción Caparrós is Manager of European Affairs in the Brussels office of ABN Amro. She is responsible for e-commerce, conduct of business rules for investment services, prospectus, investment funds and tax legislation among other issues. Before joining ABN Amro Bank, she worked in the European Commission as legal adviser in public procurement and EU citizens' rights and in the Federation of European Direct Marketing as Director of EU Affairs.

Sonia Casino-Diaz is Practice Area Manager in Weber, Shandwick, Adamson in Brussels, where she acts as Head of the Environment and Industry Practice Area. She is an environmental lawyer by training and has worked as a lawyer in Spain. Sonia specialises in European environment policy and corporate social responsibility, and part of her work involves helping to establish partnerships between companies and civil society.

Andrej Drapal is partner in Pristop Communications, leader of public affairs practice in Pristop and president of the Lobby Association within the Public Relations Society of Slovenia. He led and is leading lobby, PA and PR campaigns for various Slovene and international companies in Slovenia. He is a regular contributor on PA and related topics in Slovene general and professional media.

Christopher Fisher is Consultant to the Eurogroup for Animal Welfare. He has been an active campaigner in the voluntary sector for more than ten years, involved mainly with animal rights organizations. He has gained experience at every level – local, regional, national and international – and worked voluntarily, academically and professionally within the sector. He is an experienced lobbyist, having worked extensively in Brussels, Strasbourg and the UK, lobbying to Ministerial and Commissioner level.

Justin Greenwood is Jean Monnet, and University Professor of European Public Policy at the Robert Gordon University, Aberdeen. He is the author/editor/co-editor of seven books on interest representation in the EU, and edits the only EU studies journal published in the USA, *Current Politics and Economics of Europe*. He is a member of the Research Board of the European Centre for Public Affairs; an Advisory Board of the Brussels-based United Business Institute; and has presented and written widely for practitioner audiences interested in EU associations. His research work on EU interest intermediation has been funded, *inter alia*, by the European Commission, the European Community/Union, the British Academy, the Carnegie Foundation, and by over 20 firms and business associations.

Tomaž Ilešič (MA, LLB) is currently preparing for his bar exam as a stagiare at the High Court of Ljubljana. His previous post as a counsellor in the Governmental Office of Legislation Department of European and Comparative Law dealt with approximation of laws and general Slovenian pre-accession strategy from the legal point of view. He has written numerous articles on Europe Agreements and the association status of the Republic of Slovenia, and is the co-author of the leading handbook on EU Law which is to be published in the Slovene language in September 2001.

Stuart Kewley is Director of the Postgraduate Diploma Course in European Studies, Oxford University. His research interests include: the evolution of the political and economic relationship between the European Union and Japan and the political and economic development of the European Union. He was previously Head Teacher at the Pioneer Language School, Fujinomiya-Shi, Shizuoka-Ken, Japan, and has since held a series of teaching posts at Cambridge and Oxford Universities. He writes and lectures on Japanese society and business and Japan–EU relations.

Tony Long is Director of the WWF European Policy Office and Visiting Professor at the College of Europe, Bruges. He was previously a consultant with WWF United Kingdom and assistant director of the Council for the Protection of Rural England (CPRE). He was formerly a Harkness Fellow of the Commonwealth Fund of New York and a Congressional Fellow of the American Political Science Association working in the United States Congress and State Legislature of New Mexico. He is a member of the Editorial Advisory Board of the *Journal of European Public Policy*.

Wim Mijs is Vice-President of ABN Amro's EU Liaison Office in Brussels. He has worked for the International Court of Arbitration at the Peace Palace in The Hague during which time he co-published a book on new developments in international arbitration.

Julian Oliver is Director-General of the International Express Carriers Conference and Chief Executive of The European Policy Centre, the leading

Brussels think-tank. He has held a number of senior representative posts in Brussels and is past Chairman of the American Chamber of Commerce, EU Committee. He teaches and is course director for ECPAB.

Robin Pedler is an Associate Fellow of Templeton, the college of Oxford University that specialises in Management Studies. He is also Academic Director of the European Centre for Public Affairs, Brussels. He has had a varied career in international management, culminating as Director, External Relations Europe, with Mars. He has lived and worked in many countries, from Hong Kong to Spain, and is fluent and works in English, Spanish and French and also speaks German and Dutch. He works with both industrial managers and civil servants and has conducted 'EU Presidency' training with both Finland and Sweden and 'pre-accession' training with the countries of central Europe. He is a consultant on international trade issues and is active in UK and European food industry federations.

Irena Peterlin (LLB) is adviser to the Executive Board of Directors at Slovenian Steelworks, where she is responsible for legal and corporate affairs. She was a member of the legal team of the Commission's anti-dumping proceeding, and was in charge of managing communications and communication policy. Currently she works as a consultant to management on relations with different audiences and on the implementation of public relations strategies. She is a member of the International Association of Bussiness Communicators.

Susan Pointer is Head of EU Policy in the Confederation of British Industry (CBI)'s Brussels office, and also teaches at the ECPAB. Previously she worked as Parliamentary Adviser to Dr Caroline Jackson, MEP, in the European Parliament, and has also worked as a Parliamentary Adviser in the House of Commons.

Heikki Rautvuori is the Managing Director and senior EU consultant of EU-Info Finland Ltd. He entered the Finnish diplomatic service in 1973. After postings in France, Australia and Bulgaria he returned in 1981 to the Ministry for Foreign Affairs as First Secretary in the Department for Foreign Trade. He left the Ministry in 1985 after being nominated as Assistant Director of Foreign Trade in the Central Chamber of Commerce. He began his EU-expert tasks in 1993 when Finland started to negotiate for the membership and established one of the first private EU-consultancies in Finland in the beginning of 1994.

Liam Salter is Climate and Development Co-ordinator for the Climate Change Campaign, WWF. He joined WWF in July 1999 with the responsibility of extending the regional spread of the Campaign's work, particularly focusing on Asia. His work areas include providing international support to WWF offices working on climate issues within the region and promoting the uptake of clean energy technologies through work with governments and the private sector. Prior to joining WWF, he was Energy Specialist for Climate Network Europe, representing nearly 80 European environmental groups in Brussels. He worked extensively on the promotion of renewable energy technologies and energy efficiency within the EU, collaborating with a wide variety of groups from trade unions to heavy industry. He was previously employed as an independent consultant on energy and the environment, working on issues as diverse as power-sector planning in northern Australia and photovoltaic market development in rural Kenya.

Stephan Singer is Head of the European Climate and Energy Policy Unit at WWF, where he has close involvement in the international negotiations of the UN climate treaty and the Kyoto protocol. He also is involved with the campaigns on domestic and EU-wide clean energy policies, renewables, energy efficiency technologies and green electricity. He was previously a journalist and a campaigner for a grassroots NGO (Robin Wood) in Germany and has also worked at the German ODA agency GTZ (Society for Technical Cooperation) at the International Crops Research Institute for the Semi-Arid Tropics (IRISAT) in Hyderabad, India. While acting as a consultant he has undertaken field projects and research on various aspects of soil carbon dynamics in soils.

Ineke van der Storm is Director of ECONcept, a socially and environmentally engaged consultancy for strategies in economic and ecological development. She has long-term experience in politics both locally and regionally, and is familiar with the political culture and environment at city and province level. She has experience of the advisory work in Brussels for the Committee of the Regions. Her interests include East–West-cooperation between CEEC and EU steel regions; the balance between local and global economies, and partnerships between public and private players.

Laurentien van Oranje-Nassau is Chair of the European Corporate Practice, Weber Shandwick Worldwide. She has rich experience of representing interests in the EU, both as a corporate manager and as a consultant in strategic communications. She teaches at ECPAB.

Dejan Vercíc is a partner in Pristop, the leading political consultancy in Ljubljana, Slovenia.

Introduction
Changes in the Lobbying Arena: Real-life Cases

The arena

The arena is the space in which a lobbying campaign is played out.[1] It is defined by the institutions that the campaign seeks to influence, their relative importance and their decision-making process. It is crowded by numerous 'players'. Some are commercial, some may be organized labour. Many may be 'issue groups' or NGOs. 'Institutions', of course, seek to influence each other. In the EU context these may include member-state governments pursuing their own political agendas, or third-country governments that need to influence Europe. They all share the arena for any given issue because they all want to ensure that their views and interests contribute to the solution adopted.

Players may form alliances to promote their interests for all or part of the issue. They may equally seek very hard to frustrate the efforts of individuals or groups who promote conflicting interests. The art and science of constructing a successful campaign lies in maximizing the alliances that promote the player's views and minimizing or forestalling those that come from the opposing side. For every powerful lobby there is an equal and opposite lobby.

The cases we shall describe show a series of the most important issues for business in the EU, and through them we analyse the lobbying campaigns of different 'players': companies, NGOs, governments and formal and informal alliances. Figure I.1 shows the complex arena represented by the institutions and interests who 'play' in the case 'Chiquita Declares War and Wins'. The case will demonstrate how their interests are fully or partially linked and then played out.

In the seven years since the fieldwork for our last published series of case studies (Pedler and van Schendelen, 1994)[2] there have been substantial changes in the Brussels arena. The balance of power between the EU institutions has shifted, resulting in *de facto* changes in the decision-making process. New issues have emerged to concern both business and issue groups, notably e-commerce, environment and the greatly increased flow of EU funds into regional and structural policies.

Chiquita Declares War – the Arena

Players/issues	'Free Access'	'Protect ACP/EU'	Reference Period	First come/serve	Licence System	Peons' rights	'Fair Trade'
WTO	(MFN)	Waiver?	?	?	N		
Chiquita	?	Y	Y	N		N	
Dole	Y	Y		Y		Y(SA8000)	Y
Del Monte	Y			?		N	
Noboa	Y			Y		N	
Fyffes		Y	Y				?
Geest/Wibdeco		Y	Y				Y
Co. Fruitiere (Afrique)		Y	?				?
Pomona (Antilles)		Y		Y			N
Commission		Y		Y	Y		
Parliament		Y		Y			Y
D NL Dk S SF A B	Y			Y			
F E P Ire		Y		Y			
UK		Y		N			
USA	Y		?	Y (C tariff)			
Windward Is		Y	Y				
Africa, D'O		Y	Y				
NGOs		Y				Y	Y

Figure I.1   The Arena: Bananas example

Changes in the arena

The fieldwork for these case studies demonstrates the effect of two fundamental changes in the treaties that govern the EU: Maastricht (effective
November 1993) and Amsterdam (effective May 1999). Their implementation, following ratification by the member states, means that our first series
of cases (1992–93; *ibid.*) predates either of them while this collection
includes both.

It has been widely argued that the Single Market programme, from the
mid-1980s to the early 1990s, marked the high point of the Commission's
power and influence. The Treaty of Maastricht is then held to mark the start
of a decline, with influence increasingly taken by the member states, acting
together in the Council of Ministers and setting the EU agenda at 'summits'
of the European Council. Certainly, the Commission's reputation and influence was severely damaged by the crisis it suffered during 1999 and the
resulting mass resignation of commissioners.

These cases show, however, that on issues that affect the daily life of the
citizens of the EU and the fortunes of European companies, the Commission
remains both the initiator of policies and the key player in developing and
implementing them as they have practical effect. This is particularly clear in
Safe Harbor, Chapter 1. As the author states, at the start of industry's action,
'The EU authorities, in particular the Commission and those Member States

who had operational domestic laws, were determined not to see their hard-fought new large single market eroded or corrupted by a "black hole" in the US.' He goes on to show how the Commission then used the comitology system to entrench its position.

The primacy of the Commission as the regulating institution further emerges in Chapter 2, Consumer Confidence in e-Commerce, where the limited results achieved by the CBI were due to their focus on getting other institutions to react to and modify the Commission.

It is also significant that our cases include three that illustrate environmental issues: Lafarge and Global Warming; WWF: European and Global Climate Policy; and Clean Air and Car Emissions. In each case, the Commission is a key player and, as Chris Boyd author of Lafarge and Global Warming comments, the Commission has what approaches a clear field of action, since the member states had not addressed environmental problems to any extent individually. Further, as the implications of both cross-border pollution and global climate change became apparent, they were very happy to share sovereignty via the EU institutions to address them. (The comments were based on Chris Boyd's experience as an official of Directorate General Environment.)

The second institutional development that is usually noted is the increased power of the European Parliament, especially as it is exercised through the co-decision procedure. Many of the cases confirm that lobbying campaigns have adapted to reflect this power shift. Clean Air and Car Emissions examines in detail the interplay between Parliament and the Council of Ministers at the final stage of co-decision: conciliation. It is a good example of how the informal but extremely effective process of the trialogue operates.

Safe Harbor gives a practical example of how the Parliament may review comitology decisions since the agreement reached during the Amsterdam process (although in this case Parliament's views did not prevail). This is reported to be the first example of the review process in action.

Players in the arena often have more than one role. The cases show very interestingly the member states acting both as participants in Council of Ministers decisions and then in the role of implementing those decisions in their own countries. This latter phase may lead to actions in the European Court of Justice, either where one member state cites its fellows in the Council of Ministers for what it sees as an erroneous decision (for example Germany in Chiquita Declares War and Wins, Chapter 10), or where the Commission cites member states for failure to enact (Safe Harbor, Chapter 1).

Civil society

Players who have clearly gained influence since the first case studies are the issue groups – NGOs, often known collectively as civil society. Their campaigns are analysed in all the cases. Two of the cases – WWF and Climate

Policy, Chapter 4, and Getting Animal Welfare onto the WTO Agenda, Chapter 8 – are written from the point of view of the NGOs concerned.

Another group within civil society, as defined broadly, whose interests are related to but different from those of the member states and who have increasing access to EU funds are the regions. *CASTer*, Chapter 11, is written from that standpoint.

Changes in the global arena

While the focus is on cases 'played out' in the EU, they do not ignore the real situation that the EU is itself a very significant player in the global arena and that its institutions and the organizations that interact with them are subject to global forces. Five of the cases describe international trade issues. All of these show that the policies and decisions of the World Trade Organization (WTO) are key drivers of EU policy. This is the result of very significant changes since the last series of case studies. The WTO itself was established at Marrakech in April 1995, and all the member countries, including the EU, undertook to abide by the decisions of panels established under the new WTO dispute-resolution procedure. This was a very significant departure from the previous GATT system, under which it had been effectively possible for countries to ignore unfavourable decisions.

The Marrakech agreement also extended the remit of the WTO to cover significant new areas: Agriculture, Services and Trade in Intellectual Property – TRIPS. All of these 'new areas' impinge on EU policy and are reflected in the trade cases presented.

A separate 'global' development is the move towards international agreements, usually in the forum of the United Nations (UN) to take action to protect the environment and combat the process of global warming. These debates are reflected by cases from both company and NGO standpoints.

Businesses are increasingly global, and here one of the cases specifically examines Japanese Lobbying in the EU, Chapter 9, while three concern the differences and the potential areas of cooperation between companies that do business on both sides of the Atlantic.

The practice of public affairs

Public affairs may be defined as the management skill that internalizes the effects of the environment in which an organization operates and externalizes actions to influence that environment. The cases make clear that public affairs has become a more professional exercise, as it is practiced both by commercial interests and NGOs. One striking manifestation of this professionalism is the growing and increasingly effective role of women in public affairs. Safe Harbor, Chapter 1, particularly illustrates this development. A further practical example is that four out of these 14 cases are written or co-written by the women responsible for executing the campaigns. In the 1994 collection, we had no women authors.

The value of case studies

A good case study encapsulates what happens in a real-life situation. It also permits conclusions to be drawn that are generally applicable. In this book the reader may draw his or her own conclusions from the cases, while the final chapter will synthesise their findings and propose paradigms for application.

Fourteen cases is a large enough collection to enable us to compare approaches and results and draw conclusions. So far as possible, their selection has been made to reflect the real world of the EU, heavily focused as it is on events in Brussels. The key criteria applied in their selection were:

- the knowledge and experience of the authors;
- the quality of their writing; and
- their willingness to take part and to persuade their 'hero organizations' to contribute.

In this field, as in all case writing, there is a challenge in defining 'what is a case'? When does action on a particular issue begin and when is it complete enough to quantify the results and draw conclusions? The challenge is especially acute in defining public affairs cases. One of the internal problems for public affairs managers is that their own time scale tends to be much more extended than that of their colleagues or the institution where they work. This is not because they are dilatory, but more because issues develop over long periods, and even when they enter the arena of the EU's formal policy-making there is typically a five-year period between the commencement of policy-drafting in the Commission and the implementation of the final Directive in the member states.

When the author was writing his first banana case in 1993, one potentially valuable and generally well-disposed contributor declined to be interviewed on the grounds that 'You can't write a case because it's not over yet'. In one sense Chiquita Declares War and Wins, Chapter 10, in this volume shows how right he was. On the other hand, the first case was written and has proved a valuable and illustrative teaching example in many parts of the world. 'Bananas' may still not be finally settled, but I have every confidence that the current case will prove equally valuable.

There are two 'short' cases in this book. Slovenia and the EU: An Anti-Dumping Case, Chapter 7, was in a sense bound to be short, since the procedure for anti-dumping must be followed in a defined time period and in this case was defeated. Promoting Consumer Confidence in e-Commerce: The Brussels Regulation, Chapter 2, shows industry reacting rapidly to address a potentially serious problem posed by the language in a revised regulation, but is quite likely to prove one decisive skirmish in a 20-year war.

Slovenia and the EU is, however, an example of a 'completed' campaign, as is Safe Harbor. The other cases are all clearly defined as distinct phases in ongoing and in most cases extended campaigns.

I have set out to build a representative collection, building on my own networks, my teaching contacts in Oxford, Brussels and Bled and on recommendations received through these contacts. But it must be clear that selection was not entirely 'random'. There is a built-in prejudice in that it is much easier to persuade authors to describe cases that they consider have been 'successful'. An exception to this general rule may be found in Electricity Liberalization, Chapter 13, by Justin Greenwood. The commercial heroes are active, but have not (at least yet) secured significant influence or achieved their objectives. The authors of Consumer Confidence in e-Commerce, Chapter 2, and of Getting Animal Welfare onto the WTO Agenda, Chapter 8, in their own conclusions, rate their success as limited.

I have tried to select cases that represent both commercial and non-commercial approaches. I have also tried to spread them so that we may see the differences in various national approaches. I am delighted that we have Spanish, Slovenian, Finnish, Irish and German authors/co-authors, and that one case concerns a major French company. The largest national group, as in the previous collection, remains English and there are also several Dutch authors. This time, however, we no longer have an Anglo-Dutch majority. This clearly reflects a real change in the Brussels scene. It remains, however, hotly debated how far the EU lobbying scene is still dominated by Anglo-Dutch

Table I.1   The case framework

Layout of a case chapter

- Introduction of the organization and the 'policy playing field':

  Stakeholders
  Competitors
  Issue groups
  Size of the sector: how much are we playing for?

- The case

  Define the issue
  The lead player's objectives
  What was your 'homework'?
  Alliances for and against: *ad hoc* or organized in federations etc?
  Institutional implications: when and where was contact made?
  'Civil society' – were the NGOs allies or enemies?
  Media coverage and public interest
  The story: what happened?

- Conclusions and lessons

  Did the lead player achieve all their objectives?
  Yes or no – why?
  Lessons for the future

---

players. Certainly Daniel Guéguen, a French lobbyist, maintains in a recent article that activity is heavily 'Anglo-Saxon' (Guéguen, 2000).[3] I am particularly pleased to have been able to include two cases of 'applicant country lobbying'. I believe this to be key to successful accession.

Two of the cases are written by the company managers responsible, four by political consultants and lawyers who have handled the issue, two by officials of the federations active in Brussels, two by NGOs, one by another (regional) voluntary group and four by academics specialized in the area. To encourage practical comparison between the cases and to make each of them easier to follow, all the authors have used a common model as shown in Table I.1.

Issues and heroes

Comparison between this and the previous volume of case studies (Pedler and van Schendelen, 1994, *op. cit.*) shows clear trends in the issues that concern organizations seriously enough for them to campaign and seek to influence the result. They are grouped around a series of issues, all of which show the different approaches taken by different 'players'.

e-Europe

There are two cases that address this issue; both generated by the pressures that arise when the fast-moving world of 'new business' impacts on the duty that institutions and member states have to protect consumer interests. The authorities sometimes fulfil their duty in apparently pedestrian ways. One of our cases Promoting Consumer Confidence in e-Commerce, Chapter 2, remains in the classic regulatory field and shows the importance of lobbying all the EU institutions and the member state governments. The other case, Safe Harbor, Chapter 1, explores the rapidly developing world of self-regulation and co-regulation.

In the previous collection (Wacker in Pedler and van Schendelen, 1994, *op. cit.*) we had no cases that addressed e-commerce directly. We did have one IT case, ECIS and Competitive Softwar(e) that described what was, according to the author, 'the most heavily lobbied issue up to that time'.

This area shows how, as 'new business' develops, Public Affairs is at the cutting-edge of creating the environment in which it can flourish and grow.

Environment

Again, there are three issues concerned with legislation and conventions that seek to improve the environment and address the problem of climate change. Lafarge and Global Warming, Chapter 3; Climate Change: WWF and the Clean Development Mechanism, Chapter 4; and Clean Air and Car Emissions, Chapter 5. Each of the three shows alliances of NGOs as powerful players in the process; one is written from the NGO's standpoint, the other two explore the approaches of one large company and two powerful industry federations.

In comparing the two collections of case studies, 'environment' is a new issue for lobbyists.

Applicant country cases

At the time of writing (mid-2001) the process of negotiating the accession of a further 12–13 countries to the EU is entering its most difficult phase. While most of the 31 'Chapters' that are necessary to ensure that new members adapt to the 'acquis communautaire' are now completed and closed, there remain issues that are difficult for both sides, which may need to be resolved by derogations. At this stage it is very interesting to consider what took place at a similar phase in the last enlargement negotiations. EU Accession and the Acquis: Saving Nordic Monopolies, Chapter 6, examines how Finland, Norway and Sweden pursued their negotiations at this phase and how they succeeded.

The process of accession effectively includes the applicant countries in the single market, but until they join they are still third parties. This engenders trade tensions in sensitive industries as Slovenia and the EU: anti-Dumping Case, Chapter 7, illustrates vividly. Slovenia and the EU is doubly interesting because it demonstrates so clearly how the players in candidate countries must, and even more importantly can, deploy their lobbying skills to influence EU policy.

Global and regional issues

Three of the cases show Public Affairs addressing international trade in two distinct ways. Chapter 8, Getting Animal Welfare onto the World Trade Agenda, and Chapter 9, Japanese Lobbying in Europe, seek to profit by the agenda-setting opportunity of multilateral trade negotiations. Considering the effect that NGOs produced in Seattle it is especially interesting that Animal Welfare is written from the NGO's point of view. Japanese Lobbying is significant because 80 per cent of international trade is now conducted by foreign direct investment, rather than movement of goods and services across borders.[4]

In Chapter 10, Chiquita Declares War and Wins: Bananas – Trans-Atlantic Trade Dispute goes on to examines the intense lobbying employed in pursuing and resolving disputes following WTO procedures. It also shows the direct effect of decisions by dispute panels on EU policies.

The single market and social policy

In 1992–93, lobbying's dominant driver was the Internal Market programme and its attendant regulations and liberalization, then at its declared climax. As the new cases show, however, the process was far from complete and major issues remain to be addressed. Two cases show one multinational bank and a series of industry federations lobbying to develop and conclude the Single Market – Chapter 12, Making the Single Market in Financial Services a Reality and Chapter 13, Electricity Liberalization.

The Single Market programme of 1986–92 (278 Directives) ran in parallel with the Social Charter programme (50 Directives), and in the first series this provoked three cases of lobbying action. Since then, there has been less legislative action on Social Policy and this is reflected as there are no cases presented here.

Corporate social responsibility

The final case in the new collection reflects that the 'domain' of the Public Affairs manager covers not only lobbying and government affairs, but also and increasingly corporate social responsibility.

The 'heroes' of these cases (Tables I.2 and I.3) are clearly determined largely by the issues. As will be seen in the cases, in every one, effective lobbying depended on the building of alliances, often *ad hoc*. It appears from the 'heroes' that business maintains its reliance on formal groupings such as federations, which certainly remain numerous in Brussels (690 listed in the European Public Affairs Directory).[5]

The arena develops

These cases present a graphic and living sample of issues of concern at the start of the third millennium, how the 'players' are organizing to address them and how effective their efforts prove. They should not be taken as an immutable definition of the arena. Firstly, because the arena is of its essence defined by each issue as the players address it, and secondly because changes

Table I.2 What are the issues for our case heroes?

	e-Commerce	Enviro Policy	Applicant Countries	Global/ Regional	Single Market	Corporate Soc. Resp.	Social Policy	Other
1994–14	(1 IT)	0	0	3	5	0	2	3
2002–14	2	3	2	4	2	1	0	0

Note: 1994 refers to our previous study (Pedler and van Schendelen, 1994), and 2002 to this volume.

Table I.3 Who are the heroes?

	Companies	Trade feds. Alliances	NGOs	Countries/ Regions	Trades Unions	CSR Group
1994–14	5	5	2	0	2	0
2002–14	4	5	2	2	0	1

Note: See Table I.2.

in the balance of power and influence, in the EU and globally, will create new issues as they change its boundaries and shape.

Alert and effective organizations will already be preparing their campaigns on a new range of issues and will produce another generation of cases.

Notes

1. MPCM van Schendelen (2002) *Machiavelli in Brussels: The Art of EU Lobbying*, not published.
2. R.H. Pedler and MPCM van Schendelen (eds) (1994) *Lobbying the European Union – Companies, Trade Associations and Issue Groups*. Aldershot: Dartmouth.
3. D. Guéguen and B. Roussef (2000), article in *Public Affairs Newsletter*, December.
4. A. Rugman (2000) *The End of Globalisation*. London: Random House.
5. *European Public Affairs Directory 2001*. Brussels: Landmarks.

Part I
E-Europe Cases

1
Safe Harbor:
An Alternative Regulatory Model

Julian Oliver

> Before Safe Harbor, Europeans giving personal data to a U.S. company had little hope of privacy protection. If the company undertakes to abide by Safe Harbor, it's offering a halfway decent level of privacy, plus mechanisms for redress. That mechanism is untested but at least it exists in theory.
>
> (Jason Catlett, privacy advocate, in *Wired News*, 2 November 2000, the day after the Safe Harbor opened officially)

Introduction

This is a case study on the issues surrounding the implementation of a directive. It provides insights into some of the complexities of comitology, international negotiations, alliances, lobbying of the European parliament and the US authorities. It also provides insights into agenda-setting, Trans-Atlantic inter-agency negotiations and countervailing lobbying strategies. Finally, it features the luck that is often an essential, if unpredictable, element in a successful lobbying campaign.

The main stakeholders and the policy playing field

The issue of transfers of personal data to countries outside the European Union (and the EEA) affects many citizens and businesses, knowingly or not.[1] The issue is particularly relevant to civil liberties and to people and organizations involved in travel, tourism, journalism, research and financial services, but also and increasingly relevant to electronic commerce. Not only European companies are affected. All companies trading with or which have establishments or subsidiaries in the EU, or which conduct sales or other operations (e.g. market research) in writing, by phone or fax and through web sites accessible from within the EU, are subject to the European Union data protection directives.

No sooner had the EU adopted its general directive on data protection in October 1995 than lobbying began on one of its vital clauses. How to interpret and implement the clauses relating to the transfer of personal data to third countries became a five-year saga. Final agreement was reached in July 2000 and the Safe Harbor opened officially on 1 November 2000.

Talks between the EU and US authorities began in 1996 but started at a desultory pace. The EU authorities saw no need to do much; the EU had adopted its legislation and it was up to third countries to comply. There were essentially three potential solutions:

1. the contractual route, whereby organizations wishing to transfer data establish a contract between themselves and the data subject,
2. the legislative route, whereby the third country demonstrates that its domestic legislation provided 'adequate protection', and
3. the self-regulatory route.

Most companies regarded the first route as complex and potentially very expensive and preferred the self-regulatory route.

The US government authorities were not interested in introducing new federal legislation, which was their only option on their own. Companies on both sides of the Atlantic were increasingly concerned at the lack of urgency; and businesses that relied on the daily transfer of personal data in the rapidly growing electronic information age were concerned. The EU directive granted authority to the national data protection registrars to ban the export of data to third countries that did not have 'adequate' protection. These powers would come into force by October 1998 at the latest, and it was not inconceivable that an activist data protection authority could anticipate this date. Thus many companies and other organizations that transfer data on a regular basis saw a 'sword of Damocles' hanging over their futures.

During 1996 and early 1997 a series of representations was made to both the EU and the US authorities on the issue of transfers to third countries. In July 1997, a coalition of eight European-based trade associations signed a position paper on the Implementation of the EU Data Protection Directive.[2] Essentially, this paper argued for a dialogue with the Commission to determine whether self-regulation or, failing that, suitable contract language could be developed to avoid a ban on data exports. The EU Committee of the American Chamber of Commerce in Belgium (the EU Committee) was an interested party from early on. In effect, the EU Committee had been active continuously since 1991 throughout the negotiations of the EU's data protection directive. Another early activist on data protection issues was the Direct Marketing industry through its various configurations: EDMA, EAT, FEDIM and, latterly, the Federation of European Direct Marketing (FEDMA).

The EU Committee organized a seminar in November 1997 entitled 'The Impact of Data Protection on Global Trade', during which several industry groups, including UNICE (the European Employers Confederation) expressed their concerns about the potential risks of not being able to export data to third countries. Individual companies who were or are active include ABN-AMRO Bank, American Express, Bell Atlantic, Bertelsmann, Daimler-Chrysler, EDS, FedEx, Hewlett Packard, IBM, Intel, NCR, Reed Elsevier, Siemens and many others. The Commission now responded with a robust explanation of their intentions and an invitation to work with the private sector to achieve a structured approach. It was not yet clear whether the Commission was willing to consider the self-regulation route but at least they were now more willing to talk.

The transfer of personal data is also of considerable interest to non-governmental organizations (NGOs) and civil rights and liberties groups. Any NGO with cross-border marketing, membership or fund-raising ambitions is as equally liable as are businesses.

EU-based charities and fund-raising foundations were active in lobbying for a liberal and open general directive in the period up to 1995. They continued to express an interest in transfers but it was not an issue of overriding importance to them. There is only limited evidence of their active participation in the debate over the export of data to third countries until the European Parliament and the US Congress were about to approve the Safe Harbor provisions in 1999/2000.

Each of the EU member states are also involved since under the directive, Control of Data Exports, authority is delegated to the 15 national data protection Commissioners. Among these, Stefano Rodota, for Italy, is one of the three 'fathers' of the original Council of Europe Data Protection Convention of 1981, from which the EU directive directly descends.

Throughout the 1990s, and to date, the European Commission is the most consistently active player. The European Parliament grew in stature during the same decade (the rapporteur in the early 1990s, Geoff Hoon, is currently UK Secretary of Defence) and was influential in introducing the 'adequate protection' in place of 'equivalent protection', an even tougher hurdle.

Activity by the member states has been sporadic. Even at the time of writing, winter 2000/2001, four member states are subject to legal action by the Commission for failure to fully implement the directive within the deadline of 28 October 1998. On the other hand, those with prior domestic legislation are still active players nationally: Sweden, The Netherlands, France, Germany and the UK.

The competition

The main competition came from the United States. There was also some political opposition from the European Parliament to the final details of the Safe Harbor agreement reached by the Commission and the Department of Commerce (DoC). Among European business and NGO circles there was remarkably little opposition.

There are a very few organizations that advocate a complete free-for-all in the cross-border transfer of personal data. These are mainly US free-marketeers and defenders of journalistic freedoms. To begin with at least, there were quite a few people in the US Congress and US business who objected to the apparent extraterritorial jurisdiction which they felt the EU was trying to exert. The main US interlocutor is the Department of Commerce. The DoC has been actively involved since 1997, and is the source of the 'Safe Harbor' name and concept.

The Safe Harbor case

The issue in brief: co-regulation in the EU versus self-regulation in the USA

European countries have a long tradition of protecting personal privacy; there is said, for example, to be a Swedish law dating from 1776. In the USA, by contrast, there is no general federal law on privacy, as data protection is more commonly known in America.

In modern times the collection, manipulation, storage, use and disclosure – in short the *processing* – of personal data has been regulated in several European countries for many years. Somewhat misleadingly, this type of regulation has come to be called 'data protection' (German: *Datenschutz*; French: *protection des données*), rather than data restriction.

International guidelines, conventions and the 'godfathers' of the EU directive

OECD adopted guidelines in 1980 and the Council of Europe adopted a convention on data protection in 1981. Among the 'godfathers' of the Council convention were three important Europeans. Stefano Rodota, now the Italian Data Protection Commissioner; Professor Simitis, a Greek-born citizen and victim of the Greek military junta, who became the Data Registrar of the state of Hesse in Germany and is now a Professor in Frankfurt; and a Swede, Mr Friser. While data protection started as an issue dominated by men, this saga would only be concluded by the intervention and sustained efforts provided by several determined women. A slow fuse had been lit.

Cross-border restrictions

In general, national data protection laws commonly impose severe restrictions on the transfer of personal data across borders. As a result of increasing conflicts between various national laws of the EU member states it became clear that there was a need for a Europe-wide directive. It was also realized, some years after the famous 1985 Commission White Paper (that included a list of some 285 pieces of legislation thought necessary to complete the single market) that there would need to be a single market for personal data. Consequently, a European Directive was proposed in 1991.

The EU directive

This directive was adopted in 1995 after substantial lobbying by, *inter alia*, a loose coalition of AmCham, FEDMA, the IT industry, charities/foundations and some political parties (who were beginning to engage in cross-border fund-raising and marketing). This framework directive was due to be implemented into domestic legislation by all 15 member states within three years, by 25 October 1998.

The directive provided for a common set of rules about the collection, processing, storage and disclosure of personal data within the EU (and the European Economic Area, which includes Norway). In addition, the directive also included articles dealing with the transfer of data to third countries. It was these that became the subject of heated Trans-Atlantic debate. The fuse began to glow.

With the benefits of hindsight, it is now clear that Articles 25 and 26 (reproduced as Annex I) were poorly drafted. The first paragraph of Article 25 is reasonably straightforward; it essentially states that personal data can only be exported to third countries that provide 'an adequate level of protection'. The inclusion of the word 'adequate' was inserted as a result of lobbying to exclude the term 'equivalent' from the original Commission proposal, which certainly would have prevented most transfers from Europe. From there on it is now clear that the authors were uncertain about how to assess this 'adequacy' principle. The whole of Article 26 is devoted to exceptions to this principle and most of the rest of Article 25 describes how the Commission was then planning to assess the 'adequacy' test. And even then Commission officials have argued that a strict interpretation of Article 26 can provide conditions where Article 25 need not apply.

Persistent lobbying by businesses

Businesses were quick to raise their concerns about the uncertainty as to how the adequacy test would be applied within the EU. As often in European affairs, there were doubts about how the different member states would interpret the directive and especially the adequacy provision. The University of Edinburgh won a tender to advise the Commission on a methodology to assess the adequacy of third countries. However, their report published in September 1998 raised almost as many questions as it answered. It pointed out that there was no clear priority among the criteria in Articles 25 and 26; the difficulty of dealing with different jurisdictions within federal states such as the USA, Canada and Australia. Finally, they raised the issue of cultural and institutional non-equivalence. 'Privacy' may mean something very different in different cultures and countries. These were all to prove useful to companies arguing against a strict test of 'adequacy' in respect of the United States. Meanwhile, in Europe, there was heated talk about regulatory arbitrage; for example, moving all data processing operations to the most liberal and/or efficient country within the EU in order to avoid a mischievous or overly bureaucratic regime.

In June 1997, the Article 29 Working Party had published its first paper on how organizations could comply with the transfer provisions. This listed a variety of options including contractual clauses and a possible 'white list' of approved countries. This was in response to a growing lobby from many individual companies and industry associations but did not do much to satisfy businesses, which were now concerned about the potential costs of compliance. In July 1997 a coalition of eight trade associations sent a position paper to the Commission. This paper focuses on Articles 25 and 26 and expresses its concerns that if the Commission were to survey third countries for the degrees of 'adequacy' and produce a 'white list' it would not be long before a 'black list' of non-conforming countries would circulate. Such countries could have a *cordon sanitaire* imposed, which in turn could lead to trade disputes within the WTO. The paper goes on to argue strongly for a self-regulatory system by industry sectors or, indeed, individual companies.

In November 1997, The EU Committee hosted a public workshop on 'The Impact of Data Protection on Global Trade'. Effectively a dialogue was conducted between the major industry associations and the major Commission officials concerned. Representation included the Secretary General of UNICE, and member companies from Eurobit (the then leading IT industry association), the European Banking Association, FEDMA and the EU Committee.

The situation in the USA

While the debate within Europe over the implications of the 'adequacy' test was raging, it still had not gained much traction in the USA. However, there was a relatively high awareness among a few of the larger US multinationals with substantial operations in Europe. This was particularly true among large financial service companies who had only recently managed to lobby against the inclusion of a 'reciprocity' clause in the framework financial service directives.

Elsewhere in the States, knowledge and awareness of this 'sword of Damocles' hanging over the transfer of personal data across the Atlantic was practically non-existent. This was perhaps not so surprising given that, until recently, EU legislation had been almost exclusively concerned with 'domestic' issues. The scare stories of the EU building a 'Fortress Europe' had only just died down and there was no tradition of Europe seeking extraterritorial jurisdiction (although a growing number of countries did introduce data protection laws during the 1990s that drew heavily on the EU directive).

Personal contacts on personal data across Europe and the USA

Consequently, organizations such as the EU Committee continued to dialogue with themselves and their counterparts in the USA. They also met monthly with the US Mission to the EU (which includes representatives from most of the significant US federal departments and agencies). In the end, it was a chance personal encounter (as so often in European public affairs?) that appears to have detonated serious US government attention.

A public affairs representative of one of the larger US multinationals had recently transferred from their home EU country to Brussels. At a similar time a senior US diplomat also transferred from the same EU country to Brussels. These two people had worked on public affairs issues in this other member state and knew and respected each other. The private-sector public affairs representative queried why the US government did not seem to be reacting to this 'sword of Damocles'. The diplomat promised to look into it, and called US Under-Secretary of Commerce, Ambassador David Aaron, and action began.

At about the same time, late 1997, the concerns about the EU directive got onto the Trans-Atlantic Business Dialogue (TABD) agenda, where it was to remain until its resolution in mid-2000. Shortly afterwards, the transfer of data to third countries also appeared on the Trans-Atlantic Consumer Dialogue and the Trans-Atlantic Legislators Dialogue agendas. This was significant from a public affairs perspective because it ensured that the issue was regularly on the bilateral six-monthly EU–US summits, in turn receiving top-level political attention and maintaining pressure on the officials to produce results.

Why was the USA so agitated about EU legislation?

During the negotiations on the original EU directive, the EU Committee quickly became aware of US opposition to any data protection legislation. There was one simple but overriding reason: the USA has no equivalent federal law. Nor did the US Congress take kindly to suggestions that it might draft something in response to the EU directive. More than most legislatures, the US Congress is intensely proud of its prerogatives. During the late 1990s it was perhaps also increasingly focused on domestic issues. However, as will be shown later, the publicity and NGO interests associated with the non-legislative Safe Harbor Privacy Principles fuelled a growing list of bills in the US Congress.

Furthermore, according to Ambassador Aaron, Under-Secretary for International Trade, US Dept. of Commerce, 1997–2000, the USA and the EU clashed over a fundamental difference of approach. Aaron stated that:

the Europeans are seeking to develop a comprehensive system of regulation that covers every eventuality. The US cares about privacy protection, but that [*sic*] the US prefers a system of specific laws targeted to prevent specific abuses. Furthermore, private sector self-regulation, backed up by the Federal Trade Commission [and the implied threat of potential legal redress] is a major component of the US system.

This quote, apart from the bracketed text which has been added for clarity, is taken from US State Dept. minutes of the 16th meeting of the Advisory Committee on International Communications and Information Policy (ACICIP).

A further concern expressed by Aaron included a desire to avoid any discrimination against US firms. The EU directive allows differentiation for different countries, but the USA wants the same exceptions as are available to EU companies to apply to US companies. European industry, according to Aaron, did not want that to happen.

Position in late 1997

By late 1997, the EU directive was due to be fully implemented within a year. Yet no decisions had been taken on how third countries would be assessed as to their 'adequacy'. In addition to the obligations on organizations wishing to transfer data out of the EU, the directive also contained two articles relating to governance. These comitology articles established two authorities to advise the Commission. The Article 29 working party consists of representatives from the 15 national data protection authorities and is responsible for the protection of individuals in relation to the processing of personal data. The Article 31 Committee is the authority that judges the adequacy of third countries. Both committees met many times during 1997 and throughout the next three years, and many of their reports were strongly critical of both the Commission and the DoC proposals.

The EU authorities, in particular the Commission and those member states who had operational domestic laws, were determined not to see their hard-fought new large single market eroded or corrupted by a 'black hole' in the USA. It was well-known that with the widespread use of computers and relatively low telecommunication costs large users of personal data in the USA often vacuumed up huge quantities of data on US citizens to perform 'data-mining' and many other analyses. Among the more common practices in the USA are the pre-screening of credit records without the knowledge of the data subject, the sale of drivers' license data and many other procedures banned in Europe. The collection, manipulation, storage and processing of these data are often contracted out to third parties so there was little direct control exerted by the original organization who had requested the data, or the marketing company who were now using the processed data. It was real or imagined fears like these that drove the EU authorities to vigorously defend their legislation.

Meanwhile in the USA, concerns were rising that there was increasingly little time to find an administrative solution before the deadline of October 1998. Then national Data Protection Commissioners would be able to take a decision to ban the export of personal data to third countries without 'adequate protection'.

Threat of trans-atlantic trade war

In summary, the issue of the potential threat to the ever-increasing flows of personal data out of the EU had got onto the Trans-Atlantic political agenda. An early meeting of the incoming second term Clinton team with the EU representatives included references to a 'potential trade war' unless the issue of data transfers was resolved soon. The December 1997 biannual EU–US summit included an agenda item on data privacy. Little did the participants realize that it would remain on the agenda for another three years.

Alliances for and against a strict interpretation of articles 25 and 26

Prior to the December 1997 summit, the line-up of the major forces looked something like that shown in Table 1.1. At their 1997 meeting in Rome, the Trans-Atlantic Business Dialogue (TABD) called for 'mutual recognition by governments of industry-led, market driven privacy protection principles in order to ensure and increase consumer trust in electronic commerce'. It also went on to talk about national policies allowing for protection based on national political systems and local cultures, with government regulation as a last resort.

The arrival of Clinton's second-term team in the second half of 1997 coincided with a determination by the Commission to try and avoid another damaging trade dispute. As a result there were increasingly intensive discussions between the US and EU administrations throughout 1998. Up to half a dozen meetings at ambassadorial level, innumerable sessions in person, by video, phone and email but, consultations rather than negotiations. The Article 29 working party met regularly and in July issued a 'synthesis' document summarizing many of the cohesive views of the 15 data protection registrars in respect of the manner in which articles 25 and 26 should be applied. The Article 31 Committee increased the rhythm of its meetings on how to assess the adequacy of third countries. But by mid-October 1998, Aaron admitted

Table 1.1   Interested parties prior to the December 1997 summit

For	*Against*	*Self-regulation + legal sanctions*
The European Commission	The US Government	Leading Trans-Atlantic
Article 29 Working Party	The US Congress	traders and investors
Article 31 Committee	Some US companies	represented in the
The European Parliament	Some libertarian activists	TABD
Some European companies		
Some Privacy & consumer activists		

negotiations had not even started, although the directive was due to take effect within two weeks. Worse still, and to the shame of the EU side, only four of the 15 member states had fully implemented the directive by the due date of 25 October 1998. Although it is not uncommon for countries to miss these deadlines, it was to be a continuing thorn in the side of the EU authorities while they were negotiating with third countries. In the event, the Commission has initiated infringement proceedings against eight members for their tardiness.

However, ten days after the 25 October deadline, the US DoC published its first 'Safe Harbor' principles. The following box includes extracts from a letter sent by the DoC to US industry representatives on 4 November 1998.

Dear Industry Representative,

The European Union's comprehensive privacy legislation, the Directive on Data Protection, which became effective on October 25, 1998, prohibits the transfer of personally identifiable data to third countries that do not provide an 'adequate' level of privacy protection. Because the United States relies largely on a sectoral and self-regulatory, rather than legislative, approach to effective privacy protection, many U.S. organizations are uncertain about the impact of the 'adequacy' standard on personal data transfers from the European Community to the United States.

In an effort to find ways to bridge differences in our approaches to privacy, the U.S. Department of Commerce, on behalf of the U.S. Government, and Directorate General XV of the European Commission have been engaged in a dialogue on privacy for the past several months. We have discovered that, despite our differences in approach, there is a great deal of overlap between U.S. and EU views on privacy. Given that and to minimize the uncertainty that has arisen about the Directive's effect on transborder data transfers from the European Community to the United States, the Department of Commerce and the European Commission have discussed creating a *safe harbor* for U.S. companies that choose voluntarily to adhere to certain privacy principles.

Organizations within the safe harbor would have a presumption of adequacy and data transfers from the European Community to them would continue. Organizations could come within the safe harbor by self-certifying that they adhere to these privacy principles. The status quo ante would exist for firms that choose not to take advantage of the safe harbor.

Safe Harbor Principles. Identifying the appropriate privacy principles is clearly central to this approach. Such principles must provide 'adequate' privacy protection for European citizens. They must also reflect U.S. views on privacy, allow for relevant U.S. legislation, regulation, and other public interest requirements, and provide a predictable and cost effective framework for the private sector. Accordingly, we have drafted the attached principles, based on the Department's discussion paper, 'The Elements for Effective Privacy Protection,' the 1980 OECD Privacy Guidelines, private sector self-regulatory, on-line privacy programs, and discussions with industry and the European Commission.

Adoption of the principles is voluntary and their use is intended solely by U.S. organizations receiving personal data from the European Union for the purpose of qualifying for the safe harbor.

Benefits of the Safe Harbor. While the specific terms of the safe harbor arrangement are still under discussion with the European Commission, it is our position that organizations that decide to take advantage of the safe harbor would also benefit in the following ways:

- All fifteen Member States would be bound by the Commission's recognition of the safe harbor principles as adequate;
- The scope of any legal action by European citizens contesting data transfers under the Directive would be narrowed to alleged non-compliance with stated practices rather than addressing adequacy of the safe harbor privacy principles;
- In those EU Member States that require prior approval before data transfers can occur, organizations that belong in the safe harbor would either not have to seek such approval or would, as a general rule, have their applications automatically approved;
- The organization would have access to streamlined and expedited procedures in the event of a dispute; and
- A grace period for safe harbor participants to give them time to implement the principles.

Exceptions. It is important to bear in mind that the exceptions listed in Article 26 of the EU Directive are still applicable to all data transfers from the European Union to the United States. Those include transfers to third countries where

1. an individual has given unambiguous consent;
2. the transfer is necessary to complete a contract between the individual and the organization or a contract is concluded in the interest of the individual between the organization and a third party;
3. the transfer is necessary or legally required on important public interest grounds or for legal actions;
4. the transfer is necessary to protect the vital interests of the individual; or
5. the data comes directly from public records. We have also tried to capture all the relevant exceptions created by U.S. law and regulation in the preamble to the principles.

Source: www.ita.doc.gov/td/ecom/aaron114.html

The DoC invited comments from industry. Several dozen organizations responded, including some non-business complaints that consumer, trade union and journalistic concerns were not addressed. The bulk of responses were supportive of this set of self-regulatory proposals, although there were a number of questions about coverage, compliance and enforcement.

Consumers generally objected to the fact that Europeans had stronger protection than US citizens did. Opposition from a few academics and businesses either argued that the Safe Harbor proposals were unnecessary or that they were too burdensome (see: www.ita.doc.gov/td/ecom/com.html). The EU quickly responded on 23 November that its Article 31 committee of member states found the Safe Harbor plan flawed and unacceptable. The major concerns were that European citizens would have inadequate access to their files and be unable to stop the sale and unauthorized use of their personal data.

FAQs become part of the regulatory regime

During the early months of 1999, industry worked to enhance the protection of personal data, especially in an on-line environment. Enforcement was clearly a critical area to be resolved across the Atlantic. The TABD endorsed the principles of the On-line Privacy Alliance, as well as supporting self-enforcement mechanisms such as provided by the Better Business Bureau On-line, TrustE and FEDMA.

In April 1999 the DoC published revised Safe Harbor principles and an additional nine 'Frequently Asked Questions' to the original six FAQs. The new drafts produced a further round of comments and suggestions from a growing list of interested parties on both sides of the Atlantic. The Article 29 Working Party and the Article 31 Committee were detailed and highly technical. Among the more vocal was the Trans-Atlantic Consumer Dialogue, representing over 60 European and American consumer groups. They were particularly critical of the lack of effective enforcement and redress for violations. The TACD contended that the Safe Harbor proposals place unreasonable burdens on consumers and unfairly require European citizens to sacrifice their legal rights to pursue privacy complaints through their national authorities.

Negotiations dragged on throughout 1999 and into the early months of 2000, with the debate focusing increasingly on the issues of dispute resolution and enforcement.

2000

Finally, on the ides of March, officials from the Commission and the USA declared victory! They announced that they had reached agreement on the two outstanding issues: enforcement within the USA and how existing US laws could be integrated into the system. Exchanges of draft letters between the two administrations were published. On the EU side the Commission sent the Safe Harbor principles to the two EU legislative branches: the Council of Ministers and the European Parliament. Precisely, the Commission was seeking the approval of the legislative branches that it had properly executed its responsibilities in assessing the adequacy of the US proposals. So the action moved into the parliamentary arena. However, the enforcement and dispute settlement procedures continued to be tweaked right up until 16 June 2000. In the end, enforcement is ensured via a two-stage process of self-verification in the first instance, which respects the predominantly self-regulatory system in the USA. This is reinforced by the fact that any findings of non-compliance are then referred to the Federal Trade Commission or other statutory body with similar powers depending on the sector. Serious cases of non-compliance will result in companies being thrown out of the privacy programmes of which they are members and being struck off the DoC's list. This means that they will no longer receive data transfers from the EU under the Safe Harbor agreement. This was a considerable toughening-up of the rather lighter regime originally envisaged, and eventually passed muster with the EU authorities.

Comitology

Before examining how the legislative branches reacted to the accord reached between the executive branches of the EU and the USA it is worth looking at two other aspects of EU legislative practice. Firstly, between the adoption of the Data Protection directive in 1995 and its implementation, the Amsterdam Treaty was negotiated. This came into force on 1 May 1999. The new Treaty places a higher obligation on the EU to guarantee the protection of personal data, an obligation ensuing from the fundamental right to the protection of privacy laid down in Article 8 of the European Convention on Human Rights. The reference to the Convention appears in Article 6 of the EU Treaty. The European Parliament, in particular, saw itself as having a particular and extra responsibility as a result.

The second novelty was that the Commission proposed to exercise its 'comitology' powers under the Data Protection Directive. Again the goalposts had moved since 1995. In 1999, following the fall of the Santer Commission, new constraints and timetables were agreed between the institutions. Now the Parliament was being invited to state whether the Commission was using these powers correctly. This Parliament, newly elected in June 1999, was keen to be seen to be using these enhanced powers meticulously.

Legislators' comment

The EP had been debating the draft Safe Harbor proposals for a couple of years. Mrs Elena Piaciotti, a member of the Socialist Group (PSE), was elected as an MEP in June 1999 and immediately took a leading interest in the Safe Harbor principles. Mrs Piaciotti was a senior judge in Italy with a strong interest in citizens' rights and consumer protection. In July 1999, the Socialist Group appointed her as rapporteur and the committee debated the Safe Harbor principles regularly.

Two European Parliament committees (Legal Affairs and the Internal Market, together with Citizen's Freedoms, Rights, Justice and Home Affairs) had already held a joint hearing on data protection in February 2000. This gave a further airing and increased media attention to the almost 18-month EU/US negotiations. In April 2000 Mrs Piaciotti was appointed rapporteur of the Citizens Freedoms, Rights, Justice and Home Affairs (LIBE) Committee for a report on the adequacy of the protection provided by the Safe Harbor privacy principles.

Lobbying of the European Parliament

The EP and the Committee were then under a lot of pressure from the Commission, member states, the international business community and the US government to deliver a favourable judgement quickly. There was also pressure from the US Congress. The request came initially from the Trans-Atlantic Legislators Dialogue. Congress turned out to be more sceptical of the Safe Harbor agreement than the Commission had alleged to the Committee. At least a couple of the Congressional delegation that visited the European Parliament expressed some envy of the EU legislation; though this was not endorsed by the chair of the relevant US Congressional committee.

The European Consumer association (BEUC), and EICTA, the IT industry association produced position papers but otherwise there was little input from industry or from the usually active European-based NGOs: Amnesty International, Liberty and Privacy International were conspicuous by their absence. EPIC, a US-based alliance sent materials. To an extent there was a general desire, after over five years to put this deal to bed. Professors Simitis and Rodota, godfathers of the Council of Europe Data Protection Convention in 1981 were among the most assiduous lobbyists and attendees in the committee hearings.

The Italian connections worked in favour of the rapporteur. The chief clerk to the (British) chair of the LIBE Committee is Italian and was close to Rodota. It is the Chair's impression that the Piaciotti report received more time and attention than any other in the 1999/2000 session despite the fact that the LIBE Committee has 20 per cent of all the legislation going through the EP.

The Commission continued throughout to push for unqualified support from the EP. The Chair was not convinced that they had a watertight case and so put in some tougher amendments than might otherwise have been justified. There was a widespread feeling among MEPs that data protection legislation in the EU was either not implemented or it was not working as intended. No great support, therefore, to offer the USA an 'easy' way out. The Committee was not convinced that the Commission had got the best deal available, and they were not satisfied with the safeguards in Safe Harbor provisions. But perhaps most of all, the EP felt that the Commissioner had failed to recognize the MEPs' unease and had not worked the corridors or sought out the doubters to try and get them on-side.

European Parliament rejects the Safe Harbor proposals

As a result, the LIBE Committee adopted the Piaciotti report which expresses serious doubts about the adequacy of data protection in the United States. At about the same time, the Council of Ministers on the advice of the Article 31 Committee and the Commission delivered a positive opinion in favour of adopting the Safe Harbor principles as adequate protection. In the subsequent plenary session of the European Parliament, the Committee's rejection was endorsed by the whole of the Parliament.

Consequently, in the inter-institutional balancing act that governs much of EU legislation, the member states had supported the Commission's proposal but the Parliament had rejected it.

This posed the Commission with a delicate political dilemma. The Parliament's opinion was required as part of the new comitology introduced as a result of the Amsterdam Treaty in May 1999. Since the resignation of the Santer Commission in March 1999, the Commission had not overridden a negative opinion in the Parliament. On the other hand, Parliament had stopped short of adopting an amendment that claimed that the Commission had exceeded its authority. In effect, the European Parliament had chosen to examine the substance of the implementation of the adequacy provisions of the Directive. However, technically all they were required to do was to determine whether the Commission had executed the implementing authority granted by the Directive. So, after a few days of intensive internal consultations, the Commissioner responsible, Mr Frits Bolkestein, NL, told Parliament that he would propose to the College of Commissioners that they adopt a formal decision recognizing that the Safe Harbor arrangement with the United States represents 'adequate protection'. The opinion of the Parliament was summarized by Sarah Ludford, MEP, who stated 'it's better to have some protection than none at all'. She added that the Parliament 'reluctantly accepts' that it cannot fight the Commission over the Safe Harbor accord.

Partly as a result of complaints like these, the Commissioner went on to offer further reassurances to Parliament. He promised to report regularly on the functioning of the agreement, to convey any concerns to the US authorities and to make it clear that the Commission would seek to re-open negotiations if, as the European Parliament fears, the remedies open to individuals are too weak. At the same time, in July 2000, as the EU finalized its negotiations with the US, it also concluded agreements with Hungary and Switzerland.

On 1 November 2000, five years and a few days after the adoption of the Directive, and two years after their first publication, the Safe Harbor was officially opened and a major Trans-Atlantic trade dispute averted.

Conclusions

The users of personal data from the EU now have greater legal certainty and a relatively cheap method of compliance. Users can transfer personal data to the USA in a number of ways: but probably the easiest and most accessible is to register under the Safe Harbor process. Industry managed to persuade the EU and US authorities to adopt a self-regulatory mechanism backed by the threat of legal action for non-compliance. This was a different outcome than either the EU or US authorities had sought initially. The EU either wanted companies to use the contractual route, or for the USA to adopt a comprehensive federal law. The US authorities initially sought an entirely self-regulatory solution. Pressures from other stakeholders, notably consumers and civil rights groups, ensured that the enforcement procedures are tougher than industry or the US authorities would have liked. The European Parliament registered its strongest doubts and unease at the legal redress and enforcement procedures short of blocking the deal. The Commission overrode the Parliament's more exaggerated concerns but has undertaken to report back regularly on the operations of the agreement.

Who were the winners and losers?

The clearest beneficiaries are the hundreds and thousands of small, medium and large companies engaged in moving personal data across the Atlantic. However, it is doubtful whether more than a minority of these is yet aware. It will be interesting to see who and how many organizations opt to register in the Safe Harbor; in particular whether any more than the few per cent noted by the Dutch authorities some 30 years ago, mentioned in the first pages of this chapter.

The large multinationals and their respective trade associations on both sides of the Atlantic deserve credit for having persisted in pressing for a self-regulatory system. They persuaded an initially indifferent and occasionally reluctant European Union regime to adopt a pragmatic solution, and there was a lot of initial scepticism across Europe that a self-regulatory system would be enforceable. To date there have not been any contested cases, and it is possible that these will find that the system fails. However, the point is that the companies persuaded the Commission and the other EU authorities that it was worth trying.

The officials of the European Commission and the Department of Commerce deserve industry's appreciation for many hours, days, weeks and months of detailed negotiations. In particular, praise is due to the two women who took on the bulk of the 'heavy-lifting' of these detailed negotiations. Sue Binns, Director, Directorate A of Directorate General Internal Market of the Commission, and Barbara Wellbery, Counsellor to the Under-Secretary for Electronic Commerce at the US Department of Commerce. From January 1998 until March 2000 these two women reported to John Mogg, Director General Internal Market, and David Aaron, US Under-Secretary of State for Commerce. These two ambassadors provided the leadership and energy necessary to drive these negotiations through the toughest times.

Tribute should also be paid to the many other unnamed officials on both sides of the Atlantic who worked diligently in many of the supporting teams, committees, working parties, agencies and missions. The US embassies in the member states worked hard to identify the 'bottom-line' for each of the member-state host authorities in the run-up to the last crucial meeting of the Article 31 Committee. The US Mission to the EU is, as far as the author is aware, the only US representative organization supported by the Congress which is not affiliated to the organization to which it is accredited. It more than justified its existence on this case.

It is more difficult and invidious to identify losers in this saga. Suffice it to say that since the story is not yet over some of the apparent losers in the short term may yet have their day.

The privacy activists in the United States have certainly had awareness of the issue raised substantially. During these negotiations, in May 1998, Vice-President Gore proposed 'an electronic bill of rights for this electronic age'. He continued:

> Americans should have the right to choose whether their personal information is disclosed; they should have the right to know how, when and how much of that information is being used; and they should have the right to see it themselves, to know if it's accurate.

Public affairs lessons

What are the public affairs lessons from these negotiations?

1. Be prepared for the long haul – 'it ain't over till the fat lady sings'. Implementation of the Data Protection Directive took longer than the drafting and adoption of the original proposal. Even when the Directive was adopted in 1995, the 'adequacy' test was already recognized by industry experts as a key hurdle for Trans-Atlantic trade. But there can have been few public affairs professionals who would have thought that it would take five more years for the USA to be in full compliance. Public affairs issues often exceed one, two or three-year business-planning cycles.
2. Many big issues are increasingly global, so understand the language and culture of the other party. Oscar Wilde's aphorism of a century ago in regard to the UK and the USA still holds true: 'two peoples divided by a common language'. Even though many of the most active negotiators involved had English as a common mother tongue it did not prevent misunderstandings. Data protection, or privacy, is increasingly recognized as a legitimate right, even and perhaps especially in an increasingly global, transparent and electronic age. Initially, at least, there was ignorance and scepticism on the EU side that US self-regulation could work. On the US side there was an underestimate of the seriousness with which the EU regarded data protection. There needed to be a fair amount of mutual education and knowledge of the other sides' cultures, systems and priorities. Education is a sizeable part of the public affairs process.
3. Coalitions work. While individual companies and industry sectors delivered a series of consistent messages about the need for action on Articles 25 and 26, it was only after they began to coalesce in 1997 that they began to have an effect. The European Commission had become increasingly wary, if not sceptical, of producer industry lobbies during the 1990s.

Alliances, partnerships and working with *ad hoc* coalitions is a routine public affairs practice in the twenty-first century.

4. The Trans-Atlantic Dialogue works. It is a decade since the biannual US–EU summits started, and the Dialogues are now an integral part of the supporting infrastructure. They provide the opportunity for groups of business, consumers and legislators to raise issues of common concern before they have escalated into crises. In this case, the potential banning of Trans-Atlantic trade in personal data was a 'hot button' issue for most of the last five years. It was on the front page of the website of the US Mission to the EU for four of those years.

5. It is possible to meld the different US and EU traditions into workable and enforceable rules. The Commission is now applying the same principle to the electronic commerce directive. Structured partnerships between regulatory authorities are likely to increase as globalization continues to spread.

6. The Safe Harbor principles are a good topical working example of an 'alternative regulatory model', which could usefully be used in other circumstances to the benefit of the EU and third countries alike. The Global Business Dialogue on Electronic Commerce (GBDe) endorsed them in September 2000. It is possible that if the same approach had been used elsewhere the crises over hush-kits, beef hormones and bananas might have been avoided. Although the Safe Harbor approach emerged from an implementation challenge, there is no reason why the principle should not be applied from the beginning in other cases.

7. Companies and trade associations change: issues don't. Over a period of five years there were inevitably, in a quickly growing market, a number of mergers. Interestingly, many of the personalities remained fairly consistent, people moved from one company or trade association to the successor, or occasionally a competitor.

8. Managing EU issues and global issue groups. In a more classic EU lobbying scenario, one might initially expect to find a number of disparate organizations concerned about an issue but either unaware of the others or uncertain about how or whether to form a coalition. In this case, the issue of the transfer of data protection to third countries arose directly from the adoption of the EU Directive. As far as Europe was concerned, the issue groups already existed: FEDMA, The EU Committee, the financial services coalitions and the IT industry associations, for example. The novel aspect was the escalation of the issue into the Trans-Atlantic arena. Here the challenge was to manage an issue in two very different jurisdictions: the EU and the USA. The Trans-Atlantic Dialogues proved useful and eventually effective in keeping the issue in front of the two administrations at the highest political levels. Finally, in 1999 and 2000 it also reached the agenda of GBDe and the final deal won praise and endorsement from this new global forum. However, this was not always plain sailing nor were all the Dialogues equally effective. The public affairs lesson

is that managing issue groups is as important as managing the issue, and as issues become more global this will be an increasing challenge.

9. Best lobbyists – women! Several of the most active participants in the Safe Harbor negotiations were women, in both the US and European administrations as well as among the European-based companies and trade associations. This was not true in the late 1980s or early 1990s. The emergence of women as active leaders in European public affairs marks a welcome maturing of the profession.

Specific lessons learnt from the European Parliamentary process are as follows:

1. There was no natural European Parliament majority for a totally liberal market solution proposed by the Commission. While not inherently protectionist, most MEPs wanted to see a more codified and legally watertight formula than that proposed by Safe Harbor. There are also strong concerns about any move away from established legal rights for citizens.

2. The Chair of the relevant committee took a risk in opposing a Commissioner of his own party, and although he split the Liberal vote in the EP, he carried his committee and a good proportion of Liberal MEPs. Lesson: political groups are not necessarily cohesive and in this case the split was on the issue and not by nationality.

3. Best lobbyists: Rodota and Simitis – these godfathers of European data protection legislation adopted an intelligent approach to a newly-elected European Parliament, a new Committee and a new rapporteur. They lobbied frequently and via various channels. Although they failed to defeat the Safe Harbor arrangements, as finally negotiated, they came too close for anyone to take comfort.

4. Parliaments, like elephants, have long memories. The European Parliament will look at this again and will take a tough line on any signs of backsliding or failure to implement a tight regime.

5. On the US side, the debates on the European legislation and the wave of similar laws that have followed in third countries has produced a veritable forest of bills in Congress. To date none has become law, but federal legislation on the protection of personal privacy is a lot closer than before the Safe Harbor, so watch this space …

Annex I

Chapter IV transfer of personal data to third countries
Article 25

Principles

1. The Member States shall provide that the transfer to a third country of personal data which are undergoing processing or are intended for processing after transfer may take place only if, without prejudice to compliance with the national

provisions adopted pursuant to the other provisions of this Directive, the third country in question ensures an adequate level of protection.

2. The adequacy of the level of protection afforded by a third country shall be assessed in the light of all the circumstances surrounding a data transfer operation or set of data transfer operations; particular consideration shall be given to the nature of the data, the purpose and duration of the proposed processing operation or operations, the country of origin and country of final destination, the rules of law, both general and sectoral, in force in the third country in question and the professional rules and security measures which are complied with in that country.

3. The Member States and the Commission shall inform each other of cases where they consider that a third country does not ensure an adequate level of protection within the meaning of paragraph 2.

4. Where the Commission finds, under the procedure provided for in Article 31 (2), that a third country does not ensure an adequate level of protection within the meaning of paragraph 2 of this Article, Member States shall take the measures necessary to prevent any transfer of data of the same type to the third country in question.

5. At the appropriate time, the Commission shall enter into negotiations with a view to remedying the situation resulting from the finding made pursuant to paragraph 4.

6. The Commission may find, in accordance with the procedure referred to in Article 31 (2), that a third country ensures an adequate level of protection within the meaning of paragraph 2 of this Article, by reason of its domestic law or of the international commitments it has entered into, particularly upon conclusion of the negotiations referred to in paragraph 5, for the protection of the private lives and basic freedoms and rights of individuals.

Member States shall take the measures necessary to comply with the Commission's decision.

Article 26

Derogations

1. By way of derogation from Article 25 and save where otherwise provided by domestic law governing particular cases, Member States shall provide that a transfer or a set of transfers of personal data to a third country which does not ensure an adequate level of protection within the meaning of Article 25 (2) may take place on condition that:

   a. the data subject has given his consent unambiguously to the proposed transfer; or

   b. the transfer is necessary for the performance of a contract between the data subject and the controller or the implementation of precontractual measures taken in response to the data subject's request; or

   c. the transfer is necessary for the conclusion or performance of a contract concluded in the interest of the data subject between the controller and a third party; or

   d. the transfer is necessary or legally required on important public interest grounds, or for the establishment, exercise or defence of legal claims; or

   e. the transfer is necessary in order to protect the vital interests of the data subject; or

   f. the transfer is made from a register which according to laws or regulations is intended to provide information to the public and which is open to consultation either by the public in general or by any person who can demonstrate legitimate interest, to the extent that the conditions laid down in law for consultation are fulfilled in the particular case.

2. Without prejudice to paragraph 1, a Member State may authorize a transfer or a set of transfers of personal data to a third country which does not ensure an adequate level of protection within the meaning of Article 25 (2), where the controller adduces adequate safeguards with respect to the protection of the privacy and fundamental rights and freedoms of individuals and as regards the exercise of the corresponding rights; such safeguards may in particular result from appropriate contractual clauses.

3. The Member State shall inform the Commission and the other Member States of the authorizations it grants pursuant to paragraph 2.

   If a Member State or the Commission objects on justified grounds involving the protection of the privacy and fundamental rights and freedoms of individuals, the Commission shall take appropriate measures in accordance with the procedure laid down in Article 31 (2).

   Member States shall take the necessary measures to comply with the Commission's decision.

4. Where the Commission decides, in accordance with the procedure referred to in Article 31 (2), that certain standard contractual clauses offer sufficient safeguards as required by paragraph 2, Member States shall take the necessary measures to comply with the Commission's decision.

Source: EU Data Protection Directive 95/46/EC.

Annex II

Chapter VII community Implementing measures
Article 31

The committee

1. The Commission shall be assisted by a committee composed of the representatives of the Member States and chaired by the representative of the Commission.

2. The representative of the Commission shall submit to the committee a draft of the measures to be taken. The committee shall deliver its opinion on the draft within a time limit which the chairman may lay down according to the urgency of the matter.

   The opinion shall be delivered by the majority laid down in Article 148 (2) of the Treaty. The votes of the representatives of the Member States within the committee shall be weighted in the manner set out in that Article. The chairman shall not vote.

   The Commission shall adopt measures which shall apply immediately. However, if these measures are not in accordance with the opinion of the committee, they shall be communicated by the Commission to the Council forthwith. It that event:

   - the Commission shall defer application of the measures which it has decided for a period of three months from the date of communication,
   - the Council, acting by a qualified majority, may take a different decision within the time limit referred to in the first indent.

Source: EU Data Protection Directive 95/46/EC.

Notes

1. In the UK it has been estimated that at least one-third of data users have not registered their data processing operations (House of Common Public Affairs
   Committee, Data Protection Controls and Safeguards, 1994). Other estimates are
   even higher. In The Netherlands there is a massive discrepancy between the number of companies in the Companies register and the number of registered data
   users, the latter being just 2 per cent of the former (Douwe Korff, Korff Consultants
   in a November 1997 paper for the EU Committee seminar on 'The Impact of Data
   Protection on Global Trade').
2. Business Software Alliance, European Publishers Council, European Public
   Telecommunications Network Operators' association, The EU Committee of
   AmCham, Federation of European Direct Marketing, Federation of European
   Magazine Publishers, Euro-Commerce, and the International Communications
   Round Table.

The official web sites listed below contain a lot of the official sites and many associated
links. A good starting point for current Information Society activities can be found on
the EurActiv.com portal site under their Information Society section:

<www.euractiv.com> This EU portal compares official and other stakeholder positions.
<www.ita.doc.gov/KPIFrameset.html> US government site.
<www.europa.eu.int/comm/internal_market/en/media/dataprot/index.htm> EU site.

2
Promoting Consumer Confidence in e-Commerce: The 'Brussels Regulation' – Real or Illusory Consumer Benefit? The Business Case

Susan Pointer

Introduction

The Confederation of British Industry

Founded in 1965, the Confederation of British Industry (CBI) is a non-profit-making non-party political organization, funded by members' subscriptions. The CBI has a direct corporate membership employing over four million workers and a trade association membership representing over six million of the UK workforce. Members come from every sector of industrial and commercial activity, with – contrary to popular belief – around 90 per cent of our members being small- and medium-sized enterprises.

The CBI's objectives are 'to help create and sustain the conditions in which British business can compete and prosper'. Through its network of offices around the UK and in Brussels, it represents members' views on all cross-sectoral issues to national, European and international policy-makers. The CBI Brussels Office acts as the CBI's channel for gathering intelligence on EU developments for feed-in to policy positions, advises on EU lobbying strategies, and leads on the CBI's representation of policy positions to the EU institutions. The CBI is also the UK member of the European employers' and industry federation, UNICE,[1] which is based in Brussels.

Electronic commerce and the EU

With the development of electronic (or e-) commerce offering enormous potential for job-creation, greater supply-chain efficiency, extended markets and wider consumer choice, the economic, social and political benefits of exploiting e-commerce are clearly goals which policy-makers at all levels want to promote. Correspondingly, there are initiatives such as <e-commerce@its.best.uk> in the UK and the eEurope Programme at EU level which try to do just this.

One of the most active e-commerce issues at all levels, however, is the question of how to encourage consumers to have the confidence to buy goods electronically and thereby increase the overall use of e-commerce. There is no doubt that the growth of B2C (business-to-consumer) e-commerce has been relatively weak in comparison with B2B (business-to-business) growth, and the response to this challenge differs among different players.

The rapid expansion of e-commerce has also been a prime example of a major technological development, whose implications have tested the capacity of traditional political and legislative structures to keep pace with the novel questions that it throws up, and indeed to decide whether these developments require legislative intervention at all. This is already true within national regimes, but the global nature of e-commerce has clearly added a supra-national level of analysis in addition.

The case study

This chapter will look at one specific recent EU policy development – that of the 'Brussels Regulation', its background, the legislative process, the key players involved, and the lobbying response of the CBI and others. Unlike many of the other case studies in this publication, this particular example does not illustrate the co-decision procedure under which the majority of EU policy proposals affecting business proceed, and on which the CBI lobbies most often in Brussels. Rather, it has been selected deliberately in order to illustrate the importance of staying alert to the potential impact of *all* new initiatives in Brussels, however irrelevant they may at first seem to one's own particular organization, and whatever the legislative process they follow. It also illustrates the importance of building contacts within the EU institutions and among ally organizations for the purpose of intelligence-gathering as well as for channelling direct lobbying. And it focuses on the specific challenges involved in dealing with a 'consultation' decision-making process.

It is important to realize that the 'Brussels Regulation' did not start life as a piece of e-commerce legislation at all! Of a 58-page proposal, just *one recital* and *one article* were to become the focus of a high-profile debate, which was to centre on the potential damage that this proposal would do to the growth of e-commerce across the European Union. Indeed, were it not for the CBI and others' continuous monitoring of new initiatives emerging from the corridors of Brussels and for our network of contacts, it may not even have been an active dossier long enough to allow time for the connection between these elements of the proposal and the issue of e-commerce to have been made at all! A damaging Regulation could easily have been proposed and adopted within weeks, without any consideration of its wider impact. Instead, high-profile discussions continue to this day and new policy responses are still being formulated.

The background

The proposal for a Brussels Regulation[2] came about as a direct result of the Amsterdam Treaty[3] and of the commitment made to bringing intergovernmental judicial cooperation measures (so-called third-pillar issues) with a cross-border impact within the direct competence of the European Union.[4] In theory, this would imply a simple conversion of an existing Convention – in this case the one on 'Jurisdiction and Enforcement of Judgements in Civil and Commercial Matters' (known as the Brussels Convention and agreed at intergovernmental level in September 1968[5]) – to a Council Regulation (hence the name Brussels Regulation). The aim of the 1968 Convention and of the subsequent Regulation was primarily to facilitate and simplify the circulation and recognition of court judgements in the EU.

Whilst clearly of legal and procedural interest, this was not obviously an issue to which organizations such as the CBI would automatically accord priority in terms of attention and lobbying resources – and indeed in the very early stages we did not.

However, at the very heart of all effective and targeted EU lobbying is early intelligence-gathering, both in Brussels and in the national capitals, on *potential* developments within the European institutions. Whilst we might not have been drawn automatically to such a proposal, it was this ongoing monitoring and intelligence-gathering that alerted us to the potential problems for business of two specific paragraphs within this broader text, and therefore of the need for active CBI involvement.

The issue

The issue was one of *applicable jurisdiction* in respect of disputes arising from purchases between suppliers and customers based in different member states – or put simply, in which court can a consumer sue a supplier and vice versa where disputes arise? In the pre-e-commerce, pre-single market world of the 1968 Brussels Convention, this was primarily an issue of cross-border distance-selling through mail shots and so forth, and the Brussels Convention dealt with the limited number of such consumer contracts by exempting them from a general rule (that jurisdiction is held in *the producer's domicile*) in cases where the company *had approached and solicited* the presumed-passive consumer. In such cases, the consumer was given the right to sue a foreign company in his/her own country, rather than in the country of the company. Hence, Article 13 of the 1968 Convention read as follows:

Article 13 of the 1968 Brussels Convention

13. In proceedings concerning a contract concluded by a person for a purpose which can be regarded as being outside his trade or profession, hereinafter called 'the consumer', jurisdiction shall be determined by this Section (ie exemption from above-stated general rule) ... if ...

13.3(a) in the State of the consumer's domicile the conclusion of the contract was preceded by a specific invitation addressed to him or by advertising ...

In the corresponding text (Article 15) of a *draft* Regulation,[6] which we knew was being drawn up internally within the European Commission in conjunction with an *ad hoc* Council Justice and Home Affairs working group, the text to exclude consumer contracts from supplier-state jurisdiction read as follows:

Article 15 of pre-proposal draft Regulation (unofficial)

If … (3) in all other cases, the contract has been concluded with a person who pursues commercial or professional activities in the Member State of the consumer's domicile or, by any means, *directs* such activities to that Member State or to several countries including that Member State, and the contract falls within the scope of such activities.

This was further supplemented by an *additional recital* entered at the beginning of the draft document[7] which stated:

Recital 13 of pre-proposal draft (unofficial)

electronic commerce in goods or services by a means *accessible* in another Member State *constitutes an activity directed* to that State …

The combined implication of the draft Article 15 and draft recital 13 meant that any company simply operating a website which could be seen by a consumer in another member state, even if the company were not actively targeting that consumer's country, could be liable to being sued in the court of the consumer's place of domicile (the so-called 'principle of *destination*' as opposed to '*origin*' approach) if that consumer had, after actively entering the website, concluded a purchase with the company and a dispute later arose (that is, even where the consumer is not a *passive* consumer at all).

For the CBI, whose members are being encouraged at all levels to go on-line and to allow themselves and their customers to enjoy the many benefits of B2C e-commerce, this draft text was regarded as strongly counter-productive. The impact on our SME members in particular was potentially enormous – to the extent that the risk of litigation and of defending even a single case brought by a consumer in another member state and the costs involved in this could far outweigh any benefit to them of having a website. They might therefore be strongly discouraged by lawyers from going on-line in the first place – to the detriment of their own business potential and consumer choice and convenience alike. The draft Brussels Regulation clearly went much further in scope than the existing Brussels Convention, and had also disappointingly failed to reassess the Convention in light of technological changes since 1968.

Although the damage would apply to on-line businesses across the EU, the additional risk element in this for British business was the wide accessibility of the English language throughout other EU countries, which meant that UK websites were far more likely to be accessed by consumers outside the UK than in some other member states.

CBI objectives and strategic response at the pre-proposal stage

Regular CBI one-to-one contact with individuals in the European Commission, some of whom were not at all supportive of this approach of the Justice and Home Affairs (JHA) Directorate, alerted us back in mid-1998 to the draft text in play in the Commission. At this relatively early stage – and with no formal proposal yet released by the Commission – our overriding concern was that despite knowing that the proposal was due to be released very imminently, there had been *no prior process of consultation* with interested parties – either at national level through ministries or at European level from the Commission departments concerned. The potential impact of this text had not, it seemed, either been noticed or properly assessed.

We were in serious danger, therefore, of the Regulation being rushed through the legislative process as just a formality, and of little significance beyond legal circles. This risk was all the greater given that the *ad hoc* JHA working party of member-state representatives had already been established in December 1997 and was reaching informal agreement on an internal text – based on the draft texts described above – updating the Convention.[8] This text was therefore circulating in the Commission as the near final draft. Furthermore, we were aware that those Commission departments such as the Directorate General for the Internal Market, which had their own concerns about the document, were failing in their attempts to introduce internal changes to the document during the inter-service process. In addition, if the Commission were to release this proposal quickly, before the potential policy implications for e-commerce were widely appreciated, MEPs might simply nod through the proposal under the consultation process and Council could adopt it as a formality – feeling they were simply converting a Convention to a Regulation. Within weeks the Regulation would be set in stone, and directly applicable in member states.

Our first aim, therefore, was for a proper external consultation process. We knew that the proposal was to be discussed in the Commission with a view to formal release on 14 July 1999, and so urgent CBI action was focused on:

- calling for public consultation;
- calling for postponement of the proposal's release pending the above; and
- calling for an economic impact assessment of the proposal.

This action was undertaken at a range of levels:

CBI in the UK and Brussels

Early drafting in the JHA *ad hoc* working group had only involved the UK's Lord Chancellor's Department, given the nature of the majority of the Convention's content (this was generally true in other member states also). It was important, therefore, that we alert other UK departments such as the Department of Trade and Industry (DTI) to the specific consequences in respect of e-commerce so that these concerns were reflected in the overall UK position in the EU's Council of Ministers. This was done through the latter part of 1998 and early 1999 by means of numerous meetings and letters. This effort was reinforced in Brussels through the UK's Permanent Representative to the EU (UKREP). Representations were also made in Brussels to the European Commissioners, seeking delay of the proposal's formal release pending further and open consultation.

CBI and alliances

On national e-commerce issues, the CBI often joins forces with a number of its sectoral industry association members with a particular interest in information society issues through the Alliance for Electronic Business (AEB).[9] Given the common concerns about the draft EU Regulation, this same channel – and the combined lobbying forces – was also used for this EU-level issue. As well as collective and individual organization meetings with policy-makers, joint letters were sent from the AEB to the UK Secretary of State for Trade and Industry, the Lord Chancellor, the opposition parties, the UK Permanent Representative to the EU and to the EU Commissioners. We again drew attention to the imminent proposal from the Commission, clearly dispelling the notion that this was simply a technical adjustment of the Brussels Convention, and highlighting the lack of Commission consultation on the impact of such a Regulation. We urged that every possible step be taken to ensure that proper and thorough consultation with business was instigated. (Such pressure subsequently led to a DTI consultative Seminar in the UK in October 1999.)

CBI and UNICE

It was important for us also that this was not just seen as an issue for UK business but for the wider business community. One of the main channels for this was through our European confederation, UNICE. On 16 June 1999, through UNICE, the European business community wrote to the caretaking Commission President Jacques Santer, President-Elect Romano Prodi, and to Commission Secretary General Mr Trojan, expressing 'serious concern' about the Regulation in preparation in the Commission, believing that it would:

- omit to take account of the major economic impact of such a regulation (no economic impact assessment conducted);

- disregard fall-out on other policies, for example the development of electronic commerce; and
- fail to ascertain the appropriateness of such a regulation through democratic consultation and public scrutiny.

Furthermore, it stressed that the 'Protocol on application of the principles of proportionality and subsidiarity' imposed on the Commission the obligation to consult widely before proposing legislation, and a duty to assess the burden falling on economic operators. UNICE also urged the Commission to hold a public consultation with interested parties before adopting its proposal. With no immediate response from the Commission, nor apparently any signs of further consideration within the Commission services, UNICE issued a further Press Release,[10] entitled 'Electronic Commerce – Is Europe Missing the Boat?', which highlighted this lack of response and the Commission's failure to consult. Attention was again drawn to the threat to the development of e-commerce and its employment potential, the lack of an economic impact assessment, and noting that this was being done by a reduced caretaking Commission[11] which surely had to question its own legitimacy.

At all levels, such press releases ensured that the press coverage of the issue – and the indirect pressure put on the Commission as a result – also intensified. The CBI and UNICE also maintained close contacts with other EU sectoral business associations in Brussels with the purpose of sharing information about latest developments and thinking within the Commission.

Of course, consumer organizations such as BEUC[12] were also very active – for their part claiming that the Brussels Regulation as drafted was essential for consumer confidence in e-commerce – although they also admitted that the wording of the draft proposal was uncertain.[13]

The commission's formal proposal

Despite the above efforts, we were disappointed to see that the Commissioners' meeting on 14 July 1999 did indeed result in the formal release of a proposal for a Regulation.[14]

In line with pre-proposal drafts that we had seen – and criticised – recital 13 also introduced the statement that 'electronic commerce in goods or services by a means *accessible* in another Member State constitutes an activity *directed* to that state', thereby triggering the possibility of consumer-state jurisdiction under Article 15 of the Regulation when the commercial/professional party to the contract '*directs* such activities to that Member State…'. Furthermore, any notion of 'directed at' was completely missing the point in an on-line world where there are no barriers to where a site may be seen, even though the supplier may only be seeking to attract customers in the local area. How would such a legal statement distinguish between the two?

Nonetheless, what our lobbying had achieved was a concession from the Commission within the proposal to holding a Public Hearing in view of the fact that the wording of Article 15 had 'given rise to certain anxieties among part of the industry looking to develop electronic commerce'.[15] The Commission's text also recognized that these concerns were based on

> the fact that companies engaging in electronic commerce will have to contend with potential litigation in every Member State, or will have to specify that their products or services are not intended for consumers domiciled in certain Member States.

It is clear that, ideally, we would have wanted the Commission to hold such a consultative hearing *prior to* releasing a proposal which closely resembled the much criticized internal drafts. However, the CBI's priority now was to identify the time, place and date of this hearing, to obtain all the necessary background papers, to send a formal CBI submission to the hearing, and to ensure that we had a good turn-out of members and allies at the meeting itself.

The Commission's public hearing

Through the CBI, AEB, UNICE and others, we were able to publicize the November 1999 Hearing, deliver a formal response[16] to the list of some 25 questions raised in advance by the Commission, and be well-represented by member companies.

The 550 registered participants at the Hearing clearly confirmed that the interested parties fell into two main groups. On the one hand, consumer organizations calling for legally binding consumer-state jurisdiction – often in alliance with legal academics; and on the other, individual businesses and business organizations – often supported by private law firms[17] – warning that this would only bring illusory benefits to consumers, and urging that alternative dispute resolution (ADR) mechanisms were the more effective and cheaper option for consumers to get redress in cases of on-line disputes. Some of the associations and interests represented at the Hearing are listed in Table 2.1.

As one journal described the hearing:

> the debate highlighted the not unexpected gulf that exists between on the one hand industry, and more broadly all suppliers of products and services on the Net, hostile to Commission proposals in this area laying down jurisdiction of the destination country, and on the other, consumer

Table 2.1   Examples of associations/interests represented at the Hearing

Business	Consumers
Confederation of British Industry & Alliance for Electronic Business	BEUC (European Bureau of Consumers' Unions)
UNICE	German Consumers Association
European Association of Advertising Agencies (EAAA)	Finnish Consumer Protection Agency
FEDMA (European Direct Marketing Association)	Danish Consumers Organization
FAEP (European Magazine Publishers Federation)	Italian Consumers Association
Eurocommerce	Norwegian Consumer Council
German media associations (including German CBI-equivalent, the BDI)	UK Consumers Association
UK Advertising Association	French Consumers Association
Microsoft	
German insurance industry	European Housing Association
Barclays	Austrian Federal Labour Chamber
European Banking Federation	Austrian Employment Chamber
DLA	
Italian Lawyer association	University law faculties
BDI	
Law firms	
E-music	
Commercial Television Association	
TV3, Vivendi Group	

representatives who remain attached to a principle they regard as being essential to the development of electronic commerce.[18]

It was reported also how

the majority of speakers … claimed the wording of article 15 of the draft Regulation is ambiguous and … the notion of 'activity directed towards' cannot be applied to a website which is a window but cannot be considered an active approach of a consumer.

Having forced a hearing, our priorities and attention in the CBI now had to shift away from attacking the lack of consultation in general terms to focusing in on the specific arguments against the content of the Commission's proposed Regulation.

The *arguments put forward by business* prior to the hearing, during the hearing and throughout the subsequent legislative process can be summarized as follows:

The draft Brussels Regulation...

1. *Is a Disincentive to Business exploiting the economic and employment benefits of e-commerce.*

   - Requires all business, including SMEs operating in local markets only, to face the risk of litigation and defending an action in any other EU country; is a deterrent therefore to going on-line, or to being based or investing in the EU.
   - How can business tell where an on-line consumer is domiciled (what about...@hotmail.com?); Furthermore, the EU is urging higher levels of data privacy, which make this even more difficult.
   - Contradicts the Commission's E-Europe Programme and e-commerce framework directive designed to promote the take-up of e-commerce.

2. *Offers No Benefit to Consumers either.*

   - Apparent increased protection in law; but requires consumer to pursue an expensive lengthy and complex cross-border court case – where legal expense will almost always greatly exceed the value of the original transaction in dispute.[19]
   - Deterrent to business (as above) will reduce availability of web-based retail services for consumers; and thereby restrict consumer convenience.
   - The above in turn reduces competition and increases consumer prices.

3. *There is a Better Way of Doing things.*

   - Alternative (on-line) dispute resolution (ADR) mechanisms are cheaper/free and quicker for the consumer, and should be used as first resort.
   - No denial of ultimate court back-up where ADR does not exist, or consumer does not accept.

It was point 3 of the above which was to be brought to the fore during the European Parliament's consideration of the proposal, as we shall see below.

The legislative process

Now that we had a formal Commission proposal, we were also entering a formal legislative process, and as with all proposals needed to refer to the process of a specific EU legal base given in the EU Treaties – in this case, we were dealing with a *Consultation* procedure. The proposal had been introduced in line with Articles 65 and 67 of the EU Treaties. Article 65 gives the EU competence to introduce certain stated 'measures in the field of judicial cooperation in civil matters having cross-border implications', whilst Article 67 outlines the decision-making process for such measures, as reproduced in the Box below. The procedure is summarized in Figure 2.1.

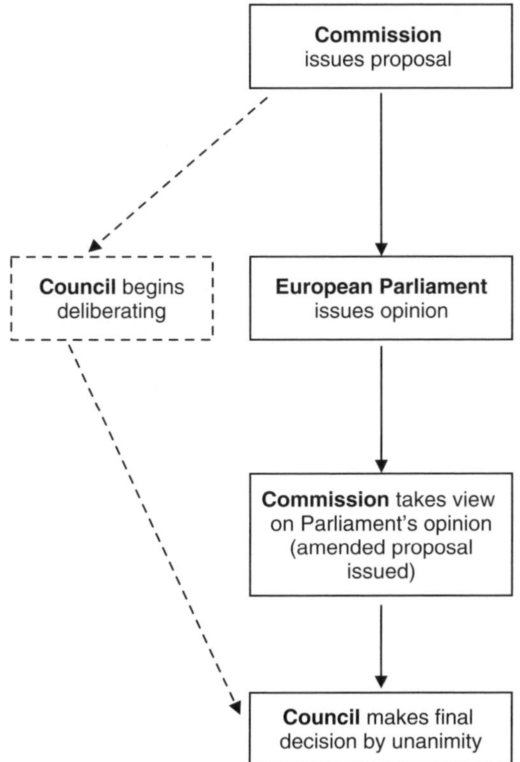

Figure 2.1   Decision-making procedure under Treaty Article 67, paragraph 1

Article 67, para. 1:

During a transitional period of five years following the entry into force of the Treaty of Amsterdam, the Council shall act unanimously on a proposal from the Commission or on the initiative of a Member State and after consulting the European Parliament.

[N.B. further paragraphs of Article 67 outline the situation following this five-year period and certain derogations.]

Consultation of the European parliament

The next objective, therefore, in view of the forthcoming European Parliament consultation, was for ourselves, the AEB, UNICE and others to sensitize Members of the European Parliament (MEPs) to our concerns prior to their formal consideration of the proposal. Whilst the opinion of MEPs is not binding on the Council in a Consultation procedure, the fact that the process required them to provide an Opinion before the Council could legally adopt the Regulation meant that the Council could not instantly rush into a decision. This was therefore a further opportunity and platform that we needed to use in order to raise the profile of the issue, make sure the proposal was taken seriously and that a full debate was initiated. Essentially, we had to ensure that this obscure-looking, consultation-procedure proposal was raised from the piles of paperwork on MEPs' desks and given proper consideration, not rushed through due to lack of interest. Ideally, of course, we also hoped it would result in a parliamentary Opinion that reflected our concerns, and which would persuade the Council of Ministers of these also.

We therefore entered into a period of intensive discussions with MEPs, even before the proposal had formally been presented to them at a Plenary session. And, indeed, the subsequent debate in the European Parliament – particularly in the Legal Affairs Committee (the lead committee) – was surprisingly in-depth and high-profile, and also clearly indicated how the Parliament has gained in confidence and is maturing as an institution. Despite its formal powers being restricted in comparison with co-decision procedure proposals, the consultation was nonetheless accorded considerable parliamentary and MEP time and commitment – even, unusually, during the recess month of August!

The lead committee in the European Parliament on this proposal was the newly-strengthened Legal Affairs and Internal Market Committee, with an Opinion also to be provided by the Citizens' Freedoms and Rights Committee. The rapporteur in the Legal Affairs Committee was the UK Liberal Democrat MEP, Diana Wallis; the draftsman in the Citizens' Freedoms Committee, the French Socialist, Adeline Hazan.

At first it appeared that this was going to be extremely difficult for business, given the Parliament's traditional leaning in favour of what was presented as consumer-protection arguments. The Opinion from the Citizens' Freedoms committee to the Legal Affairs committee called for the Commission's proposed Regulation to be adopted in its entirety as soon as possible; although it did concede that

> in view of the cost and complexity that legal proceedings represent for the consumer, even at his national courts, it would be desirable for the Commission to submit a proposal designed to simplify and speed up settlement of trans-border disputes over small claims …[and] that the introduction of alternative procedures outside the courts would be highly advisable.[20]

A growing number of industry representations ensured that the discussions in the Legal Affairs Committee were more intense – and very complex. (In fact an entire book could be written on this stage alone!) Interestingly, the majority of MEPs in this committee accepted very early on that court procedures – wherever the jurisdiction – did not offer the ideal route for consumers who needed quicker and, in particular, cheaper/free options. Strengthening their theoretical legal rights was not necessarily of any benefit to the average consumer. Very much in line with the point that the CBI had been making – that there is a better way forward – the debate focused immediately on the type of alternative dispute resolution (ADR) system which could be used, and how such a system would interact with jurisdiction possibilities without deterring business from going on-line.

Proactively, we then worked with groups of MEPs to suggest possible amendments to the proposal that they could table to the text to reflect this option. Two main ADR options subsequently emerged in the committee:

1. Allowing websites to display a 'disclaimer clause' which would alert the consumer prior to the purchase being made that the supplier-court principle would apply, but providing an on-line ADR system that the consumer could use to avoid the courts altogether, and giving the consumer the option as to whether or not to accept this and proceed with the purchase.[21]
2. The second[22] would establish ADR as the first resort for consumers with the outcome binding on all parties, but still allow the consumer ultimate recourse to his/her court where there were matters of general legal principles at stake.

Having successfully persuaded MEPs of the value of ADR, we were in the unusually pleasant position of having to choose which of the two options – both based on ADR and acceptable to the CBI – to favour.

In the earlier stages, we pushed for a variation of the disclaimer option – and indeed it was this line that was adopted by a very narrow majority of votes in the final Legal Affairs Committee report.[23] However, our subsequent toing and froing with MEPs of all parties to refine amendments over the course of August 2000 (when MEPs and lobbyists alike would have traditionally been enjoying the Brussels recess!) convinced us that an amended version of the second option was now the more realistic route – more realistic in terms of its increased likelihood of being accepted by consumers, a majority of MEPs across the Parliament and Council members alike. Furthermore, the emergence of an ECJ ruling – the 'Oceana ruling' – over the summer appeared to outlaw so-called jurisdiction clauses because of the EU Unfair Contract Terms Directive. Amendments in line with our approach were re-tabled by a rapporteur-led group of MEPs direct to the Parliament's Plenary Session. The subsequent Plenary vote meant that the European Parliament's final Resolution[24] did indeed favour this approach. The Resolution also underlined the deterrent effect on new entrants to the e-commerce market of allowing consumer-state jurisdiction, and the inappropriateness of the judicial system for consumers seeking redress. It attempted to better define 'directed at' and, with CBI support, suggested that ADR schemes be established and properly accredited.

The amended Commission proposal

However, we were again knocked back when in spite of the very useful and extended debate in Parliament, in October 2000 the Commission issued its amended proposal,[25] which made it clear that, unlike the Parliament, the Commission had still not appreciated or had chosen to dismiss what we saw as the full implications of the proposal. As a result of the above lobbying and of the Parliamentary debates, the Commission had conceded to delete the original recital 13. However, the Commission still stuck to its original text on Article 15 ('or by any means directs such activities...'). Furthermore, it rejected the Parliament's amendment calling for a new Article 17a which would allow the consumer and supplier to agree a contractual clause referring disputes to a Commission-approved ADR scheme prior to court action, feeling that this needed 'further study'. Instead the Commission made a minor concession to conducting a Review of the situation 'on the basis of alternative dispute-settlement schemes'[26] no later than five years after entry into force of the Regulation.

Although, we were pleased that recital 13 had been dropped, business remained extremely concerned about Article 15 – particularly given that in a note to the text,[27] it was suggested that Article 15 would be nonetheless interpreted as if recital 13 were still present! This completely failed to recognize that the world had changed since 1968 with the expansion of the Single Market and information society. Under this text, on-line businesses would still be exposed to the *uncertainty* of facing litigation elsewhere – and uncertainty itself is a major cost for business. For those that chose to stay on-line, they would probably be encouraged to minimize this risk by specific website statements denying use by purchasers from other member states (for example, 'no Portuguese consumers may use this website' or 'UK customers only'. Such fragmentation of European markets would mean consumers having significantly less choice than the European Single Market should allow. And, despite this ongoing damage to e-business, the consumer was still very unlikely to make use of this apparent increased court-based protection.

Lobbying the Council of Ministers

Although we had been speaking to member state representatives throughout the decision-making process, now was the last chance to influence their views prior to their adoption of the final Regulation. Unanimity was required in Council. This last stage in the process only took a matter of weeks between the amended draft proposal and the final agreement in Council in November 2000, but was extremely intensive in terms of CBI lobbying. Although UNICE had a role to play in profiling the debate in Brussels,[28] the real focus had to be within the member states. For the CBI and our allies, this meant daily – if not hourly – contact with the UK authorities during the preparation for the JHA Council, and also ensuring that our counterparts in other member states were doing the same. In retrospect, we can see that there were two main stages to our lobbying: intelligence on Council developments revealed that whilst we had convinced the UK of our concerns, many of the other delegations were prepared not only to support the Commission proposal, but some – led by the French Presidency – were even prepared to reinsert the recital 13 that had been dropped in the Commission's amended proposal.

The *first stage* therefore focused on preventing this. By the COREPER[29] meeting of 22 November, we were happy that the UK and Ireland had persuaded others (Luxembourg, Spain, Greece, Netherlands and Portugal) to resist this. Having apparently seen off recital 13, the *second stage* focused again on the implications of Article 15. Even without the recital, we still felt that the notion of 'directed at' was irrelevant in an internet environment. Ideally, we would have liked to delay the adoption of the Regulation altogether until a mechanism based on an accepted ADR mechanism could be established. Politically, this was looking unlikely. Again, we had persuaded the UK Government of the value of delay through meetings with Ministers and letters/phone calls to key players, but we knew that a lower profile accorded to this issue in other member states was going to make it very difficult – and it was not an issue on which the UK particularly wanted to use the explosive veto option.[30] Furthermore, the UK, together with Ireland and Denmark, was in the slightly awkward position of having the option available to it of an opt-out clause from Title IV of the EU Treaties,[31] which covered visas, asylum, immigration and so forth. This ironically reduced any possible impact of a veto, since other member states could press on ahead anyway. In this situation it was better to be in the negotiations, influencing the outcome, particularly given the cross-border implications of e-commerce rules.[32] The CBI had to work therefore within this political scenario.

Whilst maintaining that delay was the best option and keeping the pressure on this to the wire,[33] we knew in the final days that the Council was more likely to agree a non-binding statement attached to the Regulation's text to underline the importance of ADR, whilst not establishing these processes within the Regulation itself. Whilst in some sense this was a longer-tem victory in terms of paving the way for further detailed discussions on ADR, in the short term we were very aware that a statement, although useful in its content and for interpretation purposes, has no legal force and could not therefore be deemed adequate.

There was no doubt that the key difficulty for the Council in taking another approach was the fact that they would be seen to be going against that early draft agreement in the JHA *ad hoc* working group all those months ago in which all member states were represented.

The final 'Brussels Regulation'

On 30 November 2000, the EU's Justice and Home Affairs Council reached agreement on the Regulation. This was formalized on 22 December with the adoption of the Council Regulation on Jurisdiction and the Recognition and Enforcement of Judgements in Civil and Commercial Matters.[34] The controversial recital 13 did not appear, and Article 15.1.c was adopted as follows:

> A consumer may bring proceedings against the commercial party...in the courts in the place the consumer is domiciled.

Article 15. 1. c final

if...the contract has been concluded with a person who pursues commercial or profession activities in the Member State of the consumer's domicile or, by any means, *directs* such activities to that Member State, and the contract falls within the scope of such activities.

In an unusual appended joint Council and Commission statement,[35] some 10 paragraphs were inserted in order to clarify the interpretation of Article 15. These emphasized many of the points that business had made throughout the process, namely:

- the changes brought about by the development of e-commerce;
- the importance of establishing consumer confidence;
- that the mere fact that an internet site is accessible is *not sufficient* for Article 15 to be applicable;
- that the language or currency used is not a relevant factor in ascertaining whether active solicitation of a distance contract has taken place;
- that there is considerable value in consumers and undertakings settling disputes amicably outside of the courts;
- that the purpose of the Regulation is not to prohibit the parties from making use of alternative methods of dispute settlement (ADR);
- emphasized the importance of continuing work on ADR methods[36]
- that ADR has a useful and complementary role to play; and
- that in drawing up a future report on the application of the Regulation, 'essential attention' should be paid to the provisions relating to consumers and SMEs and e-commerce

The Regulation is to enter into force on 1 March 2002 and be directly binding on and applicable in the member states. The final text also commits the Commission[37] to reporting on its application within five years of its entry into force,[38] and to submitting proposals for adaptations within this period if necessary.

The outcome

Given the circumstances in which the draft Regulation was born from the Commission, based on a draft elaborated and endorsed within a closed *ad hoc* JHA working group, and without exposure to prior consultation of any nature, it is clear that the process for business was not ideal, and – out of necessity – was primarily one of damage limitation.

We ended up with a text similar to the original Brussels Convention. Our lobbying had prevented a considerably worse outcome than had been first proposed by the Commission in its early drafts, and we had, in addition, obtained recognition of the validity of our concerns and a not unhelpful Statement on the Regulation's interpretation and application which will help minimize although not eradicate some of the outstanding uncertainties for business.

Is business satisfied? Well, it can be argued that since little has at the end of the day fundamentally changed since the Convention, business is no worse off. On the other hand, we would have preferred to see the EU properly analyse whether a piece of 1968 legislation is really relevant to modern e-business. The Internet, by definition, allows companies to offer their services on a world market *without* specifically targeting one particular country.

Should the consumer be satisfied with the Regulation? We believe not. Whilst it could have pointed more directly to useful and cost-efficient dispute resolution procedures, the Regulation simply gave consumers the costly right to sue in their own courts, which is of little use to them in cases of most (low-cost) purchases. And will the German or Italian consumer really thank the Council of Ministers when they find, for example, sites in the UK providing cheaper and better goods discontinuing their on-line sales to those countries? What impression will they be left of the European Single Market?

Furthermore, we feel that this was a lost opportunity by the EU to establish a process by which businesses would be *encouraged* to sign up to and fund accredited and low-cost ADR schemes for consumers in return for greater legal certainty.

The future

As with most lobbying issues – and particularly at EU level – the comments above mean that the campaign is by no means over. The Regulation in itself leaves many issues unresolved, but also opens some useful doors – particularly in respect of exploring ADR mechanisms – and there is the forthcoming review. Furthermore, with the emergence of ADR systems at the European level pending, the chance still exists that the Regulation may itself be modified to reflect this before its implementation in March 2002.

But the lobbying on this issue achieved much much more than simply limiting the considerable damage which might otherwise have been caused, and opening the door for alternative dispute mechanisms. We were only too aware throughout the process that a linked proposal – on *applicable law* (a Regulation to convert the Rome II Convention into a Regulation) – was also in the pipeline from the Commission.[39] The damage to e-commerce that this could cause if a similar 'destination principle' route were to be taken would be far greater still than the Brussels Regulation, since it would take as its starting point a questioning of the principle of 'origin', under which a supplier who meets the legal requirements of his/her own country can freely export these goods throughout the Single Market under the already long-established mutual recognition principles.

The lobbying efforts outlined above have already ensured that the formal proposals on Rome II have been postponed within the Commission machinery for many months, fearing similar controversy were the process to in any way replicate the Brussels Regulation process. Clearly, we would hope that when this proposal does finally emerge, it will have been preceded by a full and open consultation with interested parties and ideally have gone through a consultation document/Green Paper stage first. Furthermore, it would be hoped that all relevant Commission departments, Commissioners and national ministries would be fully involved this time round, prior to any decisions being taken in *ad hoc* groups. CBI work has long been undertaken to ensure that this is the case.

General conclusions and lessons for the EU lobbyist

The case study above can only, I suggest, re-confirm the eternal EU lobbying rules:

- one can never be involved too early in a process;
- or overestimate the range of policy areas which might have an impact on your activities (the CBI has certainly paid closer attention to the new EU-competence area of justice and home affairs developments at their earliest drafting stages in the light of the above case);
- it is never enough to work just at the national level; as a national organization, we can never afford to rely on convincing our own MEPs/national delegation alone, who constitute just one-fifteenth of the decision-making machine;
- every vehicle should be used to raise concerns and seek support;
- alliances are helpful in reaffirming the policy message and for sharing information on developments;
- national business organizations always need to continue to develop better ways of harnessing business concerns on EU issues, and to increase resources on EU activities;
- the case is never closed! work is ever only just beginning!
- and there's still the national transposition and implementation process to go!

Notes

1. UNICE: Unions des Confédérations de l'Industrie et des Employeurs d'Europe.
2. COM 1999 348 final of 14 July 1999.
3. Signed on 2 October 1997 and entered into force on 1 May 1999.
4. Article 61c of the EU Treaties.
5. Subsequently extended to EFTA states through the Lugano Convention and to all new EU states by accession conventions; consolidated version published OJ C27 of 26 January 1998.
6. For example in a draft text of 26 February 1999.
7. Recital 13 of the draft Brussels Regulation.
8. Informal agreement of 27 May 1999.
9. Comprises the Confederation of British Industry (CBI), the Computing Software and Services Association (CSSA), the Direct Marketing Association (DMA), eCentre UK and the Federation of the Electronics Industry (FEI).
10. 5 July 1999 UNICE Press Release 'Electronic Commerce – Is Europe Missing the Boat? Commission fails to Consult Consumers and Companies'.
11. Commissioner Bangemann, for example, had already departed the caretaking Commission, and Commissioner Gradin had already implied the Commissioners' support for this text.
12. European Bureau of Consumers' Association.
13. See European Report of 10 July 1999.
14. COM 1999 348 final.
15. Explanatory Memorandum pertaining to COM 1999 348 final, p. 17.
16. AEB Memorandum on 'Electronic Commerce: Jurisdiction and applicable law' for the Public Hearing, issued 13 October 1999, and UNICE Preliminary Statement for the Public Hearing, dated 28 October 1999.
17. It is not clear why there was this difference between law academics and privately-practising lawyers – perhaps this was due to academics focusing on the legal transition of a Convention into a Regulation, whereas private lawyers were more focused on the practical functioning and implications of the Regulation for consumers and business on the ground.
18. European Report 11, November 1999
19. A 1995 study for the Commission estimated that the cost of pursuing a cross-border claim for 2000 euros would be 2500 euros, excluding the cost of having the judgement enforced.
20. Committee Opinion given 27 January 2000; PE 232.464/fin.
21. this 'disclaimer clause' approach was promoted mainly by UK Conservative MEPs, and by Committee Chairman Mrs Palacio (Spanish Centre-Right).
22. To be gradually developed by rapporteur Diana Wallis MEP (UK Liberal Democrat).
23. Committee final report of 21 September 2000 (A5 0253/2000).
24. On 21 September 2000 (R5 0401/2000).
25. COM 2000 689 final of 26 October 2000.
26. Hence addition of a new recital 14a.
27. Paragraph 2.2.2 of the explanatory statement.
28. Through press releases and speeches.
29. Council of Permanent Representatives.
30. Under Article 67, the Regulation had to be adopted by unanimity.
31. Article 69.

32. Whilst having the choice of whether to opt out or not, the UK government had decided to participate in the negotiations, but was not legally bound by the Treaty to accept the final Regulation.
33. CBI Press Release 29 November 2000 'Hold Off Adopting E-Business Regulations – CBI Warns Government'; UNICE Press Release 'UNICE Supports ADR Concept' 24 November 2000.
34. Published OJ L12/1 of 16 January 2001.
35. Section II Statement on Article 15.
36. See Council Conclusions of 29 May 2000.
37. In Article 68 of the Regulation.
38. At time of writing, due to enter into force.
39. In fact, it had been in the pipeline since the first drafts of the Brussels regulation were floating in the Commission and indeed the November 1999 public hearing addressed this too.

Part II

Environmental Cases

3
Lafarge and Global Warming

Chris Boyd

Introduction

At Lafarge we take the view that the way to persuade someone of your ideas is through rational argument. It is also an excellent way of gaining an understanding of the opposing views. This is the story of how our philosophy has been put to the test over the issue of global warming in which Lafarge, as the world leader of the cement industry, plays a crucial role.

Some believe that lobbying, or public affairs to give it a less negative connotation, is carried out in a hazy world of expensive dinners, golf games and power politics. Influence, it is therefore argued, is little related to the force of argument, more to cosy relationships and implicit threats. Of course in lobbying, just as in other areas of business and politics, there are questionable practices, but they do not produce results over the long term. Indeed, our view is that quite apart from ethical considerations, they represent an unacceptable risk to a company's credibility and image. But this does not mean that lobbying has no skill. It remains that getting the right result requires not only good arguments, but they must be well-presented, to the right people and at the right time.

The jury is still out on this case study, in fact it is still hearing the evidence because the case is far from over, so we cannot be sure whether Lafarge's strategy will pay off. Nevertheless, I hope this case gives some insight into how one company lobbies on a global issue of crucial importance not only to the company itself, but also to the world we live in.

I will start by introducing Lafarge and by giving an outline of the climate change issue to help understand the case.

Lafarge

Founded in 1833 in south-eastern France, Lafarge is world leader in construction materials, holding top-ranking positions in each of its four divisions: Cement, Aggregates and Concrete, Roofing, and Gypsum (Figure 3.1). In 2000, the Group recorded sales of €12.2bn. Lafarge currently employs 66 000

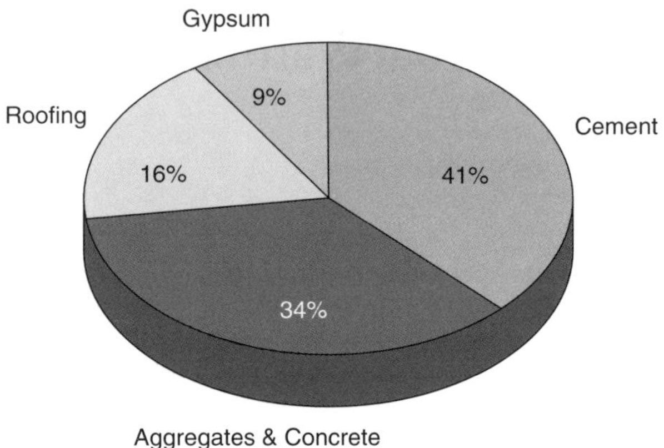

Figure 3.1   Lafarge sales, 2000

people and operates in 71 countries. Through its commitment to the development of building materials, Lafarge offers construction industry professionals 'new solutions for a new century', bringing greater safety, comfort and attractiveness to our everyday lives. While combining its traditions with dynamism and innovation, Lafarge has developed into the largest, most international construction materials company in the world.

Unlike many of its competitors in the cement industry, such as Holcim, Heidelberger, Cemex or Italcementi, Lafarge is not a family-controlled company. It has long been a traditional 'blue chip' on the Paris stock exchange with a broad-based ownership structure now dominated by international financial institutions.

Lafarge is a global, multi-local company, present all over the world. Our international expansion started in the 1950s in Brazil and Canada, and it has continued to cover much of the world. At the time of writing, Lafarge has announced an agreed take-over of Blue Circle Industries plc, the UK's leading cement manufacturer, due to be finalized in the summer of 2001. The combination of the two groups will add to the size and geographical coverage of Lafarge, especially in the UK, Asia and Africa, making Lafarge the largest cement producer in the world (Figure 3.2).

Lafarge has a long tradition of ethical management and proactive behaviour in the social and environmental fields. For example, it developed its socalled 'Principles of Action'[1] as far back as 1975 and did so in a process involving the personnel. It has only had four CEOs in the last half century, demonstrating an unrivalled stability and solidity in management terms.

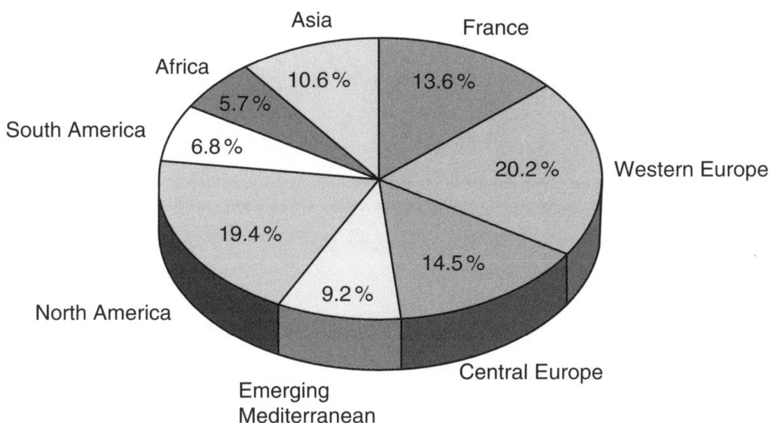

Figure 3.2   Lafarge employees, 2000

Our policy of appointing local management has led to a culturally diverse company, though the strong French roots remain clearly in evidence. Lafarge lays special emphasis on training and maintaining the decentralized, team culture that is Lafarge's trademark in the industry. This special Lafarge culture is of course reflected in our lobbying strategy.

The issue of global warming

Global warming, or climate change as it is sometimes called, is a truly global problem. It has come to attention in recent years as scientists' fears about climate change have come more and more to be supported by evidence of rising temperatures and more frequent extreme weather events. The latest work from the UN-sponsored International Panel on Climate Change suggests that the average surface temperature will rise by from 1.5 to 6.0 degrees centigrade up to the year 2100 under present trends of greenhouse gas emission.[2] The causes and consequences of global warming are still disputed by some, although the overwhelming majority of scientists agree that human activity is the main cause.

The Earth's surface temperature this century is clearly warmer than any other century during the last thousand years. The Earth has warmed by between 0.4 and 0.8 degrees centigrade over the last one hundred years (see Figure 3.3), with land areas warming more than the oceans, and with the last two decades being the hottest in the twentieth century. In addition, there is evidence that precipitation patterns are changing, that sea level is increasing, that glaciers are

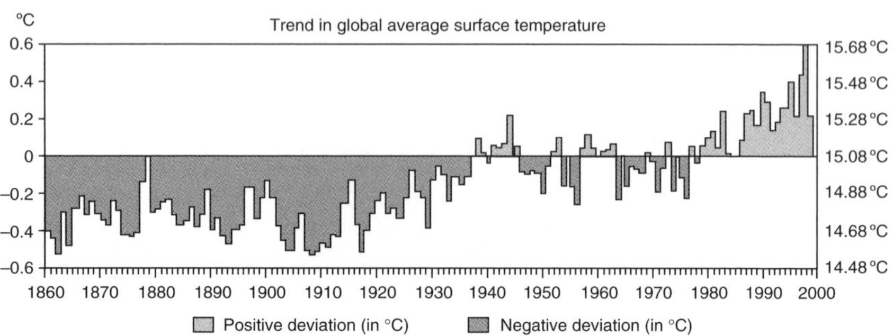

Figure 3.3   Global temperatures

Source: School of Environmental Sciences, Climatic Research Unit, University of East Anglia, Norwich, United Kingdom, 1999.

retreating worldwide, that Arctic sea ice is thinning, and that the incidence of extreme weather events is increasing in some parts of the world.

It is generally believed that global warming is caused by the emission of greenhouse gases (GHGs), principally carbon dioxide (CO_2) from burning of fossil fuels. Atmospheric GHGs, such as water vapour, CO_2 and other gases, absorb some energy radiated out from the earth that would otherwise be lost in space. This natural greenhouse effect is one basic condition for human survival, since Earth would otherwise be completely cold (see Figure 3.4).

The atmospheric concentrations of greenhouse gases have increased because of human activities, primarily due to the combustion of fossil fuels (coal, oil and gas), deforestation and agricultural practices. Cement manufacture is a major contributor to CO_2 emissions, hence the interest for Lafarge. Since the beginning of the pre-industrial era around 1750, carbon dioxide concentrations have risen by nearly 30 per cent, methane by more than a factor of two, and nitrous oxide by about 15 per cent. Their concentrations are higher now than at any time during the last 420 000 years, the period for which there are reliable ice-core data, and probably significantly longer. Continuing GHG emissions in a business-as-usual scenario would mean that the atmospheric concentration of carbon dioxide would increase from today's level of about 365 ppmv (parts per million by volume) to between about 550 and 1000 ppmv by 2100.

Even with all this evidence, the link between climate change and human activity is nevertheless difficult to prove. Although temperatures and GHG concentrations are clearly rising, some argue that this is part of nature's normal cycle of climate fluctuations. While we would expect to experience more frequent extreme weather events if there is global warming, it is not possible to attribute the cause of any particular storm or drought directly to climate change.

Figure 3.4   The greenhouse effect

Sources: Okanagan University College in Canada, Department of Geography, University of Oxford, School of Geography; United States Environmental Protection Agency (EPA), Washington; Climate change 1995, The science of climate change, contribution of working group 1 to the second assessment report of the Intergovernmental Panel on Climate Change, UNEP and WMO, Cambridge University Press, 1996. With permission of GRID-Arendal (http://www.grida.no/climate/vital/03.htm).

As to the consequences of climate change, these may not only be gradual. Some scientists also point to the risk of catastrophic climate events, such as a diversion of the North Atlantic Gulf Stream which would condemn Western Europe to an ice-age climate, or the melting of the Siberian tundra which would release enormous further quantities of CO_2 into the atmosphere.

The principal method put forward to combat climate change is to reduce emissions of greenhouse gases, which effectively means cutting use of fossil fuels, such as oil, coal and gas. But the changes will need to be drastic if we are even just to slow climate change. The long-term challenge of stabilizing the atmospheric concentrations of greenhouse gas concentrations will eventually require global emissions of greenhouse gases to be significantly lower than today. Given the economic growth that is to be expected in the meantime, it is evident that the kind of improvements in energy efficiency required to mitigate global warming could mean either genuine shifts in lifestyle or substantial economic disruption. Whatever the case, technological change will have to play a major role.

The case

Lafarge's cement business will be substantially affected by policies to mitigate climate change. Some policies would be very harmful to our business, others less so. Lafarge's public affairs objective is to get the least harmful policies. If we can forecast and adapt to these new conditions early, then it may even be possible for Lafarge to gain, but this depends on hard work, both lobbying for reasonable policies and preparing the company to really cut greenhouse gas emissions.

The stakes for Lafarge

Lafarge emits more than 45 m tonnes of CO_2 per year, almost entirely from the production of cement. That is more than Switzerland's total annual emissions of greenhouse gases. In common with the rest of the cement industry, the production of one tonne of cement at Lafarge involves emitting about three-quarters of a tonne of CO_2. Indeed, per € of turnover, the cement industry is one of the highest emitters of greenhouse gases. Given that cement is sold for $60–$70 per tonne and that econometric models show that if the Kyoto targets are to be achieved the price of a tonne of CO_2 would be anything from $10 to over $100 per tonne, clearly, climate change is important for Lafarge.

To manufacture cement, as shown in Figure 3.5, ground limestone is heated to 1450°C in a long rotary kiln. The resulting clinker is cooled quickly, then after the addition of some gypsum and clay is ground to the very fine powder that is cement. This process involves using large amounts of energy, usually coal, heavy fuel oil or petcoke, to fuel the 20 m long flame

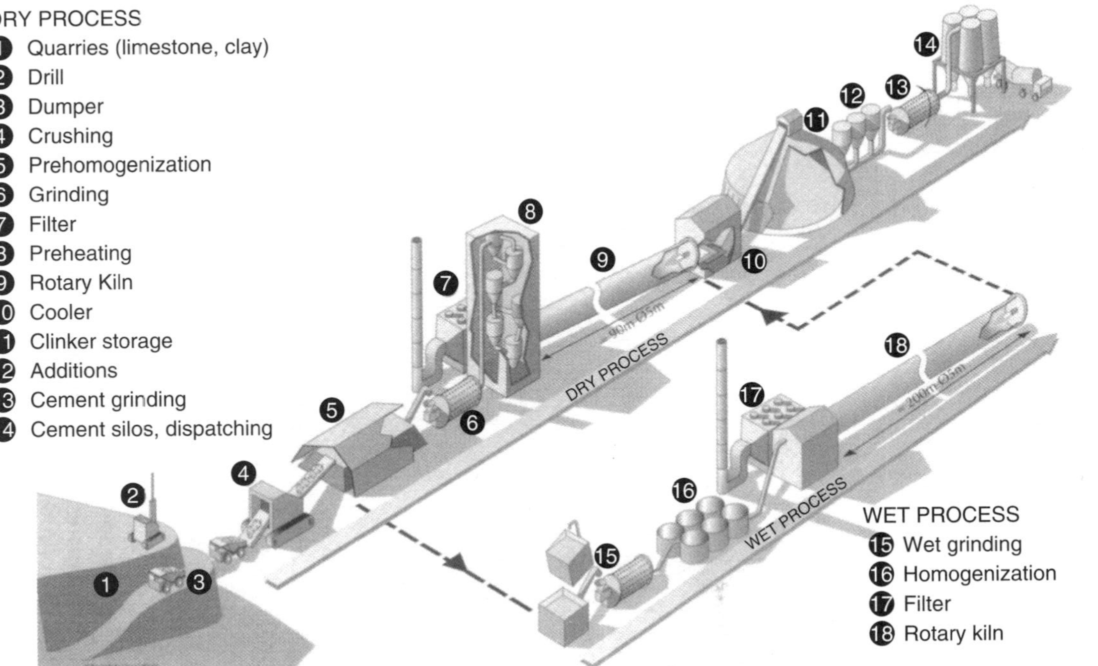

Figure 3.5   Cement manufacturing process
Source: Lafarge.

Table 3.1 Cement production and CO_2 emissions by region (1994, million tonnes)[3]

	Cement production	Total CO_2 emissions	Kg CO_2/tonne cement
OECD Pacific	151.3	104.9	693
Europe	181.9	129.4	711
Latin America	97.4	71.1	730
EE/FSU	100.7	79.6	788
Africa	41.0	33.0	803
Other Asia	123.8	104.9	847
Middle East	111.2	94.6	851
China	423.0	371.8	880
North America	88.4	78.5	887
India	62.4	57.9	928
Total	1380.9	1126	814

that heats the kiln. Also the electricity used to power the mills that grind the raw mix and the clinker gives rise to CO_2 emissions if it comes from a conventional source.

The CO_2 emissions from burning such fossil fuels count for some 40 per cent of the total emitted by the cement industry. The other 60 per cent come from the decarbonisation process that is part of the chemical transformation of the limestone from $CaCO_3$ to CaO that takes place as it is heated in the kiln and clinker is formed.

As Table 3.1 shows, the energy efficiency of the cement industry varies widely across regions in line with the level and history of economic development of each region. This demonstrates how the opportunities to reduce emissions differ widely. The USA, for example, has relatively high emissions linked to the low cost of power and the mature nature of the industry.

Political reaction to climate change

Popular opinion has been slow to take an interest in climate change. Given the complicated and uncertain nature of the phenomenon and the long time lags involved, the public policy debate has tended to involve only the few people especially interested in the environment and those directly affected by the policy measures being proposed. Resistance to abatement measures is focused among those most affected, whereas the costs of climate change are diffuse or uncertain. This means that support for action to combat climate change is often diffuse whereas opposition to particular measures is focused. Nevertheless, the occurrence of various extreme weather events, such as storms and droughts, has raised public awareness.

Pressure to reduce emissions is led by environmental groups and others convinced by the scientific arguments. The political process reflects these pressures in that countries where environmental awareness is high, such as

Germany or Scandinavian countries, have been the forerunners in pushing for action to be taken. Nevertheless, political leadership in most countries, led by environment ministers, has supported the need to take action. In Europe the need for action is broadly supported by the population; in the USA this is much less evident, with the Bush administration taking a more sceptical line that the previous administration. The open question, therefore, is what action should be taken.

International action to combat climate change

Since measures taken at the level of an individual country would be ineffective unless other countries follow suit, the policy response to the global warming has to occur at the international level. However, the very different levels of greenhouse gas emissions between the industrialized and the developing world (see Figure 3.6) complicate the international negotiating process. Nevertheless, the Framework Convention on Climate Change was agreed in 1992 at the Rio Earth Summit under the aegis of the UN, and the Kyoto Protocol agreed five years later in which countries committed themselves to targets for reducing their emissions.

At Kyoto, it was agreed to cut greenhouse gases emissions from developed countries by 5 per cent from 1990 to 2010. Because the developed world is largely responsible for causing climate change, the less-developed countries have differentiated obligations that do not involve commitments to reduce emissions, although this is expected to be the case after 2010.

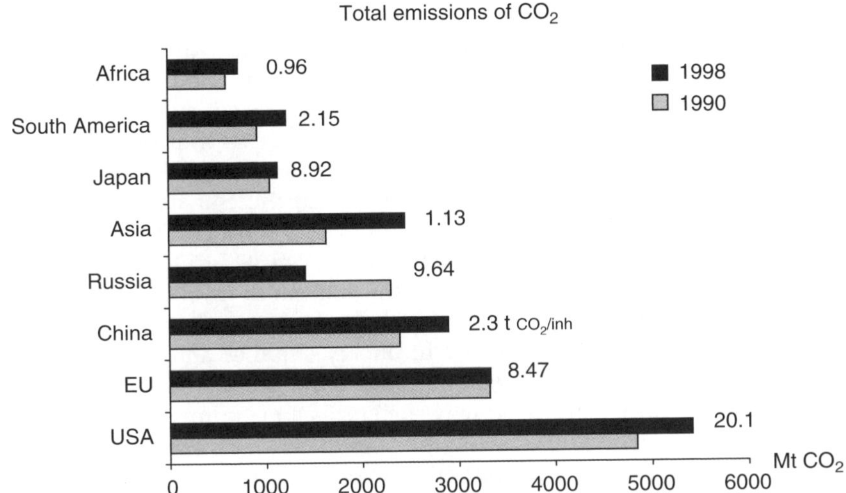

Figure 3.6 Emissions of CO$_2$ by region and by inhabitant

Source: International Energy Agency, *United Nations* Framework Convention on Climate Change.

Although the Kyoto Protocol is not yet ratified and may never be so given the extent of opposition in the USA, the Kyoto process to combat climate change represents a remarkable international effort to jointly agree on the need to take measures to deal with a global problem. The Montreal Protocol, signed in 1987, phasing out substances that deplete the ozone layer was a forerunner to the Kyoto process. However, the problems in achieving agreement on climate change are unprecedented given the much higher economic stakes and the interest each party has in seeing other countries take the burden of change.

The policy process in Europe

While climate change is a global phenomenon and Lafarge is a global company, it is important to realize that the main political pressure for action to combat global warming is coming from Europe. As a leader in the cement industry and with our main industry rival, Holcim, a company based in Switzerland – not an EU member – Lafarge is thrust into the centre of European public affairs work on this controversial subject.

In Europe, the European Union has been the principal forum for agreeing the public policy stance on global warming. The countries of Eastern Europe, many of them candidates to join the EU anyway, have generally taken their lead from the EU. Several factors would argue for the EU institutions, such as the Council of Ministers and the European Commission, to play a strong role in climate change policy relative to the EU member countries. First, it is a truly global problem that needs to be dealt with jointly. In addition, the subject is new enough for few member countries to have developed their own particular policies, which could act as a brake on developing a common position at EU level. It is also the case that environment ministers in most countries have relatively little power within their national governments, whereas their decisions at EU level are less subject to interference from other ministries.

In fact, other factors have meant that climate change is subject to a complicated hodgepodge of EU and national influences. One important element is the proposed CO_2 tax, first put forward by the European Commission in 1992 and still officially on the table. This linked the climate change issue practically from the start to that of taxation, which some countries regard as a domain of exclusively national competence. The EU CO_2 tax has since been superseded by a proposal to raise the minimum level of harmonized energy taxation. However, energy taxation itself has its roots in national policies to maintain self-sufficiency in energy supplies and has remained blocked at the level of the Council of finance ministers for many years.

This may be a principal reason why the European Commission has found it hard to obtain exclusive EU negotiating competence for the UN process of climate change negotiations, something that would probably increase efficiency. However, the European Commission has found it very difficult in recent years to take the lead in any policy area amid perceptions that it has gained too much power in the past. Nor has the European Parliament been particularly influential, something that relates also to its minor role when it comes to tax affairs, which largely remain a national responsibility.

Another factor influencing the mix of national and European responsibilities is that many of the policies and measures to combat climate change are likely to be developed at national level. For example, measures to improve public transport or to encourage the better insulation of houses are essentially national, regional or local responsibilities. Even the negotiation with industry of commitments to reduce CO_2 emissions takes place largely at national level, in spite of the evident potential to distort competition between countries.

National ministers and particular national positions have therefore taken a more prominent role in the EU context than might be justified by the subject. Nevertheless, the European Commission plays an important role in setting the tone for the debate at EU level, especially in the area of taxation and on tradable CO_2 permits. The European Parliament on the other hand is still on the sidelines. The consequence for public affairs work on climate change is that the EU debates and decisions taken in Brussels remain key, but influential national capitals such as London, Berlin and Paris also require attention. Strasbourg, the home of the European Parliament, has little to say for the time being, but might become more important should legal measures be proposed by the Commission.

Developments so far

The Kyoto commitments

Although an EU CO_2 tax was proposed as far back as 1992, the subject of climate change only really became topical for companies during the negotiation of the Kyoto Protocol which was agreed in late 1997. In Kyoto, the industrialised world, essentially the OECD countries together with those of the former Soviet Union, took on commitments to reduce their greenhouse gas emissions in 2010 by 5.2 per cent below their 1990 level (see Table 3.2).

Table 3.2 CO_2 emission commitment by country (million tonnes of CO_2 equivalent[4])

Country	Kyoto commitment (%)[5]	Emissions 1990
EU	−8	3469
US	−7	5174
Japan	−6	1170
Canada	−6	458
Russia, Ukraine, Baltics	0	2948
Australia, NZ	+8	304
Central Europe	−8	928
Total	−5.2	14450
Rest of the world		7740

Given the economic growth that can be expected in the meantime, the commitments represent cuts of 20–30 per cent or more compared to a business-as-usual scenario. This has been the basis of the rejection by many in the USA of the Kyoto Protocol. To them the Kyoto targets are simply too demanding, especially given the economic growth the USA has seen over the past decade, and would require changes that are too costly to be worthwhile. On the other side are the environmentalists who argue that even Kyoto will only have a negligible effect in mitigating global warming and that the targets should be much stricter.

The Kyoto Protocol is expected to be only the first step in a much longer-term process that will need to extend for many more years if global warming is to be kept in check. In particular the developing world will need to take on reduction commitments as their emissions are set to overtake those of the richer countries by 2010. Thus many of the elements of Kyoto will be with us much beyond 2010, which only adds to the significance of lobbying efforts in this field.

The EU arrangements

The EU negotiated in Kyoto as a unit, agreeing to its −8 per cent target on the condition that it has differentiated national targets within the EU 'bubble'. For each EU country, the commitments are as set out in Table 3.3.

Table 3.3 CO_2 emission commitment by country, EU (million tonnes of CO_2 equivalent[6])

Country	Kyoto commitment (%)[7]	Emissions 1990/5
Belgium	−7.5	139
Denmark	−21	72
Germany	−21	1201
Greece	+25	104
Spain	+15	301
France	0	637
Ireland	+13	57
Italy	−6.5	542
Luxembourg	−28	14
Netherlands	−6	208
Austria	−13	74
Portugal	+27	69
Finland	0	73
Sweden	+4	69
United Kingdom	−12.5	775
EU	−8.0	4334

These differentiated EU national targets were the subject of intense negotiation after the Kyoto Protocol had been agreed. While the different national targets for EU countries may at first sight seem unfair, they are meant to take into account the different situations. The main element is the need for economic growth of the less-prosperous countries. There are also countries' different industrial structures, such as the nuclear power industry in France, or the hydropower industry in Austria, both of which emit no CO_2 and thus cannot reduce emissions. Finally, Germany took on a target that takes account of the collapse of industry in the former DDR.

Interestingly, the differentiated commitments negotiated within the EU can be interpreted as the countries trading in tonnes of CO_2 at a price of zero. Assuming a price per tonne of CO_2 at, say, a relatively conservative $20, the result is actually some quite substantial transfers between EU member countries. Yet the decision was taken with virtually no economic analysis, without much involvement of finance ministers or even much coordination at national level. This illustrates the immaturity of the EU decision-making process in the area of climate change.

Nevertheless, the resulting burden of adjustment for each country might not be too unfair if recent emissions figures can be taken as an indicator. For example, Germany's emissions in 1998 had fallen by −7.5 per cent compared to 1990, whereas in Spain emissions have risen by over 13 per cent over the same period.

Policy initiatives

Naturally, effort will be required to reduce greenhouse gas emissions beyond business as usual and this effort needs to be stimulated through policy initiatives led by government. The burden of adjustment needs to be shared out between the sectors that emit greenhouse gases: transport, electricity, industry (including cement), domestic households and agriculture. The European average figures for emissions of CO_2 equivalent in 1990 are transport (20%), electricity (33%), industry (19%), domestic (20%) and agriculture (8%).[8]

Because the emissions from some sectors such as road transport are growing faster than the general economy, the pressure on industry to reduce emissions will be even greater than the −8 per cent implied by the EU target. There is therefore plenty of controversy over how to share the burden of adjustment between sectors, with much suspicion that some sectors are being advantaged because of their political sensitivity.

Another aspect is the danger, given the wide variance in national commitments within the EU, that industry sectors will be treated differently in different countries, leading to distortions of competition and unfair advantage. Some therefore argue that policies and measures to combat climate change should be agreed at EU level. There is however little indication of much action at the EU level. The energy tax remains blocked and even work on an EU emissions trading scheme is painfully slow.

In the EU and elsewhere, countries have already started taking policy initiatives, such as imposing energy taxes or setting up voluntary schemes to encourage reductions in emissions. Often industry has been the first sector to be targeted, since it is politically less costly and policies are more easily implemented than for other sectors.

The Kyoto mechanisms

At Kyoto, two important instruments were agreed that use market-based incentives to encourage reductions in the emissions of greenhouse gases.

Emissions trading

A significant element of the Kyoto agreement, especially from the point of view of business, is the provision to allow the use of tradable CO_2 permits. This is intended to introduce an element of flexibility into the framework, since it does not matter from the environmental point of view where the reductions in greenhouse gas emission take place.

Under such a system, tonnes of CO_2 could be traded. Thus, if a company reduces its emissions by more than required, it would sell the excess and vice versa. For a company, its costs of reducing greenhouse gas emissions would be capped by the price of a tonne of CO_2 equivalent, since it would always have the option to buy a permit rather than make the actual cut.

From the point of view of industry, tradable permits would provide an element of flexibility that would reduce the cost of compliance without compromising the environmental objective. Studies of the US system of SO_2 permits set up in the 1990s to control the emissions from power stations that cause acid rain show that the costs of compliance were reduced by around 50 per cent through the use of tradable permits. The European Commission expects that a system of tradable permits in the EU could save up to one-third of the costs of achieving the Kyoto targets or even more if the trading extended throughout the developed world.[9]

The environmental lobby is, however, very suspicious of tradable permits. Many green non-governmental organizations and even some European governments argue that allowing tradable permits will allow 'hot air' into the Kyoto framework. Tradable permits, they argue, would allow Russia and the Ukraine to sell the tonnes of CO_2 in reduced emissions that have come about from their post-Communist economic collapse. This is termed 'hot air' because it has not occurred through any special effort on their part, but through economic developments beyond their control.

Some also feel that it is not morally right to have a system that allows the rich to pay for the right to pollute. In this way, they argue, tradable permits would allow companies to escape the burden of reducing emissions themselves.

Tradable permits are important for the cement industry because their use will lessen the incentive to move production in order to meet reduction commitments. CO_2 trading would be especially useful in the cement industry since it is basically a local industry because it is so expensive to transport cement due to its low value and its bulk.

Clean development mechanism

Another flexible mechanism agreed at Kyoto is the Clean Development Mechanism (CDM). This is intended as a way to use the value of certified emissions reductions from projects sponsored by rich countries in developing countries as an incentive to encourage such investments. Basically, the tonnes of greenhouse gases reduced beyond a 'business-as-usual' baseline are made available as credits to the investment partners.

A third Kyoto mechanism, Joint Implementation, allows credits for projects in developed countries to be used as incentives. It is similar to CDM, except between two developed countries.

Many environmentalists object to the possibility that the CDM could be used for projects other than small-scale renewable energy investments. Industry argues that any project that cuts emissions of greenhouse gases should be eligible.

Another issue relates to the bureaucracy and controls surrounding the Clean Development Mechanism with the green lobby arguing for strict eligibility criteria and monitoring which industry fears will render the instrument unusable.

Lafarge's climate change strategy and objectives

Lafarge believes that we need to act to fight climate change. Our world is facing a problem that requires effort from all concerned, and it requires an international effort such as the Kyoto Protocol or something like it. This does not mean that we are totally convinced by the scientific arguments put forward in support of the global-warming thesis, but we should nevertheless take precautions. This is the first step in a proactive strategy. Other companies have not gone so far. Moreover, recognizing political and scientific realities, Lafarge has taken the basic decision to prepare itself to be operating in a carbon-constrained world in the medium term.

To some extent this decision is made easier by the fact that many of its consequences are, anyway, clearly in our interest. For example, to become more energy efficient will reduce energy consumption, helping cut our energy bills. However, other aspects are not so evident. The CO_2 from decarbonization, which is the major source of greenhouse gas emissions from the cement industry, is the inevitable physical consequence of heating limestone to make clinker. To avoid such emissions will take substantial technical research and a rethinking of the way the industry operates and may never be achievable.

Lafarge's objectives for its climate change strategy are manifold:

- Gain efficiency and thereby competitive advantage over competitors both from other industries like glass and steel and within our own industry.

- Avoid costly regulation that would hamper our business without contributing to the environmental objective of reducing the emissions of greenhouse gases.
- Achieve a flexible and efficient regulatory regime that works with the grain of business, not against it.
- Obtain fair share of burden of adjustment compared to other emitters.
- Reinforce our image as a proactive industry leader in a rapidly changing world.

Lafarge has a long tradition of responsible management and good business sense that have helped it become the largest construction materials company in the world. Climate change is but the latest challenge that it has faced. Our experience has shown us that it is better (and cheaper) to move before being pushed.

Taking a proactive stance also gives the company advantage over slower-moving competitors in a number of ways. First, it gives first-mover advantage, provided we are right in our analysis that we are heading for a carbon-constrained world in the medium term. Second, it is good for the morale of current employees and positive for future employees. Third, Lafarge's strategy in response to climate change rests in the research and technological know-how. Lafarge believes it has a competitive advantage through its advanced research facilities and technological capabilities. As an industry leader, we have an interest in raising the standards in environmental terms, helping improve the situation in the cement industry. Thus, although combating climate change is costly for us, it may be even more costly for our competitors, so adding to our competitive advantage.

In common with the rest of the cement industry, Lafarge has three main levers with which to reduce its emissions of CO_2:

- *Increase the energy efficiency of cement plants.* This is probably the least efficient lever because much has already been done and it involves large investments.
- *Use cementitious waste materials from other industries.* Blast furnace slags from the steel industry have cementitious properties provided they are properly cooled and handled. Also fly ash from coal-fired power stations can be blended with Portland cement. It has been estimated that some 150 m tons of slag is produced and 450 m tons of fly ash accounting together for around 40 per cent of cement production. Again substantial investment in technology and equipment is required to make use of these industrial waste products that are generally discarded for the time being. However, provided the quality and the logistics can be made to work, there is potential to use these products economically as a substitute for cement, thus saving CO_2.
- *Replace fossil fuels with alternative waste fuels.* Since a cement kiln burns much hotter than a commercial incinerator, waste products, such as old

engine oil, used tires and animal meal, can be used to replace fossil fuels that usually fire the kiln. This requires considerable investment in the technology to burn the wastes efficiently and safely without compromising the quality of the cement. There are also costs in the equipment needed to handle the flows of waste. However, charging these costs to those responsible for the waste sometimes offsets this.

Our allies and opponents

Global warming is a controversial subject with different countries taking very different positions, which makes predicting the effects for Lafarge all the more difficult. It is the subject of much debate in public policy circles, making for a complex lobbying strategy for industry because of the rapidly moving agenda, the numerous interest groups and the ways in which they all interact.

Environmental NGOs

The main pressure on politicians to act on climate change is coming from environmental non-governmental organizations such as Greenpeace and the Worldwide Fund for Nature (WWF). Such groups are well-organized, they network effectively and they have considerable technical expertise. Their tactics vary depending on the organization, but there are three main varieties:

- Some groups, such as Greenpeace, do little work on the ground, but specialize in exerting political pressure on governments and companies to take action. They sometimes use high-profile publicity tactics designed to bring public attention to the cause. Greenpeace, for example, insists on maintaining a strict independence from any government or company, refusing to accept contributions from anybody but individuals.
- Other NGOs, such as WWF, do much conservation work on the ground as well as acting as a pressure group on environmental causes. They are prepared to form partnerships with industry in order to help improve environmental performance, which they see as a better way of influencing behaviour.
- Yet a third group are quasi-academic NGOs, such as the Pew Centre or World Resources Institute, both based in the USA as most such organizations are. These groups link closely to academia and focus their efforts on examining the possible solutions to global warming. They develop and apply the latest science and are in the forefront of public policy approaches to the problem.

In contrast to much of industry, which remains suspicious of, if not antagonistic to, environmental NGOs, Lafarge has tried to develop close links with the second and third categories of NGOs. Our view is that these NGOs are important actors in the policy debate and that dialogue can help bring both sides closer.

Lafarge has a formal partnership with WWF that started in 2000 with climate change as one of its elements. Our goal is to work together to develop Lafarge's climate-change strategy. We also have contacts with Environmental Defense, a Washington-based NGO that has set up an initiative to encourage companies to take voluntary measures to reduce greenhouse gas emissions linked to trading in CO_2. Through our membership of the World Business Council for Sustainable Development (WBCSD) and other business organizations, Lafarge also has contacts with numerous other environmental NGOs active in the climate change debate.

Media and public interest

Much of the public and most of the political world in the USA can be characterized as indifferent to the issue of climate change. Some even go so far as to regard it as some kind of plot by European green activists to undermine the American way of life. However, paradoxically, President Bush's opposition to the Kyoto Protocol may actually raise the public profile of climate change in the USA.

In Europe, on the other hand, public opinion in environmentally aware regions such as Germany or Scandinavia shows substantial support for action to combat climate change. Whereas in southern Europe there is much less grasp of the issue or sympathy for changing policy. The public in other OECD countries, such as Japan, Canada and Australia, tend to be somewhere between the USA and European positions.

The developing world is more concerned with the desire for economic development than with climate change, even though some of the poorest countries could be hardest hit, especially by rising sea levels. The developing world is therefore suspicious of richer countries' efforts to persuade them to take a different, less-CO_2-intensive growth path. They see the global warming problem as one created by the rich countries and which those countries should therefore solve.

Governments

Naturally, national governments tend to reflect the state of public opinion in their countries; however, there are differences of approach that are important for industry to take into account.

In the US, the Clinton administration tended to take a rather progressive line compared to public opinion perhaps because of the personal interest of the President. This resulted in a large gap opening between the policy of the administration and the attitude of Congress, which remained very negative to Kyoto. The US line was nevertheless very market-oriented. The approach of the Bush administration appears to be more conservative.

In Europe, the traditional splits have opened between the more market-oriented countries such as Britain and the Netherlands and the more dirigiste, principally Germany and France. These differences of opinion are also reflected in the Commission and the European Parliament.

For industry, especially in Europe, this has meant occupying a difficult position between governments that are opponents of taking significant action and those that are supporters. The temptation is to take a reactive stance in line with the USA, but which clearly antagonizes many European governments.

The governments of developing countries have started to take more prominent positions regarding climate change, and China, India and Brazil have played prominent, but very different roles. Some developing countries are interested in the Clean Development Mechanism, but more as a source of development aid than for its environmental value.

Industry

Of course, the positions taken by industry reflect the scientific and policy controversies on global warming. It is interesting to look at the oil industry where there is a clear difference in the way that leading companies approach the subject.

On the one side are Exxon and other US-based oil giants, who have strongly resisted the environmental arguments for change, for example through the Climate Change Coalition. On the other side are BP and Shell, European-based companies who are making the environment a plank of their business plan. BP has even re-christened itself 'Beyond Petroleum' as part of its new corporate identity. Other industries and companies tend to fall between the two extremes seen in the oil industry.

Our lobbying strategy

As is often the case in public affairs work, Lafarge is faced with the choice between taking a proactive stance and a reactive stance. Reaction is often the initial choice, especially in a policy area like climate change that is subject to scientific uncertainty and implies substantial change. Reaction takes the form of resisting the proposed changes, such as taxes or restrictions on CO_2 emissions, but it does not put anything in their place. Proactivity, in contrast, implies the recognition that change is necessary and is about influencing the choice of policy measures, for example by proposing voluntary commitments to reduce emissions instead of taxes.

Lafarge is firmly committed to being proactive on climate change; we recognize that global warming is a phenomenon for which the application of the precautionary principle is justified. To deny this, as some parts of industry appear to do, would in our view damage our credibility and make us less able to achieve our objectives. Nevertheless, Lafarge has strong views on the policies that should be introduced to combat climate change. For example, Lafarge:

- opposes energy taxes on energy-intensive industry, as being inefficient from the environmental point of view and unfair economically;
- supports negotiated commitments as the most efficient way for industry to reduce emissions;

- sees emissions-trading as a useful way to make explicit incentives to reduce emissions and to reduce the costs of compliance without compromising the environmental objective;
- wants the Clean Development Mechanism to act as an incentive for investments that reduce CO_2 emissions in developing countries; and
- is concerned that the burden of adjustment is shared fairly between different sectors, since this is the basis of an efficient response.

In order to get these views accepted, the arguments must be brought across to the opinion-formers and the public. This means refining the arguments and targeting lobbying actions on the most influential groups at the right time.

Lafarge rarely has the opportunity to influence the debate on its own. We therefore act where possible in various industry groupings agreeing and communicating common positions on climate change. The main groupings are as follows:

- At the global level, Bertrand Collomb, our Chairman and CEO, is an enthusiastic and founding member of the World Business Council for Sustainable Development (WBCSD) which acts as a voice for some 150 proactive multinational businesses on issues such as climate change. As well, Lafarge is active in the OECD Business and Industry Advisory Committee (BIAC) where I co-chair the climate change sub-committee.
- At the European level, an important vehicle for Lafarge is the European Roundtable of Industrialists (ERT). Lafarge's previous CEO, Olivier Lecerf, was a founding member of the ERT in which now Bertrand Collomb, too, plays a prominent role. Another grouping is Cembureau, the European cement industry federation.
- Finally, at the national level, Lafarge is active in national cement industry federations wherever we are present. In France, we are also active in the 'Entreprises pour l'Environnement', which is a proactive grouping of French-based companies.

Of course, joining with others in such groupings means agreeing common positions that sometimes involve compromises. But this is balanced by the greater number of ideas and the opportunities to persuade and convince others that are available by working in a group. Lafarge works hard to avoid the 'lowest-common-denominator' problems that often afflict such associations, in that the least progressive members determine their positions. We are generally satisfied that alliances with others are an important way to put our arguments forward.

What is happening?

Climate change has been gradually rising in the public's perception, triggered by extreme weather events and by pressure from environmentalists. Governments and the European Commission are embroiled in a marathon intergovernmental negotiating process. Actual policies and measures are beginning to be put in place, earlier in some countries than in others, depending on their administrative efficiency and their enthusiasm about the issue.

Business is engaged in the public debate, as well as discussing with European and national government officials dealing with the subject. Energy-intensive industry is highly mobilized at this point in the debate in a cooperative effort, although some countries and some sectors are putting in a particular effort. The cement industry is one of them, which is understandable given the stakes for us.

Some would characterize the debate as governments and the public sitting between the convictions of the environmentalists and the influence of big business. Of course there is some truth to that, but in fact some governments have Green Party environment ministers, including France and Germany, and other governments are adopting the kind of frameworks that business is putting forward. Also, many businesses, such as Lafarge, are eager to be seen as part of the solution rather than part of the problem. At the same time some environmental NGOs are beginning to see the merits of moving forward into actions to reduce emissions, rather than continuing to argue for their ideal solutions.

It is useful to distinguish several areas within the climate change debate that are highly interrelated, but which have their own characteristics as far as the lobbying process is concerned.

The Kyoto process

The UN intergovernmental negotiating process involves governments, including the European Commission, in a massively complex set of negotiations around the Kyoto Protocol. NGOs and business are generally present in the margins of the negotiations, if not as part of national delegations. The annual Conference of the Parties (COP) has become a media circus as was the most recent COP6 at The Hague in November 2000. It is an ideal opportunity to lobby because all the main actors are present, as is the world's press. However, the timing is not perfect since the governments tend to have their positions well-developed and therefore inflexible. Also, most have recognized the lobbying opportunity of COPs and the stage is therefore crowded.

Lafarge is generally present for part or all of the COP meetings and takes part in side events. We tend to concentrate on the topical issues of interest to us, however the bulk of the lobbying at such meeting is left to industry groups, such as the WBCSD.

Energy taxes

Several European countries, as well as the EU, are trying to set up energy taxes as part of their efforts of combat climate change. This has led to extensive lobbying efforts, especially on the part of energy-intensive industry including Lafarge, that have been criticized by environmentalists. They argue that big industry has used its power wrongly to defeat a good policy.

Our position is that the energy taxes proposed are neither environmentally efficient, nor economically fair. We would prefer to find our own ways to make the necessary cuts in emissions, negotiating with the government what is a fair objective compared to other industries and sectors. Such a system, like that in place in Germany, has the advantage of letting industry find the best way to avoid becoming uncompetitive in a world without uniform energy taxes. It is not our position to argue that energy taxes are wrong for all parts of the economy, but rather for energy-intensive industry, which has special characteristics.

Lobbying work on energy taxes has concentrated on Brussels and Paris as far as Lafarge is concerned. Brussels, as it was the origin of the first CO_2 tax proposal in 1992, which would apply throughout Europe, and Paris, where Lafarge is based, because of the écotaxe proposals of the French government. Nevertheless, our position on energy taxes, which is shared throughout energy-intensive industry, is argued whenever useful, such as at the OECD, in Brussels or in the capitals concerned.

It is perhaps useful to distinguish a number of different stages in the life of any EU piece of legislation, which require different tactics. These apply as much to the EU energy tax as to other issues.

Stage 1: the idea is debated

Here Lafarge takes the view that we need, above all, to participate in the discussions rather than snipe from the sidelines, as has often been the case for business in the past over issues such as the energy tax. Since we believe in the power of our arguments, it is important to explain why we consider energy or CO_2 taxes are the wrong instrument for combating climate change – why it is environmentally inefficient and economically unfair. The target audiences are the ministers or commissioners involved and especially their ministries or officials, but also those involved in the public debate such as politicians, NGOs and academics.

In addition, at this stage, building and maintaining consensus among the wider business constituency is also a vital element of the job, since different companies are affected in different ways. If business can speak with one consistent message, then it will come across more forcefully. Our positions are the subject of fairly intense debate within business organizations at the sector level and across industry, both at national, European and international levels. There is, however, a strong sense of solidarity within the business community.

The forums used to get our message across vary widely. Individual contacts with ministers or their officials, either at the level of Bertrand Collomb, the Chairman and CEO of Lafarge, or at my level are relatively rare. Just as important are letters to the press, public interviews, participation at conferences or working groups, or formal position papers – for example in response to discussion papers from the European Commission or from national government, or other means.

Industry federations or other groupings play an especially prominent role for us, especially on the European lobbying scene where Lafarge does not really have the weight to influence matters by itself. The WBCSD and ERT are especially important since both these organizations have built credibility from past actions that help add weight to the messages they give. Our European industry federation, Cembureau, has a major role, too, in Brussels and Lafarge spends much effort developing common positions within the European cement industry.

Another area not to be forgotten is our own staff. Plant directors are encouraged as good corporate citizens to develop contacts with local communities and politicians. In countries where we are present, Lafarge staff generally play active roles in national industry associations and through them in Cembureau. Therefore our own people, too, should carry the same climate change message. This means spending time and effort to ensure that they understand our position on energy taxes and why we have adopted it.

Stage 2: the criticism is made and even accepted by some, but what to do instead?

Since Lafarge wants to be proactive in the climate change debate, it is important to be able to move beyond the basic anti-tax message to address the question of what should take their place. We believe that voluntary or negotiated commitments are the right way forward.

Support for negotiated commitments is the subject of controversy within business circles, with some companies reluctant to offer commitments, especially accompanied by sanctions, if they are not respected. They are no doubt worried by the costs of such commitments and hope to avoid them altogether. Lafarge sees them as the most flexible way to contribute towards efforts to mitigate climate change. More important, we believe that for credibility it is necessary to be explicit on which policies should be put in place instead of energy taxes. Anyway, solidarity between businesses has its limits; if Lafarge is seen to be more proactive than others, it may help our image and influence.

In general, the move to stage 2 in lobbying terms is often neglected, perhaps because it is not easy to accept the need to change. It is nevertheless important to be able to respond to the evolution of the debate. Naturally, this evolution happens at different times for different participants, so the approach must be well-matched to the requirements. The target audiences are basically the same as those of the first stage; it is the content of the arguments and the timing that are the delicate issues. Moving too early to a proactive stance can fog the message of opposition, moving too late can compromise a proactive strategy. Above all, preparation is vital to prepare future positions to ensure that they are robust.

Stage 3: the drafting stage

Here matters move to a different level. Looking at the European context, the European Commission is the exclusive initial drafter of legislation, which is the principal source of its influence on the Brussels scene. This means that at the outset there is probably a single European Commission official working on your dossier that should be your first port of call.

One of the positive points about Brussels in lobbying terms is that it is relatively transparent. It is also a fact that Europe is large and the European Commission is understaffed. Officials are therefore usually happy to dialogue and receive information on their dossier, especially if it is constructive. This leads to an open-door policy on the part of most officials, which should be used. Coming up with practical suggestions and comments at an early stage can save many hours of lobbying energy spent later. The key is to prepare yourself well, which is not easy at an early stage of an issue, and to gear your arguments to the objectives of the drafter. In other words, one needs to be proactive in approach to influence the text.

Naturally, other officials get involved in drafting the text, as well as cabinets and finally Commissioners, so arguing for your suggestions needs to be geared to the various stages that any legal text follows in the Commission.

On the energy tax, given the enormous financial stakes there was naturally much effort devoted to lobbying at all stages. Energy-intensive industry concentrated on the clauses excluding certain products or reducing rates for their sector. Indeed the exclusion for chemical reduction processes (Article 13 of the Commission proposal) can be seen as a victory for the industries concerned (aluminium), compared to other industries like cement which have conceptually very similar process emissions.

Once a draft proposal leaves the Commission, lobbying efforts need to move to the national capitals, where national positions are usually prepared, and to the European Parliament. Here the argumentation often needs to start from the beginning once more.

Negotiated commitments

Lafarge takes the view that energy-intensive companies should undertake their share of the adjustment burden through commitments to reduce CO_2 emissions negotiated with the government. Effectively, we are asking governments to tell us what they need in terms of emissions reductions and then let us get on with it. Naturally, we are reluctant to do the reductions *and* to transfer money to governments.

At European level, progress on negotiated agreements has been frustratingly slow, not because there is much opposition to the ideas, but because the European Parliament is worried about losing its influence. It sees negotiated commitments between the European Commission and industry as replacing legislation by the back door. Indeed, such accords are negotiated by the Commission, agreed by the Council and have a similar effect to formal legislation. Thus, their agreement at the European level is opposed by the European Parliament. The European Commission does not appear particularly concerned about this state of affairs, probably thinking that such agreements are more trouble than they are worth. The Council, on the other hand, is content to adopt such accords at the national level where ministers can adapt to their national situation.

However justifiable the institutional problems may be, the result is little progress at the European level. The resulting national free-for-all can only make the level playing field for industry in each country yet more uneven. But this is often the case for controversial subjects at the European level. If negotiated agreements do become standard practice, then it will be because some countries showed that they really work.

So our strategy is to concentrate on willing countries. At the time I write this, in Germany there is an accord at the level of the whole industry. Commitments are being negotiated in the UK, due to start in 2001. Plans were moving ahead in France, but the draft law instituting a new energy tax was declared to be against the constitution just before it was due to take effect at the start of 2001. Our prospective take-over of Blue Circle Industries, the leading UK cement manufacturer, will hopefully allow us to widen Lafarge's experience in such negotiations.

Emissions trading

This is where economists meet the real world. In theory, allowing companies to trade emission permits cuts the costs of compliance overall. If it has an emissions cap, the benefits of trading from a company's point of view are clear, since it can purchase a permit representing a tonne of CO_2 if it costs less than the company's own cost of reducing a tonne of CO_2. So the emissions cuts will tend to be made where they are the least costly. Overall the amount of reduced emissions is the same, but they take place where they cost least to do.

While this may seem clear to most business people, others see trading as some kind of immoral system that would allow the rich to pollute. But this attitude has tended to be most widespread in Latin countries. Emissions trading has been most enthusiastically supported by the Anglo-Saxon world, but other countries are also keen.

Not surprisingly, the European Commission has taken an interest in the subject of emissions trading. It has produced a green paper on the subject, looking into the need for a European framework. This is quite justified in the view of business, because the wider is a trading system, the more it can reduce costs. The European Commission has set up a working group on the subject involving Commission officials, business, governments and environmental NGOs. Lafarge is a member of this group representing the European Round Table of industrialists. The working group is still very much in the exploratory stage with a genuine attempt by the European Commission to learn from all sides about the subject. To a large extent we are advancing together into unknown territory relating to the interaction of different emissions trading systems.

The advantage, from the lobbying point of view is the access to the officials who are likely to be involved in the drafting of any proposal from the Commission. Although the group involves a lot of work, it will hopefully move things forwards at least as far as common understanding is concerned.

Conclusions and lessons

What have we achieved?

Lafarge and others that feel the same about the threat of global warning have achieved some advances, however progress has been frustratingly slow especially in the intergovernmental negotiations.

Put the business case

Most important in terms of public affairs, the business voice is being heard loud and clear in the global-warming debate arguing for practical approaches that will provide incentives to business to help in the fight against climate change. This was not evident at the outset, after all the instinct of business is basically introverted until a threat is clearly evident. Moreover, business is up against environmental organizations with well-developed communications skills, many of who see industry as the main culprit.

Most serious participants in the debate now recognize that the only way to effectively combat climate change is through harnessing the power of business to come up with solutions. While many proposals still circulate that would not act in this way, there is at least a strong body of support for an efficient system of incentives.

Avoided energy taxes, but threats remain

Up to now the application of higher energy taxes on energy-intensive industry has been largely avoided. Sometimes energy taxes have not been adopted, or if they have, energy-intensive sectors have not been hard hit either through sectoral exemptions or by way of negotiated agreements. Nevertheless there is still strong pressure from many quarters, not least finance ministries looking for resources, so the threat remains.

International negotiations process leaning towards business model, but blocked

The Kyoto negotiations process, judging from the near accord at the November 2000 COP6 in The Hague, was moving towards a business-friendly model. Heavy rules and regulations are generally regarded as the wrong way to go. Market-friendly mechanisms that involve incentives, such as emissions trading and a simple Clean Development Mechanism look more likely.

However, the Bush administration's rejection of the Kyoto process has brought further uncertainty to the international negotiations, which is unhelpful for business that is trying to prepare for the future.

Negotiated commitments are gaining, but too early to judge

In the area of implementation of national greenhouse gas reduction targets through policies and measures, governments are generally embracing negotiated agreements with industry as a way forward. Although such agreements do have drawbacks concerning enforcement and free-riders, they give industry the flexibility to implement cuts in greenhouse gas emissions in a least-cost way that they choose without transferring resources to national treasuries.

Emissions trading increasingly accepted, but not yet in place

One of the most prominent tests of whether the Kyoto framework will be an efficient way to encourage reductions in greenhouse gas emissions is whether emissions trading will be a component. My judgement is that there has been significant progress in convincing sceptics, especially the environmental NGOs, that such a system can work without endangering the environmental integrity. In particular, the European Commission now takes a clear line in favour of emissions trading.

How did we do it?

Of course Lafarge has just a small voice in a global debate; however, some elements of our approach have, I believe, helped move things forward in a way that will better encourage business to look for solutions to reducing greenhouse gas emissions.

Not a hopeless case

Perhaps most important, we have been able to convince others of our arguments because they have some merit as ways to solve the problem. There is little to be done without good arguments, although good arguments are not necessarily enough.

Proactive strategy

Comparing the European situation with that in the United States, one could characterize US industry as having chosen simply to block any measures to combat climate change, whereas European industry has taken a more proactive line. Which has been more successful?

At the time of writing, US industry looks to have won because President Bush has declared Kyoto dead and refused to impose limits on CO_2 emissions. However, the question is whether that is a long-term strategy. I believe not. Sooner or later, emissions of greenhouse gases will be constrained, so it might be less costly to move early and be prepared, than to resist and be forced to move later.

Engagement: WWF

Lafarge's partnership with WWF is still in its early stages, but already we have influenced each other. In particular our relationship with WWF, as well as numerous other dialogues and contacts with environmental NGOs, has helped persuade them of the advantages of trading, while we have appreciated the importance of ensuring environmental integrity in the system.

Hard work

Global warming is a vitally important and highly controversial issue that is actively debated in many forums. To influence the debate requires much time and effort. If this hard work is not put in, then it will not be surprising that poor decisions are made.

Right time, right place, right message

Finally, the usual principles of lobbying apply in that it is no use having a good message or argument if it is not applied at the right time and in the right place.

Lessons for the future

What should we do differently in the future?

Catch the issue earlier

There is no doubt in my view that industry tends to come late to this kind of debate. Perhaps this is natural given the competitive nature of the private sector, which leads to concentration on short-term survival. However, introversion can be risky when major threats appear from unexpected directions, such as climate change.

One way to appreciate whether such changes are likely to be real or not is to engage in dialogue with outside stakeholders, such as customers, suppliers, local communities, NGOs and governments. This is one reason why Lafarge has set up its partnership with WWF. However, becoming transparent and receptive to external influences requires a change of culture that will take time and effort.

Become part of the solution

In the context of a global problem such as climate change, it is only when industry is perceived to be part of the solution that it is able to truly influence the policy debate. This comes back to the question of whether to adopt a proactive or a reactive stance. In terms of lobbying for an efficient policy response, more work needs to be put into developing the efficient policy responses rather than resisting the inefficient ones.

Build an industry-common position efficiently

There is nothing a bureaucrat or policy-maker prefers than to have his or her opponents divided. This allows the imposition of policies that may otherwise be resisted or amended.

It will therefore be important for the future to make the effort to build common positions that can be supported by all sides of industry. Up to now, we have been fairly successful. Even European and North American industry have remained remarkably united on most points of substance throughout much of the debate, although German industry has taken a largely anti-trading stance.

Objectives for the future

The debate has only just begun on global warming and how to respond in order to prevent it from having catastrophic consequences for our planet. Whatever the state of negotiations at present, at Lafarge we believe that we are heading for a world in which carbon emissions will be constrained in one way or another in the medium term. This determines our objectives for the future.

Find the opportunities

Most importantly if Lafarge is to prosper in the long-term, we need to be at the forefront of finding the business opportunities that will arise when we are in the carbon-constrained world that we foresee. The strategy of being an early mover is designed to achieve this.

As a company we need to mobilize research efforts to develop the products and processes that will be needed in future. We should already be looking at how our customers and suppliers will react to a carbon-constrained world. History is littered with companies and even whole industries that have not reacted to changes in the marketplace and have therefore declined or even died out. At Lafarge, we are convinced that there will be as many opportunities as threats from global warming.

Improve awareness within Lafarge

The people who work at Lafarge are not very different from any cross-section of society. Most of us are therefore not well-informed on what climate change means and how best to tackle the problem. Clearly, given the serious implications for the cement industry especially, this must be corrected. Only when it is clearly understood within Lafarge why climate change is important and how we intend to prepare the company, will we be able to best harness the potential that we have to find the opportunities.

Satisfy WWF

An important element of our partnership with WWF is related to climate change. Together with WWF, we want to be an industry leader in environmental performance and especially relating to climate change, and we are discussing with them how best to do that. Our objective is to find agreement with WWF in a way that satisfies their environmental objectives as well as our business objectives.

Cut CO$_2$ emissions

Finally, Lafarge's performance as far as climate change is concerned has to be measured in terms of our CO$_2$ emissions. We will need to cut our emissions over the next decades, not only measured per tonne of cement produced, but also in absolute terms if we are to measure up to the challenge ahead of us.

Notes

1. See <www.lafarge.com> for more information.
2. See the speech by Robert T Watson, the Chairman of the IPCC, to the COP6 in The Hague, 20 November 2000.
3. C.A. Hendriks, E. Worrell, L. Price, N. Martin and L. Ozawa Meida, January 1999, Ecofys.
4. Million tons of CO$_2$ equivalents for the six greenhouse gases (CO$_2$, CH$_4$, N$_2$O, PFCs, HFCs, SF$_6$); EU Commission.
5. Reductions from 1990 level to the average of 2008–12.
6. EU Commission, *Preparing for Implementation of the Kyoto Protocol*, COM (1999) 230.
7. Reductions from 1990 level to the average of 2008–12.
8. EU Commission, *Climate change – Towards an EU Post-Kyoto Strategy*, COM (98) 353, pp. 10–11.
9. See Annex 1 of the European Commission's Green Paper on 'Emissions Trading within the European Union', COM(2000)87 dated 8 March 2000.

4

WWF: European and Global Climate Policy

Tony Long, Liam Salter and Stephan Singer

Introduction

WWF is the world's largest private conservation organization. It has 4.7 million members and supporters worldwide and an annual expenditure of € 400m, euro over half of it raised from individual contributions. Its mission is to halt and reverse the accelerating degradation of the planet's natural environment and build a future in which mankind lives in harmony with Nature. The mission statement clearly positions WWF in a broader and more environmentally encompassing way than the more traditional view of the organization as being mainly concerned with wildlife protection.

WWF began 40 years ago. With projects in over 100 countries, the organization's strongest institutional representation has always been in Europe. This is the region with the greatest number of national organizations, fund-raising support and members. The organization has also invested in building a considerable lobbying presence in Brussels. WWF opened a European Policy Office (EPO) in 1989 with one staff person, partly as a response to the growing importance of the European Union in setting environmental policy and adopting binding legislation. The EU's influence in the environmental field had been given an important boost by the passage of the Single European Act in 1986 and the adoption for the first time of an environmental chapter in the Treaty (Articles 130r–t). Twelve years later the EPO staff now numbers over 20 people.

From its inception, the EPO placed an important emphasis on seeking to influence the policy and legislation of the EU institutions beyond the conventional relationship with the Directorate General for the Environment or the Parliament's Environment, Public Health and Consumer Affairs Committee. This wider scope for the EPO's work was a recognition that some of the most profound impacts on the environment came from other economic sectors lying outside the scope of more narrowly conceived environmental policy.

This 'integrationist' approach of looking at environmental policy as a cross-cutting issue across many different sectors was given formal expression in a European WWF strategic-planning exercise conducted in 1995. The exercise involved all the formal institutional WWF presences in the WWF European network – in other words, 15 WWF national organizations, five programme offices and several regional coordination and project offices. The result was an agreement amongst the whole network to concentrate its activities and resources on eight priority themes. These were: forest protection; freshwater conservation; fisheries and marine work; habitat and species protection; agriculture and rural development; regional policy, including the EU's structural funds; energy policy and climate change; and, Europe's global relations including trade, development aid and foreign investment.

These eight strategic objectives were further prioritized in 1998 and 1999 when four were selected to become the focus of global campaigns affecting the entire global WWF network: forests, fisheries, freshwater and climate change. It was at this time that a decision was taken to increase the resources and capacity of the European Policy Office to work on energy and climate issues in Brussels, especially in view of the growing importance of the European Union in international conventions dealing with climate change issues. Three staff persons in the European Policy Office are dedicated exclusively to working on energy and climate change issues.

The remainder of this chapter looks at two examples of WWF's lobbying approach and style in respect of climate and energy objectives. The first case study outlines WWF's efforts to keep EU policy-makers focused on domestic policies and measures (PAMs) in its lobbying positions in international climate negotiations. This contrasts with the US position, for example, which concentrates on emissions trading and carbon sinks rather than on managing domestic energy through energy-saving measures.

The second case study concerns WWF's successful attempt to ensure that the European Union would take an environmentally progressive position concerning the rules for new economic instrument, the Clean Development Mechanism, being developed under the United Nations Framework Convention on Climate Change (UNFCCC).

Case study 1: EU support for policies and measures to reduce carbon dioxide emissions from burning fossil fuels

Background

Climate change poses one of the most challenging threats to sustainable development and to survival of many already strained and fragile ecosystems such as coral reefs, cloud rain forests in the tropics and boreal forests in the High North. But the implied rise of sea level also endangers low-lying coastal settlements and small island nations. Many human activities such as dry-land agriculture and freshwater management, mainly in poorer tropical countries, are likely to be affected negatively by climate change.

Despite this overarching threat, solutions to climate change are not that easy to implement. Most of them are widely acknowledged to be cost-effective and provide many ancillary benefits to society such as creating new jobs, but climate policies are not environmental policies any more – they are pure economics. Carbon dioxide, or CO_2, the most prominent and important greenhouse gas is derived from burning fossil fuels – oil, coal and gas. Attempts to reduce the use of fossil fuels have a huge impact on the economy. Growing and inexpensive energy availability is the motor of increased industrial activities, one key reason for the wealth of the OECD and of rich communities wherever they may live.

Whereas most toxins or pollutants such as heavy metals, sulphur and nitrogen oxides can be removed from manufacturing processes or from cars by catalytic converters, CO_2 cannot. Reductions of CO_2 require shifts to other forms of energy, energy efficiency measures and completely new technologies.

Key constraints

Unlike many other forms of pollution or environmental threats, climate change does not happen immediately in one's backyard, for instance if the neighbours waste energy or one is driving a less-efficient car. Greenhouse gases impact globally and take time to have effect. The climate system is based on many inertias such as the heat flux in the oceans to balance the often chaotic weather conditions. Climate is nothing other than the average of the prevailing weather conditions over the past 30 years. But we know from science that climate change hits first those who are most innocent, such as fragile and poorer human communities in the Southern hemisphere who may already be living at the limits of harsh weather conditions. Ironically, they are the least likely to emit greenhouse gases. It also hits those who have not yet been born. Causes and impacts of climate change could not differ more – both in terms of timing and of regions.

Thus, climate policy is very much linked to equity – North–South as well as inter-generational. The international climate process takes notice of this fact; but it still requires an enormous exercise of responsibility and full acceptance of the precautionary principle to make the right decisions – not easy for most politicians.

Timeframe and events

The evolution of climate change as a major concern in national and international public policy has broadly followed the following stages.

The warm up period, 1988–92

In this period climate change/global warming turns into an issue on the global agenda as the UN Assembly supports the creation of a Framework Convention (UNFCCC). It also agrees on the setting-up of the

UN Intergovernmental Panel on Climate Change (IPCC), composed of thousands of scientists globally.

Meanwhile, the EU develops its position as the most progressive group among all industrialized nations in the run-up to the Earth Summit in Rio de Janeiro in 1992. Unilaterally, in Rio, the EU commits publicly to *stabilize* its emissions by the year 2000 based on 1990 emission levels and not to increase them thereafter. This objective represented more than was being required of all industrialized nations in the UNFCCC and had been agreed and signed by Heads of State in Rio, namely that industrialized nations were being asked to *return voluntarily to* 1990 emissions levels by 2000. This wording would have allowed them to increase emissions again post-2000, not to stabilize them in other words.

Within the EU, the Netherlands and Germany are the first nations globally that introduce national greenhouse gas reduction targets. The work of Germany's First Parliamentary Inquiry Commission on Climate Change (PEC) was instrumental in helping Germany to take a lead in the EU. The ongoing work and high-level consultations of the PEC (1988–96) impacted on the EU as a whole and prevented the emergence of those confusing and strange theories of the climate sceptics that successfully prevented progress in the USA and Canada. In the UK, the Conservative Party's successful showdown with the coal-miners in the 1980s benefited the growth of natural gas – and thus protection of climate.

At the EU level in these years, however, no single, coordinated climate or energy policy was agreed by the Council. During this period, the proposed joint carbon/energy tax failed to emerge or even to be taken terribly seriously.

'Rise to the challenge' period, 1993–95

Science on the dangers of climate change became more consolidated through the ongoing work of the IPCC. The UNFCCC entered into force globally as more than 50 nations had ratified it by 1994. The First Conference of the Parties to the Climate Convention in Germany (COP1, March 1995) laid the basis for the Kyoto Protocol (KP) through a mandate requiring negotiating parties to agree on a protocol by the end of 1997. Together with the developing nations, the EU was responsible for that 'Berlin-Mandate'.

The core of the mandate confirmed that present commitments by industrialized nations to cut greenhouse gas emissions would not be adequate. By the end of 1995, the Second Assessment Report of the IPCC, representing a consensus of scientists – including many climate sceptics – strengthened the conclusion that 'human activities have a discernible influence on the global climate'.

During the period, there was a lack of agreed, coordinated Policies and Measures (PAMs) in the EU. On the other hand, the first EU nations had started to implement domestic measures

'Professionals needed' period, 1996–97

As the EU had now become a club of 15, internal coordination did not get any easier. The Berlin Mandate led to eight official UN preparation meetings before Kyoto, each lasting for two weeks. Various informal ministerial meetings and COP2 added to the global 'climate marathon'. As a result of a fundamental change in the US position, COP2 agreed that any targets agreed in Kyoto should be legally binding. In these years the EU now tried to define PAMs for all OECD and industrialized nations in order to address:

1. the most important greenhouse gas emissions sectors of all countries concerned; and
2. industrial competitiveness.

Led by the USA, the other non-EU OECD nations rejected the proposal of any legally binding PAMs under the process leading to the Kyoto Protocol by insisting on full subsidiarity. At Kyoto, the EU insisted that industrialized nations should cut emissions by 2010 to 15 per cent below 1990 levels. The proposal was based on PAMs analysis for its own reduction potentials. While supported by the developing nations, this figure was far away from the proposals by Canada, Japan and the USA.

Finally, at the end of 1997, COP3 in Japan agreed on differentiated targets. Industrialized nations must, on average, cut greenhouse gas emissions by 5 per cent below 1990 levels, as measured on the average of five years of a 'commitment period' – 2008–12. Whereas the EU and most Eastern European nations must reduce their emissions by 8 per cent, Japan, Canada and the USA must reduce them by 6 and 7 per cent, respectively.

However, a 'deal' was made between the USA on one side and Russia and Ukraine on the other. These latter countries were given emissions-stabilization targets only (although both nations, due to their economic collapse, had already reduced their CO_2 emissions since 1990 by 30 per cent and 50 per cent respectively). And most economic forecasts foresaw emission levels staying pretty much below 1990 by 2008–12 for both countries even under fast economic recovery and high GDP growth. This would open the way for so-called 'Hot Air' emissions trading between Russia, Ukraine and the USA.

However, policies and measures figured prominently in the KP (Article 2), even before the eventual emissions reduction commitments under Article 3 or indeed any mention of Emissions Trading (Article 17).

At home, EU-wide programmes to fund energy efficiency (SAVE) and renewable energy (ALTENER) pilot projects are the only 'policies' that can be described as cross-border activities, but they offer no quantitative objectives to cut emissions. The stakeholder process of doubling renewable energies in the EU by 2010 had led to the emergence of a Green Paper (1997) with no legally binding consequences or commitments by member states. Similarly, agreement by the Energy Council to double co-generation of heat and power had been watered down by the new lower status of the commitment as a

'Communication'. Directives with legally binding targets to underline the EU's leading position in the climate negotiations were still missing.

The 'moment of truth', 1998–2001

The KP is far from being ratified globally; rules of the game are still unclear. In 1998, the EU confirmed and revised a 'burden-sharing' regime that described the emissions reductions duties that each member state would have to undertake to produce a result averaging out at the overall EU commitment from the KP. That burden-sharing regime is close to a microcosm of the real world – emission growth allowances for the poorer EU nations and reduction targets for the richer ones.

In 1998 and 1999 the EU was also very busy in defining a ceiling for emissions trading for both sellers and buyers in order to ensure that the majority of Kyoto commitments are met domestically and not by Hot Air trading. COP4 in Buenos Aires in 1998 called upon nations to clarify many outstanding issues such as the use of sinks and emissions trading by no later than COP6 in The Hague. COP5 in Bonn (1999) saw the first emergence of the EU's position on 'integrity of the protocol'. The EU has made its ratification of the KP dependent on the results and clarifications achieved in The Hague. Entry into force of the KP is still targeted for 2002, ideally to be announced at 'Rio plus 10' in South Africa, the Earth Summit 10 years after Rio.

In 2000, the EU confirmed its strong position on 'domestic action first' and rejected the broad use of sinks and Hot Air. The EU argued that these would destroy the integrity of the KP and allow key OECD countries to actually *increase* their fossil fuel emissions to the atmosphere rather than reduce them. The EU position was backed by science, most European industries and all NGOs.

The strong EU approach led to the breakdown of COP6 in The Hague in 2000. The EU resisted attempts by the USA and others to follow this weaker policy line. In contrast with earlier conferences, the EU remained strong and did not bow to the 'realpolitic' which claimed that the USA, Canada and Japan needed 'some' flexibility (that is, unlimited emissions trading, use of sinks) to able them to meet Kyoto commitments *and* ensure economic growth. Since 1990, CO_2 emissions by the USA, Australia, Japan and Canada have grown by some 6–12 per cent, whereas the EU has managed to meet the target it set itself in Rio to stabilize emissions by 2000.

Since 1998, the EU has been busy both at the Community level and also in domestic policies to elaborate, define and implement some policies that underlay their strong stand in The Hague. In early 2000, the EU started its European Climate Change Programme (ECCP) which should result in an EU-internal Emissions Trading scheme by 2005 but based on real targets, and coordinated PAMs in the sectors of energy demand, energy supply, industry, transport and agriculture. All these policies are being elaborated and defined currently in working groups with stakeholders from NGOs, industry, country experts and academia.

In early 2001, a draft Directive on doubling renewables in the EU from 6 to 12 per cent by 2010 has been agreed in principle by the Energy Council despite a few outstanding issues. Surprisingly, a new initiative for a Directive on energy efficiency in houses is under preparation by the Commission. This will tackle the high CO_2 emission-reduction potentials in that sector. Moreover, environmentally-friendly amendments to the Directive on liberalization of the EU-wide electricity and gas are under active consideration. A draft Directive on doubling co-generation of heat and power is under internal discussion by the Commission and is receiving much support from key member states.

At the national level, only eight member states have domestic carbon and energy taxes in place; but there is some domestic action. Most of those EU countries that have published their domestic Kyoto implementation plans have confirmed that they intend to achieve all greenhouse gas emissions reductions domestically and without the use of sinks. For example, Germany's revenue-neutral fuel and electricity tax accounts now for 10 per cent and 20 per cent respectively of the average consumer sales price of these commodities. Spain, Germany and Denmark implemented legislation for privileged increase of renewable energy. Not surprisingly, more than three-quarters of new wind capacity installed globally is now in these three countries. Scandinavian member states and the Netherlands have contributed to a high share of domestic co-generation. The shift from coal to natural gas, mainly in Germany and the UK, has led to substantial decreases of CO_2 emissions in the Community. In the past 10 years, many governments in the EU decided to either not embark on or to phase out nuclear energy and to attempt to build up a sustainable energy system without recourse to nuclear energy.

All these factors show that so far as climate policies and domestic action are concerned, the EU is already far and away ahead of the USA. Interestingly, the same divide is also true not only for industries but also sometimes NGOs. European industries now broadly back the EU approach for domestic action first. US companies, on the other hand, still prefer planting trees and buying Hot Air in Russia or receiving carbon emission credits for simple forest conservation in the Amazon basin. Sadly, a few US NGOs are also following this official government line – a distinctive split between the major global NGOs (Friends of the Earth, Greenpeace, WWF) and some US NGOs (Environmental Defense, for instance) became visible at COP6 in The Hague in 2000.

Present situation and outlook

As domestic actions in the EU show their positive effects – contributing to curtailing emissions while not compromising economic growth – much more is still to be done if the EU wants to achieve its Kyoto target of 8 per cent reduction in emissions. First, just three countries account for the EU's present emissions reductions of 2.5 per cent below 1990 levels.[1] The UK and Germany have pulled the EU to that level, assisted by Luxembourg; these two large nations have reduced their greenhouse gas emissions below 1990 levels by 10 per cent and 16 per cent respectively. All other EU member states have increased their emissions. In the coming years, the EU cannot rely any longer on these nations alone; more coordinated PAMs are needed in the *entire* EU.

Second, the Kyoto commitments do not account for the fact that greenhouse gas emissions eventually have to be reduced by more than 50 per cent globally in the next decades if the climate system is to stay within a safe corridor. Fundamental structural and energy policy changes are needed in industrialized countries in the subsequent commitment periods post-2012 if that reduction is to happen in harmony with the economy. The EU is far from ready to take these steps.

WWF's activities

Helping the 'Berlin Mandate' to emerge

By 1992, WWF entered the scene of the international as well as the national climate change debates as a visible player. Two years earlier, WWF had become a member of the global 'Climate Action Network' (CAN) representing more than 250 NGOs worldwide.

The first WWF initiatives were undertaken prior to, during and shortly after the Rio Summit in the context of the UNFCCC meetings in Geneva, focusing on the impact of climate change on ecosystems. Activities were mainly steered by the international WWF secretariat in Switzerland. Although public awareness on the issue was rising, WWF's contribution to solving the problem was rather marginal. For the public and the policy stakeholders, Greenpeace and other NGOs were seen to take the lead on climate and energy issues. This may be partly due to the slow internal process of WWF as it changed from being a largely field-based, nature conservation organization towards a more policy and advocacy-oriented international NGO.

However, this perception of WWF as a somewhat marginal player in climate change debates changed fundamentally in the run-up to and during COP3 in Berlin. As soon as it became clear that COP3 would take place in Germany – a key country for climate change mitigation – WWF strengthened its approaches to reaching policy decision-makers. Founding a climate team to accompany the COP1 preparatory meetings was instrumental. Clear decision-making capability in the WWF team, expertise from some key WWF staff, professional media work and awareness-raising in Germany and elsewhere as well as simple policy papers for delegates all helped to achieve the first success of WWF in that area.

WWF staff helped to draft a paper in Berlin in the second week of COP1 that was instrumental in launching the 'Berlin Mandate'. As things went, the EU and the developing nations (G77 and China) were internally paralysed on how to proceed as the USA, Russia and the OPEC nations were successfully blocking the introduction of a clear timetable for a protocol that would provide emissions reductions for greenhouse gases. Such a timetable (laid down in a mandate) would have been the logical consequence from the acknowledgement by the parties in the first days of COP1 that the present commitments to control greenhouse gas emissions – to voluntarily return to 1990 emission levels by the year 2000 – were not adequate.

'Isolate and embarrass' – this was the strategy CAN used in the corridors to polarize the positions of the USA and the EU. Thus, the EU was pushed into alliance with the G77. However, although the majority of the G77 supported a clear reduction of greenhouse gases by developed nations – such as the protocol proposal by the Small Island Nations (AOSIS) to cut CO_2 by 20 per cent by 2005 – its decision-making was paralysed by the mighty oil exporting nations assembled in OPEC. Together with India, WWF was working on text that would support the AOSIS protocol but would also take account of key concerns of China and other mighty developing nations as well. This paper was special insofar as it would split away OPEC from the G77 (the first and last time in climate history so far!) but would allow the hesitant EU to join. This new and powerful 'green group' emerged from the joint negotiating of the parties involved. Consequently, when all parties debated, the USA could not afford to publicly resist the principle of a Berlin Mandate (BM) anymore.

Serious involvement in PAMs

With the start of the international negotiations of countries of the 'Adhoc group on the Berlin Mandate' (AGBM) in autumn 1995, the EU tried to reach consensus within that particular UNFCCC body for common and coordinated PAMs in all industrialized countries. Although the USA initially indicated sympathy for this approach, there was hardly any strategic analysis on the potentials in sectors for PAMs to cut greenhouse gas emissions.

But, one year later, the USA completely changed course. It promoted 'legally binding targets' to be agreed in Kyoto but not coordinated PAMs. The well-known issue of 'subsidiarity' came onto the scene. Most NGOs favoured the US stance on targets rather than on policies and measures and jumped on this particular bandwagon. WWF, however, concluded that any greenhouse gas reduction target countries that might be agreed upon in Kyoto should be based on sound policies and measures; these should clearly demonstrate what can be done economically and technically. Without this knowledge, WWF concluded, countries would hardly be in a position to agree on legally binding emission cuts.

Consequently, WWF commissioned a report from the Utrecht University in the Netherlands whose starting point was on how the EU could achieve a

20 per cent reduction of CO_2 by 2005 – in other words, the same amount as the AOSIS protocol proposal for all industrialized countries supported by the global NGO community.[2] During 1996, WWF shared the outcome of this study with all EU negotiators in several workshops. Interestingly, the study concluded that a CO_2 reduction of 'only' 14 per cent was achievable by 2005 in the EU. This was based on the assumption that, apart from the extension of renewable energy in the EU, all measures taken were cost-effective and did not lead to capital destruction such as enforced early decommissioning of power plants.

From this study WWF achieved a credible reputation in parts of the business community and among government climate negotiators. The reason was that WWF's own study did not comply with the 'political correctness' of the 20 per cent target. WWF argued to get around this that in order to meet the 20 per cent target, measures on reductions of other greenhouse gases could be added which were not included in the study. Also, we supported that some of the overall reduction could be met through environmentally-sound joint-implementation schemes in Eastern Europe and Russia where huge emission-reduction potentials prevailed.

The Utrecht study set the scene for those measures taken in the energy supply and energy demand sector that are still discussed or are in the pipeline in the EU climate and energy policy currently. This is true for proposals such as doubling the renewable energy in the EU, increasing co-generation, efficient space heating in buildings and progressive standards for appliances.

The EU could not, of course, adopt the WWF-commissioned report's conclusions and recommendations for PAMs. Nevertheless, the Dutch government with its forthcoming Presidency of the European Union in mind for the first half of 1997 appointed the same researchers from Utrecht University for 'official' government purposes on the same subject. Utrecht researchers now undertook for the Dutch government an unusual project. Using a 'triptyche' approach, the researchers tried to find out how many emissions reductions each member state could achieve in the three key greenhouse-gas-intensive sectors – energy production, housing and industry. The result was a unique and comprehensive report with detailed calculations and clear allocations to member states.

Ultimately, the findings did not differ greatly from the WWF report and displayed emission reduction potentials in similar orders of magnitude. However, in order to be accepted by governments for a negotiation position on an overall Kyoto target proposal, these research findings needed approval by governments. The horsetrading among governments that became the 'EU Burden-Sharing Scheme' thus started. This burden-sharing scheme comprised a commitment by the 15 EU member states on what they should each contribute to the overall EU reduction target. The resulting aggregate EU number was a 10 per cent reduction target of three greenhouse gases (CO_2,

CH_4 and N_2O) by 2010 below 1990 levels. This 10 per cent reduction agreement included individual country targets that were far removed from any scientific justification and were largely different from each other. For instance, Portugal was allowed to increase its emissions by 40 per cent and Austria agreed to cut its emissions by 25 per cent in the same period.

Parallel to the 'tryptiche approach', the Commission had published an 'EU strategy for Kyoto' in the middle of 1997. The surprising result showed that the EU could cut CO_2 emissions by about 800 million tons by 2010 – and all this in a cost-effective way. This would represent a cut of approximately 17 per cent below 1990 levels. As the EU needed a kind of 'radical' idea to counter strongly-anticipated weak proposals for targets by the USA and Japan, the EU simply proposed for Kyoto a position to cut emissions of CO_2, CH_4 and N_2O by 15 per cent by 2010. This happened regardless of the fact that the EU internally had not agreed at all on how to meet the last 5 per cent. WWF and other NGOs confronted governments and the Commission with their own research and warned them not to cave in to the USA and others' pressure.

Not surprisingly, the 15 per cent 'negotiation target' for Kyoto helped the EU to move the other players towards more ambitious targets in the final Kyoto Protocol. The developing countries supported the EU position in principal, and in the end the USA, Japan and Canada were forced to move from their original proposal to cut emissions by only 0–2 per cent below 1990 levels to accept targets of minus 7 per cent and minus 6 per cent respectively. For the EU, a Kyoto target of 8 per cent emissions reduction by 2010 was established.

These targets must be considered a success given the resistance of certain countries to take climate policy seriously and given the rise of greenhouse gas emissions in many OECD nations in the 1990s. They would not have been possible to agree if the EU had relied solely on their earlier 10 per cent internal agreement. Efforts aimed at getting other industrialized nations to agree on absolute emission-reduction targets in Kyoto were only successful because the EU had backed their proposal with policies and measures which were reasonable and were widely supported by WWF and other NGOs.

Case study 2: The clean development mechanism

Background

In 1997 the Kyoto Protocol created an instrument for investing in energy projects in developing countries called the Clean Development Mechanism (CDM). By internalizing a dollar value for reduced carbon emissions, CDM projects promote lower carbon technologies. Little guidance was given by the Protocol on the rules and standards for putting into operation what is in practice a complex instrument. The elaboration of those rules and standards for the CDM can be expected to determine which energy technologies stand to benefit. Broadly speaking, a weak set of rules and standards could be expected to benefit marginal improvements in fossil and other business-as-usual energy practices. Weak rules would therefore offer little incentive for shifts in technology or business practices and, worse, could lead to a large number of fictitious carbon reductions from 'free-rider' projects.

WWF felt that as carbon credits accruing through the CDM can be directly used to comply with industrialized-country emission targets under the Kyoto Protocol, such credits come at a premium. WWF's position was that the CDM should be directed towards innovative demand-side and renewable energy activities, to act as a catalyst for driving real change in patterns of energy consumption and supply. The result was a more or less classic split. NGOs (North and South) and the emerging sustainable industry lobby in favour of tighter rules on one side were ranged against the conventional fossil, nuclear and large hydropower industry groupings in favour of maximum flexibility on the other. Caught between the two were those companies which have interests in both camps, for example oil companies such as BP and Shell with investments in renewable energy and a purchased public image as responsible multinationals of the future.

Prior to WWF's advocacy work, at the end of 1999 the question of what sorts of investment the CDM would drive and which sorts of technology options were most likely to benefit were not political priorities. WWF's intention was to develop a proactive position within the EU which could then be used to drive the debate at the international level through the Climate Convention. The following analysis will concentrate on the work which led to the adoption of a particular EU position at the Environment Council in June 2000. The case study will not examine the resulting impact of the EU decision on the international negotiations in The Hague in November 2000, which in any case remains an open issue.

How much are we playing for?

The CDM is an important issue for a number of reasons:

- Integrity of the Kyoto Protocol. Weak rules for the CDM could undermine the Kyoto targets by authorizing the import of free-rider carbon credits in hydro, coal, gas and nuclear sectors from developing countries to meet the industrialized-country Kyoto targets. Under weak, but by no means worst-case, scenarios free-rider credits alone could be used to meet 25 per cent of the industrialized-country reduction targets with zero climate benefit.

- As a potential major driver for renewables and sustainable energy markets worldwide. A well-constructed CDM could lead to a 300 per cent increase in renewables markets in developing countries by 2010. Conversely, a regime where renewables CDM projects are forced to compete against free-rider projects let in through weak rules would send a very limited market signal to renewables investors.

- As regards marketing, the CDM as a new economic instrument has been the centre of considerable media promotion in terms of conferences, publications, pilot projects and so forth. It should provide a useful vehicle for driving supporting market infrastructure development, for example international awareness-raising and policy work, should sustainable energy projects be substantial and realistic options.

Why the EU?

The EU was of central importance in the debate over the CDM for two reasons. Firstly, the Union negotiates at the Climate Convention as a bloc and is a signatory to the Kyoto Protocol in its own right. Secondly the EU views itself (rightly) as the environmental leader in the negotiations and is a logical vehicle for bringing environmentally-proactive new ideas to the negotiations backed with considerable political clout.

From the process perspective, member-state civil servants and Commission staff negotiate internal common EU positions which are agreed by ministers at the Environment Council and then used as the basis for the ensuing international Convention discussions. The Presidency is responsible for coordination and is very influential. The Commission is closely involved, has good technical expertise and usually tries to position itself in the centre of the EU position where it can act as a broker if necessary. The European Parliament is not a major player in this debate; although the Parliament will issue resolutions on climate issues, these are rarely followed up and are not normally influential in formulating common EU positions.

Timelines

The timing for WWF's work in lobbying for a proactive EU position on the CDM more or less covered the period of the Portuguese Presidency – the first six months of 2000. The target was to reach a decision from ministers on the issue at the June Environment Council which could then be used to drive the intensive international negotiation process unfolding in the second half of the year.

Techniques

The advocacy strategy concentrated on a very specific issue. It was necessary to deliver a clear and credible message to a limited group of the right people and then to back that message up through alliances and limited media work. In such cases it is crucial to get the message right. Not only must it be simple but it should also be tied into as many existing EU positions and desires as possible. Once key arguments had been developed a short draft briefing was put together and circulated not just to WWF experts but also to a limited number of individuals within governments and EU institutions where informal contact was possible to gauge initial response. Once the rigour and logic of the ideas had been reviewed in this way a product could be developed.

WWF advocated that the CDM should be focused on a 'positive list' of renewable and demand-side energy efficiency projects. The vehicle for the message was a four-page lobbying document which laid out the issue and clearly explained the logic behind WWF's position.

Getting on the agenda

The first task was to place the positive list on the EU agenda, and two things were therefore necessary – (a) a general awareness amongst the target group of the concept, and (b) champions willing to back the issue.

The target group was readily identifiable from WWF's previous work on climate issues. In cases where identifying the correct national or Commission representative was difficult, WWF was able to use its network of national offices. The location of champions was based upon personal contacts. Again this was not a problem given the organization's long-standing work and connections on the issue.

The focus document was therefore distributed to the entire target group slightly in advance of the first major internal meeting under the Portuguese Presidency. Four or five key member states with good track records on the CDM were asked to raise the positive-list issue as a central component of an EU strategy. The result was not agreement but the beginnings of a discussion around WWF's ideas. In fact, some disagreement between some of the proponents actually helped – internal discussion actually helps to cement an issue on the agenda.

Consolidation

The next steps involved consolidating the issue on the agenda and turning it into a priority. Continued contact with key officials, direct lobbying of problem countries, using national offices or other NGOs if possible and plenty of informal meetings took place week by week. Tasks were to maintain the profile of the issue, gather good intelligence, deal with bureaucratic blockages and defuse counter-arguments.

In addition mobilizing support from other organizations and constituencies was important so that the issue was not perceived solely as a WWF concern.

Alliances and opponents

The NGO community on climate issues is loosely federated around the Climate Action Network (CAN). The European branch of CAN is the Climate Network Europe (CNE), representing some 75 European NGOs on climate issues (including WWF, Greenpeace, Friends of the Earth) and based in Brussels. Consolidation meant gaining the support of CNE and its members and turning the WWF position into a CNE position – and eventually a CAN one as well. This was a relatively straightforward process as the positive-list concept was based on existing NGO positions and aspirations. With CNE members' backing, the positive-list idea then quickly became the EU

NGO position. Support also came from other areas such as GLOBE – the green parliamentarians network. Such widespread consensus substantially reinforced the geographical coverage and the intensity with which the issue was presented to EU governments and institutions.

The business community was split on the CDM. Brussels-based groups like COGEN Europe, the European Wind Energy Association and the European Photovoltaic Industry Association (solar) were supportive when engaged, and concerned about losing business opportunities abroad. EWEA and EPIA wrote letters to ministers on the issue, with COGEN producing and disseminating position papers on the CDM with the positive list as the central issue.

Companies and groups such as BP, Shell and World Business Council for Sustainable Development were more reluctant because of concerns from their oil and gas interests which also saw lost business opportunities from a CDM slanted towards a positive list. Despite considerable discussion, middle-of-the-road industry was not prepared to come out publicly and support the concept. Nevertheless, they learned two things. Firstly that the issue was a major one and they would have to be careful about publicly opposing it. Secondly, that there would be very limited benefits from the CDM to their renewables operations unless the CDM rules were rigorous enough to exclude free-rider competition. This led either to their silence on the issue or attempts at defining some middle ground between the NGOs and the conservative industry positions.

The conservative industry groups – oil, gas, coal and nuclear companies and trade associations such as UNICE, ERT and Eurelectric – were opposed to the positive list. However the issue was not considered a high enough priority for them to engage in much active lobbying and they were not really on the ball. The issue was very focused and demanded an insider's knowledge of the climate process and the individuals concerned; that is, a limited target group of government specialists. The conservative industry lobby did not really have the background to engage without considerable efforts – which they were not prepared to put in.

Media

Detailed policy issues are difficult media topics at the best of times. Given the complexities surrounding the CDM and the Climate Convention in particular, little coverage of the positive-list issue was expected. The main task with general media was to get across the concept of what the CDM actually was, and this was achieved using the nuclear debate.

The idea that an environmental convention could directly support the spread of nuclear power was of interest to some journalists and was also very well picked up by the anti-nuclear movement. Coordination with anti-nuclear groups meant that they could be kept abreast of latest political developments on the CDM and that the issue in general would continue to get some limited general press as a result of their responses. This helped to remind the civil servants and their ministers that the CDM was potentially a politically charged issue and that they needed to look good on it. One way of looking good was to support a positive list, which obviously would not include nuclear power.

Specialist press was accessible on a limited basis. Energy-trade media covered issues such as the potential for the CDM to deliver market incentives for sustainable energy in developing countries. Climate-related press, such as journals and newsletters, also produced or printed pieces discussing the positive list. These avenues were useful in legitimizing the concept and broadening the base of support but were not key components of the advocacy work centred on the EU.

Getting the result

By May, the positive list issue was high up the agenda of the forthcoming Environment Council, but exactly how to put it into operation was causing considerable internal discussion among the different countries.

Prior to the key Council meeting, two weeks of preparatory international negotiations took place in early June where the EU failed to go public with the concept – despite the fact that other countries were already voicing opinions. These negotiations were used by WWF to achieve three goals:

- An increase in pressure through direct contact, using the negotiations journal, side events and so forth.
- The gathering of excellent intelligence on the state of the debate within the EU and key lobby countries.
- The soliciting of support from other countries prepared to support an EU initiative on a positive list – and telling the EU about it.

After the negotiations – which also covered a whole range of other climate issues – and running into the Council meeting itself, the EU was still split. However, intelligence was good enough to understand the nature of the problem and what was causing it, and from this perspective WWF was able to propose a solution. This was achieved with a letter circulated through priority channels to ministers and key aides, and timed to coincide with the pre-Council briefings that ministers receive before coming to Brussels.

Against a background of growing urgency to reach a decision, the WWF letter helped to broker a useful compromise. This resulted in Council conclusions stating that the EU supported:

> a positive list of safe, environmentally sound eligible projects based on renewable energy sources, energy efficiency improvements and demand side management in the fields of energy and transport.

A mere three lines of text, but the ministerial conclusions underpinned the EU's negotiating position on the CDM in the international climate negotiations and at the Climate Summit in the Hague, in November 2000.

Lessons learned

From the perspective of lobbying at the EU level a number of lessons can be learned – some are obvious, others less so. For example:

- Access to key personnel is not difficult providing that your arguments provide value-added to the debate. Personal contact is easy but should be used judiciously.
- Process is time-intensive and continuous.
- Within a complex bureaucracy such as the Council and internal EU negotiations, good intelligence from a variety of sources is essential.
- Avoiding perceptions of national bias is essential – overreliance on support from a single country undermines that state's own credibility.
- The EU Presidency can be extremely important.
- Timing is key. Understanding the internal agenda and which decisions are taken where and when is essential.
- The situation within the EU is extremely unpredictable and fluid. Decisions and actions may have to be taken rapidly at short notice in order to limit damage or maximize opportunities. In addition, operating slavishly to a very detailed timetable reduces flexibility and freedom and can prove counter-productive.

Conclusion

These two case studies have sought to show how an international conservation organization, in this case WWF, works at a policy level in Brussels, in Europe and globally in EU decision-making and international conventions to shape the development of public policy as it relates to climate change. The distinctiveness of the EU position in international climate negotiations over the past decade, especially with its focus on domestic policies and measures to reduce energy demand, is due in no small part to the activities of environmental organizations throughout this period. The growing Trans-Atlantic divide on approaches to tackling greenhouse gas emissions, evident in President George W. Bush's rejection of the Kyoto Protocol within his first hundred days in office, is likely to place environmental NGOs in an even more influential position in the future. It seems that EU political leaders may be prepared to take a go-it-alone position *vis-à-vis* the USA. If so, it can be assumed that NGOs will become key agents in helping to raise public awareness and support for the implementation of the domestic policies and measures that will be necessary to reach the targets.

Notes

1. *European Environment Agency Topic Report*, Copenhagen, No. 6/2000. Summary in *ENDS DAILY*, 28 January 2000.
2. *Policies and Measures to Reduce CO$_2$ Emissions by Efficiency and Renewables – a Preliminary Survey for the Period to 2005*, WWF and Utrecht University, 1996.

5

Clean Air and Car Emissions: What Industries and Issue Groups Can and Can't Achieve

Robin Pedler

Los Angeles, USA is a remarkable city. It has similarities with cities in Europe, as well as a lot of differences. There is, however, one negative characteristic many of them share: they suffer from bad air pollution. Los Angeles is more notorious than, for instance, Madrid, but in both cities you can see the pall of pollution as you fly in. The major contributor to this worrying pollution is the motor vehicle, so this case concerns an issue that is important in all our lives.

The case tracks the development and eventual adoption of two parallel Directives that aim to address the issue and diminish the pollution. Like many Directives, Exhaust Emissions, and Petrol and Diesel Fuels, have technical and apparently boring titles. They do, however, affect us all. We all breathe air and nearly all of us also drive cars, if indeed cars can still move! The case shows us how EU policy develops in an important area and how it is increasingly concerned with the detail of our lives. It provides a good illustration of how the EU's decision-making process works in practice, how coalitions of interest groups try to influence it, and how successful they can or can't be.

Who are the stakeholders?

Firstly, and importantly, there are the *EU institutions*. We can see how the *Commission* develops policy; that's its job. As we move through the case, we can also see the growing power of the *European Parliament* and the way in which the members use their power. It is generally assumed that when the Parliament addresses an issue, if it concerns environmental policy, the members will be 'greener' than the Commission has been in its proposal. This case, as we shall see, is no exception.

The member states of the EU, all 15, are also stakeholders. They have at heart not only the interests of their citizens, but also the interests of their motor industry. Until the present day, a flourishing motor industry has been an important national symbol, almost like an army or a national airline. This led the member states, during the discussion of the Exhaust Emissions Directive, into some strong arguments, even some confrontations. Then, once they have agreed and decided, it is the member state administrations that will have to enforce the directive, which raises another set of issues.

Industry is of course a stakeholder. Very small variances in the reductions and controls mandated can cost or save industry millions of €. It should not be assumed that industry speaks with one voice; that is one of the ongoing facts about public affairs. In this case, industries organize themselves into federations. There are two large and powerful industries – ACEA, the motor manufacturers, and Europia, the oil refining companies – and as we shall see they have conflicting interests. Even within the same industry, the positions of competing manufacturers have sometimes been so far apart that they have split up the federation which represented them.

Issue groups, also known as non-governmental organizations (NGOs) are stakeholders, both informally because they want to be, and formally because their participation is now an accepted part of the decision-making process. This case is especially interesting because it shows the first example of an alliance of NGOs – 'Working for Environmental Sustainability' formally gaining 'a seat at the table'. They are pressing, however, to be recognized round many other tables. NGOs are stakeholders whom public affairs ignores at its peril.

To bring the catalogue of stakeholders full circle, let's not forget *ourselves*. While the processes of the EU institutions and public affairs are fascinating, in the end this is all about the air you and I have to breathe.

The final point this study will show is the time scale of EU decision-making, both how long it takes the institutions to arrive at a decision and the period which that decision covers. In both cases, it can be an amazingly long time.

The costs of the issue

Solving the problem of exhaust emissions is like many other issues in environmental improvement: the cleaner you make it the more expensive it becomes. As an Italian manager put it to the author forcefully: 'Look, then you come to a Fiat CinqueCento the cat [catalytic converter] costs more than the engine.'

For this reason, while the makers of large cars favoured the 'catalytic converter' solution, the makers of smaller cars favoured other, less-expensive control systems and so did the governments which supported them. Their differences fuelled an argument which raged for a very long time. It has now been largely resolved within the car industry, but we shall see strong arguments between that group and the oil companies over how to assign costs between extensive modifications to oil refineries and expensive exhaust cleaning systems on every car sold.

Table 5.1 Chronology of exhaust emissions controls

1970	First limits to emissions of CO and HC by petrol engines
1971–93	Progressive reduction in limits. Extension of controls to other types of vehicle (with Spanish Presidency compromise, 1987)
1994	Common (reduced) limits on CO, HC and NO_X for all passenger cars, with variations between diesel and petrol. Commission mandated to develop '2000' limits
1995	EPEFE: tripartite research enterprise – European Commission/ACEA (car manufacturers)/Europia (oil companies)
1996	Commission proposals to 2005
1998	European Parliament votes for more stringent proposals
1998	October – new directives agreed after conciliation

The EU began trying to limit exhaust emissions in 1970, and even the most recent legislation harks back to those first measures (Figure 5.1). Controls became progressively tighter and were extended to all kinds of vehicles. The latest directives, whose development and adoption this case examines, project increasingly stringent controls through the first decade of the current century and provide for research to develop them even further. We can see that EU policy aims to cover a very long period and reaches progressively deeper into our lives. This case also shows that it takes a surprisingly long time to develop one single piece of legislation within the process.

The Exhaust Emissions Directive was adopted in the 'First Pillar', so that is the relevant process. A policy is developed and a formal proposal is made by the Commission. The decision process then passes to and is concluded by the European Parliament and the Council, who debate, amend and argue until they agree on a 'co-decision'.

Although the struggle to control exhaust emissions had a long history, 1994 saw a significant change in the Commission's approach, demonstrated by the shift in 'lead' Directorate General. The directives adopted up to and including that of 1994 had been led by the Industry Directorate General (then DGIII). For these directives, the 'lead passed to Environment (then DGXI), although DGIII remained interested and played an active part in driving policy in at least one direction favoured by the car manufacturers.

The *legal base* for the new directives was therefore environment, and the Council which would take part in the process was the Environment Council. Environmental policy is subject to co-decision, allowing the European Parliament to exercise its powers. In this case, as we shall see, the Parliament had considerable influence on the outcome.

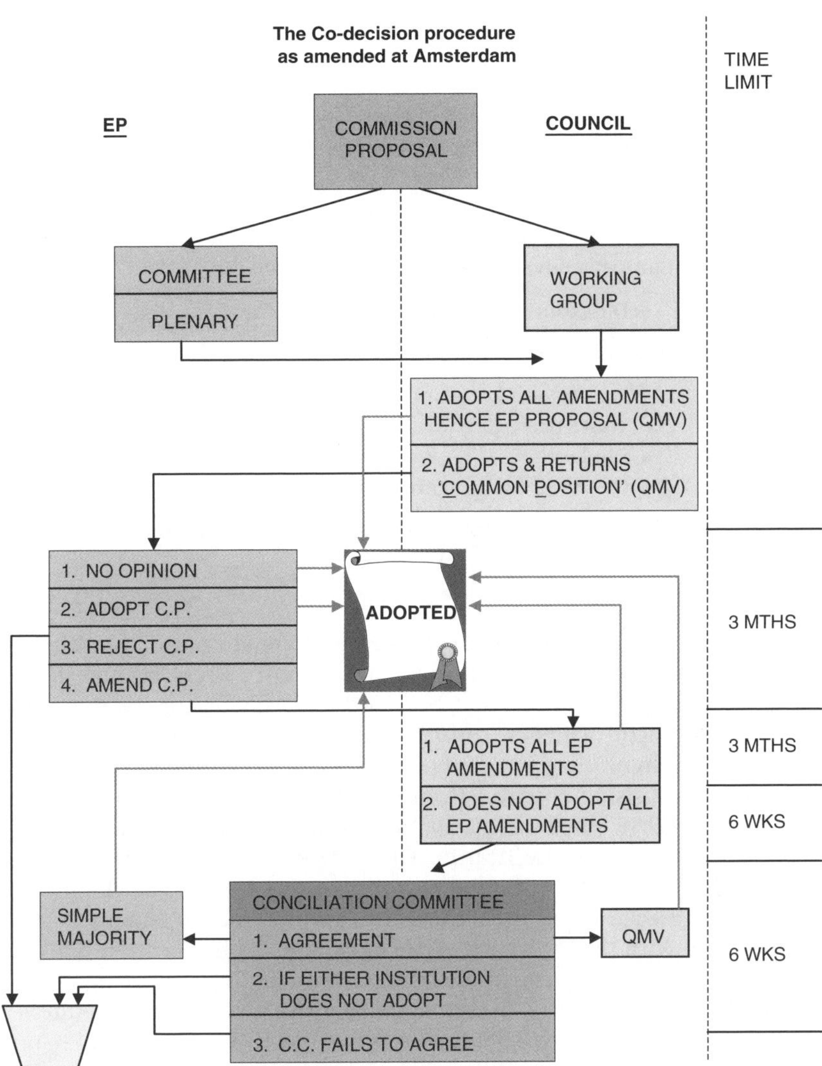

Figure 5.1   Co-decision procedure

Table 5.2 shows the names of the senior individuals involved and their nationalities as well as the issues under consideration. The Directorate General (DG) within the Commission for developing environmental policy was then responsible to the Danish Commissioner, Ritt Bjeregaard. The table also shows the other Directorates General within the Commission with an interest in environmental matters. It is usual to find several of the 27 DGs concerned

Table 5.2   EU environmental policy

Legal Base

- Single European Act, Arts 130 (r, s, t)
- (but also 100a – minimum standards)

Competence: concurrent member states and EU
Commissioner: Ritt Bjerregaard (Dk)
DG XI: Director General: James Currie (UK)
European Environment Agency – Copenhagen

- Director General: Jimenez Beltran

Areas of current action/interest

- Pollution of water and air
- Waste/packaging waste
- Eco-labelling
- CO_2 tax (conflict with member states)

Other DGs in the area: III (Industry), XII (R&T), XV
(Internal Market) XVII (Energy)

---

with any issue, which can complicate the development of policy within the
Commission. Apart from DGIII, mentioned above, these include DGVII,
Transport, although it appears that Transport had in practice little role to play
in the development of policy, surprising given that enhanced use of public
transport was a significant part of the policy to improve air quality.

The other surprising absentee from the debates and the decision-making
process was Health, since the motive for promoting improved air quality is
very much to promote the health of EU citizens. The Commission's own
responsibility for health is limited, but it does not appear that the member
states involved their own health ministries and the matter remained one of
environment, with the health effects included only by implication. This may
be an example of 'compartmentalized' decision-making.

Figure 5.1 illustrates the co-decision procedure followed by the measure. The
figure may look complicated, but it reflects real life; this *is* what has to happen
as a measure goes through. When the European Parliament (EP) and the
Council fail to agree at an earlier stage, the final text of the measure is settled
round the table at a Conciliation Committee, made up of representatives of the
15 member states and 15 members of the Parliament. One may say the matter
is settled, because, again, this is reality. Should the Conciliation Committee fail
to agree, the measure falls, giving the Parliament an effective right of veto. This
has, however, happened only three times in the seven years since the process
was established, while conciliation has worked in some 300 cases.

Both the Directives were decided by conciliation. The process towards the
new directives (Table 5.3) began in 1994, as soon as the previous Exhaust
Emissions Directive was adopted. In the 1994 Directive, the institutions

Table 5.3   Background from the previous directive

Exhaust emission directive 'towards 2000'

1   The Commission is mandated to propose new limits, and the European Parliament has indicated that these should not be above half of those settled in 1994

2   The car industry complains that EU limits have up to new followed US standards, whereas cars and roads are quite different. 'Can't we have a European solution?'

3   The European Programme on Emissions, Fuels and Engine Technology (EPEFE) – Auto-Oil Programme: the Commission 'co-opts' the car and the oil industries. They embark on a tripartite research programme, with ECU 10 million finance

4   Research begins to address the problem of CO_2 emissions and EU commitments (after Rio)

responded to some extent to vigorous criticism from the motor industry. This might be taken as a limited success for a powerful lobby. True, the Directive imposed stringent controls, which implied costs for the industry amounting to millions of ecus. The industry had, however, been successful in 1993/94 in fighting off proposals for even more stringent controls. They also convinced the institutions that they should, in further developments of policy, be treated not as arm's-length lobbyists, but as part of the process. They should have 'a seat at the table' – a development of what management academics call 'neo-corporatism'.

The main issue, which the motor industry wanted to address 'at the table', was that of the research which would underlie the next Directive in the long series. They hoped very much that it would lead to a 'European' solution, arguing that previous legislation had been far too ready to adopt the detail of US legislation which, the industry believed, had been developed for very different conditions and was not applicable directly.

A second issue was that future legislation should focus not only on output (exhaust emissions), but also input (fuels) and that there would be much potential environmental improvement from cleaning up petrol and diesel inputs. This brought the oil refining industry directly into play. While the two industries were to a large extent opposed, since saving of costs for one might well mean their imposition on the other, they were united in seeking to have the concept of 'cost-effective' included in any future legislation. They saw past legislation as driven essentially by 'best-environment' considerations, without considering cost-effectiveness.

They were successful to the extent that, in parallel to the technical research, chaired by DGXI, there was a cost-effectiveness study commissioned by DGIII and carried out by Touche Ross on data supplied by the two industries (Friedrich, 2000).[1] DGXI, meanwhile, commissioned its own parallel studies on ambient air quality. These sought to predict ground levels of ozone in 2010 across the EU.[2]

A specific issue for the motor industry was to seek legal approval for measures to encourage consumers to dump old vehicles in favour of new 'cleaner' models. This desire generated tensions between the institutional stakeholders. The member states jealously guard the right to impose and collect taxes, and they are therefore opposed on principle to any EU measure that deals with tax. So strong is the feeling that argument over this very point nearly destroyed an earlier Exhaust Emissions Directive in the mid-1980s and indeed held up its implementation for 18 months.

Technical research

DG XI established a research programme – The European Programme on Emissions, Fuels and Engine Technology (EPEFE). It was a tripartite operation, co-funded by the EU and bringing together the Commission with the two major industries concerned. EPEFE included both powerful industries, car manufacturers, represented by The European Vehicle Manufacturers' Federation (ACEA) and the oil industry, represented by Europia. Industry assisted

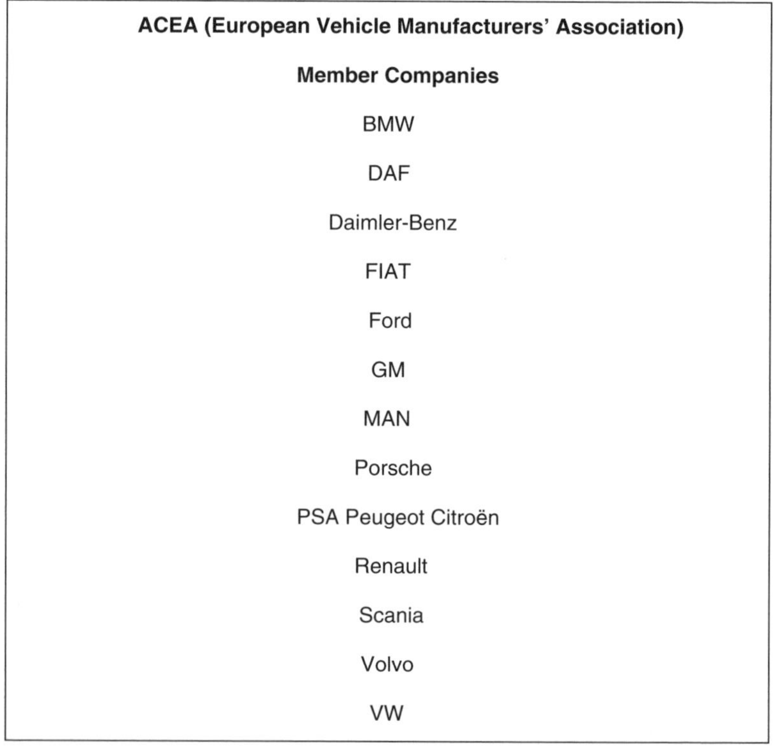

Figure 5.2   Membership of ACEA

Figure 5.3   Leading company members of Europia (out of a total of 75)

actively with the research, applying their own resources and technical back up. Membership of ACEA is shown in Figure 5.2, and of Europia in Figure 5.3.

Both the industry groups include companies of several nationalities. The car manufacturers have embraced the two American giants Ford and General Motors, long-established in Europe. They do not, however, include any of the Japanese or Korean manufacturers, who also produce in Europe. The representative of Toyota in Brussels told the author that the Japanese Auto Manufacturers Association (JAMA), and Toyota itself, had pressed hard with the commission to be included in the process, but had been forced to continue as a separate lobby. It has been commented that the Japanese manufacturers, in particular, were technically very advanced in emissions control.

While it was a logical approach to examine, in the interests of a cleaner environment, what goes into a vehicle as well as what comes out, the presence of these two powerful industries gave rise to some very strong arguments. Once again, decisions as to where the process should be 'cleaned up' – in the oil refineries or at the back of vehicles – had cost implications of millions for one or other of the industries, a level of costs reflected in the vigour of their lobbying.

The outcome of the EPEFE process was the Commission's proposals of June 1996 (Tables 5.4 and 5.5) for Directives to regulate the motor and oil industries. These proposals grew in parallel and developed into the Directives adopted just over two years later. As they went through the process, they were seen by the officials and politicians involved as a 'package'. The tables show in detail the limits proposed for the Exhaust Emissions and Motor Fuel Directives which concerned the members of ACEA and Europia.

Although these are particularly controversial directives, the timing is quite typical: two years of hard work and research to develop a policy into Commission proposals – 1994–96 – and then another two years of strong argument and amendment for it to go through the full process to adoption – 1996–98.

Table 5.4   Commission proposals, 1996: vehicles

	Emission target (gms/km)	
	---	---
Emissions	*2000* *(mandatory)*	*2005* *(targets)*
Petrol passenger cars		
CO	2.3	1.00
HC	0.20	0.10
NO_x	0.15	0.08
Diesel passenger cars		
CO	0.54	0.50
$HC + NO_x$	0.56	0.30
NO_x	0.50	0.25
Particulate matter	0.05	0.025

Source: Exhaust Emissions Directive, the Commission's Proposals, June 1996.

Table 5.5   The draft directive for motor fuels

	Gas	*Diesel*
Benzene (%)	2	
Aromatics (%)	45	
Olefins (%)	18	
Oxygen (%)	2.3	
Sulphur (ppm)	200	350
Cetane number		49
Density (kg/m^3)		845
PAH (%)		11
T-95 (°C)		360

Source: Commission proposals: fuels, July 1996.

The proposals are detailed, in that they set limits for each of the noxious chemicals associated with vehicle emissions: carbon monoxide (CO), Hydrocarbons (HC) and Nitrous Oxide (NO_x). They also distinguish limits for petrol-driven and diesel cars; and for diesels, for the first time, they identify a new and dangerous emission – 'particulate matter'.

The burden which these proposals laid on the industries may be summarized as a demand for a reduction of up to 40 per cent in the level of emissions. The 'good news' for the industries was that the reduction was less severe than the European Parliament had demanded when debating the 1994 Directive, although, as we shall see, the Parliament was able to use the co-decision procedure to reintroduce some of its demands.

The reaction of the vehicle manufacturers was to complain that the burden had been divided unfairly between the two industries. They felt that the emphasis was almost entirely on their requirement to clean up vehicle exhausts at their or their customers' cost, while little effort had been made to require the fuel suppliers to clean up their products, which would of course have imposed costs on them in their refineries. The motor industry claimed that the 'unfair burden' they suffered amounted to millions of ecus (now euros) per year. The Commission's own estimate was that the burden would be ecus 765 million.[3] A DGXI official commented 'The automobile industry liked the procedure. They did not like the outcome.'[4] They were not, however, able to shift the burden in subsequent lobbying, but neither did it materially increase as the measure went through the co-decision process.

The Commission's estimate of the cost of its 1996 proposals to the oil industry was ecus 3.1 billion.[5] The industry's own estimate of the likely cost was ecus 11.5 billion. They go on to estimate that amendments introduced during the legislative process cost them an additional €23.5 billion, though the cost could have been much higher had all the European Parliament's amendments survived the process.

The NGOs commented that the Commission's proposals were insufficient and demanded that, rather than take into account cost-effectiveness, the Commission should have based itself on the principle of best available technology (BAT) (European Environment Bureau, 1997; Transport and the Environment, 1997).[6]

The co-decision process

European Parliament

The Commission's formal proposals of July 1996 now began their progress through the co-decision procedure. They went to the European Parliament and the Council of Ministers for consideration, amendment and, hopefully, agreement.

The lead committee in the European Parliament was Environment, then chaired by a tough Scottish Socialist, Ken Collins. The rapporteur on the Exhaust Emissions Directive, whose job was to coordinate his colleagues' views and draft their joint opinion, was Bernd Lange, a German member, also a Socialist. He retained the post throughout the Parliament's two readings. The rapporteur on the Motor Fuels Directive was Noël Mamére (Radicals) At the second reading, the role of rapporteur passed to Heidi Hautala, a Finnish Green member.

Parliamentary committees were subject to vigorous and sustained lobbying, both by person-to-person contact and by written submissions. This applied not only to the Environment Committee but to others required to give opinions. The assistant to the Chairman of the Legal Affairs Committee told the author that his boss had received 27 submissions, two from industry and 25 from NGOs. (He also commented that most of them were useless, as they were too long and nearly all in English, a language that his boss, a Spanish MEP, does not read.)

The responsible official of ACEA told the author that, for person-to-person contacts, the member companies were careful to send persons who represented the nationality and so far as possible the regional interests of the MEP concerned.

Individual car companies, notably Renault, formed an unusual temporary alliance with the NGOs to argue for tougher controls on fuel. They were able to agree on the basis that cleaner fuels could be used in older cars, whereas the full effect of the Emissions Directive would only be apparent in models manufactured after January 2000 (AIT *et al.*, 1998;[7] Friedrich *et al.*, 1998;[8] Warleigh, 2000[9]).

It is a truism that the European Parliament is the 'greenest' of the three institutions and may therefore be expected to amend Commission proposals or Council opinions towards stricter environmental controls. This case was no exception. Collins and Lange had to bear in mind, however, that during the debate on the previous Exhaust Emissions Directive in 1993–94, while their committee had produced a long list of strong amendments, they had not been able to muster the votes amongst their fellow members in the plenary session to sustain their amendments in the Council position. (Very heavy lobbying was reported ahead of this vote.) They were therefore going for fewer, but stronger amendments, and this was to prove an effective tactic. The key amendments, which were introduced at first reading and survived into the Directive, were to make the proposed limits for 2005 mandatory and to introduce 'on-board diagnosis'.

On the Fuels Directive, the Committee was more aggressive, substantially reducing the Commission's proposed limits on all the chemicals concerned and inserting, for the first time, lower but mandatory levels for 2005. That would, by the industry's calculations, have cost them an additional € 50 billion, had all amendments found their way into the final directive.

On exhaust emissions, as we noted, the Environment Committee of the European Parliament decided to go for 'fewer but stronger' amendments. They nevertheless recommended 100 amendments

The Parliament's Environment Committee took their recommendations to the Plenary Session in the spring of 1998 and secured an absolute majority vote from their fellow members (auto-emissions 340 in favour 36 against, fuels 325 in favour 40 against). This put the Parliament in a very strong position in the co-decision procedure.

Environment Council: co-decision and conciliation

Both the industries concerned included large companies able to play the 'national champion' card to individual member-state governments. This was particularly the case in Germany, France, Italy, Spain and Belgium for the car industry, and in the UK, the Netherlands and France for the oil industry.

Responding to the Parliament, the Council faced 'more than 100 amendments which contributed to the complexity of the negotiations but also provided the material for trade-offs' (Shackleton, 2000).[10] Most of them were retained, again by substantial voting majorities, when Parliament considered the common position and passed its second reading in February 1998.

This triggered a conciliation procedure, whilst the Environment Council was led by the British Presidency. Ken Collins told the author that he felt the conciliation process on these two Directives was a prime example of the effective working of the 'trialogue process' (of which Collins is considered by many to be the originator). In these 'trialogues', the three players were Collins himself, The Deputy Permanent Representative from the UK, and the Director General of DGXI (James Currie).

At the final conciliation meeting on 29 June 1998, Parliament found itself facing a British Presidency with a strong domestic interest in finding a solution. The Deputy Prime Minster, John Prescott, had returned from the Kyoto summit at the end of 1997, committed to reducing the level of CO_2 emissions in Europe. He was therefore eager to ensure that a deal was reached on

Table 5.6   Exhaust Emissions Directive 98/69EC

1 Reduces permitted emissions as follows: (figures in grams per kilometer – all mandatory)

Petrol Passenger Cars	2000	2005
CO	2.3	1.0
HC	0.2	0.1
NO_x	0.15	0.08
Diesel Passenger Cars		
CO	0.64	0.5
$HC + NO_x$	0.56	0.3
NO_x	0.5	0.25
Particulate matter	0.05	0.025

2 Encourages more 'environmentally friendly' vehicles and notes the Commission's 'Car of Tomorrow' project

3 Encourages the fitting of 'on board diagnosis' (OBD)

4 Permits member states to encourage 'cleaner' vehicles by tax incentives

5 The Commission will 'monitor technological developments' and carry out research projects to propose future legislation after 2005

6 Petrol and Diesel Fuels Directive 98/70/EC adopted simultaneously. Sets limits for 2000 not 2005

Source: European Parliament and the Council, 13 October 1998.

the auto-oil package as a way of showing to the outside world that the EU was respecting the Kyoto deal. The British Presidency made it clear that it wanted to find a compromise with the Parliament. It suggested that the central element of that compromise should be an acceptance by the Parliament of the limit values laid down in the common position and by the council that those standards should be compulsory by the year 2005 rather than optional as proposed in the common position. (The 'mandatory in 2005' measure was indeed adopted for automobiles, but not for the Fuels Directive.) It was reported that the meeting took only 20 minutes to reach a conclusion 'because most of the contentious issues had been resolved by then' (Friedrich, 2000).[11]

The EP adopted the conciliation committee compromise on 15 September and the Directives were published in parallel on 13 October 1998 (Table 5.6). So far as exhaust emissions were concerned, with one minor variation in respect of diesel vehicles the maximum emission levels for the chemicals designated were set for 2000 and 2005 at the levels proposed by the Commission (though the Commission had limited itself to calling them 'targets' for 2005). Table 5.6 shows the key features of the Directive; in addition there are four other important elements in the text:

- 'More environmentally friendly vehicles'. The car industry recognizes this as an inevitable development, and most large companies have their own research programme. The issue was also taken up by the commission and the then research and technology commissioner, Edith Cresson, launched a project to develop the 'car of the future'.
- 'On board diagnosis' implies that the car industry will, in new models, use its advanced computer technology to improve emission elimination performance in every car.
- 'Member states may encourage "cleaner" vehicles with tax incentives'. This was a surprisingly controversial part of the directive, since some member states saw it as a small breach in the armour by which they protect all tax issues as being *their* concern, in which the EU institutions have no role. They accepted it during conciliation, however, and most member states are already applying it – France for instance by the 'Jospin FF 500' policy that encourages consumers to scrap elderly cars, and the UK by a complicated system of reduced road fund taxes. They seek to address the basic problem that, because of increasingly restrictive legislation, new cars are 'cleaner' than old ones.
- Probably the most significant new proposal in the document is item 5: the mandate to continue research in order to set further standards beyond 2005. The earlier, 1994, Directive which had set in motion the process described in this case, broke new ground in terms of EU policy-making by giving the Commission a formal mandate to research and develop further controls. This process is now legally continued. As we shall see, the prospect of further, research-based limits in 8–10 years' time is already generating vigorous preparation and lobbying.

Table 5.7   Directive 98/70 EC: potential costs to
the oil industry during the negotiation process

Stage	Costs (€ bn)
Commission proposals	11.5
Council common position	20
With EP amendments	60
Conciliation outcome	35

Source: Europia.

The potential costs to the oil industry varied as the negotiation process progressed, as shown in Table 5.7. In the case of auto fuels, the industry, as we see here, faced much more severe costs if the Parliament's amendments were to be adopted. The outcome of the co-decision process, however, while it meant that the industry still faced costs that it estimated to be three times as high as those proposed by the Commission, arising out of EPEFE, faced only 58 per cent of the much higher costs proposed in Parliament's amendments. One may speculate on the reasons for these reductions. It is clear, however, that the oil industries, established in almost all member states, would have put strong pressure on the national governments.

Public affairs lessons from the case

We may ask, What did the stakeholders get for all their lobbying? and Where do we go from here?

On the face of it, the *motor industry* did not achieve much. The emission levels proposed by the Commission were, with one very minor amendment, those imposed by co-decision of the Parliament and the Council, indeed they had been strengthened by making the medium-term limits mandatory. We must remember, however, that the proposals came out of the EPEFE programme, in which industry had been an equal partner with the Commission and the oil industry. Even if there were some complaints about the outcome being in favour of petroleum, we may take it that, in general, the motor industry is, as they themselves say, 'not unhappy with the challenge set' (interview with Margari, 1998).

The industry has also gained substantial advantages in the detail of the text. The first of these is that the words 'cost-effective' appear in the Directive, thus realizing one of industry's key objectives. They were keen that the limits set should not be those proposed by, for instance, the NGOs, who argued for the application of BAT without thought to economics.

The industry also achieved considerable modifications in the duty imposed by the Directive that vehicles respecting emission limits should be not only produced by them, but also maintained. It remains a keenly debated issue to see, once you or I have bought a car, whose responsibility it is that everything remains in perfect working order, the manufacturer's or ours. The original text proposed put, in industry's view, too much responsibility on them and opened them to the ultimate horror situation, a model recall, on what they held to be scanty evidence.

Finally, the Directive's authorization to member states to vary tax regimes in order to encourage 'clean' vehicles is very good for the industry. It is a reasonable proposition that if markedly 'cleaner' new vehicles are mandated, the environment will benefit if people drive those rather than older, 'dirty' vehicles. It will, of course, benefit the industry's sales if governments use tax incentives to encourage consumers to dump their old cars more quickly and drive new ones. It is partly for these reasons that the industry 'accepts the challenge'. Their technical efforts will be devoted to meeting it and their lobbying efforts are already focused on the standards to be determined by the next round of research, which has now started.

The *oil industry*'s achievements and conclusions are very different. On balance (at least in the car industry's view), they seem to have done better in the early stages of the process. The limits proposed for them, however, were materially and potentially expensively lowered by Council and, especially, Parliament. The final settlement reflected to a large extent the Council's common position ahead of a second reading. This meant that, while limits were reduced, reductions did not go as far as Parliament wished and that limits were mandatory only for 2000, not 2005.

There is one interesting effect of this final detail. Under the Auto-Oil II programme now under way (discussed below), the oil industry feels vulnerable because the motor industry is already subject to mandatory limits for 2005, so the subject cannot be reopened. This would remain true even if, as the oil industry suggests, there might be scope to combine some modifications to fuel specifications with modifications to vehicle design.

The *NGOs* did not succeed in getting legislation based on BAT, rather than cost-effectiveness. They did, however, as we have seen, play an active role in an *ad hoc* alliance to tighten up the limits imposed on the oil companies (and increase the costs to those companies).

NGOs become formal players in policy-making

We have seen how major European industries organized themselves to play a key role in this case at the stage of policy formation. We shall now examine how another increasingly powerful group of interests, the NGOs, achieved a similar status. They were of course already strongly, but up to now informally, involved. A senior official of DG XI commented to the author that the Auto-Oil proposals 'were not seen as credible, because industry was so openly involved and the NGOs were not'.

'If you have an issue to manage, you will have an issue driving it' (Pedler, 1999).[12] Issue groups, that is NGOs, are numerous. At the European level there are some 600 recognized and listed, and many are well-organized and funded. For a long time they have been expressing their views to officials and politicians, trying to influence policy. Now they are becoming better organized and, in the case of the Auto-Oil programme, for the first time they assume a semi-official role.

This is a trend which will continue. NGO representation is already under discussion in other policy areas, and their adoption into the system is encouraged by a European Commission policy of an 'open dialogue' which effectively means involving NGOs. The phrase 'open dialogue' was first used by the former President of the Commission, Jacques Delors, but it has been substantially developed since then. Like all organized lobbying, it raises serious issues of representation.

In this concrete case of the Auto-Oil proposals we may see how the NGOs became involved and what their influence has been. One may recall that the proposals which the Commission had published in 1996 were in two stages: mandatory limits to be imposed in 2000 and targets to be established for 2005. In February 1997 the Commission moved to consider the next stage: how to meet new (more severe) air quality targets for 2010. They launched a new programme of consultation and development, beginning with a 'stakeholders' meeting'; at which the major industries were again present as stakeholders. They were now joined by the NGOs and by officials representing member-state governments.

The NGOs, like the industries involved, formed themselves into a campaigning alliance, 'working for environmental sustainability'. The eight issue groups are shown in Figure 5.4. The member states are significant 'stakeholders' in three ways:

- First, they have a duty to protect and improve the safety and health of their citizens, a duty which at times may conflict with their second 'stake':
- Many member states are moral, or even financial, supporters of national vehicle manufacturing and oil industries.
- Thirdly, the member states have the technical infrastructure of laboratories and scientists to contribute to policy formation and, once the policy is adopted, will have the duty of enforcing it.

The 'stakeholders' were organized into seven very large working groups (Table 5.8) to look at different aspects of the policy. These groups still exist and continue to debate, so that the next stage of legislation had begun its process even before the previous measures had been adopted.

Both industries' going-in position is that exhaust emissions are no longer the main contributor to pollution, hence our environment will be improved by concentrating on other polluters. This underlies their emphasis on the 'base case'. We shall watch developments with interest and, I hope, encouragement.

Auto-Oil II

'Working for Environmental Sustainability'

NGOs in the Alliance

Bird Life International

Climate Network Europe

EEB - European Environment Bureau

Friends of the Earth

Greenpeace

T&E – Transport and the Environment

WWF – World Wide Fund

Figure 5.4   Auto-Oil II: the NGO alliance 'Working for Environmental Sustainability'

Table 5.8   Working groups in Auto-Oil II

Objective: To meet new (more severe) EU air quality targets for 2010

February 1997: 'Stakeholders' meeting

- Seven working groups set up
- Member states and *NGOs* now have a seat at the table

Project management: Commission through 7 working groups

Technical programme:

- Existing data
- No conventional auto technology
- Covers: fuels, vehicles, inspection and maintenance, non-technical measures, stationary sources (tax)

We can see the Commission seeking to re-establish its role as the proponent of 'Clean Air for Europe' and the initiator of the legislation to achieve its goals. At the same time, it is keeping large industries close to the process and profiting from their technical expertise. Legislation that may come over the next decade is still in the crucial 'ideas' stage and it is significant that there is already a scientific debate developing over the optimum research on which to found the 'base case'. The Joint Research Committee and the European Environment Agency are working on different projects. Table 5.9 summarizes the outlook and developments following the Exhaust Emissions Directive.

Table 5.9   Outlook and developments

1.1   'ACEA accepts the challenge of 2005'
- Petrol: industry can get there with existing technology
- Diesel: more work needed

1.2   ACEA believes that 2000/2005 programme 'definitively solves the air quality problem from a vehicle point of view.'

2   European Commission has launched a 'Clean Air for Europe' programme and plans five directives:
- Air Quality Data Directive
- Acidity Directive
- National limits or acidity
- Ozone Directive and reduction strategy
- Auto Oil II

3   Industry and Commission are working together on a 'base case' for emissions reductions, against which to measure any proposed improvements

4   A Joint Research Committee (JRC) is developing, for the Commission, a 'bottom-up' approach, based on detailed studies in 10 key cities

5   European Environment Agency is developing a 'top-down' approach, which measures total volumes of pollutants in European air, divided by population, ranking cities with 10%, 20% etc. scores

---

Table 5.10   Benchmarking and further developments

Reducing exhaust emissions	EU	USA
Catalytic converters mandatory	1994	1984
Levels proposed for new Directive	1996	1994
Passenger car levels mandated	2000	2000
Heavy duty levels achieved	2005	ULV behind

European industry now plans 'global harmonization'

We began this case with a review of the 'stakeholders', including the most important of all, ourselves the citizens of the EU. After studying the policy formation, the lobbying and the decision-making, we must demand to know: 'How much good has it done us?' A way of approaching this question is to set 'benchmarks' (Table 5.10). One may recall that, at the start of the case, the motor industry was complaining that the EU was 'constantly following US policy'. Table 5.10 based on information from the motor industry itself, shows that, in a sense, the EU had to follow US policy because the EU was a full 10 years behind. The result of the intense activity, which we have been examining, should be that the two systems are now 'level-pegging', and within five years EU policy will have overtaken and be leading US policy. It is significant in this context that the European industry is now calling for the imposition of 'global standards'. When an industry in any economic area emits that call, it is usually a sign that it considers itself more severely regulated than its competitors in other zones.

In so far as the controls are adequate and effective on either side of the Atlantic, that should be good for citizens' health.

Notes

The author would especially like to thank the following persons: Ken Collins (now of the Scottish Environment Agency) and Heide Jekel of the German Federal Ministry of the Environment for their supportive comments on an early version of this study and enlightenment on the trialogue process; Giovanni Margaria of ACEA, John Price of Europia and Tony Long of WWF for the time they devoted to interviews; Professor Rinus van Schendelen of Erasmus University for his active help and constructive criticism in the course of developing the study.

1. Axel Friedrich, Matthias Tappe and Rüdiger Wurzel, 'A New Approach to EU Environmental Policy-Making? The Auto-Oil 1 Programme', *Journal of European Public Policy*, 7(4) October 2000, pp. 593–612.
2. *Ibid.*
3. (EC, 1996a, p. 21)
4. Friedrich *et al.*, *op. cit.*
5. CEC, 1996a, p. 21, *op. cit.*
6. EEB (1997) *Auto Emissions 2000 EEB Comments on the Common Position of September 1997* Brussels European Environment Bureau. Transport and Environment (1997) *Updated Response to the EU Auto Oil Proposals*, Brussels, European Federation for Transport and the Environment.
7. AIT, FIA, BEUC, ECAS, EEB, EPHA and T&E (1998) 'NGO Appeal to MEPs to Reduce Traffic Pollution', Brussels press release, February 1998.
8. Axel Friedrich, Matthias Tappe and Rüdige Wurzel 'The Auto-Oil Programme, a Critical Interim Assessment', *European Environmental Law Review* 7(4), pp. 104–11.
9. Alex Warleigh, 'The Hustle – Citizenship Practice, NGOs and "Policy Coalitions" in the EU – the Cases of Auto Oil, Drinking Water and and Unit Pricing', *Journal of European Public Policy*, 7(2), pp. 229–43.
10. Michel Shackleton, 'The Politics of Co-Decision', *Journal of Common Market Studies*, 38 (2), June 2000.
11. Friedrich *et al.*, *op. cit.*
12. Robin Pedler, 'EU Public Affairs: The Growing Role of NOGs in the Decision-Making Process', *Journal of Communication Management*, 3(3), April 1999, pp. 235–47.

Part III

Applicant Country Cases

6
EU Accession and the 'Acquis': Saving Nordic Monopolies

Robin Pedler and Heikki Rautvuori

Introduction

The alcohol case was one of the 'Big Hits' on the EU accession negotiation agenda. Three of the four Nordic countries (Finland, Sweden and Norway) have similar retail monopolies for the sale of alcohol, and all three were negotiating to accede to the EU on 1 January 1995 (although Norway later decided not to do so). The study therefore examines the similarities and the differences in their approaches.

Sweden has a monopoly over the retail sale of alcohol, operated by the state-owned company Systembolaget, which it was determined to preserve. It also had monopolies over imports and wholesale distribution, but not production.

In *Finland* the monopoly was more extensive, since the activities of its state-owned company, Alko, extended over production as well as imports, wholesale and retail. Alko was broken up and reorganized as a result of changes to the alcohol legislation. Government negotiators saw monopoly defence as a crucial national item because of its symbolic meaning to Finnish people who were used to the strict national alcohol policy.

In *Norway*, imports, wholesale and retail sales were controlled by Vinmonopolet. They sought to preserve this monopoly, but by the time the referendum in October 1994 ended their move to join the EU, they had still not negotiated a solution.

This study goes beyond the phase of negotiation to describe the decisions of the European Court of Justice (ECJ) regarding the exemptions to Articles 30 and 37 of the Treaty of Rome. The Swedish 'Franzén' case is especially significant for the principle of monopolies. It should be valuable for the countries that are now negotiating to join the EU, showing how in two out of the three cases, applicant countries were able to preserve a monopoly that they judged important, even though the Commission's initial opinion recommended abolition.

The Nordic countries and their attitudes at the beginning of the European integration process

Four Nordic countries have negotiated to join the European Union. Three of them – Denmark, Finland and Sweden – are now members. The fourth, Norway, although she has not yet joined, has twice completed the full process of negotiation. Three of the four – Finland, Norway and Sweden – had national monopoly systems which they were determined to maintain. Denmark did not have monopolies, but since the advent of the Internal Market has negotiated special conditions, restricting the right of citizens to import alcohol, an issue which is also of great concern to her northern neighbours with their continuing monopolies.

Denmark did not have monopolies on the retailing or import of alcohol and therefore it was not an issue in its negotiations. Long after they joined, however, Denmark restricted the quantity of alcohol that might be imported by individuals and has got permission to keep the restrictions until the end of the year 2003. Finland has negotiated the same derogation. Sweden secured the exemption only until the end of June 2000 (then extended until the end of 2003). It will be very interesting to see how these three EU member states will be treated by the Commission. Geography dictates that the question of importing 'normal EU alcohol quantities' is very closely linked for the Finns and the Swedes.

In Finland only the state-owned company, Alko Ltd, may sell alcohol to private citizens. The same company further enjoyed monopolies over import and production. That monopoly's history goes back to the 12 years of total prohibition in the early years of independence (1919–31). Prohibition was finally abolished by referendum, and the Monopoly set up at the same time. It therefore has a long history and a well-developed culture. There is also a strong public health argument, and this concern cannot be overemphasized. For instance, the management of the Alcohol Monopoly is in the hands of the Ministry of Social Affairs and Health, Department for Promotion and Prevention. There is strong and widespread concern over the health effects of 'freeing'. From a health point of view, 'High taxes limit consumption'. They also provide a significant source of government revenue – 6.3 per cent of the national budget.

Thus the system was based upon the risks to health and the social problems in this heavy-drinking nation. The wholesale, production and alcohol import agencies are free to act in Finland. Alko and its operating divisions are described below.

Norway Also had total prohibition from 1919 to 1926. Since a referendum in that year again allowed the consumption of alcohol, Vinmonopolet controls imports and wholesale and retail sales. Monopoly profits and alcohol taxes account for 2 per cent of state revenues. Norway was the first Nordic country to take the alcohol monopoly case to the accession negotiations at the beginning of 1970s. Norway informed the Commission that it would keep the monopoly for 'health and social reasons' and got a positive answer from the Commission.

Later, in spring 1972, the Norwegian referendum result was negative and Norway withdrew its membership application. The first step in the monopoly case, however, was taken as a reference 20 years later when all three Nordic countries decided to act the same way on this question of principle.

Sweden also has a long tradition of control. The country never went as far as prohibition, but from 1917 to 1955 consumption was limited by a system of ration books. In 1982, the government banned Saturday sales after a four-month experiment suggested that this reduced 'drunk and disorderly conduct, assaults and burglaries'. (Saturday sales were restored in 1999.) The national retail company is called Systembolaget; they were never allowed to import or wholesale alcohol, these activities being restricted to Vinospritcentralen A.G. Vinosprit also produced alcohol, but did not have monopoly protection. Monopoly profits and alcohol taxes contribute 4.6 per cent of national revenue.

The monopoly system certainly seems to have maintained a low level of alcohol consumption in the three Nordic countries that maintain it; they figure at the bottom of a list of EU member states as shown in Table 6.1 (Denmark is quite well up).

These are 'official' figures. Interviewing two senior Swedish officials, both commented that they represent only about half of the 'real' consumption, the rest being accounted for by illicit distilling and smuggling. (One of the

Table 6.1 Annual consumption of alcohol: EU member states and Norway

Member state	*Litres per capita (adult)*
France	14.1
Portugal	13.6
Denmark	**12.1**
Austria	11.9
Germany	11.8
Belgium	11.7
Ireland	11.5
Spain	11.4
Greece	10.4
Netherlands	9.8
Italy	9.4
UK	9.4
Finland	**8.4**
Sweden	**6.4**
Norway	**4.8**
EU average	11.1

Source: Eurostat *Yearbook*, 1999.

officials was from the customs administration.) Alcohol monopoly companies are owned by the state but they function as if they were 'normal' businesses. The three national companies played a minor role in the accession negotiations because their owners, governments, were able to make decisions independently on their behalf.

EEA, the starting point for the negotiations

Austria, Finland, Norway and Sweden greeted with pleasure Jacques Delors' initiative towards the end of the 1980s to encourage closer integration between EFTA countries and the existing Community. This led then to the European Economic Area (EEA) negotiations in 1990–92. This phase of negotiations was essential to the contents of the alcohol monopoly clause, because all the stipulations were already made at this early stage.

The three Nordic countries declared their intention to maintain their alcohol monopolies in Appendix I to the Treaty of Oporto of 2 May 1992. They recall that their monopolies 'are based on important health and social policy considerations' (Holder *et al.*, 1998).[1] The EU did not comment on this declaration and it had no legal bearing on the Agreement, as expressly stated in the Declaration itself.

The articles in the EEA and EU treaties are similar

As stated above, the EEA Treaty was the cornerstone when the Commission accepted the retail alcohol monopolies. The mere word 'monopoly' sounds quite suspicious in the Internal Market and in the context of the Free Movement of Goods, but monopolies are defined precisely in Article 37 of the Treaty of Rome.

Finland had at that time three monopolies which were apparently excluded by the application of Article 37: Alko Ltd.; the special calendar rights of Helsinki university; and the State Grain Stock Ltd.

Swedish monopolies were: Systembolaget, and retail pharmacy stores.

Finland had to give undertakings to the Commission that monopolies were going to be abolished or reformed and that they would have a transparent status. The Swedish pharmacy monopoly 'was not contested'.

The following Articles were negotiated in the EEA Treaty (1992), and there are equivalent Articles in the Finnish EU Accession Treaty as follows:

EEA	EU
Art.11	Art.30
Art.12	Art.34
Art.13	Art.36
Art.16	Art.37

Article 30 (Now 28)

Quantitative restrictions on imports and all measures having equivalent effect shall, without prejudice to the following provisions, be prohibited between Member States.

Article 34 (Now 29)

Quantitative restrictions on exports, and all measures having equivalent effect, shall be prohibited between Member States.[1]

Article 36 (Now 30)

The provisions of Articles 30 to 34 shall not preclude prohibitions or restrictions on imports, exports or goods in transit justified on grounds of public morality, public policy or public security; the protection of life of humans, animals and plants; the protection of national treasures possessing artistic, historic or archaeological value; or the protection of industrial and commerical property. Such prohibitions or restrictions shall not, however, constitute a means of arbitrary discrimination or a disguised restriction on trade between Member States.

Article 37 (Now 31)

1. Member States shall progressively adjust any State monopolies of a commercial character so as to ensure that when the transitional period has ended no discrimination regarding the conditions under which the goods are procured and marketed exists between nationals of Member States.

   The provisions of this article shall apply to any body through which a Member State, in law or in fact, either directly or indirectly supervises determines or appreciably influences imports or exports bteween Member States. These provisions shall likewise apply to monopolies delegated by the State to others.
2. Member States shall refrain from introducing any new measure which is contrary to the principles laid down in paragraph 1 or which restricts the scope of the Articles dealing with the abolition of customs duties and quantitative restrictions between Member States.
3. The timetable for the measures referred to in paragraph 1 shall be harmonized with the abolition of quantitative restrictions on the same products provided for in Articles 30 to 34.

   If a product is subject to a State monopoly of a commercial character in only one or some Member States, the Commission may authroize the other Member States to apply protective measures until the adjustment provided for in paragraph 1 has been effected; the Commission shall determine the conditions and details of such measures.
4. If a state monopoly of a commercial character has rules which are designed to make it easier to dipose of agricultural products or obtain for them the best return, steps should be taken in applying the rules contained in this

Article to ensure equivalent safeguards for the employment and standard of living of the producers concerned, account being taken of the adjustments that will be possible and the spcialization that will be needed with the passage of time.

5. The obligations on Member States shall be binding only in so far as they are compatible with existing international agreements.

6. With effect from the first stage the Commission shall make recommendations as to the manner in which and the timetable according to which the adjustment provided for in this Article shall be carried out.[2]

The EEA articles are reproduced in Appendix 1 where the important words are underlined.

1992: reaction to the Nordic countries' application to join the EU

The Commission delivered its opinion on the applications in late 1992 and early 1993, and in all three cases it stated that the alcohol monopolies would have to be abolished. Its sharpest language, in the case of Norway, was that:

> the protection of public health could not be allowed to obstruct free trade unless there was no alternative. Reserving retail sale to one organisation, which moreover holds the national production monopoly, is not necessarily the only way to protect health. There exist other forms of regulations (for instance, restrictions on advertising, prohibitions of sales by unauthorised shops, prohibitions on selling to the young, limited business hours of outlets and increased fiscal duties) which would be less detrimental to trade but pursue the same goal. (Commission of the European Communities, 1993a)[3]

Finland: negotiations develop

Companies, including Alko, were fully involved in the EEA negotiations. They covered 'all the technical rules on wines and spirits',[4] so it was very important for industry to be involved, 'as we know the market mechanisms: competition, branding, quality, service e.g. delivery to restaurants'.[5] For the EEA negotiations, Finland set up an EFTA/EC committee, and the alcohol industry set up a 'Strategy Group for European Integration'. There were distinct groups, one for Alko itself and the other for 'Nordic Industries'. Dr Bertil Roslin of Alko chaired both. Their work resulted in the alcohol producers being 'well prepared when membership did come, unlike the brewers'.[6]

Alko began by making it clear that: 'This will not be good for the company'. They wanted to establish the importance of keeping the *retail and wholesale monopoly* but were willing to free *imports*. The Ministry of Social and Health Affairs, however, saw immediately that this would cause a curious situation: how can a private company import alcohol if it cannot sell or consume it? Alko was naturally disappointed, but it could only accept the owner's decision when the Ministry informed the Commission that Finland, along with Sweden and Norway, was going to free the import and wholesale distribution of alcohol. The production of alcoholic drinks had already been licensed and the same system would continue.

The 'EU' negotiations were 'political discussions', though it should be noted that the Finnish Foreign Ministry founded an industry advice group, which met ten times a year. The role of the Ministry for Foreign Affairs during this phase was important but not decisive. The Ministry of Social and Health Affairs gave instructions to the negotiators in Brussels. The role of the Alko Concern was not remarkable, but the directors were actively involved in the domestic preparations.

Domestic attitude towards liberalization

The Finnish Minister of Health and Social Affairs in 1992 was from the Christian Party, and he was unwilling to abolish all aspects of alcohol monopoly rules in Finland. He established a committee to revise Finnish alcohol legislation to meet EEA requirements, but it soon came out with the recommendation that *wholesaling, production* (under 4.7%) and *imports* (but only those below 60% of alcohol) should be free but *retailing* should be left to Alko. Despite objections from 'sober-minded' politicians the new Finnish alcohol law was adopted in December 1994. This law had been drafted under the EEA procedure and therefore had to be adjusted to EU membership that would begin in 1995.

A minor change to Article 10 was made very quickly. It allowed the import of alcohol from third countries without time limits, in line with EU rules. This led to vast legal and also illegal imports by citizens from Finland's neighbouring countries Russia and Estonia. The Commission threatened Finland that they would take the case to the EC J because of discriminatory actions that violated the Community rules concerning imports from third countries. Finland defended itself by referring to the time limits granted to, for example, Denmark. Finally the law (Article 10) was formulated so that the authorities can restrict the import of alcohol from 'outside the European Economic Area' during short visits when it is necessary for 'the general order and security to the citizens'. This ruling is explained later in this study.

The people in Finland remained unbelievably quiet during the EEA procedure, and only in 1994, during the EU negotiations, were some voices heard demanding a more liberal retail policy in Finland. There was a debate whether the sale of wine should be allowed in grocery stores, but people had obviously forgotten that this demand should have been made at an earlier stage!

It was evident that the EEA Article 16 required the abolition of Alko's privileges except the retail monopoly. In maintaining the latter right it was taken for granted that all imported alcoholic drinks would be treated equally. During the EU negotiations this was fully understood and it didn't cause any problems for the Finnish negotiators. It is interesting to note, however, that the EU allowed certain exemptions from the general line. These are defined in EEA Article 13. The text is clear:

> The provisions of Arts. 11 and 12 shall not preclude prohibitions or restrictions on imports, exports or goods in transit justified on grounds of public morality, public policy or public security; *the protection of health and life of humans*. (Emphasis added)

Finland has used this argument on several occasions when it wanted to place restrictions on alcohol imports or on rights of sale.

Finland remained with two difficult questions linked with the import of alcohol:

1. *The obligation to change national import legislation regarding short-term trips abroad.* Finland had to change the content of Article 10 in the national alcohol law. The text was: 'The import of alcoholic drinks for own use and deliveries containing alcohol are subject to special regulations' (free translation).

   This was not acceptable because third countries had to be treated similarly to EU countries. The transparency was obviously lost in this wording and the government had to prepare more suitable legislation. It remained a fact that since Finnish accession to EU the import of alcohol 'for own use' from neighbours Russia and Estonia had increased enormously. The short distance also tempted many people to challenge Alko's domestic and official monopoly over alcohol retailing. Alcohol was brought to Finland even from trips lasting less than eight hours.

   Finland referred to the exemptions given to Sweden and Denmark to restrict the import in connection with short-term trips abroad. To make the import of alcohol legal, Sweden requires an absence of 24 hrs, and Denmark requires 36 hours to secure entitlement to import alcohol up to the EU limits. Therefore it was quite natural that Finland also set time limits and it changed Article 10 of the alcohol law as follows:

   > The amount of alcohol imported for 'own use' by persons arriving in Finland from third countries after trips lasting a short time may be restricted, as required for common order and security and for the health of people. This restriction can be imposed by regulation. (Free translation)

   Finland has set the minimum limit to 20 hours to trips from third countries.

   This Article 10 was taken to the Court of Justice in Luxembourg. The case is still open but the Advocate General has already given a positive statement about the final Court decision. It would be difficult to imagine that Sweden and Denmark could continue their restrictions if the same right were denied to Finland. The real problems actually lie after the year 2004 when the quantitative restrictions will be the same as those existing inside the Union.

2. *The import of alcohol stronger than 60 per cent*
The Commission (DG IV) has asked the Finnish Government for clarification regarding the limits on the import of alcohol stronger than 60 per cent. The Commission presumes that the Finnish interpretation of the strong alcohol regulation violates Articles 30 and 37 of the Treaty of Rome.

In 1997, a Finnish law student imported a couple of bottles containing 96 per cent of alcohol. These bottles were confiscated and he took the case to the Court of Justice. The decision was given in December 1998 and it was favourable to the Finnish legislation. This legislation is based on the limit that had already been set in the 1970s when there were several deaths caused by drinking very strong alcohol. Finland has now changed the system and imposes higher prices for over-proof spirits. This will change the situation when over-proof drinks and spirits are defined as 'drinkable products' and thus separated from all other alcohol. It is noteworthy that especially spirits from Russia have caused problems because of their high alcohol content.

Finland and Sweden: correspondence with and declarations to the commission

The three Nordic applicants were invited to exchange letters with the Commission in order to clarify their situation and intentions over alcohol monopolies. Norway declined, saying that the matter had already been resolved in the EEA treaty negotiations, but Finland and Sweden accepted and issued correspondence and declarations. The declarations about the alcohol monopoly were given at the 5th ministerial-level meeting on 21 December 1993, in the chapter on Competition Policy containing the documents CONF-SF 78/93 and CONF-S 82/93.

These declarations are based on the correspondence between the Commissioner for competition policy, Hans van den Broek, and the Finnish Minister for Foreign Trade, Pertti Salolainen, and are reproduced in Appendix 2. Commissioner van den Broek points out in his letter that the Commission assumes that Finland will abolish *the exclusive import, export, wholesale and production rights for its alcohol monopolies, including the wholesale function to bars and restaurants.* The Commission is of the opinion that this is the only possibility in order to bring Finnish legislation in line with Community *Acquis*.

This statement is the key issue because the Commission here defines the limits of its tolerance! The Commission also gives the Court of Justice the last word in interpreting this clause. It recalls that Finland has already committed itself to apply the Community *Acquis* concerning monopolies under the provisions of the EEA Agreement. It also wanted to retain the right to closely monitor the implementation of this procedure.

One may have the impression that the Commission took a brave step backwards in allowing the retention of a monopoly (retail sale of alcohol). The Swedish 'Franzén Case' showed that the risk of interpretation by the Court of Justice was real. If that Swedish case had shown that the retail monopoly is illegal and against the Community *Acquis* it would also have damaged the Finnish position. It goes without saying that the authority of the Commission (and especially of Commissioner Hans van den Broek) would have suffered a lot.

Pertti Salolainen confirmed on behalf of the Finnish Government that it totally accepted the contents of the Commission's letter. Later the Finnish decision was accepted in a Government ministerial meeting and it didn't cause any further domestic public or political debate. Sweden also agreed in December 1993 to remove 'the institutional link between the monopoly on alcohol production and the off-premise retail monopoly on alcoholic beverages'. The Swedish Secretary of State of the Ministry of Health and Social Affairs justified this step to his own parliament as necessary to end a state of uncertainty. It was also, presumably, an attempt to get away with the minimum possible change while still retaining the retail monopoly.[6]

This was reflected in the political understanding between Finland and Sweden and the European Commission:

> Without prejudice to the future jurisprudence of the European Court of Justice and the Commission's role as guardian of the Treaty of European Union, the Commission does not see any reason to proceed on its own initiative, either now or after the Swedish and Finnish accession to the Union, against the maintenance of the retail monopoly on the basis of the current Acquis. (Commission of the European Communities, 1993b, 1993c)[7]

The political understanding was accompanied by a detailed series of measures that would be necessary to ensure that the retail monopolies were non-discriminatory.

Norway continued to defend its position and refuse to negotiate, and the country was indeed under threat of legal action before the EFTA court when the negative referendum ended its application negotiations. Remaining a member of EFTA, however, Norway did agree to partial abolition of the monopoly, effective 1 January 1996.

The ECJ: leading alcohol monopoly cases

The Court of Justice has tried two important alcohol cases: the one which allowed the retail monopoly in Nordic countries and the one which allows Finland to restrict the import of alcohol from third countries in connection with trips lasting less than 20 hours. The latter case will be described later in this Study.

The Swedish 'Franzén' case

Grocery store owner Harry Franzén bought wine from Denmark and sold it in his store on 1 January 1995 (the date when Sweden joined the European Union). The General Prosecutor accused him of illegal retail sale of alcohol. Franzén denied the accusation, relying on Articles 30 and 36 of the Treaty of Rome. The local Court referred the case to the ECJ, where the Swedish government was joined by France, Finland, Norway and the Commission as interested parties. They all gave written statements to the Court. The Commission, in particular, 'did not consider the retail monopoly's activity in any way contrary to EC law'.

Danish Advocate General, Michael B. Elmer, who prepared the case for the Court of Justice, was of the opinion that the Swedish retail monopoly was not consistent with the *Acquis Communautaire*. The Swedish legal services, however, judged his arguments 'weak' and were not therefore surprised that the Court subsequently found in their Government's favour. The decision was given on 23 October 1997 and the Court of Justice totally accepted the agreement made between the Commission and Sweden denying the right of retail sale to stores other than Systembolaget.

It was clear that another Court decision might have totally changed the previous work done by the accession negotiators. Former monopoly cases cited were: 3.2.1976, 7.6.1983/Italy, 13.12.1990/Greece and 14.12.1995/ 'Banchero case'.

Obviously, transparency was the key element in the Court's favourable decision; the retail monopoly should stock a range of alcohol without discrimination in favour of any alcohol producer. Systembolaget might not have a certain product available in its retail store; it must be prepared, however, to supply that product to the client. The same system is applies to the other Nordic monopoly companies – Alko and Vinmonopolet. The Court observed that Swedish legislation was not totally in line with the EU Articles 30 and 36 (import, wholesale and production). Sweden had made, however, the same corrections to national legislation as Finland. Sweden also pointed out that the Government has the right to protect the people's health by keeping the retail monopoly in the hands of the Government-owned retail chain of stores. This is allowed even according to the Article 36 in the Treaty of Rome.

They clarified that the monopoly must be in the public interest, and it is. The Franzén case was very important, because it was the first clarification of the application of Article 37. Even when compared to Articles 30 and 36, this shows that member states *may* have monopolies.[8]

There were parallel cases before the EFTA court concerning the Norwegian monopoly (1994, 1997), with a similar outcome.

Since these decisions of the Courts of Justice there has been no further debate concerning the retail monopoly of alcohol.

The case dealing with the import from third countries in connection with short trips

EU legislation allows people to freely import alcoholic drinks *for their own use only*. The amounts are normally the following:

- 10 litres of strong alcohol (< 22%)
- 20 litres of aperitifs (> 22%)
- 90 litres of wine, only 60 sparkling
- 110 litres of beer

Ireland has certain restrictions to these amounts. An even higher amount of alcohol is allowed if one can prove the reason: wedding, anniversary and so forth. The import is free of taxes.

The tax-free sale of alcohol onboard ships and aeroplanes and in the ports and airports was abolished inside the EU on 30 June 1999. There will be no exceptions and only the Ahvenanmaa Islands (Åland) between Finland and Sweden remain as a tax-free zone.

Because of its geographical position at the frontier of the European Union, Finland faces an enormous pressure from third countries that offer an easy access to the Finnish alcohol market. When the Government referred to the need to protect the health of the people in restricting the retail sale of alcohol, it had to adjust the local legislation to this need. Finland, together with other Nordic countries, negotiated the following modification of the above import amounts:

Denmark, Finland, Sweden	*Other EU members*
1 litre of spirits	10 litres of spirits
5 litres of wine	20 litres of 'intermediate products'
	90 litres of table wine
15 litres of beer	110 litres of beer

Finland along with Denmark will obey the EU rules from the beginning of the year 2004. The Swedish exemption was only valid until 30 June 2000. Sweden repeated several times that it would continue to restrict imports 'because of needs to protect the health of the people'. It succeeded in negotiating a further three-year extension of its limitation policy, against vigorous opposition from the Commission, so all the Nordic countries are now in line for liberalization at the end of 2003.

Status and composition of the Finnish alcohol monopoly *Oy Alko Ab*

The production, import, wholesale and retail of alcohol have been the monopoly of the company Oy Alko Ab (former 'Oy Alkoholiliike Ab') since the 1930s when prohibition was abolished. At the beginning of the 1990s it was evident that this monopoly had to come to an end. The owner, the Government, decided to split the company into five separate divisions. At the end of 1998 the de-merger was completed and the company will face the challenges of the next millennium in the following form:

1. *Altia Group*: Primalco Ltd. in charge of production. The main product is Finlandia vodka. Avistra Ltd. in charge of wholesale and distribution of Primalco's brands and of imported alcoholic products, mainly from the Baltic states
2. *Alko Group*: Alko Ltd. and Vistalko Ltd. Operates the retail alcohol monopoly and acts as agent.
3. *Arctia Group*: Arctia Ltd, until 1998 a hotel and restaurant chain, has now become a real estate company. The restaurants and hotels were sold to Swedish-owned Scandic Hotels which sold the restaurants on to a privately-owned Finnish company 'Royal Ravintolat Oy' (Royal Restaurants Ltd).

Primalco hopes that Finlandia vodka will increase its exports and is therefore investing large amounts of money into advertising and promotion (for example, on the helmet of the Finnish Formula 1 star Mika Hakkinen). The former monopoly is now an international company that has top products for sale! The Commission (DGs Competition and Internal Market) is following the activities of the company closely. The owner, the State of Finland, has to report to Competition at least once a year on the transparency and neutrality of the whole Alko Concern.

The Product Control Authority was created at the beginning of 1995 for administrative tasks connected with alcohol licenses, production licenses and so forth. This Authority is linked with the Ministry of Social and Health Affairs, which still has overall authority in alcohol matters.

The challenges to applicant countries of keeping exceptional institutions and privileges

The Nordic Alcohol Case is an interesting example of how small nations can tackle a difficult task: keep their own national interest and still obey Community law. The Commission has long experience in dealing with derogations and exceptions granted to member states. It has shown, however, very little understanding towards clear violations of the Community *Acquis*. It is therefore recommended that candidate countries prepare their positions carefully since it might be impossible subsequently to change rulings accepted by both sides. The ECJ may always decide that things have to be changed. The alcohol monopoly case shows that there will be hardly any changes to the agreed legislation.

The starting point of the accession negotiation was the Commission's recommendation of full abolition of the monopoly system in all three countries. Yet Sweden and Finland negotiated with sufficient skill and determination that they retained at least some of it. The process of negotiation, however, forced them to decide what was their *real* objective – to retain their retail monopoly. They were constrained to make other compromises to their original monopoly system to achieve this.

The other important conclusion from the case is that accession negotiations are not purely 'foreign' or external. The decision to join the EU and the conditions of accession will have important consequences for all the citizens of the applicant country. The way domestic politics and opinion are handled is also crucial. In this context it is interesting to see that Finland and Sweden, who concluded their alcohol monopoly negotiations successfully, both to some extent 'de-politicized' the debate by using a special body (a government-industry 'working group' in Finland and a parliamentary commission in Sweden). In Norway, however, the issue remained in mainstream politics and became part of the strident overall debate about joining the EU. Partly as a result, had the 1994 referendum said 'yes', the Norwegians would still have faced an unresolved problem.[9]

Looking at the countries now negotiating future membership with the EU Commission, one has to bear in mind that the starting point on difficult questions like existing monopolies had already been passed in the EEA/EU negotiations. It might be a good idea to have a similar pattern now! During the negotiations for accession in 1995, the Finnish Accession Team of diplomats and their advisors kept in close contact with their Swedish counterparts. Even so, there was an important difference in the outcome – the Finns won three years' longer of import restriction (though the Swedes ironed out the difference in negotiations five years after they joined.) It will also be important for future candidate countries to keep other candidates informed about positions that may affect them all.

Appendix 1: text of the European economic area treaty
Part II – free movement of goods

Article 8

1. Free movement of goods between the Contracting Parties shall be established in conformity with the provisions of the Agreement.

2. Unless otherwise specified therein, the provisions of this Agreement shall apply only to:

   a. Products falling within Chapters 25 to 97 of the Harmonized Commodity Description and Coding system, excluding the products listed in Protocol 2:
   b. Products specified in Protocol 3 subject to the specific arrangements set out in that Protocol.

Article 9

1. The rules of origin are set out in Protocol 4. They are without prejudice to any international obligations which have been or may be subscribed to by the Contracting Parties under the General Agreement on Tariffs and Trade.
2. With a view to developing the results achieved in this Agreement, the Contracting Parties will continue their efforts in order to further improve and simplify all aspects of rules of origin and to increase cooperation in customs matters.
3. A first review will take place before the end of 1993. Subsequent reviews will take place at two-yearly intervals. On the basis of these reviews the Contracting Parties undertake to decide on the appropriate measures to be included in this agreement.

Article 10

Customs duties on imports and exports and any charges having equivalent effect shall be prohibited between the Contracting Parties. Without prejudice to the arrangements set out in Protocol 5, this shall also apply to customs duties of a fiscal nature.

Article 11

Quantitive restrictions on imports and all measures having equivalent effect shall be prohibited between the contracting parties.

Article 12

Quantitive restricitions on exports and all measures having equivalent effect shall be prohibited between the contracting parties.

Article 13

The provisions of Articles 11 and 12 shall not preclude prohibitions or restrictions on imports, exports or goods in transit justified on grounds of public morality, public policy or public security: the protection of health and life of humans, animals and plants: the protections of national treasures possessing artistic, historic or archaeological value: or the protection of industrial and commercial property. Such prohibitions or restrictions shall not, however, constitute a means of arbitrary discrimination or a disguised restriction on trade between the Contracting Parties.

Article 14

No Contracting Party shall impose, directly or indirectly, on the products of other Contracting Parties any internal taxation or any kind in excess of that imposed directly or indirectly on similar domestic products.

Futhermore, no Contracting Party shall impose on the products of other Contracting Parties any internal taxation of such a nature as to afford indirect protection to other products.

Article 15

Where products are exported to the territory of any Contracting Party, any repayment of internal taxation shall not exceed the internal taxation imposed on them whether directly or indirectly.

Article 16

1. The Contracting Parties shall ensure that <u>any state monopoly of a commercial character</u> be adjusted so that <u>no discrimination</u> regarding the conditions under which goods are procured and marketed <u>will exist</u> between nationals of EC Member States and EFTA States.
2. The provisions of this Article shall apply to any body through which the competent authorities of the Contracting Parties, in law or in fact, either directly or indirectly supervise, determine or appreciably influence <u>imports or exports</u> between Contracting Parties. These provisions shall likewise apply to monopolies designated by the state to others.

Appendix 2: exchange of correspondence between commissioner van den Broek and the Finnish minister for foreign trade

Hans van den Broek
MEMBER OF THE COMMISSION
OF THE EUROPEAN COMMUNITIES

Dear Mr Salolainen,

As a result of the exploratory contacts which have taken place between Finland and Commission services, the Commission assumes that Finland will abolish the exclusive import, export, wholesale and production rights for its respective alcohol monpolies including the wholesale function to bars and restaurants. It is the Commission's opinion that this is indeed necessary in order to bring Finnish legislation in line with Community acquis.

In relation to the Finnish retail monopoly, the Commission considers that any discriminatory effects between national products and products imported from EC Member States must be eliminated. Without prejudice to future jurisprudence of the Court of Justice and the Commission's role as guardian of the Treaty on European Union, the Commission does not see any reason to proceed on its own initiative, either now or after the Finnish accession to the Union, against the maintenance of the retail monopoly on the basis of the current acquis.

I take the opportunity to recall that Finland has already committed itself to apply the Community acquis concerning monopolies under the provisions of the EEA Agreement. The Commission therefore considers that the above elements are applicable as from the entry into force of the EEA Agreement.

Expert discussions with the responsible Commission services should take place as soon as possible, and in any case before the entry into force of the EEA Agreement, in order to identify the elements necessary to ensure that the retail monopoly will function in a non- discriminatory way.

In order to ensure that the practices of the retail monopoly conforn1 to the Community acquis, it is of paramount importance that the European Commission will be involved in close and regular monitoring.

sincerely,

I would be grateful if you could inform me whether Finland agrees with the Commission's views.

H.E. Mr P. Salolainen, Minister for Foreign Trade, Helsinki.

Minister for Foreign Trade

Helsinki, Finland

21 December, 1993

Dear Commissioner,

I hereby wish to confirm, that the Finnish Government is in agreement with the principles outlined in your letter on 21 December regarding the Finnish alcohol monopolies.

Sincerely yours,

Pertti Salolainen
Ministeri for Foreign Trade

Mr. Hans van den Broek
Member of the Commission
Brussels

Acknowledgements

The authors are grateful to the following persons for the time and attention they gave in interview in researching this study: Dr Jaako Eskola, Ministry of Health, Helsinki, MR Pertti Karhu, Inspector, Alcohol Surveillance Authority, Helsinki, Ambassador Lotty Nordling, Director of Legal Service, Foreign Ministry, Stockholm, Dr Kari Paaso, Ministry of Health, Helsinki, Dr Bertil Rosin, Executive Vice President, Alko Group, Helsinki, Dr Stefan Schepers, Director EPPA, Brussels, MR Olli Zinn, Director, Customs Administration, Stockholm.

Notes

1. Külhorn F. Holder, S. Norlund, F. Osterberg, A. Rommelsjö, and T. Ugland, *European Integration and Nordic Alcohol Policies*, Aldershot, Ashgate, 1998.
2. Treaty on European Union, 1992. New article numbers refer to amendments in the Treaty of Amsterdam 1997.
3. Accession negotiation chapter on Competition Policy CONF-SF 78/93 and CONF – S 82/93 December 21 1993.
4. Dr Bertil Roslin, Alko, Personal communication.
5. *Ibid.*
6. *Ibid.*
7. Holder *et al., op. cit.*
8. CONF – SF 78/93 AND CONF – S 82/93 *op. cit.*
9. Holder *et al., op. cit.*

7
Slovenia and the EU:
An Anti-Dumping Case

Andrej Drapal, Dejan Vercíc, Irena Peterlin and Tomaž Ilešiě

Introduction

In June 1998, management of the Slovenian Steelworks learned informally that one of its companies, Acroni might be accused of 'dumping' its exports to the European Union. This indeed materialized when on 4 August 1998 the Association of European Steelworks, EUROFER, presented a complaint to the Commission on the alleged dumping by Acroni in the EU market (specifically in Germany, France and Italy). On 17 September 1998, the Notice of Initiation was published in the *Official Journal of the European Communities*. The complaint by EUROFER was withdrawn in a letter to the Commission on 4 March 1999.

The case is interesting because Slovenia and the three European Communities and their member states have concluded the so-called 'Europe Agreement' (EA). The EA with Slovenia is specific in that Slovenia was already a WTO member at the time of EA negotiations and its EA refers to WTO rules. The EA in reference to WTO Anti-Dumping Agreements introduced different (additional) procedural rules as a general principle that, before any measures can be taken, the Association Council shall be supplied with all relevant information, with a view to seeking a solution acceptable to both parties. In the Acroni anti-dumping case these specific EA rules were not applied.

Since the Commission did not submit the information to the Association Council, Slovenia was unable legally to defend its case until the publication of the Notice of Initiation. If Slovenian Steelworks had been given a possibility to explain its case to the Association Council, the anti-dumping procedure would very probably never have taken place. While this procedural omission by the Commission might have decided the case, had it ever got to a court, Slovenian Steelworks nevertheless had to defend itself in an anti-dumping procedure.

The focal player

Acroni has over 600 years of long and rich tradition in iron and steel production. Today it is the largest 'mini-mill' steel producer in Slovenia and a part of Slovenian Steelworks. The term 'mini-mill' refers to a steel production facility that recycles scrap using electric-arc furnaces, continuous casters and rolling mills. The use of secondary metallurgy enables the production of high-quality steels that are used for various demanding industrial applications. The core business is based on high-quality flat-rolled electrical, stainless and structural steel products.

In 1999, Acroni sold 200/200 tons of steel products and billed DM 248 million. Almost half of this turnover was realized on the European Union markets. The most important markets for Acroni are the domestic (40.2%) and the European Union (49.1%). To its domestic market, Acroni mainly sells common steel grades and more than half of its electrical steel production, whereas for the sale of stainless steel the domestic market is less important. Exports to Central European Free Trade Area (CEFTA) countries (primarily the Czech Republic and Hungary) represented 4 per cent of total exports and included all programmes in 1999. Acroni exported only stainless steel to the American market, amounting to 3.5 per cent of total exports in 1999.

Among the export markets the most important is the European Union, with an 82.1 per cent share of Acroni's total exports in 1999; 28.4 per cent of exports went to Italy, 24.7 per cent to Germany, 13.7 per cent to Austria and 9.2 per cent to France. The German market is particularly important for the export of stainless steel and electrical steel. The Italian market is, besides the above-mentioned groups of steel, a big consumer of special types of steel – namely heat-treatable and micro-alloy steel grades. The Austrian market also imports construction steel besides stainless steel and electrical steel. The French market is primarily the buyer of heavy stainless steel plates. The electrical steel and special steel are sold mostly to final consumers, where, besides price and quality, the producer's service has an important role.

The major force behind this successful orientation to the EU markets lies in the loss of almost all of Acroni's market after Slovenia declared independence from Yugoslavia in 1991. Acroni had to find new markets literally overnight. This heavy economic crisis in combination with the general political and public reorientation from heavy industry to a small and mid-size entrepreneurial economy and later the 'new economy' was reflected in a poor and still declining reputation of the steel industry in Slovenia.

The issue for the focal player

With almost 54 per cent of its production sold to EU markets and its operations producing minimal but continuous losses over the years, it was clear that the immediate consequence of a possible negative outcome of the anti-dumping case could be disastrous for Acroni. After nine years of continuous restructuring, market reorientation and negative operation, Acroni had no means to adapt to the threat of an anti-dumping duty imposed by the Commission. The issue was thus very clear in this respect – to win the case. But there was a much more obscure issue behind this main one: how to involve state institutions whose formal and informal support of this case in Brussels was of key importance, but who so far had almost no experience in affairs that would need such wide cooperation and coordination of different institutions and individuals.

The other side

The complaint was lodged by the European Confederation of Iron and Steel Industries (EUROFER) on behalf of Krupp Thyssen Nirosta GmbH, Germany; CLI-Usine du Creusot, France; and Fabrique de Fer de Charleroi S.A., Belgium.

The issue for the other side

EU steel producers had started to consider Acroni, with an almost 10 per cent share of stainless steel heavy plates (18 000t of the total of 220 000t in the EU in 1997) as a serious competitor. They argued that the price of such steel had dropped heavily in that year mainly because of the larger quantity of steel at a dumped price from some CEE and Asian producers. Eurofer finally decided to initiate an anti-dumping proceeding concerning imports of certain stainless-steel heavy plates originating in Slovenia and South Africa.

The case

Slovenia is one of the Central and Eastern European Countries (CEECs) with which the three European Communities and their member states have concluded international agreements establishing an association, the so called 'Europe Agreements' (EAs). A network of EAs was gradually established between 1991 and 1996 with the following ten countries in Central and Eastern Europe: Hungary, Poland and the Czech and Slovak Federal Republic (in 1991)[7], Bulgaria and Romania (1993), the Baltic States (1995), and Slovenia (1996). According to Maresceau (1997b: 7): 'It is very unlikely that in the future similar agreements will be signed with other countries in Central and Eastern Europe.'

All ten CEESs have applied for membership of the European Union. The ten countries and their dates of application are: Hungary – 31 March 1994, Poland – 5 April 1994, Slovakia – 27 June 1995, Romania – 22 June 1995, Latvia – 13 October 1995, Estonia – 24 November 1995, Lithuania – 8 December 1995, Bulgaria – 14 December 1995, Czech Republic – 17 January 1996, and Slovenia – 10 June 1996. (For an overview of relations between the EU and CEESs see Maresceau 1997a.)

On the other side the recognition of EA countries as market economies resulted, among other things, in the calculation of dumping margins as one of a number of trade measures. Dumping is defined as 'introducing the products of one country into the commerce of another country at less than its normal value, which is, as a rule, the comparable price, in the ordinary course of trade, for the like products when destined for consumption in the exporting country' (Art. VI of GATT, 1994). Since the beginning of 1994, treatment as a market economy in anti-dumping procedures has become a progressively established practice in respect of all the EA countries.[1] More than half of all anti-dumping procedures were against steel producers. It is thus very common that government bureaucrats determine whether domestically produced steel is substituted by imports and whether cost advantages of imported steel are genuine or a result of unfair practices by foreign suppliers. It is thus comprehensible that the success rate of steel dumping cases has fallen from 90 to 73 per cent in recent years.

It should be mentioned that it is not only the measure imposed that damages the producer. The mere opening of an inquiry also damages producers in that it causes exports to decline and deters potential foreign investments, particularly in the CEECs. It is clear that the investor, once aware of an anti-dumping proceeding, would rather invest somewhere else in the Community, since if dumping is finally proved he will be locked out of the EU by heavy anti-dumping measures.[2] The best defence is therefore a quick response in order to try to prevent the official initiation of the investigation procedure.

Although the anti-dumping proceeding was not yet formally filed, Acroni started defence activities immediately after the first warning. The Slovenian government urged all institutions involved (Acroni, Ministry of the Economy, and the Competition Protection Office) to start the necessary activities. Already by August 1998 Acroni had formed a defence team of representatives from the above-mentioned institutions and several in-house experts. Acroni's general manager, Dr Vasilij Prešern, led the team but the preparation of the legal part of the defence was handed to Prof. Dr Mirko Ilešiè from the University of Maribor who had already successfully defeated some anti-dumping allegations. The power of attorney was given to the European Law firm Van Bael & Bellis to represent company interests in the investigation. To avoid misunderstandings among different audiences and to keep control of all necessary working documents, a person responsible for the coordination was appointed. Strategy was then formulated with experienced professionals and the defence team.

Although it was initially decided to try to prevent the formal anti-dumping proceeding there was not much to be done since the Commission handed over a 'Note Verbal' on 31 August 1998, and the Notice of Initiation was published in the *Official Journal of the European Communities* on 17 September 1998.[3] With this act the investigation by the Commission started. At the same time as the Commission publishes the Notice of Initiation, it forwards questionnaires to all exporters and importers known to be involved. Once the questionnaire has been answered, there is a short period while the Commission review the answers to the questionnaire. The Commission then arranges to visit the offices of the various companies involved.

There were 40 days left to prepare answers to the questionnaire that accompanied allegations, a very short period for such a huge task. A verification meeting in Acroni in November 1998 was the company's unique direct contact with the representatives of the Commission except for the oral hearing in January 1999.

Every member of the defence team was cautious that any mistake might result in higher dumping duties being imposed and that the tiniest procedural fault would cause damage to the case. So it was greatly in Acroni's interest to cooperate with the Commission. The company went on to lodge its injury submission. It set out to rebut the allegations regarding dumping, injury and Community interest contained in the Complaint lodged by Eurofer.

Major points alleged were:

- Acroni dumped its price by 30 per cent.
- Complaining companies lost ecus 70.1 million due to lower prices and suffered 12 per cent lower sales.
- Hence:

  - a 35 per cent decrease of profit;
  - 10 per cent lower utilization; and
  - 439 newly unemployed workers.

Acroni decided to run the defence on three levels:

- Economic expertise
- Legal expertise
- Political

The team spotted two critical success factors:

- Coordination between their team (focused on expertise and formal procedures) and diplomats (political level), which should support the case through formal and informal contacts with EU representatives on all levels.
- Involvement of Slovene media and other stakeholders who might otherwise intensify their public attacks on Acroni and all Slovenian steel producers.

The team member responsible for coordination, Irena Peterlin, consultant to the board of Slovenian Steelworks, took over those two critical success factors.

Economic expertise

A simple analysis of world steel production, consumption and trade showed clear explanations for a drop of steel prices. In all world regions but especially in Western Europe, Japan and South America capacity growth had been two or three times as high as consumption growth over the last ten years. The situation became even worse after the Asian crisis that heavily delayed the growth of Asian (excluding Japan and China) steel consumption and inflated their production that represented 11 per cent of global production in 1990 but as much as 20 per cent in 1997. Prices of electrical steel on the world market were really falling, but mainly due to cheaper raw material and cheaper steel from the Far East. But the major argument against dumping allegations was that some of Eurofer members were found guilty and heavily punished by the Commission for their illegal cartel agreements in 1997.[4] One might therefore suspect that losses and price reductions were caused by the before-mentioned cartel agreement rather than directly by Slovenian steel exports. It is clear that the complaints filed should fail due to the cartel agreement (previously condemned). The Eurofer companies had obviously intended to seek the protection of their market share through the imposition of the anti-dumping duties.

This case is not unique. Mayhew mentions a similar case where, shortly after lodging a complaint against producers from the Czech Republic, Poland and Slovakia, the Association of Cement Producers from the Community was fined by the Commission for price fixing.[5]

Legal expertise

The major background for legal expertise was a clear understanding of the anti-dumping procedures.

The calculation of dumping is entirely in the hands of the Commission, which was bad news for Acroni since the Commission could use the most unfavourable method of valuation. The danger was enhanced by the fact that Acroni's share had risen significantly in last few years. The Commission could find the Community industry to be suffering material injury, which is the second major point of the submission. So the above-mentioned cartel agreements between Krupp and other Eurofer members were found to be the major argument against allegations. And even if both dumping and damage is found, the Commission can stop the proceeding if such a measure would be 'against the interests of the Community'. It is clear that the direct political and lobby power of countries involved play the major role in this respect.

The expertise also found that the Commission had made a serious procedural mistake by not following Article 28 of the Interim Agreement which states that all relevant important information regarding the case should be handed to the Cooperation Council before the proceeding is filed. This mistake was even more serious since the Council could find a need for reconstruction that would be funded by PHARE and supported by the EU.

Political involvement and coordination

The Government, Ministry of Economy, Competition Protection Office, the Office of European Affairs and the Slovene Mission to the EU were regularly briefed about the strategy, arguments and changes by the team coordinator. There were several coordination meetings, some of them called by Igor Bavèar, Minister of European Affairs, that generated formal and informal meetings of Slovene diplomats with EU representatives. Marija Adanja, state Undersecretary of the Government Office for European Affairs, took care to ensure good and permanent relationships with the relevant authorities in the Office of European Affairs, the relevant national authorities, the Slovene Mission to the EU, EU institutions, the Government of the Republic of Slovenia and Acroni's team member responsible for coordination.

On the EU side as well, coordination between different departments of the Commission must have taken place. As the subject covers several areas, it is normal that DG Competition has to be consulted by DG Trade to assess the impact of the case. The Slovenian team and the law firm Van Bael & Bellis therefore made direct contacts with each of those sections of the Commission involved. Although the procedure was run by DG I (External Trade), contacts were also made with DG III (Industry) and DG IV (Competition).

Media and other stakeholder involvement

There was a serious threat that the general 'anti-steel' opinion supported by the Slovene media could harm the defence. This could be done by false information in the Slovene media which could mislead the Commission. It is worth mentioning that there are very few (if any) Slovene journalists that understood or supported the reconstruction of the Slovenian steel industry, and on the basis of such ignorance there was a risk they could construct even more misleading and harmful information regarding the anti-dumping proceeding.

Another even more serious threat was that misleading information could weaken the internal coherence of the defence team and all supporters involved. It is easy to confuse supporters of heavy industry in times when the 'new economy' is fashionable.

The team coordinator thus established regular relations to all media covering the issue with regular updates, briefing meetings and many informal meetings with editors and media opinion leaders. These activities proved to be efficient since this case was one of few 'critical' issues that received heavy but technically balanced and correct coverage.

Nevertheless, besides economic damage for the producer caused by an anti-dumping proceeding, considerable political damage might be done by improper media coverage of the case. Trade instruments – if not well explained – may result in loss of confidence in the trading partner and in worsening public opinion on accession to European integration. It might also cause and/or support renewal of trade (and political) protectionism.

The result

Simultaneously with the above-mentioned expertise and critical communications activities, the in-house team prepared answers to the questionnaire. After a short period while the Commission reviewed the answers, the Commission then arranged to visit the offices of Acroni and also the offices of some of Acroni's partners to verify the information contained in the answers. The Commission did not find any false or misleading information or absence of cooperation with the relevant department of the European Commission.

The first official oral hearing in which the representatives of Acroni presented their arguments relating to the injury was held on 21 January 1999. *Metal Bulletin*, 16 March 1999, writes:

> The European Commission is poised to request that steel producers withdraw their anti-dumping complaint against imports of stainless steel plate from South Africa and Slovenia. According to a source close to negotiations, the Commission has been unable to establish any evidence of damage to EU stainless producers resulting from imports and within the next few weeks will ask complainants to withdraw their AD claims.

On 17 March 1999, Acroni received information from DG I that the allegation had been withdrawn on 3 March 1999. The Slovene Mission to the EU received a Note Verbal that the proceeding was withdrawn on 22 March 1999, and the Commission Decision terminating the procedures was published in the *Official Journal* on 28 May 1999.[6]

Conclusions and lessons

The Acroni case is an example of the triple nature of EU anti-dumping procedures. Firstly, it cannot be denied that 'the core' argument in these procedures is an economic one. The more detailed and holistic a picture that the team can develop, the higher are their chances of presenting the case from the right angle.

Secondly, an anti-dumping procedure is a legal case in which every minor legal and procedural detail should be thoroughly examined, understood and reacted to.

And thirdly, an anti-dumping procedure is also a political game though which institutions of the EU (under pressure from domestic producers and their lobbies) try to restrict competitive imports from non-member countries. It is a chess game in which every player is equally important if he or she follows a common strategy plan. Acroni successfully went through this particular case without any harm.

Acroni's success was based on several factors that are lessons for the future:

- React to the first information.
- Form a multidisciplinary defence team.
- Do not skimp on time and effort on necessary expertise.
- Do not forget about 'internal' stakeholders.
- Do not overestimate the opponent.

Notes

1. M. Maresceau (ed.) (1997) *Enlarging the European Union: Relations between the EU and Central and Eastern Europe*, London and New York: Longman. See also M. Maresceau (1997) 'On Association, Partnership, Pre-accession and Accession', in M. Maresceau (ed.), *Enlarging the European Union: Relations between the EU and Central and Eastern Europe*, London and New York: Longman, pp. 3–22.
2. A. Mayhew (1998) *Recreating Europe – The European Union's Policy towards Central and Eastern Europe*, Cambridge University Press.
3. *Official Journal of the European Communities*, vol. C289, p. 12.
4. See Commission Decision 98/247/ECSC of 21 January 1998. *Official Journal of the European Communities*, vol. L100/55.
5. Mayhew (1998), *op. cit.*
6. See Commission Decision 99/353/ECSC of 28 May 1999. *Official Journal of the European Communities*, vol. L135/95.

Part IV
Global and Regional Cases

8
Getting Animal Welfare on to the World Trade Agenda

Christopher Fisher

Introduction

This case study will examine how the establishment of the World Trade Organization is influencing domestic policy within the EU and, as a result, changing the way that NGOs, EC and government officials behave in the political and policy arena. It will consider the case of animal welfare, an interesting and in some cases atypical field of EU policy-making, but one which illustrates the issues and problems raised in the World Trade Organization (WTO) era. It will cover the period from late 1994 to the present (January 2001), and of necessity will have to do so briefly. Three specific areas of policy will be addressed:

1. The prohibition on importation of certain furs from countries that permit use of 'leghold traps' which was established under Regulation 5241/92/EEC.
2. The various minimum farm animal welfare standards existing in the Community,[1] and related measures such as labelling schemes;
3. The animal testing and marketing restrictions adopted under Directive 93/35/EC with regard to cosmetic products – the subject of a case study in the previous edition.[2]

The main 'stakeholder' in this case study is the Eurogroup for Animal Welfare.[3] Eurogroup was established in 1980 and acts as an umbrella organization for its member societies, typically the major animal welfare organization in each member state. In addition, Eurogroup has a number of 'observer' members including prospective member organizations from the accession countries, international animal welfare groups and other national groups based outside the EU. Eurogroup also liaises and cooperates with other animal welfare/rights organizations on specific campaigns and initiatives, but does not represent them as such in its contacts with the EU institutions. For much of its history, Eurogroup has had a particularly strong presence in the European Parliament where it also provides the secretariat for the Parliamentary

Intergroup on the Welfare and Conservation of Animals.[4] Eurogroup nominees are represented on various advisory committees established by the European Commission and also at the Council of Europe.

The basic approach adopted by Eurogroup has been to lobby for the introduction of minimum welfare standards, principally in relation to farm animals, laboratory animals and wildlife; thereafter, to press for supporting policy initiatives and the ongoing improvement and extension of such standards. The gradual progress achieved since 1980 was reflected in the Treaty of Amsterdam which included a 'Protocol on Protection and Welfare of Animals' which states:

> In formulating the Community's agriculture, transport, internal market and research policies, the Community and Member States shall pay full regard to the welfare requirements of animals.[5]

The other main actor throughout this case study is the European Commission (EC). On the one hand the EC has responsibility for proposing new animal welfare legislation and ensuring that member states carry out their obligations; on the other it has responsibility for negotiating international treaties and ensuring compliance by the European Community – it also represents the Community at the WTO and is responsible for both developing and implementing most aspects of its Common Commercial Policy. This analysis requires that the conduct of the EC be considered both collectively and separately with regard to the relevant responsible Directorates General (DG). First and foremost DG Trade, where the Commissioner was formerly Sir Leon Brittan and is now Mr Pascal Lamy; DG Agriculture, where the Commissioner is Mr Franz Fischler; DG Environment, where the Commissioner was formerly Mrs Ritt Bjerregaard and is now Mrs Margot Wallstrom; DG Sanco (formerly Consumer Policy) where the Commissioner was formerly Ms Emma Bonino and is now Mr David Byrne; DG Industry, where the Commissioner is Mr Erik Liikaanen. These are the main players, but others are also relevant, notably the DGs for External Relations and Development and also the Legal Services of the EC.

It is important to note that some animal welfare competences have changed during the relevant period; DG Industry has assumed responsibility for the Cosmetics Directive from DG SANCO, while SANCO has assumed responsibility for proposing new farm animal welfare standards from DG Agriculture. DG Agriculture continues to retain some animal welfare related competences and moreover, it represents the EC in trade negotiations for the sector. DG Trade, meanwhile, has overall responsibility for Trade Policy and WTO-related issues. It takes an active role on issues deemed to be 'difficult' or 'controversial', such as animal welfare.

The member states are also key stakeholders in this case study and special attention will be given to the role of the Presidency. Some differentiation will be made between the role of member states on specific policy problems such as 'leghold traps' and their role in the development of overall trade policy.

The European Parliament has often been the 'champion' of specific animal welfare measures, notably on leghold traps and cosmetics. However, its role is limited because it has relatively little influence over common commercial policy or agriculture policy. This fact affected Eurogroup's lobbying strategy and priorities.

When considering other relevant stakeholders, competitors and issue groups it is important to appreciate the context in which the matter is being addressed. Throughout much of the period, a broader debate has been raging about the pros and cons of 'globalization' as represented by international trade managed by the WTO. Related to this has been the debate about the so-called 'Millennium Round' of trade negotiations, proposed by the EU as the best means of achieving further trade liberalization. The reasoning of those advocating the round, is that the only way to reach an agreement satisfactory to all parties is to have wide-ranging negotiations within which everyone can identify some gains to offset against any losses or concessions they might have to incur in other sectors. For the EU, these losses are widely predicted to fall in agriculture, where the sector is highly protected, while the expected gains would be in areas such as investment, competition and services.

The existence of such a highly charged and complex negotiating scenario creates a lobbying environment very different to that normally associated with EU policy. It is not just a matter of reconciling internal differences and competing interests, but also external interests too. Moreover, these interests may potentially become subordinate to others considered more important in the overall trade negotiations and therefore risk being compromised or abandoned altogether in pursuit of a higher political or economic objective. In this climate, a multitude of outcomes and alliances are possible and these may not follow predictable patterns. Thus, EU farmers may feel they have more common cause with animal welfare NGOs than with third-country farmers seeking to gain access to the EU market – development and consumer NGOs may feel exactly the opposite. In summary, the situation is very fluid and mostly unfamiliar to many of the actors.

The case

Eurogroup and other animal welfare organizations based in the EU became aware of the WTO as an issue in the summer of 1994. They were alerted to it by US colleagues, who gained experience of the General Agreements on Tariffs and Trade (GATT) when they had become involved in trade issues as a result of the 'Tuna-Dolphin' GATT dispute between the USA, Mexico *et al.*,[6, 7] and also as a result of the creation of the North American Free Trade Agreement (NAFTA). Eurogroup was not alone in being late to recognize the potential significance of the ongoing trade negotiations known as the 'Uruguay Round' (UR) – most NGOs had not followed these in any detail, and only a small minority were actively lobbying governments. As the conclusion of the UR approached, a Ministerial Meeting was organized in Marrakech with a view to finalizing the text of the new Agreements which would transform the GATT into the WTO – it was only at this stage that many of those affected, not just NGOs, became aware and started to get involved – other actors such as the European Parliament, which had to give its assent, were not much better informed. The UR was negotiated by trade specialists from national governments and from other bodies such as the EC and the GATT, there was little by way of public scrutiny or even cross-departmental scrutiny. Whether this was by design or default is hard to say, but the result was that many only came to realize the full significance of the WTO Agreements to their own interests after they had been adopted. This is true of governments as well as NGOs and may go some way towards explaining the public and political backlash that has subsequently emerged.

Interest groups have different reasons to be concerned about the WTO. Some commentators have argued that many of the fundamental issues now deemed to be of concern existed in the GATT, which may be true in some respects but it also serves to highlight the fundamental change introduced under the WTO regime. Disputes between parties are now subject to a binding resolution mechanism – for the first time, international trade rules have teeth. The consequences have been dramatic and often plain to see in high-profile WTO disputes such as 'beef-hormone',[8] 'bananas'[9, 10] and 'shrimp-turtle'[11] – cases which might respectively also be described as reflecting 'consumer', 'development' and 'environment' concerns. Beyond these examples, there is a further and deeper layer of concerns – these have started to affect a wide range of national and international policy measures and initiatives at various levels including adoption, development, enforcement and implementation. To date, this is the level at which animal welfare measures have been affected.

The animal welfare problem with regard to the WTO is at least three distinct but related problems, namely:

1. Scope to use trade-related policy mechanisms to improve animal welfare standards in third countries.
2. Ability to prevent domestic welfare policies being undermined by trade, for example by an influx of (cheap) imports which do not respect domestic welfare standards.
3. Right to refuse products which do not meet domestic welfare standards.

In practice, policy measures can combine more than one of these options, but each can be demonstrated as follows

1. the leghold-trap Regulation was mainly external in focus in that it prohibited imports of all furs of specific species until such time as the exporting

country banned the use of leghold traps or applied internationally agreed humane trapping standards.

2. Farm animal welfare standards in the EU are higher than in many of its potential competitors. Such standards tend to increase costs to domestic producers and thereby make them less competitive in terms of price. Thus, unless adjusted for, raising domestic standards could lead to more lower welfare imports and consequently undermine the domestic policy goal – the focus is primarily internal.

3. The Cosmetics Directive seeks to apply a common practice or standard – it effectively prohibits the marketing of products tested on animals when humane alternatives could have been used instead (the EU policy).

Thus, while all being concerned with animal welfare, these three types of measure each one has a different emphasis. The first is essentially external while the second is essentially internal. The third is neutral in that it seeks to ensure all products meet the same welfare (ethical) standard, although the standard itself is determined by EU concerns and not by an agreed 'common value'.

The reasons why such policy measures may contravene WTO rules are complex but can be simplified as follows:

- WTO rules require all 'like' products of a specific type to be treated equally. Distinctions based upon the manner in which a product is produced are therefore not generally considered as either acceptable or compatible
- Although general exceptions to the rules permit (trade-restrictive) measures relating to 'public morals', 'animal life or health' and 'conservation of exhaustible natural resources', the extent to which these cover animal welfare is unknown
- To qualify as an exception, a measure must not 'constitute a means of arbitrary or unjustifiable discrimination between countries', or be a 'disguised restriction on international trade' – furthermore, in some cases it must also be 'necessary'
- Measures such as tariffs and technical requirements are strictly controlled by WTO rules with the overall aim that such 'barriers to trade' should be reduced and eliminated wherever possible

The net result is that where policy measures seek to prohibit or regulate trade on the basis of animal welfare concerns they are likely to fall within the scope of WTO rules. In such cases it would typically be necessary to demonstrate that a measure is 'legitimate' under WTO rules and also applied in a non-discriminatory, justifiable and least-trade-restrictive manner. If found to contravene the rules, the State concerned must either withdraw the measure, adapt it to make it fully compliant, agree compensation with the plaintiff or, failing that, to accept proportionate retaliatory action sanctioned by the dispute mechanism.

From the outset it was evident that animal welfare was particularly vulnerable. Unlike other social objectives such as environmental protection, sustainable development, poverty alleviation and consumer safety, animal welfare is not acknowledged specifically in the WTO Agreements[12] although it may still be implicitly covered or accepted by them. Furthermore, animal welfare is almost exclusively concerned with the processes by which products are made.

It was necessary for animal welfare groups to undertake a steep learning curve. Rather than ask someone who understood trade policy to become familiar with animal welfare, it was decided to engage someone who understood animal welfare in the EU context, to become familiar with trade policy. Initially some joint funding was provided by NGOs and a consultant (the author) was hired to undertake the work on a part-time basis. This arrangement has been maintained ever since with a variety of animal welfare NGOs acting as sponsors. Continuity of personnel has ensured a growing body of expertize supported by an increased organizational commitment to WTO-related work. Thus, having identified the importance of the WTO, animal welfare NGOs devoted resources sufficient to achieve progress. This has proved to be an advantage in sustaining and developing the position of animal welfare *vis-à-vis* the WTO. Many NGOs in other sectors have not been able to devote (or prioritize) resources in this way, with the result that the WTO has been one among several designated issues of a staff member; or, instead, their activity has been concentrated around particular events such as ministerial conferences. Among Brussels-based NGOs, Eurogroup is unusual in having someone almost wholly focused on WTO-related issues.

Having made an initial review of the situation in 1994, an important strategic decision had to be taken. Although the dangers of the new WTO system were evident, there was also potential within the text of the WTO Agreements to find an accommodation for animal welfare. Having come late to the issue, animal welfare groups were in no position to derail the Assent process even if they had wanted to – at that time there was no strong groundswell of NGO or political opposition to the WTO. Tactically it was decided to raise relevant concerns and seek assurances – WTO was going to happen, the key question was 'what would happen next'?

With the WTO established it was necessary to consider options. Examination of the texts highlighted a number of potential obstacles to animal welfare and a good deal of uncertainty about how the current agreements might be interpreted. There were two ways of progressing this, either to seek appropriate clarifications or amendments to the WTO Agreements or, where appropriate, to let the existing text be put to the test in the context of a WTO dispute panel. At that time the argument was still a theoretical one even though some 'storm clouds' were already on the horizon with regard to leghold traps.

Changing WTO rules would first require convincing at least some members of the need to do so (and the best methods), and then persuade the large majority of the WTO membership of 140 to agree – this would have been politically very difficult, time-consuming and not likely to be considered as a high-priority for special attention so early in the WTO's existence. The WTO is essentially intergovernmental in character and only the members can bring forward proposals for reform; unlike some UN institutions there is little scope for formal input by NGOs. Because the Community is represented by the EC, it was evident that in order to raise animal welfare at the WTO or see it defended in a panel it would be necessary to secure the support of the EC. In the early stages the strategy was therefore essentially to increase knowledge, develop argumentation and make contacts at the EC, national and WTO level – there was also a need to increase awareness among the animal welfare NGOs.

This situation soon began to change as a result of Canadian and US pressure concerning the leghold-trap Regulation. With other high-profile issues on the trade agenda, such as US 'Helms–Burton' sanctions against Cuba, the EC wanted to avoid a high-profile Trans-Atlantic trade dispute which it feared it might lose. In December 1995 it took the unprecedented step of instructing member states not to implement the fur import ban so as to allow time for a negotiated settlement.

Animal welfare fears about the impact of the WTO were therefore quickly realized. Importantly, the EC's decision did not result from a WTO panel ruling, but merely from the threat of a panel being convened. Most alarming was the manner in which the fur-import ban established in the Regulation was effectively 'suspended' by the EC with the collusion of member states prior to any amending legislation being adopted. This saga has been extensively commented upon[13] and can only be dealt with briefly here.

The EC reasoned that the same welfare objective could be realized through negotiation of humane trapping standards. It also argued that this option would not be viable in the event of a negative panel ruling as the USA and Canada would no longer have any need to negotiate. The proposed agreements on trapping standards concerned welfare criteria, yet the EC was represented by DG Environment (the responsible DG) and DG Trade. At one stage there was a public falling-out between Commissioners Bjerregaard and Brittan, and by the end of the process most of the detail was being negotiated by officials from DG Trade. The final text was universally condemned by animal welfare NGOs, rejected by the European Parliament and a number of member states. The outcome in the Council remained uncertain until the final vote, which only took place after several discussions in full Council. Intensive lobbying by Eurogroup and others ensured that the whole process was subject to considerable public scrutiny and criticism. However, in December 1996 the Council finally accepted the Agreement negotiated with Canada and Russia;[14] and in July 1997 a weaker bilateral Agreement was concluded with the USA.[15]

Commissioner Brittan attempted to draw a line under the issue by suggesting that it was 'an isolated case' and not an indication of a wider problem for EU animal welfare measures. While asserting that there was no *a priori* exclusion of animal welfare from the exceptions allowed under WTO rules (something which the EC had been unwilling to put to the test in the case of leghold traps), EC officials were clearly concerned about making distinctions between products on the basis of how they are produced. Thereafter, alternative policy solutions, such as international animal welfare agreements and labelling, were increasingly highlighted in the statements of EC officials.

Also in December 1996, the first WTO Ministerial Conference was held in Singapore and Eurogroup was represented. Until that time, animal welfare NGOs had concentrated on developing their own position and had devoted little effort to wider discussion with other NGOs or with third-country and WTO officials. This process began at the Singapore Ministerial Conference.

Singapore was also where the EU first pushed its proposal for a 'new round' of trade negotiations. 'No New Round' subsequently became a rallying cry for many NGOs worldwide who, despite their differing constituencies and priorities, were united in their concern about the consequences of further and deeper trade liberalization – an underlying theme was that liberalization was being pursued to benefit corporations instead of citizens. Although sometimes misrepresented as wholly negative or 'anti-trade', in fact many of those supporting this approach have proposed constructive alternatives.

Eurogroup decided to take a different approach for several reasons:

- First, it saw no inherent problem with international trade, only with the way in which it was currently organized. Perhaps most significantly, it was aware that the creation of the Single Market had facilitated an overall improvement in animal welfare in the EU through the adoption of minimum standards throughout the Community.
- Second, there were obvious difficulties in proposing discussion of animal welfare at the WTO in isolation. Raising the issue as one among many in the context of a broader round of negotiations was more viable. It was therefore sensible for animal welfare groups to at least keep an open mind on any 'new round' providing that issues of concern to them would be addressed.
- Third, because the Community was leading the calls for a 'new round' and Eurogroup relied upon it to advocate its concerns, it was not tactically wise to push in the opposite direction.
- Fourth, in any event, further negotiations on agriculture were already programmed to commence in 2000 and these would be crucially important to animal welfare.
- Fifth, at that time, three years prior to Seattle, a 'new round' seemed highly likely. With only limited resources available, expending significant energy opposing it was unwise, especially as it might also have proved counterproductive to animal welfare objectives.

Eurogroup was not alone among NGOs in taking such an approach. It chose to remain sceptical, be positive wherever possible, and above all to be pragmatic.

Throughout 1997 Eurogroup's emphasis centred upon analysing the fundamental problems and trying to identify possible solutions. Given that the Community had shown little enthusiasm for defending an animal welfare measure at the WTO, the alternative was to try and negotiate appropriate revisions of WTO rules or to secure an adequate accommodation in an official 'clarification' or 'understanding' of the existing WTO text. A period of calm followed the leghold-trap storm during which contacts continued and were expanded. Eurogroup set out its concerns and proposals in a report entitled 'Conflict or Concord'[16] which was widely distributed to WTO members, trade officials, press and NGOs and also subsequently reproduced in a US version.

In May 1998, the second WTO Ministerial Conference was held in Geneva. It was designed to be a largely ceremonial event to celebrate the 50th Anniversary of the GATT, attended by many heads of state. For the EU and others it represented an ideal opportunity to push forward with their proposal for a 'new round'. To the apparent surprise of the authorities and organizers, the event was also the subject of substantial street protests that were at times confrontational. This produced something of a siege mentality inside the Conference venue, but at the same time led to acknowledgement of the need to engage with civil society on trade issues. This pattern was to be repeated on a grand scale 18 months later in Seattle.

In Brussels, the EC was quick to respond by organizing an *ad hoc* programme of civil society consultations on trade issues[17] to which representatives from all relevant NGOs were invited, also including business, labour and academics. This process has continued to develop. It has had a considerable impact on the interaction between EC officials and NGOs on trade issues, and also between NGOs. Sceptics have condemned it as little more than a PR exercise by the EC; however, whether or not that was the original intention it has become more than that. Largely funded and organized by DG Trade, the process has gathered momentum to the point where it would now be difficult to stop. Moreover, it appears that the EC is more than willing to continue, and not solely for reasons of PR.

A number of observations can be made about this process. First, it is an initiative of the EC, principally DG Trade – the Council and the Parliament have both been almost entirely without representation although they are not excluded. Second, it is evident that there is a large degree of common ground between 'non-profit' NGOs with regard to a scepticism towards the WTO system: for example, its lack of transparency and public participation; concerns about the negative consequences of liberalization and the manner in which its benefits are shared; and about the application and interpretation of WTO rules and the premises on which they are based. These 'common criticisms' provide a basis against which the EC can evaluate 'civil-society' (non-business) concerns. On the question of a 'new round' the position of 'civil-society' NGOs ranges between sympathetic and opposed – most are sceptical. While the EC has never wavered in its support for a 'new round', it has undoubtedly made efforts to respond to various civil-society concerns, for example by agreeing to conduct an impact assessment on social, environment, health and other issues.[18] At the same time the process has enabled NGOs to identify both common ground and differences between them, with the result that bilateral discussions have often taken place to work on these. While the relationship has not been as collaborative with business, common ground has sometimes emerged on specific points. Overall the dialogue has increased the level of understanding between the actors, but not always the level of agreement, although this could still develop.

By participating in this process, coupled with ongoing bilateral contacts with EC officials and others, such as the WTO secretariat, Eurogroup was able to build up a good picture of the many different interests and opinions, both about the specifics of concern to animal welfare and also the general situation. This was important in shaping its priorities in the run-up to the Seattle Ministerial Conference, where it was widely anticipated that with growing support from the USA a new round of negotiations would finally be agreed.

Although fundamental rule changes at the WTO would be the most beneficial to animal welfare, it was obvious that it would be very difficult to persuade the Community to argue for this. It was not just a question of assessing whether the Community could be lobbied to take such a position, but also whether it could succeed in the overall WTO negotiations. The conclusion drawn was that unfortunately such an approach was not the most viable and that to pursue it would risk coming away empty-handed from the process. Moreover, of the animal welfare measures potentially at risk, 'leghold traps' had already been lost and with one exception (cosmetics), all the others were in the field of agriculture. Thus, it was decided to focus most attention on securing a strong EC negotiating position on farm animal welfare, especially as negotiations in this sector were already agreed to start in 2000.

Thereafter, Eurogroup's main concern was to find viable solutions that would enable the Community to maintain and improve farm animal welfare standards in the context of a liberalized market and WTO rules. It was less concerned with the principle of whether trade liberalization was a good or bad thing; rather, it posed the question – assuming that further liberalization in agriculture will proceed, what steps are necessary to ensure that animal welfare policies are not undermined or rendered impracticable?

Eurogroup set about evaluating different policy options, taking account of the WTO realities which included an ongoing commitment to reduce import barriers and forms of domestic support which are trade-distorting. The bottom line of this analysis was that the Community should not agree to further liberalization in agriculture without putting in place adequate safeguards to ensure the viability of farm animal welfare standards. A number of different approaches were explored ranging from reforms to the WTO Agreements to utilizing trade liberalization to promote trade in welfare-friendly products – these were set out in a further report entitled 'Food for Thought'.[19]

These ideas were explored in an ongoing dialogue with EC officials in a non-mutually-exclusive fashion. Post-Geneva, contacts were established with DG Agriculture who would take the lead in the trade negotiations for the sector. The perspective of DG Trade and DG Agriculture is somewhat different, and it was therefore instructive to gauge their respective enthusiasms for different ideas presented. Among the options discussed several began to emerge, including making direct payments to producers to offset higher welfare costs and labelling to indicate welfare standards – both of these effectively represented new approaches to Community animal welfare policy.

Without abandoning any of the various options still being explored, Eurogroup set about refining this list and lobbying for key components to be integrated into the EC's negotiating position at Seattle. The formulation of this position was the product of a year-long process during 1999 where the EC drafted different texts for consideration by the Council all with a view to developing a final negotiating mandate for the proposed 'new round'. DG Agriculture held a special position in this regard and exercised a lot more control and input for its section of the draft text.

Recognizing that the Presidency of the Council would be of special importance during this process and at the Ministerial Conference, a Eurogroup delegation was organized to visit Helsinki for meetings with Finnish officials who would take responsibility during the crucial period in the second half of 1999. Moreover, the Finnish Presidency was seen as a good opportunity because Finland has a progressive position on animal welfare and a good record for conducting open and transparent government. With the assistance of its national member organization, Animalia, Eurogroup secured separate meetings with the Finnish Ministers for Agriculture, Trade & Environment, plus other meetings, including with the Department of Foreign Affairs. An especially good contact was made with the Minister for Agriculture who was both well-informed and sympathetic to the animal welfare problem – he gave an assurance that animal welfare would be discussed as a priority by the Presidency and he was as good as his word.

There were two other unusual factors in 1999. First there was the unprecedented resignation of the Commission, followed by the temporary continuation of existing Commissioners and the subsequent appointment of a new Commission. Second there were European Parliamentary elections. While in many respects, despite the resignation of the Commission, it remained 'business as usual', this undoubtedly had some knock-on effects. One of these was that it gave extra prominence to the Presidency at a time when the EC was not fully able (or legitimate enough) to provide leadership; it also meant that Commissioner Brittan, the main proponent of the new round, would not actually be in post in Seattle whereas it was considered highly likely that Commissioner Fischler would be reappointed to Agriculture, and inevitably this could only strengthen his hand; new Trade Commissioner Lamy would have to 'hit the ground running' and rely on the brief and mandate prescribed for him on entering office. All of this was probably to the advantage of animal welfare. Furthermore, transfer of some animal welfare competences (from Agriculture to SANCO) would not take place until the agriculture position was well-advanced and in any event would still effectively remain in Commissioner Fischler's (safe pair of) hands for negotiating purposes.

The EC crisis and the elections virtually removed the Parliament as a player in the Seattle preparations. Due to its dual lack of competence on common commercial policy and agriculture, its potential influence on behalf of animal welfare was already limited; but by the time the new Parliament had convened, organized itself and scrutinized the new Commissioners, most of the preparation for Seattle was already complete.

The final outcome was that the negotiating mandate included a specific reference with regard to animal welfare and agriculture,[20] but the issue was not taken up elsewhere and neither were any of the more fundamental WTO reforms. However, Eurogroup had achieved its primary lobbying objective – the Community would go to Seattle with a mandate to ensure that its farm animal welfare concerns would be addressed in future trade negotiations.

Unfortunately, the confused situation in Brussels and the emphasis on preparation of the Ministerial Conference meant that Eurogroup was unsuccessful in its efforts to get the EC to raise animal welfare concerns in discussions at the WTO in Geneva. The first time it did so was in Seattle where it received a hostile response. It would not have been surprising if the initial reaction of trading partners had been negative, but by then there was a fraught negotiating atmosphere so it was almost inevitable. To the credit of the Commissioner and the Presidency, the Community held its ground. In the final stages a compromise text using more general language was under discussion, but it was clear that the Community wanted to pursue animal welfare as a 'non-trade concern' item for negotiation. The final outcome was inconclusive and no text was agreed.

The Seattle Ministerial Conference was remarkable for many reasons, but compared to the two previous WTO Ministerials it represented a new level of interaction between government officials and NGOs. Despite the fact that the NGO delegates were located in a separate building and the streets were often blocked by protesters, Commissioners, ministers and EC and EU national government officials regularly came to participate in briefings and discussions. Further briefings were also held where the EC and government delegations were located. Given that the formal debates were largely cere-monial and that the negotiating sessions were entirely closed, it was there-fore at such briefings and in the corridors that lobbying and exchange of information occurred. In the animal welfare case, Eurogroup had direct con-tacts with several national delegations, including ministers, and held two meetings with the Finnish Minister of Agriculture. During these contacts, soundings were taken as to the progress of negotiation and the possible approaches – Eurogroup was therefore able to put its views at crucial moments and in a timely fashion.

The aftermath of Seattle produced a strange mix of messages and lessons to be learned. There was wide acknowledgement of the need to respect the views of developing countries and also to take account of the concerns of civil society. At the same time the hostility expressed by some nations towards discussion of issues such as labour standards, environment and animal welfare prompted some to argue that these should not be discussed, despite the fact that they were at the heart of many civil society concerns. The early message from the EC was clear, the Community was 'isolated' on animal welfare – the clear inference being that it might not be tenable to keep it on the EU's agenda. Having lobbied for animal welfare to be included, Eurogroup still had more work to do to keep it on the EU negotiating agenda.

Back in Brussels, Eurogroup continued to focus most of its effort towards the EC with regard to developing the specific ideas already proposed and also to push forward with relevant policy issues including the publication of an overdue report on welfare standards in third countries[21] and a draft labelling scheme for eggs.[22] Most important of all, to demonstrate that the EC was seri-ous about pursuing animal welfare by raising it in Geneva, where discussions on agriculture were due to begin. The general civil society consultations were also continuing and Eurogroup was among those pushing for specific issue-based groups to be established, particularly for agriculture. The transfer of competence for development of new farm animal welfare standards to DG SANCO was worrying because it might have led to less commitment from DG Agriculture. SANCO was also widely acknowledged to be underresourced as well as being less powerful in the overall EC structure compared to Agriculture and Trade. WTO-related differences between DGs on animal wel-fare issues were also evident in a number of other areas such as labelling and the introduction of new standards. For example, at a time when the EC was advocating labelling as a potential solution, it was demonstrating reluctance to bring forward a mandatory egg-labelling scheme that would have applied to imports as well as to EU-produced eggs – outside of agriculture, problems also emerged with regard to Cosmetics (see below).

Despite these tensions and discontinuities, Eurogroup persisted and a break-through was achieved in June 2000 when the EC tabled a discussion paper[23] on animal welfare in Geneva. In Brussels, it was also agreed that Agriculture would be discussed as a specific issue group with civil society. Both were particularly important because under the terms agreed for the progress of Agriculture negotiations at the WTO, the Community had to submit its basic negotiating position by the end of the year – Eurogroup's main objective was to ensure that animal welfare was adequately included within this.

During the course of the Agriculture issue-group convened in Brussels it became evident that many of the issues raised by animal welfare were also relevant to other civil-society concerns. Furthermore, farmers' representatives also demonstrated concern about the impact of liberalization on domestic welfare standards. Although EC officials still complained of hostility from trading partners on the issue, they nonetheless continued to pursue it. In a high-profile statement to the Cairns group of agricultural exporting countries, Commissioner Fischler stated 'Those who ignore these aspects that society increasingly demands have not learned the lesson from Seattle. The WTO must address broader concerns than just trade'.[24] Late in 2000, the EC's basic negotiating position was agreed and animal welfare was prominently included.[25]

Following the success of the contacts made in connection with the Finnish Presidency, the practice was continued with Portugal and France, although the significance of these was less than during the period leading to Seattle. The Swedish Presidency scheduled for the first half of 2001 was considered more significant and, like Finland, the Swedish government was potentially sympathetic to animal welfare, but also very much in favour of trade liberalization. Swedish officials had previously demonstrated interest in the idea of making compensation payments to farmers and labelling schemes. A delegation was organized to visit Stockholm prior to the Presidency. The reactions were mixed, but overall it was clear that animal welfare was considered a serious issue to be addressed by the Presidency. This was subsequently confirmed by the decision to organize a special public discussion of farm animal husbandry at the Agriculture Council scheduled for May 2001 – inevitably WTO considerations will feature in this discussion.

In Brussels, the civil society consultations continued and Eurogroup succeeded in ensuring that Agriculture will continue to be discussed as an ongoing issue throughout the WTO negotiating process – thereby providing routine interaction and increased transparency in the agriculture negotiations that might otherwise have disappeared 'underground'. Moreover, it will allow Eurogroup and others to input ideas into the development of the Community's position and to test its adequacy. A significant success of the NGO dialogue process is that the EC has taken on board the concept of conducting 'impact assessments' to evaluate the potential trade and non-trade impacts of trade liberalization. Although this is primarily concerned with sustainable development, it has other applications. Eurogroup has therefore lobbied for assessments to be conducted about the impact on specific farm animal welfare objectives. At the same time, it will also press for studies to evaluate the economic costs of animal welfare standards compared to third countries in order to assess the potential level of compensation payments required. Thus, the Eurogroup strategy on agriculture is clear, first to ensure that animal welfare remains an integrated component of the EC's negotiating mandate; second to work at a practical level to develop and assess potentially viable solutions. This is considered particularly important because many of the approaches 'flagged' by the EC in its position paper represent new policy mechanisms that are as yet untried with respect to animal welfare. Eurogroup therefore wants to ensure not only that the EC negotiates successfully in Geneva, but also that the solutions proposed will be effective and have the full support of the member states.

To further highlight the complexity and tensions of this problem, it is necessary also to say something about the situation regarding Cosmetics. After an intensive lobbying campaign and a fierce struggle between the Parliament and the Council, the sixth amendment to the Cosmetics Directive (93/35/EC) was adopted in 1993. This provided for a marketing restriction on cosmetics tested on animals in cases where humane non-animal alternatives could have been used instead. However, although some alternative tests became available, the EC (now represented by DG Industry, not SANCO) did not want to implement the marketing ban for fear of a WTO challenge.

For the second time, the EC acting in conjunction with the member states, failed to implement a Community animal welfare measure on the basis of a potential incompatibility with WTO rules. The worrying precedent is plain to see – hard fought legislation being nullified as a result of the mere possibility that it might be challenged at the WTO and found to contravene its rules. Interestingly, since 1993, the Parliament has acquired co-decision powers in relation to the Cosmetics Directive. This means that if a satisfactory compromise is not found, then the sixth amendment stands. This issue is still at an early stage in the legislative process, but for Eurogroup it represents another WTO-related challenge.

Conclusions and lessons

In drawing together some lessons and conclusions from this particular case, it is helpful to recall the title – there is more than one way of 'Getting Animal Welfare onto the World Trade Agenda'. Three specific examples have been presented; leghold traps, farm animal welfare and cosmetics – each could have been a separate case study in its own right. Moreover, if each had been examined separately, the answer would have been different. Similar case studies could also be written in other fields, for example development, environment or consumer protection, although again the conclusions might differ. The overarching issue addressed is the impact of WTO rules on a specific area of Community policy.

Certainly for animal welfare, as for many other sectors and interest groups, the creation of the WTO has substantially changed the arena in which EU policy is developed and implemented. It has introduced several new dynamics into the process, both internal and external; it is causing all the actors to consider new policy mechanisms and, in more extreme cases, to question whether the WTO system is actually compatible with pursuing their objectives. It has produced a new type of dialogue both between the EC and NGOs and also between NGOs. At times it has revealed differences within the EC, particularly between Directorates.

It has also highlighted the peripheral role still ascribed to Parliament in important policy areas such as agriculture and the common commercial policy, and the potential for legislative measures to be overridden by trade-policy concerns. Significantly, it demonstrates how what might previously have been viewed as essentially domestic policy concerns are now increasingly exposed to external scrutiny and pressure when these in some way affect the trading interests of third countries. Thus, domestic policy mechanisms are no longer mainly evaluated on their domestic utility or appeal, but increasingly with regard to their relative importance with regard to the Community's overall Common Commercial Policy.

The results for animal welfare have been mixed. Taking 1994 as a reference point, to what extent have things improved? There are many parallels between the leghold-trap case and cosmetics. In both, the EC and the member states preemptively decided not to implement a measure on the basis that it *might* be challenged and subsequently found to contravene WTO rules. If anything, the EC has been bolder with the cosmetics decision in that it knows it must also secure the support of the Parliament. Contrast these examples with the high-profile WTO disputes concerning beef-hormones and bananas, and it is clear that animal welfare measures currently enjoy a much lower level of political commitment. In both of the other cases a WTO dispute panel has actually ruled against the Community measure, yet the Community has declined to conform to it and incurred substantial penalties as a result (in practice, these penalties are incurred by EU exporters trading with the affected countries). It is notable that, in both cases, a minority of member states have strongly opposed lifting the offending measures, and this has been sufficient to prevent the Community from changing its current policy, although a negotiated settlement is eventually likely to be agreed for bananas.

Despite this observation and the fact that the outcome of the leghold-trap saga was totally unsatisfactory from Eurogroup's point of view, it nonetheless played an important role in raising the profile of animal welfare on the trade agenda. It turned into a protracted struggle for which the EC had not really bargained, including an internal schism between two Commissioners. The EC eventually got its way, but at some considerable political and PR cost – in future, it would need to think more carefully about how to handle animal welfare as an issue in the WTO. Eurogroup could therefore take some positives from an overall negative outcome.

The leghold-trap Regulation was determinedly opposed by Canada and the USA from its very beginning. However, when it was adopted in 1992, most commentators felt that was probably the end of the matter. But with effect from 1995, the WTO system offered a new approach that they quickly threatened to utilize. Subsequent events demonstrated how these new rules were perceived to have teeth, even to the point of not waiting for a panel to be convened before changing the measure in question; it also demonstrated an assumption by the EC and others that current WTO rules would likely be interpreted so as to favour the trade objective over the animal welfare objective. The fact that in 2000 the EC should follow a similar course of action with regard to cosmetics (and with the same reasoning) suggests that Eurogroup has not made significant progress in persuading it to take a stronger approach.

Why the EC, supported by the member states, has failed to modify its approach can be explained in several ways:

- First, the EC still believes that such measures will likely be found contrary to WTO rules. This point is emphasized by the fact that substantive differences exist between the leghold-trap case and that of cosmetics, which is potentially more defensible under WTO rules.
- Second, the Community lacks the political will to put these questions to the test in a WTO panel. This reluctance is often justified by the EC on the basis that a negative ruling might actually make things worse for animal welfare by establishing an unhelpful precedent. Yet, the EC is unwilling to seek rule changes that would improve the situation, arguing that these would be almost impossible to negotiate.
- Third, it believes the same objective can be achieved by other means that will be politically acceptable to the institutions, for example bilateral agreements for leghold traps and a domestic test ban for cosmetics.
- Fourth, it has not yet perceived a sufficient degree of political concern from member states or the European Parliament which would cause it to consider defending such a measure at the WTO.

Both the leghold-trap Regulation and the cosmetics Directive provide examples of existing measures due to be implemented at a specific time and fully exposed to scrutiny under WTO rules. The situation in Agriculture is somewhat different – the emphasis has not been on regulating trade on the basis of production methods, but on ensuring that higher domestic welfare standards are not undermined by cheaper imports produced to lower standards. Agricultural products are provided with varying degrees of border protection in the form of tariffs and quotas, the actual point of impact on animal welfare is therefore still in the future, not the present. Moreover, the nature of such border protection and the amount and types of support that can be given to the agricultural sector will be the essential points for discussion in future WTO negotiations – this affords the Community the opportunity to seek a negotiated settlement rather than one resulting from or caused by the WTO's dispute settlement mechanism. However, if such a negotiated solution is unsatisfactory, then it can be foreseen that farm animal welfare legislation may also become the subject of further adverse review by the EC and member states. This would not be based on incompatibility with WTO rules, but on new economic concerns arising out of trade liberalization regulated by the WTO Agreements.

A brief review of the EC's position demonstrates how much animal welfare policy choices have been influenced as a result of WTO rules:

1. Trade measures targeting poor animal welfare practices in third countries are now considered to be an unacceptable option.
2. Measures that seek to regulate trade on the basis of welfare standards acceptable to the EU are not generally considered to be defensible at the WTO and are therefore unlikely to be adopted.
3. Differences in production standards will in future be more likely be addressed through labelling schemes.
4. Loss of competitiveness due to higher welfare standards can be potentially offset through direct payments or other border measures to be negotiated at the WTO.
5. Multilateral or bilateral Agreements are to be explored to provide a potential framework criteria or minimum welfare standard, that is to minimize disparities in welfare standards.
6. Fundamental reform of WTO rules to accommodate animal welfare is considered to be too difficult and probably in conflict with the Community's overall policy, which generally does not favour distinctions based on the method of production.

Eurogroup has not accepted these outcomes as inevitable and argues that, in some cases, outright import bans or regulation of trade on the basis of production standards are justifiable and the most effective option. However, it has also accepted that the situation has changed fundamentally and has therefore been active in proposing and evaluating new types of policy mechanisms such as direct payments and mandatory labelling. Its support for such alternatives is nevertheless conditional on them being able to produce comparable results sustainable over time. This approach implicitly acknowledges that some measures, particularly those that are externally focused, will be difficult to deploy in future.

The aforementioned should not, however, overshadow Eurogroup's achievements, particularly in the field of agriculture. The fact that the Community has incorporated, defended and maintained animal welfare in its negotiating agenda under adverse conditions is a testament to Eurogroup's lobbying success. Furthermore, alternative policy approaches first proposed by Eurogroup have been taken up at the Community level and will be subject to further development. Good contacts have been maintained at various levels in the EC and with the Council, resulting in a high level of awareness and visibility of the issue. The fact that the EU continues to advocate animal welfare is recognition of its importance as a domestic constituency.

Eurogroup's overall approach has also proved effective. Despite arguing for some fundamental reforms and at times being highly critical of the actions of the EC and the member states, it has nevertheless avoided becoming marginalized. Most importantly, it has succeeded in keeping its issue on the agenda at times when it could have been pushed aside. Its overall approach was one reason why it was able to do this, another was the fact that it was sufficiently well-resourced to be able to maintain a constant and coherent presence. Unlike some NGOs which were often forced to discuss theoretical WTO problems, Eurogroup had the dubious 'advantage' of having some real ones to deal with which provided numerous and sometimes politically charged opportunities for engagement with the various actors.

Although Eurogroup did not join those (the majority of) NGOs calling for 'no new round', it has still been able to enjoy constructive relations with them. Collaboration has for the most part been confined to institutional WTO issues such as transparency; and more recently Eurogroup has started to work closely with environmental groups who share many common concerns in the field of agriculture.

Historically, Eurogroup has extensive experience in lobbying for new Community legislation dealing principally with DGs Agriculture and Environment and also Consumer Policy (now SANCO). In most cases the pattern has been the same, persuading the relevant DG to bring forward a proposal and then lobbying the usually supportive Parliament to strengthen it – the most difficult part was nearly always the Council.

With WTO the situation is entirely different, especially due to the much more limited role of the Parliament. Accordingly, almost none of Eurogroup's effort has been directed towards the Parliament except in those instances where it had some direct leverage, for example leghold traps and cosmetics. In fact, more effort has gone into lobbying third-country officials than those of the Parliament.

Prior to WTO being created, Eurogroup had almost no contact with DG Trade. First encounters proved to be something of a culture shock for both as neither really understood the perspective of the other or could appreciate their problems. Over time this situation has improved to the point where there is now a high degree of understanding between them, although both obviously have different priorities. This has been enhanced through the dialogue process to which Eurogroup has sought to make a regular and substantive contribution. The process also gives the EC an opportunity to explain its thinking in more detail to NGOs, who in turn can gain a wider appreciation of the divergent and often conflicting objectives the EC is attempting to reconcile.

It has been a common point among NGOs that other DGs with specific policy responsibilities should be better represented in the dialogue. This is in part due to a genuine desire to engage directly with those DGs, but also to an underlying suspicion that DG Trade exerts too much overall control. The EC works hard to portray a united front, but it is evident that there are sometimes tensions between DG Trade and other DGs. These differences periodically surface at the highest level between Commissioners. Such differences can be merely territorial between DGs, but often they are symptomatic of differing policy priorities. With the exception of Agriculture, which seems to exercise a high degree of influence over trade issues in the sector, the overall impression is that, elsewhere, DG Trade exercises something close to seniority – non-trade policies are increasingly seen as being operated within the overall framework (some would say straitjacket) of the Common Commercial Policy.

While the Council ultimately makes decisions concerning the Common Commercial Policy, it invests considerable authority in the EC to negotiate trade agreements. Generally such negotiations move at a slow pace and there is ample opportunity for the EC to consult and take instruction from the Council. However, in the concluding phase or at other events such as the WTO Ministerial Conference, this process can get more difficult. The EC says that it needs maximum flexibility to be able to negotiate effectively, while the member states are reluctant to see important concessions made without their consent. At key moments, the role of the Presidency becomes particularly important. In Seattle, Commissioner Lamy ran into difficulties over his approach to biotechnology, resulting in a rebuke by the Council. Normally he might have escaped such criticism from trade ministers, but in Seattle he could count himself 'unlucky' that there were several environment ministers present. This example demonstrates how, especially in the heat of negotiations, important non-trade policy concessions can be made, perhaps without the potential implications even being realized by the negotiators.

In this case Eurogroup concentrated attention on the Council, but mainly with regard to the Presidency and also at specific points where its decisions were pivotal. However, it is the EC and not the Council that it identified as being the driving force in the development and implementation of Trade policy. Furthermore, even within the EC, DG Trade is identified as highly influential, often determining whether or how a particular measure should be developed or implemented based on its own interpretation of WTO rules and its evaluation of the overall political and negotiating situation within the WTO. With some exceptions, such as DG Agriculture, this tends to cast other DGs and national government ministries as relatively passive or secondary actors in the decision-making process. The same applies to an even greater degree for the European Parliament, which notwithstanding the limitations of its competence, has thus far shown itself to be surprisingly indifferent to the impact of WTO rules on Community policy development and especially upon its own legislative freedom.

The relationship between WTO rules and Community policy is a fast developing area, and the extent to which it is changing the EU political landscape is still not yet fully appreciated. The creation of the WTO has brought trade policy out of the shadows and into the spotlight, and this has been as much a shock for trade policy specialists as it has for other actors, all of whom are still trying to adjust to the new situation. The glare of attention is unlikely to diminish for the foreseeable future because, whatever may be decided about a new round, the built-in agenda of the WTO already contains two controversial issues – Agriculture and Services. These, combined with a string of contentious disputes, particularly between the EU and the USA, and the expressed discontent of developing countries, all virtually assure that the WTO will continue to be a substantial influence within the EU policy arena – perhaps nowhere more so than in the future reform of the Common Agricultural Policy, where the growing domestic desire to produce social, environmental and animal welfare benefits may be increasingly at odds with a substantial shift towards liberalization and lower levels of domestic support favoured by many within the WTO system.

Notes

1. David B. Wilkins (ed.) (1997) *Animal Welfare in Europe: European Legislation and Concerns*, London: Kluwer International Law.
2. R.H. Pedler and M.P.C.M. van Schendelen (eds) (1994) *Lobbying the European Union*, Aldershot: Dartmouth Publishing Company.
3. http://www.eurogroupanimalwelfare.org
4. Established in 1983, 174 sessions of the Intergroup had been convened as of March 2001. In 2000, it was one of only 16 Intergroups to be accepted under new rules established by the Parliament.
5. EU (1997) *Protocol on the Protection and Welfare of Animals*, European Union Treaty of Amsterdam.
6. Anon. (1991) *United States – Restrictions on Imports of Tuna*, BISD 39S/155 (not adopted), Geneva: GATT Secretariat.
7. Anon. (1994) *United States – Restrictions on Imports of Tuna*, DS29/R (not adopted), Geneva: GATT secretariat.
8. Report of the Appellate Body (1998), *EC Measures Concerning Meat and Meat Products (Hormones)*, WT/DS26/AB/R and WT/DS48/AB/R, Geneva: WTO secretariat.
9. See Pedler in *Lobbying the European Union, op. cit.*
10. First report of the Panel (1993), *EEC-Member States' Import Regime for Bananas*, DS32/R, Geneva: GATT secretariat.
11. Report of the Panel (1998), WT/DS58/R, Geneva: WTO secretariat.
12. WTO (1994) *The Results of the Uruguay Round – The Legal Texts*, Geneva: World Trade Organization.
13. A. Nollkaemper (ed.) (1997) *Trapped by Furs? The Legality of the European Community's Fur Import Ban in EC and International Law*, Rotterdam: Faculty of Law, Erasmus University.
14. Anon. (1997) 'Amended Proposal for a Council Decision Concerning the Signing and Conclusion of an Agreement on International Humane Trapping Standards between the European Community, Canada and the Russian Federation', *Official Journal of the European Communities*, C207/14–30.
15. Anon. (1998) 'Proposal for a Council Decision Concerning the Signing and Conclusion of an International Agreement in the Form of Agreed Minute between

the European Community and the United States of America on Humane Trapping Standards', *Official Journal of the European Communities*, C32/8–24

16. RSPCA/Eurogroup (1998) *Conflict or Concord – Animal Welfare and the WTO*, Horsham: RSPCA.

17. http://europa.eu.int/comm/trade/csc/dcs_proc.htm

18. http://europa.eu.int?comm/trade/miti/envir/sia/htm

19. RSPCA/Eurogroup (1999) *Food for Thought – Farm Animal Welfare and the WTO*, Horsham: RSPCA.

20. Communication from the European Communities (1999) *Preparations for the 1999 Ministerial Conference – EC Approach on Agriculture*, WT/GC/W/273, Geneva, WTO secretariat.

21. Required under Directive 98/58/EC.

22. European Commission (2000) *Proposal for a Council Regulation Amending Regulation (EEC) No. 1907/90 on Certain Marketing Standards for Eggs*, COM(2000) 522 final.

23. Communication from the European Communities (2000) *Animal Welfare and Trade in Agriculture*, G/AG/NG/W/19, Geneva: WTO secretariat.

24. Anon. (2000) Fischler Warns Cairns Group against Hard Line', *Agra Europe*, 13 October.

25. Communication from the European Communities (2000) *EC Comprehensive Negotiating Proposal*, G/AG/NG/W/90, Geneva: WTO secretariat.

9
Japanese Lobbying in the EU

Stuart Kewley

Introduction: Japanese lobbying in the EU and in the USA – different approaches

The USA is very different to the EU; what may work there has not in the past necessarily worked here, and even in the present environment may not necessarily work in the Single European Market. To understand fully why this is the case it will be necessary to examine how relations between Japan and the EU have developed. An analysis will be made of why such relations have been, more often then not, dominated by trade issues and how this has shaped Japanese firms' lobbying efforts in the EC/EU.

In 1990, it has been estimated that some US$400 million was spent by Japanese firms on hiring lobbyists for federal and grassroots campaigns in the USA. More recent Japanese lobbying in the USA has capitalized upon the investment activities of Japanese manufacturing concerns there, whereby some commentators have alleged that jobs have been traded for political influence. This has been done to such a degree that Choate (1990) argued that the massive levels of Japanese FDI in the USA had crippled the American political system. Investment in lobbying has continued throughout the decade despite the recessionary environment in Japan, although it has been more apparent in the area of public relations as opposed to public affairs. Underpinning this strategy has been the desire to dispel the negative image that Japan had developed in the 1980s and attempt to naturalize Japanese companies in the US market. Writing in 1997, Keehn describes such companies' attempts to become inconspicuous on the American corporate landscape, via brand campaigns emphasizing local production and American values, as Japan's disappearance strategy. He notes:

> Japan is more integrated in the US economy than ever before, with Americans less aware of it than ever before. In this sense, Japan's disappearance strategy has been a brilliant success. (NIRA Review, Winter 1997)

And yet the United States is not the only country to have experienced substantial inward investment by Japanese manufacturing concerns. Throughout the 1980s and, albeit less intensively in the 1990s, there has been substantial Japanese investment in the European Community/Union. On the one hand, the forced upward revaluation of the yen in 1985 drove overseas Japanese firms that were particularly dependent upon export markets (Hartcher, 1998, p. 65). On the other hand, these firms' European investment strategies have been a very definite reaction to the vagaries of national European markets and later the Single European Market (SEM), and the regulatory environments which governed these markets (Steven, 1991, p. 51). Even in the 1990s, despite significant investment in the European Union and the Europeanization of their local production, Japanese automotive manufacturers were locked into a Voluntary Restraint Agreement (VRA) which held their share of the market to an average of 16 per cent per annum over seven years. Unlike Japan's relationship with the USA, trade issues have tended to monopolize the relationship between Japan and the EU. Even with the creation of a Joint Declaration in 1991, which introduced a political dimension into this relationship, Japan complained that the content of the Declaration, on the European side, focused too heavily on trade (*Japan Times*, 13 July 1991). One would expect then, in a climate where trade dominates and trade friction has at times been the norm, that Japan would attempt to strongly influence Community trade policy to its own benefit, much in the same manner that it has done in the USA. This has not been the case. In the European context, Japan appears not to have been able, until only recently, to generate political capital from its inward investment in the Union. Even with public-relations exercises, Japanese firms that operate in the EU have also not been able to blend into the European corporate landscape. Above all, they remain manifestly Japanese. When lobbying the European Commission, Japan has and still does prefer to lobby indirectly through the governments of sympathetic member states to secure policy objectives. Even then policy successes have been few. This begs the question, is Japan underrepresented in the EU? The answer is quite clearly no; from the Japan External Trade Relations Office (JETRO) to industry representative organizations such as the Japan Business Council for Europe, the Japan Automobile Manufacturers Association (JAMA) and the Japan Machinery Exporters Association (JMEA), and so on, all these are well-established, well-funded and have strong budget or personnel links with Japanese economic Ministries, especially the Ministry of International Trade and Industry (MITI). Links have also been established with former Commission personnel and, since the late 1980s, members of the European Parliament. Moreover, those manufacturing firms that have European production facilities typically have antennae offices in Brussels leading to, if anything overrepresentation on the ground.

Japanese lobbying in the EC in the 1970s:
ware ware nihon gin (we the Japanese)

Here we introduce MITI, the hero organization, and the stakeholders, Japanese manufacturing industries and their respective federations.

Talks between Japan and the EC on a trade agreement began in 1969. Doomed to failure from the outset, the agreement faltered over the insistence by the Council of Ministers that a safeguard clause, extra to that provided under GATT protocols, should be written into any agreement that governed trade between the EC and Japan. Japan believed that a supplementary clause was unnecessary. Moreover, the Japanese took issue with the actual content of the European safeguard clause which – with the continued absence of the UK from the Community in 1970 – bore a marked resemblance to a bilateral agreement drawn up between Japan and France in the mid-1960s which was highly protective of the French market (Economist Intelligence Unit, *European Trends* no. 25, 1976, p. 30). Japan's export industries became more serious about European markets only after seeing exports to the United States drop as a consequence of the so-called Nixon Shock in 1971, which resulted in a decline in exports from Japan to the USA by US$2 billion. This was followed by a domestic business decline in the same year when the Bank of Japan adopted a stringent money policy to curb inflationary pressures brought on by the shock. This policy not only fuelled the propensity of individuals to save, but also created slack demand leading to an inventory surplus for many firms, which then had to re-orient themselves to export markets. Caught in what seemed to be a vicious – as opposed to virtuous – circle, European markets were targeted as the only logical destination for Japan's surplus production. Despite assurances by the Japanese government to the contrary, a Council of Ministers report in 1973 accused Japan of planning a highly structured sectoral export strategy to recessionary European markets, concentrating with the view of establishing a dominant position in different member states with different products (*Guardian*, 2 April 1973).

Japan did not view the Community as a whole, as the European Commission may have wished, but preferred to conduct trade bilaterally with its constituent parts, the member states or their domestic industries. With the failure to reach a trade agreement by the early 1970s, most trade between Japan and the EC was conducted either bilaterally at the member state level, whereby Japan would agree to exercise 'prudence' in its exports by accepting Voluntary Restraint Agreements (VRAs). Or, alternatively, export restraint was exercised by Japanese firms sectorally, whereby industry-to-industry self-limitation agreements (VERs) (for the difference between VRAs and VERs see Kostecki, 1987 p. 427) were concluded with European industry without the knowledge of respective European governments.

The preference for nationally or sectorally negotiated self-limitation agreements by Japan, as an alternative to a common European agreement administered solely by the Community, is understandable. VRAs and VERs where agreed, were made possible only when an acceptable market share had been reached, making some form of managed trade for Japanese firms more palatable. As the trade regimes of the member states varied, so then did the market share allotted to a given exporter in a sector of a given member state. By 1974, the Community was composed of nine member states, the majority of which viewed themselves as essentially liberal in their trade orientation. Strict limitations on imports of, for example, tape recorders to the Italian and the French market, could be offset by less strict limitations on exports of similar products to the British, Benelux and German markets.

VRAs and VERs by their very nature are not set in stone and, depending on the health of a given market, could annually be revised upwards. Moreover, even strict limitations could be circumvented by parallel importing as was the case with tape recorders exported to the Italian market by a Japanese manufacturer with a facility in Taiwan. A final benefit of the acceptance of self-limitation agreements is that they focused exclusively on the export market in question and did not generate reciprocity requirements in trade, thus drawing attention away from the Japanese market which was overly regulated at the time. Comparing these agreements with a Community-administered pan-European VRA, shaped by the less-liberal of the member states and including a reciprocity agreement, their attraction becomes obvious. The application of a Community-administered limitation agreement was undoubtedly preferable for the Community. It would have allowed the Community to manage its trade with Japan, rather than permitting either the governments of the member states spurred on by national economic considerations, or their industries, to do so.

The Commission, although oblivious to the duration and extent of some agreements, was cognizant that such agreements were being negotiated and, as such, was legally entitled to prohibit them due to the trade-distorting impact they had upon European markets. The basic competition Articles of the Treaty of Rome are Articles 85–94. Of these, Articles 85 and 86 are crucial to the governance of competition policy within European markets (Wyatt and Dashwood, 1993, p. 379). The Commission is able to 'decide' whether or not to prosecute companies that enter into such arrangements under Articles 85 or 86. Given the tensions in the recessionary market at the time, it instead chose not to, and alternatively granted an exemption to those companies found in breach of Article 85(3). The reason was quite straightforward. To prosecute would have exacerbated political tensions within European markets at the time, a fact the Japanese were fully aware of (Report Commissioned by JETRO from the British law firm Cleary, Gottlieb, Steen and Hamilton, 1974). All the Commission could do was attempt to steer the member states back to the issue of a trade agreement with Japan which, without the inclusion of the safeguard clause, was a non-starter.

If limitation agreements when negotiated were concluded with or without the explicit knowledge of the governments of the member states, one could assume then that such agreements would be entered into on the Japanese side with or without the explicit knowledge of the Japanese government. In truth this was not the case. In order to understand how the Japanese government was able to monitor, advise upon and regulate such agreements, it is worthwhile to examine the role of the 'hero' organization, the Ministry of International Trade and Industry (MITI), and its governance capacity in relation to Japan's foreign trade. MITI, until the 1990s, exerted a disproportionate degree of influence over Japan's foreign trade with the EC. Both MITI and the Ministry of Finance (MoF) are synonymous with Japan's postwar economic success, but by the 1970s MITI saw its ability to influence the domestic market environment begin to shrink. The decline coincided with the greater penetration of European markets by Japanese exports, a situation which was highly significant for the Ministry. For while its ability to exert influence over the domestic market ebbed, in terms of controlling Japan's foreign trade MITI was able to carve out for itself a niche as the adviser, promoter and, in essence, the regulator of Japanese interests in foreign markets.

Until the deregulation initiatives of the mid-to-late 1990s, MITI had at its disposal two laws with which it could regulate the flow of exports from Japan. The first of these was the Control Law which permitted the Ministry to designate commodities which are subject to export approval (Matsushita, 1993, p. 228). If it chose to do so, the Ministry could either refuse to grant an export license or attach conditions to the export approval and, by so doing, attempt to achieve trade policy objectives. The second regulatory mechanism MITI had at its disposal was the Transactions Law which deals specifically with orderly exporting by waiving anti-competition objections of the Japan Fair Trade Committee (JFTC), permitting the creation of export agreements or export cartels overseen by MITI. MITI has thus been pivotal in providing 'leadership' to assist individual firms and their trade associations to come to some form of internal consensus on their export activity, while ensuring that such activity corresponds to the strategic policy of the state itself. MITI's ability to advise on overseas trade has been helped by the fact that officials from the Ministry have been present from the outset in important Japanese embassies, consulates and overseas delegations, and thus have hands-on knowledge of local markets. MITI's links, for example, with the Japan External Trade Relations Organization (JETRO) are well-known, with MITI personnel occupying senior positions in the organization in conjunction with senior advisors drawn from trading companies. The Ministry's ability to regulate export flows from Japan to the EC in the 1970s, 1980s and even the early 1990s is clear. Cooperating with the Ministry's trade policy aspirations was essential if Japanese companies wanted to realize their export aims in European markets.

If the 1970s were a bleak period for the Community, they were an even bleaker period for the Community's trade relations with Japan. The negotiation of self-limitation agreements sectorally or at the national level lulled the member states and their respective industries into a false sense of security that they could actually manage their trade with Japan without the assistance of the Community. Due to the political consequences of Japan's export strategy, the Community did not actively seek them out or take action against the governments of member states or their industries that had entered into them. As such, Japan, meaning this key economic Ministry operating in conjunction with Japanese firms, did not attempt to lobby the EC in the 1970s because its strategic trade objectives – through the acceptance of self-limitation agreements – were being realized. The conclusion of such agreements, done in conjunction with or under the watchful eye of MITI, ensured that the aspirations of the Japanese state and individual exporters were the same. This *ware ware* strategy meant that export markets were adequately exploited and, where possible, an acceptable market share was achieved, without the fear that reciprocity would have to be granted for European exports in the Japanese market.

Japanese lobbying in the EC in the 1980s: scaling the walls of fortress Europe

In this section the stakeholders concerned are Japanese manufacturing firms, MITI and the British Government.

If Japan did not need to lobby the Community in the 1970s, by the 1980s the situation had changed. In the 1970s, Japan had expressed a psychological desire to catch up with the West, by the 1980s it was actively overtaking it. By 1980, moreover, the ability to utilize self-limitation agreements in European markets to fragment the member states and fend off a Community-administered agreement was lost, due to the severe economic conditions of the time and Japan's export strategy to the EC. Japanese companies embarked upon another sustained export drive after the 1979 oil shock, with exports either targeting growth industries, such as consumer electronics, politically sensitive sunset industries such as ship-building, or large employers that were particularly hard hit by the oil shock, such as the European automobile industry. Increasingly, even the Community's liberal member states began to agitate for more overt and concrete national limitations to be applied to imports from Japan, with the Commission itself being increasingly petitioned to sanction the recourse to emergency import limitation under Article 115 of the Treaty of Rome.

In the UK, for example, the Society for Motor Manufacturers and Traders (SMMT) persuaded JAMA to agree to what the latter described as a gentleman's agreement, limiting Japanese automotive penetration of the UK market to 11 per cent per annum. France imposed a registration limitation of 3 per cent on Japanese cars, and Belgium and Luxembourg, despite having no indigenous automotive industry of their own, also limited Japanese automotive penetration of their markets. Although the West German market was still open, pressure began to build from the labour union IG Metall which accused auto imports from Japan as being the reason behind lay offs at Opel and Ford (*Financial Times*, 14 October 1980). MITI officials expressed anxiety that West Germany might go the same way, and lobbying began in earnest in both Bonn and Brussels.

MITI attempted to rally the more liberal of the member states, namely West Germany that had not overtly limited Japanese imports, in defence of Japanese interests within European markets. The Ministry also began to very tentatively explore the possibility of offering Brussels some form of EC-wide restraint on a short-term basis. The lobbying campaign was, however, unsuccessful, largely because there was a lack of continuity in MITI's lobbying objectives – specifically, what concessions could be offered to keep markets free from a Community-wide agreement. MITI's Okita, the External Economic Relations Minister, was sympathetic towards the Community's proposal for a European-wide VRA. Alternatively, Ito, the Head of the Ministry at the time, publicly rejected any measure that would uniformly restrict market access for Japanese imports (*Japan Times*, 18 November 1980). He did make a commitment, however, first to pursue a growth pattern based on domestic demand, and second to advise private enterprises not to export specific goods to the market of any region in a torrential manner (*Bulletin of the EC*, November 1980, p. 11).

For the Community, the fact that, increasingly, even the more liberal of the member states were petitioning for assistance or resorting to nationally administered limitation agreements meant that the less-transparent sectorally-set limitation agreements with the Japanese were failing. In light of this fact, the Community sought to wrestle the control of European trade with Japan away from the member states and their industries and create a comprehensive commercial policy towards Japan. In a *communiqué* to the Council, the Commission outlined the rationale behind this approach when it argued:

> The Community's present trade arrangements with regard to Japan are embodied in a patchwork of separate national trade restrictions which are more a relic of the 1950s than a Community policy of the 1980s ... some of these restrictions are applied selectively to a number of countries including Japan but not against other major trading partners, while a few discriminate against Japan alone. There are also a number of informal arrangements restricting imports from Japan, negotiated annually at the national level notably by certain industries. (*Bulletin of the EC*, 7 August 1980, pp. 11–12)

By 1981, Europe's economic situation had become serious. The Community's deficit with Japan had grown to US$11 600 million, while Japan boasted a trade surplus with the Community of some US$10 000 million. European unemployment had risen by over 3 million between 1980 and 1981 alone (The European Commission, *Europe 82*, p. 82). A proposal by Gaston Thorn, the Prime Minister of Luxembourg, to freeze Japanese exports to the Community at 1980s levels was flatly rejected by Tokyo. What was more difficult for the Community to accept was that Japan had, under pressure from the USA, agreed to limit automotive exports to the USA for three years. It was only when the Community, in 1982, launched a complaint against Japan at GATT (GATT, *The Agreement on the Interpretation and Application of Articles VI, XVI, XXIII*, Geneva, 1979, p. 41) over market-access issues, while simultaneously 'monitoring'(*Official Journal of the EC*, no. L 37130, December 1982). Japanese imports to the Community, that an agreement to limit imports of 10 sensitive items (The Tokyo Agreement) was reached.

Although the Community's GATT action failed, it had worried the Japanese, largely because it had highlighted reciprocity issues. Moreover, by failing to agree to voluntarily limit exports to the EC, MITI had marginalized itself from the negotiation process and thus could not determine which products, and for what duration, should be limited. What was of greater concern was that by 1982 the Community had the full support of member states for the negotiation of an EC-wide limitation agreement applied to imports of 10 sensitive items from Japan and administered by the Commission which ran in conjunction with existing limitation agreements. Hence the strategy of accepting VERs and/or VRAs that had worked so well to fragment the Community in the past, and which had kept a uniform agreement at bay, was rendered impotent, somewhat ironically due to what the Europeans described as Japan's own irresponsible exporting habits.

The negotiation of the Tokyo Agreement was seen as a success for the Community. Not only did the Japanese promise to moderate exports of politically sensitive items, but assurances were given that moderation would be applied incrementally in order to permit European industries to restructure. In truth, the more protectionist of the member states were less than satisfied with the Agreement and called for stricter enforcement measures which was picked up by the Council. Although proposals for completely new trade weaponry were never realized, the Community did agree to revise the existing regulatory mechanisms it had at its disposal and, if need be, sharpen them to suit the situation. By 1984, with exasperation in the Community towards Japan mounting due to the active circumvention of the Tokyo Agreement by export-complimentary single-firm investment, this was the path the Community followed. The weapon it chose was its revised anti-dumping regulations. Japanese firms reacted by identifying a supportive member state which could not only host single-firm investment, but could also act as an advocate of their lobbying objectives, specifically the objective of unfettered access for manufactured goods in European markets. Hence from the mid-to-late 1980s, Britain became the preferred location for inward investment from Japan.

The Plaza Accord revaluation of the yen in 1985 constituted what has been described as a push factor for Japanese inward investment, coming as it did on top of the already existing factor of trade barriers. The revision of the Community's anti-dumping codes in 1984 and again in 1987, plus their liberal application against Japanese imports, meant that an exportcentric strategy was increasingly becoming untenable. Single-firm investment, which was initially designed to complement exports from Japan, had by 1989 almost come to replace them. The attraction of Britain for Japanese manufacturers was varied. France, West Germany, the Netherlands and Italy were unsatisfactory investment locations given that the sectors in which the investment was being made – consumer electronics and automobiles – offended the sensibilities of either national governments or indigenous producers and their respective lobbies. What Britain could offer was something that Japanese firms desperately required, and that was an advocate in Europe; and not just any advocate, but rather one that had sufficient political influence to defend Japanese interests in intra-Community trade disputes.

It is clear, then, that by the mid-1980s Japan firms were becoming increasingly constrained in their ability to realize its trade aspirations in European markets. Not only were they locked into a Community-wide limitation on 10 sensitive items, but when this Agreement was circumvented by firms which were particularly dependent on export markets, the Community under pressure to show that it could enforce the agreement responded by targeting Japanese imports with dumping action. At this point, Japanese firms that had invested in the UK – the number grew after the 1984 revision of the Community's dumping codes – sought to exploit such investment, much as similar FDI in the USA had been exploited. The strategy would, however, never reap the same kind of benefits. For a start, Japanese firms had to lobby indirectly through a sole sympathetic member state, which was the recipient of the lion's share of Japanese inward investment, Britain. Despite the fact that Britain was a political heavyweight within the Community, its ability to lobby successfully on behalf of the Japanese companies was always limited, simply because it was attempting to champion the market access aspirations of Japanese firms in a trading environment that was effectively hostile to Japan; not only at the level of the member states but, it must be said at this point in time, at the level of the Community itself.

Case study: automotive disputes – from Nissan to the elements of consensus

The stakeholders here were Nissan and Japanese automotive manufactures, the British Government, MITI and the European Commission. Opposing stakeholders were ACEA.

Nissan was the first Japanese automotive manufacturer to locate in the UK. Unlike Toyota, by the late 1970s the company had become increasingly dependent on export markets. When the Tokyo Agreement limited the option of direct exports to the Community, Nissan sought other ways to address the reduction in its European market share. It did explore the possibility of tie-ups with European firms – and the Nissan/Alfa Romeo venture was a case in point. Production from this venture began in 1983 despite a bilateral agreement between the Italian and Japanese governments to limit penetration of each other's automotive markets to 2200 units per annum – but this meant that production from the joint venture was suspended in 1986 (*Japan Times*, 10 October 1980). Another option was to establish a facility in the EC, with the UK as really the only viable investment location. At the time, local component procurement, although relevant, appeared not to be too pressing an issue, and certainly if limits were applied to the amount of content that should be European they were not formally indicated to the Japanese. As such, Nissan's European competitors claimed that the plant – located in Sunderland in the north-east of England and far removed from the traditional bases of motor manufacturing in the country – was nothing more than an assembly facility or, to put it colloquially, a 'screwdriver' operation.

Traditionally, Japanese manufacturers have opted for direct export strategies in terms of completely assembled goods or components and Nissan was no exception, preferring to ship most of the component parts for the UK plant from its suppliers in Japan. The first wave of vehicles to come out of the Nissan factory in Sunderland were actually assembled from knock-down kits (KDKs), and assembly of 2000 Nissan Bluebird saloons per month from KDKs was begun in July 1986.

Nissan's preference for assembly as opposed to manufacturing is understandable. Both Japan and the EC had in 1975 signed the Kyoto Convention, stipulating that the last substantial transformation which is economically justifiable should take place locally in order to denote that product's origin; the process should include man-hours, which are perceived to form an integral element of the vehicle's value-added. It was, however, exactly the concept of value-added that both the French and Italian Governments disputed when they refused to accept the first consignment of Nissans from Sunderland as fully European. The French government argued that the Nissan vehicles contained insufficient European value-added, and further argued that to meet such requirements more of the vehicles' content should be derived from components sourced from European suppliers.

As the dispute raged, Britain came to Nissan's defence by claiming that if any such limitations were applied to the Bluebird, this would constitute a violation of the Treaty of Rome (*Financial Times*, 30 September 1988). David Young, the Trade and Industry Secretary at the time, brought the case to the attention of the internal market Commissioner David Cockfield, who leant his support to the British case with the Commission initially choosing to support the British claim as being legitimate. Later, however, after a bitter compliant was lodged against the position of the Commission by the French

Government and with the backing of the then president of the Commission Jacques Delors, the Commission appeared to backtrack on its support for the British case. Rather, it asked the French for an explanation as to why the Nissan vehicles were still subject to restriction and refused to comment any further on the substance of the case as it was still under investigation. Hence the French restraint on the sale of Nissan vehicles assembled in the UK rapidly developed into a serious Community-wide row (*Japan Times*, 21 May 1991). The Italian government also refused to accept shipments of the vehicles until the classification issue had been resolved. Ultimately a compromise was reached between the feuding parties: the British accepted the imposition of a local-content requirement, but did stipulate that its application should be examined on a case-by-case basis; the French agreed to accept Nissan vehicles produced in Sunderland as European if and only if, after a certain period of time, these vehicles reached component levels of some 80 per cent. The original consignment was diverted to other markets within the EU until 80 per cent local content had been achieved. Undoubtedly, the loser in the dispute was Nissan Motor (GB). It had been led to believe that the assembly location combined with a limited degree of local content would give the vehicles origin. Soon after, the company was obliged to meet content levels of 60 per cent and the later 80 per cent, which by the end of the 1980s all Japanese automotive manufacturers in the UK had achieved. In a bitter response to the 80 per cent local-content requirement, Yoshikazu Kawana, the company's director for European sales, complained:

> These cars have been certified as having be made in the UK. This is a very touchy issue. We were told if we reached 60 per cent local content then the cars would be British made. It was supposed to be OK. (*Financial Times*, 18 September 1988)

Despite failing to win for Nissan and later Fujitsu/ICL the type of market access requirements both companies felt they should have gained, given their levels of FDI in the UK, Britain continued to attract Japanese manufacturing investment in the run-up to the Single Market programme. Some of this had to do with the fact that there was a general insecurity amongst Japanese firms in locating in a member state where any investment made may challenge indigenous producers. More probably, however, the preference for Britain as an investment location was as much to do with the fact that, even by 1990, the Community still appeared to be a hostile trading environment for the Japanese, especially after the 1987 revision of the dumping codes which targeted components imported from abroad for assembly within the EC. As such, Britain remained the only state that was both willing and able to articulate Japanese interests in the Community at that time.

In the run up to the launching of the Single Market programme, Honda established a facility at Swindon in 1987. Toyota soon followed establishing both a manufacturing facility at Burnaston and an engine plant in Deeside in 1989 (*Guardian*, 28 February 1989). By May of the same year, the European Commission proposed to the member states and the Japanese Government that bilateral restraints on Japanese auto imports be eliminated by the end of 1992. From the perspective of the Commission, unilaterally applied limitation agreements, even with an extra Community trading partner, would inhibit trade within the Single Market and would thus be incompatible with the objectives of the Single Market programme. Instead it proposed as an alternative a jointly (Commission/MITI) administered VRA, which would run for a period of five to seven years. The VRA would limit the penetration of the European market of imports from Japan and give European automotive producers sufficient time to become competitive against Japanese producers. After the transitional period, the VRA would cease to exist and the European automotive market would, in theory, be completely liberalized.

The liberalization of such a politically sensitive sector as part of the Single Market programme would not involve a complete overnight liberalization, nor could it be done without the consensus of the member states that believed that protection in some sensitive sectors was preferable to none at all. A report by the Economist Intelligence Unit in 1989 verified this hypothesis. It noted that if import curbs against Japan by the five member states (France, Italy, Spain, Germany and the UK) were lifted and not replaced by another form of limitation agreement, then Japanese manufacturers' share of the Community market could conceivably rise from 10.6 per cent in 1986 to 18 per cent by 1995. This would result in the disappearance of at least one of Europe's six automotive producers. In terms of the European automotive market, the French and Italians would only accept the Single Market programme if some form of defensive measure to protect against competition from outside the EC was introduced (Interview with Commission Official, 6 December 1998). From 1988 to 1989, a team of Commission officials from DG I worked on the prospect of eradicating informal barriers from European automotive markets and finding an acceptable compromise. As McLaughlin and Maloney note:

> The Commission team focused on a number of possibilities in the initial policy options exercise. One was the abolition of existing national restrictions after 1992, leaving a completely open market. This option was never feasible; not even for the more liberal states such as Britain. The Commission finally settled upon an option whereby a hybrid policy could be developed that combined a negotiated EC-wide understanding on moderation along with a transitional period within which protected markets could gradually relax existing quotas. (1999, p. 164)

By December of 1989 the Commission team had created a broad-based draft policy document which suggested the limitation of Japanese automotive exports to the Community for a finite period thus allowing, in the interim, the restructuring of European producers. By August 1990, MITI, which would be responsible for creating an export cartel on the Japanese side, had agreed to explore with JAMA the issue of 'self-restraint' in the European market and, to this effect, a draft document entitled the *Elements of Consensus* was produced by the Commission. The document proposed a transitional period of five to seven years from the completion of the Single Market, during which automotive exports from Japan would be limited to a specific market share. An estimation of the number of automobiles that could be imported into the Community by the end of the transition period was agreed upon, as were fixed sub-ceilings for imports of Japanese cars into the five restricted markets of the UK, France, Italy, Spain and Portugal. A semi-annual consultation system was created to ensure the accord was efficiently executed and monitoring – the euphemism used by the Commission for limiting imports from Japan – undertaken.

Given the sensitivity of the agreement and the need to ensure it complied with the ongoing GATT Uruguay Round of talks, MITI officials were joined in the initial negotiations by officials from the Ministry of Foreign Affairs (MFA) who later dropped out of proceedings once the type of limitation agreement had been agreed upon (Abe, 1990, pp. 79–80). More importantly, JAMA acting on behalf of the Japanese automotive manufacturers, permitted MITI to take sole responsibility for conducting the negotiations on the Japanese side, thus assuring the Ministry's primacy in not only influencing, but also in articulating, the demands of the Japanese automotive manufacturers. Given past disdain for agreements that had uniformly limited market access across the Community, it may seem surprising that MITI entered into the agreement rather than challenging it at GATT. Clearly reciprocity issues were important and what the Ministry did not want was a full-scale row over access in the European market on the one hand, and the Japanese market on the other. The Ministry also did not want the Europeans and the Americans unifying in a combined assault on impediments in the Japanese market.

With the Single Market programme in place and the Community determined to make it succeed, there was little option even to revert to the VER style of limitations that were so indicative of EC–Japan trade relations the 1970s. MITI had little choice, then, but to accept the VRA and find a workable solution even if this solution was not to the liking of all the Japanese automotive producers affected by the agreement. One area that these producers had pressed the Ministry not to give ground on was the issue of transplants. The Ministry did agree to a 'no-targeting' clause that prohibited concentrated transplant sales in the five countries that maintained national restrictions. It insisted, however, that no transplant restrictions other than the 'no-targeting' clause be written into the accord (Mason, 1997, pp. 63–4).

Much to the Commission's dismay, the draft Accord was firmly rejected by the heads of the European generalist automotive producers who argued that it was too favourable to Japan. The European generalists called for a longer transition period, up to 10 years, if the challenge from Japan were to be met. Calvet, the head of PSA Citröen at the time, refused even to accept this position and demanded much longer restrictions on all Japanese automotive activity including, for the duration of the transition period, a limitation of transplant production. Calvet's opposition to the common position adopted by the other European generalists forced the remaining European producers to abandon the industry federation, The Committee of Common Market Automobile Constructors (CCMC) that had until that time served them, and start afresh without Calvet. In February 1991, a new organization, the Association des Constructeurs Européens d'Automobiles (ACEA) was created (Pedler and van Schendelen, 1994, pp. 149–50).

ACEA differed from its predecessor in a number of ways. The first was that American automotive manufacturers with European manufacturing operations were invited to join the organization. Japanese manufacturers, even those with European plants, were not invited to, or chose not to, join. The second was that in order to move towards a more meaningful collective position and to prevent any one member using a veto in group discussions which would lead to a common policy stance, ACEA adopted a majority-voting mechanism (McLaughlin, Jordan and Maloney, 1993, pp. 206–7). This was intended to improve the efficiency of decision-making procedures and the commonality in policy positions. It requires a 75 per cent threshold with decisions reached on a one-to-one vote basis. Calvet's objections were thus sidestepped.

The refusal by the European generalists to accept the Commission's initial draft policy document as being too 'soft' on the Japanese, came against the background of an increasing Japanese automotive presence in the European market. By 1990, Japanese automotive exports to the EC alone amounted to 1248 million units, with sales of Japanese cars in EFTA states rising by 30 per cent in the same year (The Economist Intelligence Unit, 1991, p. 51). Combined with European transplant production (Toyota had pledged to bring its Burnaston plant in the UK on-line by 1992), this brought the Japanese share of the European automotive market to 12 per cent, even though under the terms of the failed Tokyo Agreement MITI was obliged to monitor automotive exports and enforce a non-disruptive export policy (*Nihon Keizai Shimbun*, 16 March 1991).

In light of the sustained pressure on the European market, the Commission came under a concerted degree of pressure to take a stricter line with Japan or risk losing the initiative in securing an agreement that could be acceptable to all parties, but which could also be policed on the European side by the Commission as opposed to national governments. This was a very real concern, for despite the pending realization of the Single Market project, in the automotive sector member states still appeared willing to resort to the application of the instruments of managed trade. In the summer of the same year, both Italy and Spain had limited the penetration of their domestic automotive markets by applying for emergency measures under Article 115 of the Treaty of Rome. The measures allowed the limitation of indirect imports – in other words Japanese automobiles produced by European or North American transplants – to Italy, and automobiles, buses and trucks directly exported from Japan to Spain. (*Japan Times*, 19 July 1991). Carlo Ripa di Meana, the Italian Commissioner for the Environment at the time, appeared to anticipate the position of the Italian Government taken a few months later when he issued a letter to the other Commissioners urging them to support stricter limitations on exports from Japan. By March 1991 European automotive producers, via ACEA, had presented a revised common position to their national governments that was then passed on to the Commission. Although still stringent on certain issues, especially transplant production and market share according to market conditions, the position was less draconian than before.

The reaction of the Commission was mixed. Some were philosophical about ACEA's rejection of the initial draft Accord. Others were less so. Martin Bangeman, the Industry Commissioner at the time, angrily threatened to scrap any protective features leaving the European automotive market entirely open to unrestricted Japanese imports after 1992 (*Japan Times*, 14 May 1991), although as noted above this alternative would never have been accepted by the member states. From the Japanese perspective, a Commission-administered transitional VRA was naturally undesirable, but tolerable and preferable to the preservation of national limitations or the recourse to emergency measures under Article 115. Undoubtedly the Japanese held the view that if the agreement focused on exports limitation only, then any shortfall in market share caused by an export limitation could be redressed by transplant production, much in the same way as the Tokyo agreement had been circumvented in the case of Nissan by production in Sunderland. What the Japanese did not want was a limitation on transplant production, nor for that matter the end products of Japanese automotive transplants in the EU falling foul of local content requirements making them ineligible for a European classification but eligible for the export quota.

The Commission had little choice but to work from the revised position put forward by ACEA. The original draft Accord had to be withdrawn and an alternative had to be presented to MITI. This weakened the Commission's hand, not only in terms of its competence over the issue but in other areas such as its ability to press MITI for reciprocity for European automobiles in the Japanese market, an issue that the French had been keen to see included in the Agreement. As with the initial draft, MITI was willing to accept the seven-year transitional period but flatly refused to entertain any possibility of transplant production being tied to any limitation. It was somewhat miraculous, then, that a final Agreement was reached. What Mason describes as 'one of the most unusual understandings in modern international economic diplomacy' came into effect on 31 July 1991 in Tokyo, with the head of the Commission's External Relations Directorate General, Frans Andriessen, outlining the EC's obligations under the Agreement and MITI's Eichi Nakao doing the same on behalf of the Japanese government (Mason, 1997, pp. 64–70).

The understanding reached between the EU and MITI in July 1991 closely approximated the main elements of the ACEA position. Entitled the *Elements of Consensus*, the paper saw the Japanese Government agreeing to a transitional period of seven years within which the Japanese share of the EU market would be allowed to increase from 12 per cent in 1991 to 16 per cent by 1999. The understanding also allowed the more protected EU car markets to expose their domestic industries gradually to greater Japanese competition by continuing to implement national export restraints until 1999. The Commission and MITI also agreed to review the market situation every six months and, in addition, the situation was also to be reviewed following a downturn or an upturn in the EU market (*Financial Times*, 2 August 1991). The most significant difference between ACEA's position and the *Elements of Consensus* was over the question of Japanese transplants in the EU. The sticking point in the negotiations was that while the Japanese were prepared to see their market share increase to just 16 per cent, neither they, nor the British Government for that matter, believed that transplant production should be included in any limitation agreement. Peter Lilley the British Secretary of State at the time, sought assurances from Bangeman on the issue of transplants in a response to calls from both France and Italy that all Japanese vehicles, regardless of origin, should be restricted (*Japan Times*, 11 July 1991). ACEA and other national governments had argued that transplants should also be part of the understanding since restrictions on direct imports could be rendered meaningless if the Japanese market share was boosted by local production.

The Commission thus had to compromise. Andriessen, speaking in Tokyo in 1991, suggested that due to the transitional period Japanese manufacturers would be free to make as many cars as they wanted in the EC, but that the greater their European production the less they would be allowed to ship directly from Japan, he further noted that although the limits applied directly to imports, in effect local production was to be counted. He did, however, qualify these remarks by noting that imports from overseas plants of Japanese companies outside the EC would not be taken into account (*Nikkei Weekly*, 8 June 1991). The understanding thus allowed for a growth in EU transplant production from its 1991 output of 120 000 vehicles to a protected 1, 200 000 units by 1999, subject to market conditions.

The Japanese were thus faced with an agreement that was essentially not to their liking for a number of reasons. For a start, although the increase in market share was acceptable, it was, however, dependent on market conditions and size – an issue which later led to ill-tempered disputes between the

Commission and MITI. A second problem was that any increase in market share had realistically to be derived from either local production (which was preferable for the Commission) or from direct imports from Japan, but not both. By 1991, the Japanese had worked hard to achieve local content levels of some 80 per cent which should have meant that Japanese European transplant production was seen as just that, European. Finally, by the time the agreement was signed, it was also realized that the growth estimates for the European automotive market for 1999 had been exaggerated. Even if the Japanese automotive manufacturers did increase market share by whatever manner, the actual increase in market share would be less than expected when the deal was negotiated.

Such revelations produced bitter responses from the Japanese. The then chairman of Nissan, Yutaka Kume, argued for a shorter transitional period stating, 'we understand the need for a transitional period but it is our desire that it be dismantled as soon as possible' (*The Independent*, 4 December 1991). Representatives of Toyota were much less taciturn about the agreement, with one of the group's officials angrily claiming that, 'Japan was completely defeated!' (*Nikkei Weekly*, 17 August 1991). Why, then, was the Accord accepted? Undoubtedly MITI had a lot to do with it. Although unhappy about the transplant issue, MITI did believe the Agreement was the best option at the time. The Ministry's position had a lot to with factors that fell under its jurisdiction but were not explicitly linked to the automotive Accord. The Commission president, Jacques Delors, had also been in Japan during May of 1991 to discuss the Joint Declaration between Japan and the EC. Discussions over the Declaration naturally spilled over into the area of the automotive Accord, the negotiations on which were drawing to a close at the time, especially since Nakao was MITI's primary negotiator for both agreements. With the debate over transplant-produced vehicles' classification still unconcluded, the French and the Italian governments applied pressure on the negotiations for the Joint Declaration, by suggesting that the wording of the Declaration should include the term 'a balance of benefits'. This was basically a desire to mirror reciprocity in both the European and Japanese markets and one which the French, in particular, were anxious to have extended to the automotive Accord. MITI was thus faced with the prospect of a protracted dispute over the classification of transplant production in the automotive Accord or, alternatively, having to agree to wording in the Joint Declaration that would commit Japan to provide mirror reciprocity in manufactured goods. The Ministry gave way on the former, probably under pressure from the Ministry of Foreign Affairs (MFA) that was anxious to see the Declaration formalized. Again the British Government came to Japan's defence in refusing to endorse the French and Italian proposed wording which came to be replaced by the term 'equitable access to one another's markets', which the French criticized as being too weak (*Japan Times*, 20 July 1990).

The automotive Accord expired on 31 December 1999 and the Commission was of the view that the Single European Market for cars would be fully liberalized by that date. This included the elimination of national restrictions such as the French 3 per cent registration limitation (interview with Commission Official, 7 December 1998). Monitoring of export levels has been completely abolished as from 1 January 2000, and as such, at face value at least, the market appears to have been liberalized. JAMA officials in Brussels, when interviewed in 1998, remained to be convinced that the Commission would not ask for some kind of restrictions to remain in place. To this effect, there do appear to be areas where Japanese automotive manufacturers have been advised by the Commission on how to conduct their Single European Market strategy.

The first is that although monitoring of automotive exports from Japan has ceased, the Commission has recommended that the Japanese automotive manufacturers that produce in the EU exploit the lifting of import limitations by increasing their market share via European-produced vehicles, as opposed to vehicles directly exported from Japan. Japanese automotive manufacturers have publicly agreed to abide by such recommendations, with Toyota in particular noting that it has abandoned strategies centred around exports to the European automotive market (interview with Toyota Representative, Tokyo, 24 May 2000).

Moreover, despite the affirmation by the Commission that even national restrictions had expired, including the French registration limitation, Toyota has set up production facilities in France to guarantee unfettered access to the French and Italian markets. The vehicles produced in Toyota's Valenciennes plant, despite having much of their local content made in the UK, will thus qualify as being fully European under the French and Italian understanding of the term and, unlike the Bluebirds before them, they will not be held 'hostage' by the governments of the member states over their place of origin or content levels. In response to the announcement by Toyota to set up the first-ever Japanese automotive plant located on French soil, a representative of JETRO wryly noted that Toyota's decision to build a French factory was as much a political as a strategic decision (interview with JETRO Representative, Brussels, 8 December 1998).

Japan's European lobbying strategy for the twenty-first century: from emissions to the euro

If the Japanese tended to initiate their European lobbying campaigns at the governmental level, lobbying on the issue of automotive emissions saw a change of tack. The 1989 Automotive Emissions Directive (89/458EEC) was an issue where Japanese automotive manufacturers undertook a proactive lobbying campaign at the level of the Commission and the European Parliament, as well as utilizing the influence of sympathetic governments.

By the late 1980s, it was clear that automotive emissions standards in the EC where far behind those in the USA and Japan. Both DG III (Industry and Internal Affairs) and DG XI (Environment) led the proposal for a directive to bring EC standards up to those in the USA. The proposal was seen by the CCMC as another incurred cost on the production process. Japanese automotive manufacturers, while similarly unhappy about the added costs, felt, however, that they could meet enhanced European emissions standards. The Japanese undertook a soft lobbying campaign at the Commission, as well as the Permanent Representations, Parliament and COREPER levels, and traded technical information for being kept inside the information loop. The Japanese were thus able to build a relatively, on this issue at least, solid relationship with the Commission and for that matter the Parliament as well (Morrison, 1993, p. 62).

Throughout the 1980s, the Japanese had used actual, and the prospect of, inward investment to generate political influence. By the mid-1990s, however, the prospect of disinvestment and relocation was also used to coerce governments, specifically the British Government, to heed Japanese concerns about policy issues. From 1997 onwards, Japanese companies located in the UK, especially those in the automotive sector, entered a national debate on sterling's strength and Britain's participation in Economic and Monetary Union (EMU), a debate that has, for the Labour Government, wider political implications. The views of Japanese firms located in the EU on the benefits or detriments of participation in EMU featured in the *16th Survey of the Operations of Japanese Affiliated Manufacturing JETRO Report* (JETRO, 2000). Of the 402 businesses that responded, the general consensus was that the merits of participation in the single currency outweighed the demerits. Japanese companies that had a manufacturing facility in the UK were also surveyed, and of the 151 respondent, 41 per cent saw no business benefit for them, while 29 per cent believed the merits and demerits of euro participation cancelled each other out. Only 15 per cent saw large merits or demerits.

From the perspective of JETRO at least, it appears that Japanese companies are nonchalant about the UK joining the single currency. In reality the pronouncements and actions of Japanese companies and their respective employment federations tell a very different story. Initially, Japanese manufacturers refused to be drawn over Britain's non-participation in the euro in first wave. That was until Autumn 1997 when Hiroshi Okuda – the often controversial and outspoken head of the Toyota group at the time – ignited a political row in the UK by announcing that the firm's future European investment strategy might change if the British Government chose not to enter EMU (*Financial Times*, 31 January 1997). Okuda later attempted to mollify concerns raised by his comments by insisting that any future investment by Toyota would still be determined by basic business factors such as location, infrastructure and labour. He refused, however, to discount the view that a unified currency would be beneficial to Toyota, as it would alleviate exchange-rate fluctuations between participating states and thus bring business benefits.

The announcement in the same year by Toyota, that it had chosen Valenciennes as its latest European production base, coincided with Okuda's remarks regarding the euro. This led to the misperception that Toyota's decision to locate in France was somehow bound up in the then Conservative Government's decision not to join the single currency in the first wave (Kewley, forthcoming). Sir Ken Jackson, the General Secretary of the Amalgamated Engineering and Electrical Union (AEEU) – the only union in Toyota's Deeside plant – certainly subscribed to this view when he argued that Toyota's decision to opt for France was a 'clear result of the Government's policy on Monetary Union' (*Daily Telegraph*, 10 December 1997). Moreover, Okuda's remarks on the single currency issue was a clear backing for participation in the euro as opposed to a call for the re-weighting of either sterling or the euro.

The concern caused by the Toyota's French investment decision was compounded by a *Keidanren* (employer's federation) mission visit to Britain in November 1999, which lobbied the British Prime Minister to join the euro or jeopardize Japanese investment in the UK. Disinvestment concerns brought on by non-participation grew even more pressing when, in July 2000, a telegram from Sir Stephen Gumsersall, the British Ambassador in Tokyo, was leaked to the British press. Gumersall warned that the sit-tight attitude of Japanese manufacturing firms already in the UK was receding as the prospect of British entry receded, and until Britain was seen to be on-track to full membership of the euro the UK was perceived to be a risky investment location (*The Times*, 4 July 2000). Concern over Japanese disinvestment and job losses became a reality with warnings from Nissan over production and procurement costs in Sunderland and physical lay offs by Sony's facility in Pencoed, South Wales. An increased willingness to accept Japanese investment, by the mid-1990s, in sectors that had once been considered sensitive by member states that formerly had been hostile to the Japanese, ensured that Japanese manufacturers were able to use the threat of disinvestment to achieve national policy goals; much in the way they had used the prospect of investment to attempt to secure similar goals at the European level. Japanese manufacturers in the UK and Japanese employers' federations, for example, exerted pressure on both the representatives of the British Government in Tokyo and on the Government in the UK itself, over the sterling and euro issue. Their objective was twofold. First there was the requirement that the government make a firm commitment to participate in the single currency and educate the public to its benefits. Government vacillation on the issue and its failure to take control of the debate was seen as compounding the risks and allowing the opposition to heighten public hostility to the single currency. Secondly, the Japanese were and remain concerned about the strength of sterling against the euro.

The Nissan case and subsequent automotive VRA has shown that from the mid-1980s onwards, Japanese manufacturers were forced to rethink the efficacy of their exportcentric strategy and focus more predominantly on local production, using local parts and employing local people. The automotive VRA and subsequent recommendations by the Commission, has forced high-volume Japanese automotive manufacturers to continue the trend of servicing the European market from their transplant facilities within the EU itself. Britain, as the preferred location for Japanese investment at that time, had become Japan's export springboard into the European market. Such facilities now heavily localized are, however, prone to currency fluctuation and the benefits of the UK are being undermined by the strength of sterling. The constant increase in the value of the yen from the mid-1980s onwards has meant that Japanese managers have had to create staggering savings and production efficiencies which have been assisted, in part, by the Bank of Japan's sympathetic revision of interest rates.

Despite this, Japanese manufacturing industries have been slowly moving production offshore to the extent that from 1992 to 1994, the proportion of Japanese cars assembled overseas rose from 26.5 per cent to 31 per cent, and is still growing. In 1995, for example, it cost about the same to make a car in Japan as it did in the UK. Since then the yen appreciated sharply against all currencies including sterling, and Japan became 20 per cent more expensive (Hartcher, 1990, p. 169). The disadvantage of the strong yen means that overseas investment locations should offer the compensatory advantage of a weaker currency. In the British case, the strong yen has been replaced by the strong pound with the added attraction of a weak euro only 30 miles away across the English channel. Even if the yen declines in value, as it did in the Spring of 2001, this will not have any real benefits in the Single European Market context for Japanese automotive and consumer electronic manufacturers, as the majority of their products sold there are made in the UK.

Nissan, when announcing its decision to build the Micra at its Sunderland plant, did note that it would be using sterling's strength to source most of its components from the euro zone and, moreover, that it expected Europe's most efficient automotive factory to become even more efficient to offset the effects of sterling's strength. The company's chief executive met with the British Prime Minister over the issue of the Sunderland plant and speculation exists that he received assurances on the currency issue. This view was confirmed when the Tony Blair, only days later, announced a specific timetable for Britain's participation in the euro if the referendum proved successful, something he had neglected to do in the past (*Financial Times*, 8 February 2001).

Conclusion

Despite attempts to generate a more fruitful political relationship between Japan and the EU, trade is still the primary factor which sets the dimensions of the relationship. Changes have, however, occurred – due in the main to the 10-year-long recession in Japan which is a remarkable example of Japan's economic fallibility as opposed to infallibility. Japan's inability to disengage itself from its economic downturn has eased European anxiety over the seriousness of the competitive challenge posed by Japan. The recession has also brought about a revision of the role of the traditional architects of the Japanese economic miracle, namely the economic Ministries. Corruption scandals and allegations of mismanagement have undermined the creditability of key Ministries such as the MoF.

MITI, for its part, has also experienced changes on a number of fronts, not least in its name, which has been altered as of January 2001 from MITI to the Ministry for Economics, Trade and Industry (METI). It is also suffering from a continued dilution of its authority, a claim that Mikanagi (1996, p. 72) supports when she argues that the Ministry's ability to dominate the economic agenda in Japan has been challenged by rival Ministries such as Posts and Telecommunications (MPT) amongst others. Certainly the continued hollowing out of the Japanese economy and the abandonment, particularly in relation to the Single European Market, of an exportcentric strategy by Japanese firms, has meant the METI's ability to 'influence' how such firms conduct their European market strategy has been significantly diminished. The Ministry has also embraced economic liberalization more fully, actively courting partners for ailing Japanese firms, the Renault takeover of Nissan being a case in point. And so it seems that the sun is setting on the era of *gyosei shido* (administrative guidance). How has the change in the status of the Ministry affected the way Japanese firms operating in the EU conduct their European market strategy and how they lobby the EU?

Clearly METI still has a presence in Brussels. Interviews with public affairs specialists that have worked with Japanese industry representative offices suggest that budget and personnel links, particularly with METI, remain. But how much can such organizations influence the policy debate? The answer is only slightly. Japanese manufacturing firms such as Toyota, Fujitsu and Canon, amongst others, that have a high profile in the EU, are actively developing their own public affairs divisions and are attempting to become more embedded in the European corporate landscape. A localization policy is a primary factor in recruitment of personnel for these divisions. It is doubtful if such firms will ever become fully naturalized, or as Keehn has described in relation to the US market disappear, but certainly the government of the member states that in the past had been openly hostile to the Japanese presence in the European market are becoming less so. Indeed, Japanese inward investment has been spread more evenly throughout the EU and thus governments – other than the British government – have been drawn to the Japanese cause.

Where lobbying the institutions of the EU is undertaken at the level of the member state, METI may still provide a coordinating function and, to a degree, can still oversee the agenda of the lobbying campaign. It cannot, however, determine the agenda, under the auspices of realizing national trade policy objectives, as it had done on the past. What is of interest is that the Ministry is now more concerned with bringing foreign investment into Japan, whereas in the past this was not always the case. The governments of the member states still remain the most vocal supporters of the Japanese cause in the European Union, and this is where lobby campaigns usually start. With a less hostile environment for Japanese investment in the EU, the Japanese are, however, willing to use the threat of disinvestment and relocation to secure policy objectives.

With the creation of public affairs divisions within antennae offices in Brussels, staffed by Europeans knowledgeable in the workings of the institutions of the EU, lobbying campaigns may also be initiated directly with the Commission or the European Parliament either independently of or in conjunction with those directed at COREPER or the Council of Ministers. Members of the European Parliament have even gone so far as to actively court the Japanese and encourage them to see the Parliament as a viable channel for realizing policy objectives. One British MEP has expressed the view that if the Americans have no qualms about lobbying very hard at the Parliamentary level, then the Japanese should be encouraged to do the same. To this effect a forum has been created where issues of mutual concern can be addressed (interview with MEP, Brussels, 6 December 2000). Hence, by the end of the 1990s and given the *volte-face* by the member states in relation to Japanese investment, the Japanese are now able to exploit policy channels in the EU more fully. It remains to be seen, however, given the economic ill-health of many of Japan's former economic giants and the fragility of the Japanese economy itself, whether or not this new-found advantage will be exploited to the full.

References

Abe, A. (1999) *Japan and the European Union*, London: The Athlone Press.

Choate, P. (1990) *The Agents of Influence*, London: Business Books.

Commission of the European Communities (1982) *Eurotrends*, Brussels.

Economist Intelligence Unit (1976) *European Trends*, no. 25.

Economist Intelligence Unit (1991) *Japanese Motor Business*, June.

Hartcher, P. (1998) *The Ministry*, Boston: Harvard Business School Press.

Keehn, E. B. (1997) 'Image is Everything: Japan's Failing RR Strategy in the United States', *National Institute for Research Advancement* (NIRA) *Quarterly*, Autumn.

Japan External Trade Relations Organization (2000) *Sixteenth Survey of the Operations of Japanese Affiliated Manufacturing JETRO Report*, London: JETRO.

Kewley, S. *Japan's French Automotive Connection*, Chatham House Discussion Paper, forthcoming.

Kostecki, M. (1987) 'Voluntary Export Restraints', *World Economy*, vol. 10, no. 4, December.

Mason, M. (1997) *Europe and the Japanese Challenge*, Oxford: Oxford University Press.

Matsushita, M. (1993) *International Trade and Competition Law in Japan*, Oxford: Oxford University Press.

McLaughlin, A. M., Jordan, A. G. and Maloney, W. A. (1993) 'Corporate Lobbying in the European Community', *Journal of Common Market Studies*, vol. 31, no. 2, June.

McLaughlin, A. M. and Maloney, W. A. (1999) *The European Automotive Industry*, London: Routledge.

Mikanagi, Y. (1996) *Japan's Trade Policy*, London: Routledge.

Morrison, D. A. (1993) 'The Channels of Japanese Lobbying in the European Community', unpublished MPhil thesis, Cambridge.

Pedler, R. H. and Van Schendelen M.P.C.M (eds) (1994) *Lobbying the European Union*, Aldershot: Dartmouth.

Watanabe, T. (1999) 'The Automotive Accord Between the EU and Japan', unpublished European Studies Diploma Course thesis: Oxford.

Wyatt, D. and Dashwood, A. (1993) *European Community Law*, London: Sweet & Maxwell.

10
Chiquita Declares War and Wins: Bananas – Trans-Atlantic Trade Dispute

Robin Pedler

> When a fruit baron wanted to conquer more of the European market, he got Washington to launch a trade war for him. The victims of the cross fire? A bunch of ordinary Americans who never saw it coming. (*Time Magazine*, 2 February 2000)

In the first of a series of lead articles on 'Big Money and Politics – Who Gets Hurt?', *Time Magazine* singles out Carl Lindner and charts the sum of $5.5 million in campaign contributions to both parties, spread over the period 1991–99. The money, as they say 'bought Chiquita access in Washington'. Lindner is the President of Chiquita, one of a number of companies that have lobbied long and hard on bananas on both sides of the Atlantic.

Background to the case: how the EU got into this mess[1]

The seeds of the banana war were sown in 1945.[1] During the Second World War, the population of Europe had been totally deprived of bananas by the U-boat blockade and the fruit was one of the pleasures that populations demanded amidst austerity and rationing. (The author still remembers the excitement of eating his first banana.) Unfortunately, the traditional prewar suppliers, plantations in Central America, were in the dollar zone and European governments were desperately short of dollars. UK and France therefore launched banana growing schemes in sterling and franc zone territories in the Caribbean and Africa. Growing bananas in these areas was clearly much more expensive than in Central America, since most of the Caribbean islands with suitable climates are effectively the crests of volcanoes. This did not matter when the world was divided into currency zones and GATT had yet to be established (1948).

The EU's banana position became even more complicated with the accession of Mediterranean member states in the 1980s. Greece and Portugal grow some bananas, while Spain in its Canary Islands is a major producer. Thus the EU now had about 25 per cent of its consumption grown within the EU.

Table 10.1   Banana production efficiency

Source	Total production cost* (ecu/kg)
Latin America	0.200
Caribbean	0.460
Canary Islands	0.520
Martinique and Guadeloupe	0.550

*Includes storage, transport and export taxes.

Source: Brent Borrell, Centre for International Economics, 1992.

Once again, however, costs of production were much higher than in Central America (Table 10.1).

The Caribbean and African sources – hereafter referred to by the acronym ACP – and the EU's own banana growers are capable of producing some 40 per cent of the bananas the EU consumes. At least 60 per cent must therefore be imported from what are still known as the 'dollar' growing countries. Given the cost structures, however, if the EU and Caribbean growers are to continue to thrive, they have to be protected.

The internal market drives reform[2]

Prior to 1992, the necessary protection for EU and ACP growers was afforded by national quota systems. These not only imposed border restrictions but also limited the circulation of bananas within the EU. The determination to create the Internal Market meant that those barriers must disappear and be replaced by a common external system. The 'dollar' producers believed that the solution would be 'free trade' or at the worst a common external tariff that would permit them to benefit from their lower production costs to seize control of the market. In preparation, they 'loaded' bananas into those parts of the EU market that were accessible in 1990–92 to create a strong position. They were aided in this by the fall of the Berlin wall (1989). Once again the banana was the symbolic fruit of peace and freedom and those 17 million Germans who had been citizens of the German Democratic Republic (DDR) were each consuming 30 kg annually (EU average 10.5 kg).

In the event, however, the solution the EU adopted was indeed to unify its internal market, but to continue to apportion sourcing by tariff quotas under its Common Commercial Policy (Table 10.2).

One objective was that any company distributing bananas should source from both 'dollar' and ACP suppliers. There was also an internal division between the shipping companies and those who ripened and distributed the fruit within the EU. (Bananas are shipped underripe in refrigerated ships and finally ripened relatively close to their point of consumption.)

It was the licence system that was to be the undoing of the EU in the face of the US/Ecuador complaint to the WTO.

Table 10.2   Banana trade regime: Regulation (EEC) 404/93

	Tonnes (000s)
CAP banana regime	750
Imports	
ACP countries	
'Historic quantities' tariff free	858
Dollar bananas	
Favourable tariff quota (75 tonne)	2200
Total of EU production and imports	3808

Category C: 3.5 per cent to operators who start to import 'dollar' bananas and non-traditional ACP bananas after 1992 (newcomers).

Legal challenges to the Banana Trade Regime (BTR) before national courts and the European Court of Justice (ECJ)

Immediately on the adoption of Directive 404/93, Germany opened an ECJ case against its fellow member-states. Their government argued in Case C-280/93, *Federal Republic of Germany* v. *Council of the European Communities*, that Council Regulation 404/93 places an unacceptable burden on certain groups of German operators. However, the European Court of Justice (ECJ) found that 'Germany had not shown that Council Regulation (EEC) No. 404/93 on the Common Organization of the Market in Bananas was manifestly inappropriate as regards its objectives'.

Another case was taken by a number of German banana companies before the Financial Court of Hamburg. In an attempt to obtain interim relief, Atlanta and Weichert successfully argued that they, as German companies active in bananas, were almost on the verge of bankruptcy due to the fact that they had suddenly become subject to trade-impeding border measures which they perceived as imposing unnecessary costs for their businesses. However, the Federal Court of Germany decided to annul this decision on procedural grounds.

Subsequently, a relatively small Hamburg importer, T.Port did succeed in getting its case to the European Court of the First Instance *T.Port* v *Hauptzollamt Hamburg-Jonas*. On 10 March 1998 the ECJ delivered a negative judgement. The company had argued that the BTR countered Germany's obligations under GATT, but basically it wanted to import bananas from Ecuador, a country that never joined GATT and did not join the WTO until 1996, so the ECJ found no commitments prior to the BTR.

BTR: International obligations and legal challenges

In international trade terms, the EU faced conflicting treaty obligations. Its own policies, expressed in the Lomé Convention, meant it was bound to give preference to the suppliers from associated countries in Africa, the Caribbean and the Pacific (ACP). On the other hand, it faced a series of challenges under GATT/WTO. Two GATT dispute panels, resulting from cases brought by Central American countries, found against the EU's restrictive regime, but under that system the EU was entitled to reject the findings and on the first occasion did so.

In the second case, four Central American countries – Colombia, Costa Rica, Venezuela and Nicaragua – quickly lodged a complaint against the new regime. While they were successful, they agreed with the EU not to pursue it or seek sanctions in return for a Framework Agreement (1994) that adjusted the export licence arrangements under 404/93 to favour their supplies.

The establishment of the WTO (1995) changed the situation in two ways. Contracting parties undertook to accept panel findings under the dispute settlement mechanism and the trade system was extended to cover services.

Stakeholders: the fruit companies and the Caribbean growers

The companies lobbying may be grouped into two powerful camps. First there are those who stand to profit by free access to the EU market for 'dollar' bananas grown in Central America. Besides Chiquita, there are Dole, another US company, Del Monte, now owned by financial interests from the United Arab Emirates, and Noboa, from Ecuador.

The second group is composed of companies that have traditionally benefited from the restrictive banana regime that favours those produced on the Caribbean Islands and in the EU itself. These companies are Fyffes (Ireland), Compagnie Frutière and Pomona (France), and Geest Bananas, now owned jointly by Fyffes and the Windward Islands Banana Development and Export Company (Wibdeco).

It should not be supposed that these opposing groups are united within themselves. Particularly on the 'dollar' side, there are strong rivalries and very different agendas are pursued by the four contenders. The case shows that, as the argument developed, companies formed *ad hoc* alliances that crossed the apparent 'dollar/European' divide.

How the fruit companies acted and fared

The settlement of 1992/3 appeared to create clear 'winners' and 'losers'. The campaign in favour of restricting the access of 'dollar' bananas in order to protect those grown in the EU and the Caribbean was led and substantially organized by Geest. Fyffes were in close alliance. Those two companies were both based in English-speaking countries and their efforts were supported, in the interests especially of bananas grown in West Africa, by the French companies Compagnie Fruitière and Pomona.

Chiquita, Dole and Del Monte were all already present and were lobbying in opposition. They were convinced that they would win, because of the 'free market' ethos generated by the creation of the EU's Single Market on 1 January 1993. Indeed, they believed they *had* won and secured an open market solution right up to the crucial events that took place in the small hours of Thursday, 18 December 1992. At that moment, the EU presidency was held by the UK. British agriculture minister John Gummer, who believed very strongly that the interests of the Caribbean growers should be protected, was able to bring a Qualified Majority of his colleagues round to his point of view.

Chiquita

The 1992/93 settlement allotted 30 million 'A' licences to Chiquita, equivalent to an EU market share of 21–22 per cent. Chiquita however, maintained that it was badly treated as its market share in its own chosen 'reference period' had been around 35 per cent. This result was supported by high shares in the largest markets that were also 'liberal and open' – some 50 per cent in Germany and even up to 70 per cent in Scandinavian countries. Chiquita's lobbying efforts in the eight years during which the new regime has operated have been focused on recovering its traditional share. They are interested not in the abolition of the cake, but in being served a bigger share.

Alone amongst the competing companies, on either side of the Atlantic, Chiquita decided to keep its sourcing 100 per cent in Central America and to pursue legalistic and confrontational efforts to open the EU market.

The United States could not be a party to the complaints under GATT, as it does not export bananas to the EU. This situation changed in 1995, however, when the WTO was established and its remit extended to include 'Services'. US company Chiquita certainly provides services, transporting the 'dollar' bananas to Europe in their ships. The company reasoned that it could invoke Section 301 of the 1974 American Trade Act and, as we shall see, they did so.

Dole

Dole, formerly known as Standard Fruit, operates primarily in Guatemala, Honduras, Ecuador and Costa Rica. It seemed at first to have emerged from the 1992/93 settlement even worse than Chiquita, since its 'ensured' market share had been reduced from about 20 per cent to 5 per cent. The company nevertheless decided to opt for a pragmatic approach to the EU Banana Trade Regime. In order to maximize market access to the European Community, Dole established distribution and marketing linkages with producers in European areas such as the Canary Islands or Guadeloupe and Martinique, as well as those in banana-producing ACP countries such as Jamaica, Cameroun and Côte d'Ivoire. They added joint ventures with companies such as SCB, Pasqual Hermanos, Compagnie Fruitière and Jamaica Producers to their production in Central and Latin America, which was already well-controlled. This provided Dole not only with a foothold in the more competitive banana-producing ACP countries, but also with the opportunity to make use of distribution and marketing networks in previously closed markets: Spain, France and the United Kingdom.

In other words, unlike its competitor Chiquita, Dole followed the 'partnership' idea of Council Regulation 404/93, since it invested succesfully in both European and ACP production areas. This action resulted in both immediate access to additional volumes and future entitlements under the 'dollar quota'. The other main outcome of this investment and acquisition strategy is that Dole has slowly taken over market share from its main competitor Chiquita in the single banana market of the European Community. By establishing supply contracts with ripeners, distributors, wholesalers and retailers in France, Germany and Spain, and by opening a new harbor facility in Italy, Dole has, since the early 1990s, successfully strengthened its presence in the European community, rebuilding its market share to some 10 per cent. The licensing system means, however, that in order to achieve this Dole has had to purchase licenses from importers and ripeners. Their growth and relative success meant that they differed with regard to unilateral Section 301 and subsequently multilateral WTO action. Dole informed the Office of the United States Trade Representative that he

> recognizes the economic importance of continued banana production and trade to remote regions of the Community and to producers in the African, Caribbean and Pacific ('ACP') group of countries [and that] ... Precipitous change in current trading arrangements would cause a disproportionate amount of harm to ACP and European banana producing regions.

Del Monte

Fresh Del Monte Produce, the second largest banana company worldwide, was originally an American company. Sold by Del Monte in the United States to Polly Peck in the United Kingdom at the beginning of the 1990s, Fresh Del Monte Produce changed hands again in 1994, going to GEAM, an investor group based in Mexico, and subsequently in 1996 to IAT, a holding company from the United Arab Emirates. Like Dole, Del Monte decided to expand its production and sourcing across the various producing areas of the European Community and the more competitive ACP countries in order to secure additional volumes. However, and probably largely due to changes in ownership and legal incorporation status, Del Monte had to concentrate on its internal financial situation and management rather than Council Regulation 404/93 and subsequently the Framework Agreement on Bananas. In-house problems during the early 1990s prevented Del Monte from focusing fully on the events taking place in the European Community.

Indeed, Fresh Del Monte Produce became more competitive on the banana market of the European Community after the company moved to

IAT ownership in 1996. A combination of capital investment and cost-cutting measures provided the previously troubled company with fresh impetus in terms of production and marketing. A first visible result of these efforts was the establishment of Central and Latin American-style plantations in banana-producing ACP countries such as Cameroun and Côte d'Ivoire in order to generate future 'B' licences for quota entitlement under Council Regulation 404/93. Like Dole, Del Monte decided not to join Chiquita in its efforts to attack certain aspects of both Council Regulation 404/93 and the Framework Agreement on Bananas. Del Monte understood the structure and the rationale of the provisions governing 'trade with third countries'.

Del Monte never took action to lobby against the Regulation prior to its implementation nor has it taken action to undermine the provisions in effect. In fact, Del Monte's activities during the last few years in Cameroun and with EU business were not a reaction to the new regulations, but rather were part of a corporate strategy recognizing the EU's need to provide some form of protection to EU growers and to honour the commitments made under the Lomé Convention. Del Monte modified its production, transportation and distribution systems to accomodate changes in view of the new regulations. Del Monte is faithfully working within the system. Indeed, company continue to support Regulation 404/93. It limited its demands to wishing that when new regulations came to be issued in 2002, minor modifications would be made to eliminate distortions that were affecting the market.

It was significant Del Monte had ceased to be in American ownership at the time that Mexico decided to join Guatemala in its ongoing battle for free international trade. It is possible that Del Monte had second thoughts and that Mexico therefore stepped in on behalf of the commercial interests of Del Monte. However, with an annual production capacity of some 250 000 tonnes in the Chiapas region alone, is it more likely that Mexico was interested in receiving a country allocation in order to safeguard its potential future exports to the European Community, than safeguarding the commercial interests of a former American banana company.

Noboa

Noboa operates its own plantations in Ecuador and maintains, in addition, supply contracts with small local producers or their producer organizations in the largest banana-exporting country in the world. Sourcing in, shipping, ripening, distributing and marketing from Ecuador, the family-run banana company Noboa won approximately 13 per cent of world trade in bananas. Since the early 1990s, Noboa had managed to increase its shipments to the European Community on the basis of a marketing arrangement with an Antwerp-based importer who is ripening and subsequently distributing bananas supplied by Noboa under the Bonita trademark on the single banana market of the European Community. The main result of Noboa having successfully increased its market share is that the family-run company has placed itself in direct competition with the three other major 'dollar' suppliers.

They ship approximately 40 million cases of bananas a year to Europe. Under the 1998 system, 30 million of these go to East and Central Europe and 10 million to the EU. It was considered likely that, under the 'first-come, first-served' proposal, those proportions would be reversed, giving Noboa some 22 per cent share of the EU market.

Geest

The 'winners' in 1992/93 appeared to be the European companies, and the progress in the market value of Geest in 1992/93 seems to confirm the favourable turn of events. Subsequent management errors are then reflected in a steadily declining trend over a three-year period, until Geest sold its banana interests in January 1995 (see Figure 10.1). The recovery in the company's value may be taken to show how the markets rate Geest's fruit business without the complication of bananas.

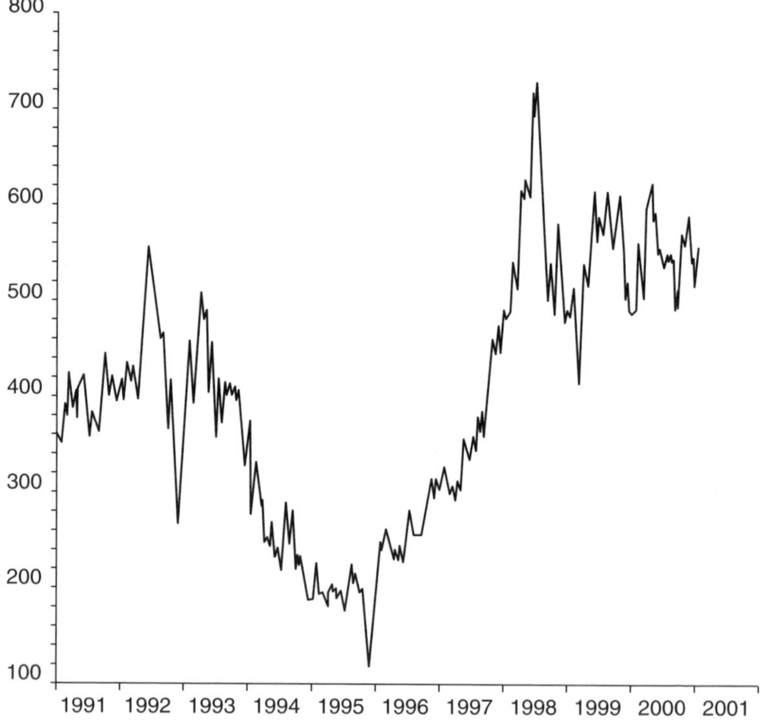

Figure 10.1   Geest market value (US$millions)
Source: Datastream.

It had proved difficult for them to manage the market they had worked hard to create, and they had made a number of strategic errors.

Opening 30 per cent of the 'dollar quota' to operators who had imported Euro bananas or traditional ACP bananas before 1992 gave Geest, like Fyffes, good prospects. Geest, however, was confronted with some criticism from its suppliers when it became clear that the shares of the company had gone up considerably once the details of Council Regulation 404/93 were known. The growers felt that Geest was reaping far too much of the profits on their crop. Refrigerated shipping was felt to be overcharged and the company was alleged to be doing too little for urgently needed cost-restructuring and competitiveness improvement. In other words, the individual grower felt increasingly frustrated that shares of the cake were not properly distributed. The perception of having 'missed the boat' resulted in discussions with Geest over a possible renegotiation of the long-established shipping and marketing contract or the setting up of a joint-venture. This step was not without danger. The bargaining position of the small individual cultivator in its producer organization was rather weak since Geest's weekly banana boat was vital to their business. Moreover, the economy of places such as Dominica or Saint-Lucia was heavily dependant on Geest vessels bringing in all kinds of daily necessities. However, Geest suddenly became more flexible over this matter, driven by an unfortunate $150 million investment in a plantation in Costa Rica, plus a few hazards of climate in the English-speaking Caribbean. Moreover, the average prices for ACP bananas appeared to be lower than expected. The Framework Agreement on Bananas only threatened to exacerbate the pricing situation. The tariff quota for 'dollar' bananas had been adjusted to generate a larger quantity and a lower in-quota tariff. Meanwhile, production in the English-speaking Caribbean had once again been adversely affected by a range of crop-destroying hurricanes and some new litigations had been opened in the World Trade Organization.

The outcome of all this was that Geest sold its banana interests to a joint venture of Fyffes and the Windward Islands Banana Development and Export Company at the end of 1995. The 50–50 per cent joint venture with Fyffes meant that the producers' own umbrella organization, Wibdeco, is now to be regarded as the exporter and therefore qualifies to receive import licences in its own right. It is, however, now questionable whether the considerable investment by a relatively small producer organization will pay off, due to current events at WTO. Moreover, it seems that a rival bid from Noboa and months of other rumours had overvalued Geest's banana business by some £75 million. Fyffes and Wibdeco negotiated to maintain the Geest brand for reasons of consumer awareness and commented on the take-over and the labour problems in its 1995 Annual Report as follows:

In January 1996 along with our partner, the Windward Islands Banana Development Company (Wibdeco), we acquired the Banana Business of

Geest plc for a total consideration of £147.5 million. The Geest Banana Business which always traded successfully in the past, has produced disappointing results over recent years, principally because of capital projects which have not generated the expected returns. Our main efforts in 1996 will be directed towards restoring the results to their historic levels. We are excited about this acquisition and believe that the opportunities for improving its performance are significant.

The long-established Geest Banana Business compromises a UK banana importing, ripening and distribution business with an extensive network of ripening and distribution facilities. Geest also has a large cargo shipping business from the UK to the Caribbean. Geest developed a large banana farm in Costa Rica which has been unsuccessful and which Fyffes and Wibdeco have decided to sell.[3]

Fyffes

Fyffes also fared well under the 1992/3 deal, which increased its market share in Europe from about 8 per cent to 21–22 per cent. This gave them the same share as Chiquita, with the difference that Fyffes moved up to that share, whereas Chiquita moved down. They remain today the main or even leading European banana company in their own right. The company is now legally incorporated in Ireland and has been owned by the McCann family since the late 1980s. (In the past it had been a wholly-owned subsidiary of Chiquita.) Fyffes may now claim to be the banana company with probably the most successful series of take-overs and joint ventures since the coming into force of Council Regulation 404/93 on 1 July 1993.

Like its American counterpart Dole, Fyffes from Ireland decided to strengthen its commercial presence on the single banana-market of the European Community by establishing effective ripening, distribution and marketing networks in virtually all member states of the European Community. Traditionally active in the English-speaking Caribbean and to a lesser extent the Canary Islands, Fyffes also tried to get a foothold in Central and Latin America. Fyffes had a competitive edge, given its access to B licences on the basis of Council Regulation 404/93 which enabled it to spread its sourcing across Central and Latin America, yet the idea proved to be less successful than expansion in the European Community. The main causes of this failure lie in both inexperience in the region and fierce competition from traditional 'dollar' companies, Dole, and even more Chiquita. Fyffes therefore decided to dsicontinue its cultivation and sourcing operations in Honduras and Guatemala. Today, Fyffes remains commercially active in plantations only in Belize, and maintains in addition a long-term shipping arrangement with Dole.

The commercial efforts of Fyffes in the European Community proved to be far more successful than its venture in Central and Latin America. Its strategy aimed to develop supply and marketing contracts with companies in European production areas such as the Canary Islands and in banana-producing ACP countries such as, primarily, Cameroun and Côte d'Ivoire. This resulted in a rapid expansion of profit, permitting vertical integration since 1992. As a result of the take-overs and joint ventures with importers, ripeners, distributors and wholesalers, Fyffes obtained a profitable foothold in Spain, Denmark, Germany, France, Italy, Austria and the Netherlands. After winning a trademark fight with its former parent company Chiquita, Fyffes was entitled to sell bananas under its own company name outside Ireland and the United Kingdom.

Dole tried to take over Fyffes in 1993 and Fyffes itself lost a bid for Del Monte in 1992, but the most interesting take-over was that by Fyffes of its main European rival Geest from the United Kingdom.

Comparison and conclusions on the the companies

Thus to maintain the EU market shares to which they had been accustomed, American banana-sourcing and marketing companies, except Chiquita, have adopted the following combination of strategies:

- Investment in the more competitive banana-producing ACP states Côte d'Ivoire and Cameroun in order to generate future entitlements under the 'dollar quota'.
- Take-overs and joint ventures with companies in the banana-producing ACP states Côte d'Ivoire and Cameroun in order to have immediate access to additional volumes.
- Take-overs and joint ventures with ripening and distribution companies in, primarily, France and Spain in order to have immediate access to additional volumes and to be able to make use of well-established ripening and distribution networks in previously closed markets.
- Purchase of import licences from the competing category-'B' operators in order to be able to dispose of higher volumes than they had been accustomed to import from Central and Latin America.

But Chiquita fights on.

Stakeholders: NGOs, European institutions and others

NGOs

A range of NGOs are actively involved. Those based in the UK and the Netherlands played an important role at the time of the 1992 settlement in persuading the ministers from their respective countries that they had a moral duty to protect the Caribbean growers.

EUROPABAN, the most active and visible, is a federation of 37 NGOs covering the countries of the EU and also Switzerland. They have two active websites <http://bananas.agoranet.be> and <http://www:bananalink.org.uk> and they publish an informative quarterly *Banana Trade News Bulletin*, distributed widely to interested parties and lobbying targets. Their overall position, however, is not so much 'in favour' of the Caribbean growers as 'against' the behaviour of major US companies in their plantations in Central America.

EUROPABAN was one of the organizers of a two-day conference in Brussels in May 1998, just ahead of the reform of the regime to publicize their views. They cooperated with Caribbean producers and with Central American trades unions.

One Europaban member Solidaridad, a Netherlands-based NGO with a Spanish name, is especially concerned about working conditions in Central America. Two others, Max Havelaar (Belgium and Netherlands) and Fairtrade Foundation (UK) have broadened their approach to promote 'fair-trade' bananas as a way of transferring more income to Caribbean growers.

The European Commission

The legal base of the Banana Trade Regime remains Article 37. It is a regime that forms part of the Common Agricultural Policy (CAP), and the lead Directorate General is therefore Agriculture, under Commissioner Frans Fischler. However there have always been tensions between Agriculture and External Trade, under Commissioner Pascal Lamy. External Trade is concerned with managing trans-Atlantic relations. It has to deal with a series of high-profile issues that have progressed from disagreement to complaint and then to trade wars. The $190 million of penalties imposed on EU exporters under the banana war is in one sense minor, since it represents only some 1 per cent of trans-Atlantic trade, but apart from being annoying and exremely damaging for the companies affected, it also creates a conflictual rather than a cooperative atmosphere.

The third Directorate General that is actively involved and has a point of view different from the first two is Development, under Commissioner Poul Nielson. They have the responsibility of promoting and protecting the interests of the African, Caribbean and Pacific countries associated with the EU under the Lomé Convention, and that includes a banana protocol.

The European Parliament (EP)

On the legal base of Article 37, the EP is required to give an Opinion. Members have strong views and indeed the language of their Opinion was influential in the detail of the 1992 settlement. In general, the EP is strongly in favour of 'taking care of' the Caribbean growers'. A leader of this group is Mrs Glenys Kinnock, Socialist UK, who has organized a number of fact-finding delegations to the Caribbean.

The Council – views of the member states

Under Article 37, the Council proceeds by qualified majority vote. It is extremely difficult for them to reach a common position because without special influence or considerations, if it comes to a vote between 'liberal traders' and 'restricters', there will be a blocking minority on either side. 'Liberals' can count on Germany, three Nordic countries and the Netherlands – 28 votes. 'Restricters' will certainly include France and Spain, and usually also the UK and Ireland – 31 votes. Other member states may be influenced by argument, by the precise detail of the proposal or, since the vote is in the Agriculture Council, by other measures that the Presidency decides to include in a package for voting.

Third countries

Third-country ambassadors are very active in Brussels and, not infrequently, their ministers and heads of state come to lend weight.

The Caribbean islands

The group of the Windward Islands – Dominica, Grenada, Jamaica, St Lucia, St Vincent and the Grenadines – are the most affected by changes in the regime. Their interests as a group are coordinated in Brussels by Ambassador Laurent. Their near neighbours, Martinique and Guadaloupe, have similar interests but are legally different as they are Départments d'Outremer of France, hence EU producers. The main African producers, Cameroun and Côte d'Ivoire, are represented by their ACP missions.

The Latino producers

The seven 'Latino' producers – Mexico, Panama, Costa Rica, Guatemala, Ecuador Colombia and Venzuela – generally cooperate and coordinate the approaches of their ambassadors in Brussels.

EU accession countries

One byproduct of the restrictive EU banana regime is that very large volumes are shipped to other countries in Europe. The progression of supplies to Hungary over a three-year period, for instance, is as shown in Table 10.3.

While the Central Americans remain dominant, they are increasingly being joined by quantities from Cameroun, the Ivory Coast and Mexico. All the exporting countries, apart from needing to move surplus production, are building up a sizeable 'reference base' for when the applicant countries finally join the EU. Sweden went through a similar process in 1992–94 and

Table 10.3   Hungarian banana imports

	Tonnes 000s		
	1996	*1997*	*1998**
Total imports	35.8	54.9	57.4
% from Central America	98	91	79

* January to November.

was very concerned that its supplies would be resticted by joining the regime. In fact, however, although prices rose somewhat, reference volume was sufficient to maintain supplies to consumers. Swedish importers also benefitted under the new regime because the two largest retail chains were distributors and ripeners and they now had a quasi-monopoly position as holders of the licences.

1995: Chiquita provokes the 'banana war'

In 1995, Chiquita sought to persuade the US administration to mount a '301 action', relying on the invitation to

> American companies to petition the US Government to investigate and seek redress against foreign trade acts, policies and practices that either violate US rights under GATT, or are unreasonable or discriminatory and burden or restrict US Commerce; Section 301 authorizes the US Government, unless satifactory relief from the unfair practices is forthcoming, to take relaliatory measures such as tariffs or withdrawal of tariff concessions against the offending countries.[4]

The main problem in invoking this domestic trade legislation appeared to be how to gather support from the American banana industry. The drafting or reading of Section 301 indicates that a representation of the industry or trade, as such, is a prerequisite for initiating a so-called 'unfairness determination' conducted by the Office of the United States Trade Representative under Section 301. For reasons of, respectively, different strategy and change of legal incorporation status, neither Dole nor Del Monte were ultimately prepared formally to support Chiquita in its efforts. Chiquita, however, was quick to solve the representation problem by inducing the Hawaiian Banana Industry Association to file a joint petition to Mickey Kantor, then the United States Trade Representative, stating that

> The petitioners stress that they have tried and failed through all other means to obtain relief against the EU Import Regime on Bananas [and that they now, in light of an] extraordinary loss of US company investment interests, service interests, market share, volume, profit opportunities, and other interests:
>
> Request the US government to take all appropriate and feasible action under the authority of Section 301.

In the event that a consistent restructuring of the EU Banana Trade Regime is not achieved within the section 301 principles of fair trade, the US government is urged to: 'Impose duties or other import restrictions on goods or services originating from respondent EU countries.'

From this point on, Chiquita was bound to furnish evidence to secure determination by the United States Trade Representative that

> the EU Banana Trade Regime effectively entailed trade impeding border measures adversely affecting the vested commercial interest of American companies in a discriminatory or unreasonable manner.

This 'unfairness determination' was facilitated by the conclusion and the entry into force of the 'Framework Agreement on Bananas'. Instead of moving to a more open banana market within the European Community as recommended in the second GATT Banana Panel, this meant that a minority of countries from the 'dollar zone', some not even recognized as actual or potential substantial suppliers, secretly negotiated an even more restrictive and discriminatory position. EU Banana Trade Regime.

American companies had once enjoyed unconditional market access for bananas produced or sourced in virtually every banana-producing country located in Central and Latin America. On 29 March 1994, Colombia, Costa Rica, Venezuela and Nicaragua became able to require that American companies source specified quantities from their national producers or producer organizations. In return for dropping charges under GATT, they had been assigned not only country allocations, but also the right to open these allocations up to 70 per cent with export certificates to be matched with import licences. Taking the preceeding events into consideration, one may suppose that the Office of the United States Trade Representative must have been split as to whether or not to open a formal investigation under American trade legislation. The main reason for this doubt may be that the industry or trade was apparently not properly represented in the petition, as required under Section 301. Dole, for instance, decided that it would abstain. The modifications they sought were minor and they therefore opted for a pragmatic approach. Del Monte had in the meantime become a Mexico-based company in terms of both ownership and legal incorporation status. In any event, the Office of the United States Trade Representative accepted the allegations petitioned on 2 September 1994, and declared on 27 September 1995, on the basis of the investigations conducted, that

> We have repeatedly sought changes in the European banana regime to address the discrimination against US companies, but unfortunately the EU has been inflexible. We think it is appropriate at this time to resort to WTO dispute settlement procedures and we are pleased that other countries in our region that are also adversely affected by the regime are joining us.

Commenting on Mickey Kantor's statement, the President and Chief Operating Officer of Chiquita said in a company press release that

> We applaud the US government's decision to accept this action and compliment Ambassador Kantor for his strong commitment to upholding the

principles of free trade and fair world trade. The US Government now becomes a significant, major player in this dispute and will fight to achieve fair treatment of the US industry's interests on all fronts. Based on two victories previously achieved in this matter at the GATT, we trust that the WTO will declare the EU's protectionist, discriminatory and anti-consumer banana policy contrary to all international principles of free trade, and will order substantial reform.

At the time of these announcements, aspects of Council Regulation 404/93 had already been condemned under GATT, and the sole distributor of bananas supplied by Chiquita in Germany had already referred the matter to the European Court of Justice. A number of arguments were advanced questioning why the United States should flex its muscles against the European Community over bananas.

The European Community and its banana-producing ACP partners vigorously claimed that the United States did not actually or potentially export considerable quantities of domestically-produced bananas. Chiquita alone had problems of market access to the European Community, not because of Council Regulation 404/93 or the Framework Agreement on Bananas, but because of their own unfortunate business strategy. The vexed question was why a country such as the United States, which exported almost no bananas, entered into a long-running banana dispute with the European Community. Some reasoned it was because of generous election donations to both Democrats and Republicans by Carl Lindner, the politically well-connected head of Chiquita Brands International. Others argued it was in order to test the recently introduced WTO agreements in general and its modified dispute-settlement procedures in particular. Due to a similar and parallel market-access dispute on hormone-treated beef, it is also possible to say that the United States used or saw the banana case as 'crowbar' to obtain market access for agricultural produce as a whole. This kind of 'precedent seeking' is not illogical, and was reinforced by the fact that the United States is already well-advanced in the large and fast-growing high-tech sector of genetically-modified organisms or GMOs

The United States decided to go to the WTO on a matter involving bananas, a product not actually or potentially exported from its own country borders. They reasoned that the EU Banana Trade Regime continued to discriminate against banana-marketing firms from the United States in terms of import licences, and that it became even more restrictive as a result of the share-out or administration of the 'dollar quota' whereby import licences have to be matched with export certificates. Moreover, and certainly no less important, failure to challenge new WTO agreements on services with a cross-border element and international investments related to trade could be regarded by the global community as permission to employ similar illegal trade practices against other US sectors or companies. On the controversial question as to why the United States became involved on behalf of just one American banana-marketing company, it is possible to answer that Chiquita was joined by the Hawaiian Banana Trade Industry Association and that some other American umbrella organizations such as the American Farm Bureau, the National Foreign Trade Council and the Grocery Manufactures of America supported the Section 301 action for the sake of American commerce as a whole, reasoning that

> The potential damage to long-term US agricultural exports if similar import restrictions were to be extended to additional commodities by the EU or other countries.

Moreover, the newly-appointed United States Trade Representative, Charlene Barshefsky, remarked in a statement on the WTO verdict of 29 April 1997 that

> This final report sets an important precedent for all US exporters of services and agricultural goods. I am gratified that the WTO has denounced a variety of egregious non-tariff barriers that impede US exports.[5]

In other words, the banana dispute has become much more than just a row over import rights or trade impeding border measures as such. However, it remains strange that the United States continues to press the European Community over a commodity grown only marginally within its domestic borders or customs territory, and therefore not destined for direct export to the European community.

The United States had been joined in its action by Ecuador, the largest Central American producer. Following the finding in April 1997, they had to wait while the EU mounted an appeal. This was in turn rejected and in September 1997 the EU regime was confirmed to be incompatible with WTO rules. The whole area of the WTO complaint procedure is new and under development, but the EU considered it had 15 months to modify its regime to meet the WTO's criticisms and undertook to do so.

The proposal moved relatively rapidly through the EU's decision-making process, heavily lobbied all the way. The critical Agriculture Council at which the new regime had to be decided took place in late June 1998. Once again, it was under UK presidency, but the UK government had changed in the meantime and the Minister in charge was Labour's Nick Brown. He tabled a package that included not only bananas but also modifications to the Olive Oil Regime. The meeting was long, stormy and extremely active. The result was surprisingly favourable to the presidency. The proposal that they had made, to retain a restrictive Banana Trade Regime with just some modification of the licensing system, got the support of all the member states except

Denmark and the Netherlands (see Table 10.4). Even apparently convinced and committed liberals like Germany and Sweden voted in favour. (One commentator took the view that they were quite relaxed because they were convinced that the new proposal would not survive presentation to the WTO, so there would have to be a new and more radical reform in very short order.)

Reform was indeed adjudged not to have gone far enough, and first the United States and then Ecuador were given the right to impose trade sanctions. The United States has already done so, as Table 10.5 shows. The regime in force and being applied in the EU therefore became that decreed in 1998.

Table 10.4   The 1998 banana trade regime

	Tonnes (000s)
'Domestic' production under CAP regime	750*
Imports	
ACP countries 0 tariff	858
'dollar' bananas 'bound' @ 75 ecu/tonne	2200
'Enlargement compensation' @ 200 ecu	353
Total	4161

'Non traditional' ACP quantities could enter with a 200 ecu/t tariff allowance (e.g. @ ecu 500/t)

Other (mainly dollar) quantities face ecu 700/t tariff

Licences
  Export: (basis of problem with WTO); four countries receive tariff rate quota as 'major exporters' – historically above 10%: Colombia, Ecuador, Panama, Costa Rica; rest of $ quota unallocated
  Import: 'internal' problem to be solved by Commission regulation. Proposed traditional/newcomers' system

* Estimated quantity. 'It is what it is'. Increased support for EU growers.

Table 10.5   Bananas: developments 1999–2000

April 1999: USA receives WTO clearance for 'hit list' worth $191 m (had requested $520 m).

May 2000: Congress directs 'carousel tariffs'

April 2000: Ecuador receives WTO clearance for 'hit list' worth $201.5 m. May apply it to services.

October 2000: Council agrees to propose a 'tariff only' system, with an interim period of six years to be administered on a 'first-come, first-served' basis.

October 2000: Nine Central American exporters reject the EU's plan of tariffication with licences to 'first-come, first-served'. 'They will develop their proposal.'

But so long as it continued, a selection of European producers of goods and services, most of whom have nothing to do with bananas, would continue to suffer penal duties on their exports to the USA.

Pascal Lamy decided to address this situation vigorously in late 1999. He reasoned that since there was an active trade dispute, it should be his task, mandated by the General Affairs Council, to solve it. He tried on three occasions to secure a broad mandate, but the divisions and tensions within the Council made this difficult (France, Spain, Portugal, Ireland and Greece were a very solid blocking minority). Finally, in October 2000, the General Affairs Council agreed by Qualified Majority that the solution should be sought by a two-stage proposal (Germany, Italy and Belgium voted against). The final objective would be to move to a 'tariff-only' regime. There was little doubt that this would be acceptable to the US government and compatible with WTO rules. In order, however, to give the Caribbean and EU producers the opportunity to adjust to and prepare for the 'liberal and open situation', its arrival would be delayed until 2006 and, in the meantime, the licensing system would move from the present matching of export and import licences to operate a 'first-come, first-served' system:

The meaning of 'first-come, first-served'

Rather than try to guess banana consumption ahead of time and control supply by a complicated (and clearly, so far as the WTO is concerned, illegal) system of licences, the EU will declare its requirements every 15 days and invite those who have bananas available to bid for licences. They must then fulfil the licence supply, under penalty. ('Available' in this context means aboard a ship that has already sailed, to avoid the risk of EU ports becoming clogged by ships with cargoes of rotting bananas.)

In order to become a formal EU offer, the proposal had first to gain an Opinion in the European Parliament and then be adopted at yet another Agriculture Council, this time under the French Presidency, on 19–20 December 2000. France was very keen to achieve a result under its presidency, as from 1 January 2001 the chair would pass to Sweden, notoriously 'liberal' on bananas.

Lobbying by the stakeholders

As the prospect of a solution to the EU's difficulties loomed, the lobbying on all sides intensified. Chiquita had made its desired solution very clear in 1999, when it formed an *ad hoc* alliance with Fyffes to produce a 'Caribbean' proposal (Table 10.6). The key words in this proposal, that distinguish Chiquita–Fyffes from their competitors, are 'established' and 'reference period pre-1993'. It is a clear declaration of Chiquita's ambition to regain its market share of some 35 per cent.

Table 10.6 'Caribbean' (Chiquita–Fyffes) proposal, November 1999

	Tonnes (millions)
Tariff 'equal for all comers'	2.700
ACP tariff free, Latinos pay €115	0.850
EU-grown bananas	0.750
Total	4.300

Note: 96.5% of the licences in each tier will be granted to 'established' importers. *Reference period 'pre-1993'* for tier 1, 1995–97 for tier 2. Must be used or will be lost. 3.5% in each tier reserved for 'newcomers'.

The effect of this would be to lock out other suppliers from the 'dollar' quota. In this proposal, at least from Chiquita's perspective, 'reference period' is the key phrase, just as in other trade disputes 'origin' may be the key. In opposition, Dole and Noboa were both convinced that they would gain share from Chiquita if the 'first-come, first-served' solution were to be applied. The Caribbean producers opposed the 'first-come, first-served' system. A split occurred in the 'Latino' camp, with Ecuador, feeling that it had both volume and cost advantages, prepared to back the 'first-come, first-served' approach.

All sides deployed their ambassadors as appropriate and employed trade lawyers and consultants in Brussels to argue their cases with the Commission, Parliament and with member-state governments.

Chiquita was of course also active in Washington. In November 2000, they persuaded the US Trade Representative (USTR) to present a very slightly modified version of its 1999 proposal as the 'official' US position. The US position, sent 1 December 2000, proposed to allocate market access on the basis of a historical reference period that is modified from earlier proposals and still included provisions designed to increase Chiquita Brands International sales in the EU market.

The proposal not only maintained the 'reference period', it also reduced the ACP share, got rid of what Chiquita found to be the inconvenience of the Framework Agreement, and removed the ability of European competitors to source Latino bananas under the 1992/93 settlement.

It was discussed in a series of letters and a face-to-face meeting between Greg Frazier for the USTR and Bernhard Zepter for the EU Commission, that took place in Nice on 14 December. Since the two sides were far from agreeing, it was then on the agenda of the EU/US summit in Washington on 18 December. The EU was represented by France, as the member state holding the presidency, so its line could be expected to be strong in supporting the EU position. Whatever the relative positions, the US proposal made no headway. Agriculture Commissioner Frans Fischler commented afterwards: 'We shall continue the dialogue, but we are simply not ready to satisfy a completely unacceptable series of demands'.

The Parliament expressed its favourable opinion on 14 December, adopting the Dary Report on the proposed changes to the regime. The French Presidency achieved its objective of having the Commission's proposal to modify regulation 404/93 adopted 'in principle' and by Qualified Majority at the Agriculture Council on 19/20 December 2000, with only the UK voting against. The UK stated its reasons for its negative vote: 'We do not believe that this is a solution to the trade dispute. It won't satisfy the WTO, the US or the Caribbean producers. This will be back before long.'

As in 1992/93, the regime was referred to a future council for final adoption, to be taken as an 'A' point after the legal and linguistic details of the text had been finalized.

The war goes on

Round Two of the War continued. As Figure 10.2 suggests, Chiquita in particular was 'wounded' – in serious financial trouble. On 16 January 2001, the

Figure 10.2   The market value of Chiquita, Geest and Fyffes related to the MSCI world index

Source: Datastream.

company was forced to reschedule its heavy load of debts and to persuade some of its creditors to exchange debt for equity. One week later Chiquita opened an action in the ECJ, suing the Commission for €564 million. The grounds for the action are that 'The Commission violated a clear mandate from the member states by introducing in January 1999 a new import regime that continued to violate WTO rules'.

On a broader front, it was said in early 2001 that the incoming Bush administration would bring a more 'robust' approach to US trade policy. An early presidential appointment was Joseph Hagin, 'drafted in from Chiquita's Cincinnati HQ as Deputy Chief of Staff of Operations'.[2] On the other hand, his appointed Trade Representative, Robert Zoellick, though reputed to be a hard player, was also said to be a good and long-standing friend of EU Trade Commissioner Pascal Lamy. Following his appointment, Lamy made an initial, 'fence-mending' visit to Washington in March 2001. After the meeting Lamy announced that: 'The EU would delay implementation of its controversial new regime for importing bananas and attempt to strike a deal with the US.' He went on to say that: 'Europe would be willing to negotiate further on an alternative US approach favoured by Chiquita Brands, the banana company that has made the issue a top priority for the US'. It was apparently agreed that a settlement should be reached before July 2001.

So Chiquita resumed its place in the heat of the battle. Public affairs would continue to be essential to the survival and prosperity of all the companies playing on either side of the Atlantic. Trans-Atlantic negotiations continued, and led up to a potential settlement agreed between Pascal Lamy and Robert Zoellick in a late-night telephone dialogue on 11 April 2001 (Table 10.7).

Table 10.7   The EU–US settlement of April 2001

	Tonnes (000s)
Bananas produced in the EU	750
Imports	
A & B: 'dollar' bananas (reference 1994–96)	1832
'Newcomers' (all sources)	721
C: phase I, Caribbean 'traditional quantities'	858
Total imports	3411
Total EU banana supply	4161

Notes: 1 Tariffs will be €75/tonne in classes A & B.

2 In class C, ACP bananas will enter free of duty, others pay €300/tonne.

3 The US will support the granting of a WTO waiver to allow a specific quota of ACP bananas to be imported tariff-free until 2006.

4 By 31 December 2001 the EU will move to 'Phase II' by transferring 100 000 tonnes from the Caribbean quota into the 'dollar' bananas pool.

5 Because quotas continue, so do licensing systems. Licences for newcomers will be granted on 'simultaneous examination'.

The significance of the agreement lay in there being two phases. Phase I is seen by both the EU and the USA as being an administrative arrangement that may be made between senior officials. Thus Lamy does not have to submit his compromise to the European Parliament and the Council of Ministers in order to implement it. Equally, Zoellick does not have to await or submit to the opinion of Congress. Phase II, which involves moving a significant proportion of the ACP quota, will require Parliamentary and Council approval on the EU side.

Reactions to the deal were varied. Lamy and Zoellick said the solution

> Demonstrates that the US and the EU can resolve some tough problems, even those trade issues that have resisted solution for years. We have a common agenda and have indicated that we shall try to reduce the number of trade disputes rather than increase it.

Of the players in the banana arena, the most clearly satisfied was Chiquita. They had achieved a reference period (though not the one they had proposed or that was absolutely favourable to them) and had seen the constraints on their Central American sourcing removed. Chief operating officer Steven Warshaw stated:

> The conclusion that's been reached, while it does not restore the company to the position it had prior to the initial regime, it does provide opportunity that we have not had. (*Financial Times*, 12 April 2001)

His company's share price rose 50 per cent overnight (Figure 10.3).

Pedro Rodriguez of the Canary Islands Government (the islands are by far the largest producer area in the EU) said: 'The agreement will result in much greater price stability for Canaries producers' (*El Pais*, 12 April 2001). Dole, on the other hand, had already stated that: 'A deal of this type would fossilise licence allocation and essentially cartelise trade in Chiquita's favour.' It was also immediately clear that the wholesale revision of the licence regime would create substantial winners and losers amongst EU importers and ripeners and that there would be complaints from the losing companies and even countries.

Ecuador indicated that it was not fully happy with the EU/US settlement and there followed another two weeks of intensive negotiations. Agreement was announced on 30 April 2001. Within the settlement so recently agreed

> It provides increased opportunities for Ecuadorian exports. It abolishes the EU's import breakdown on a country quota basis, increases the export volumes from Latin America by 100 000 tonnes and improves market access for traditional and non-traditional importers from Ecuador, following the WTO ruling on GATS.

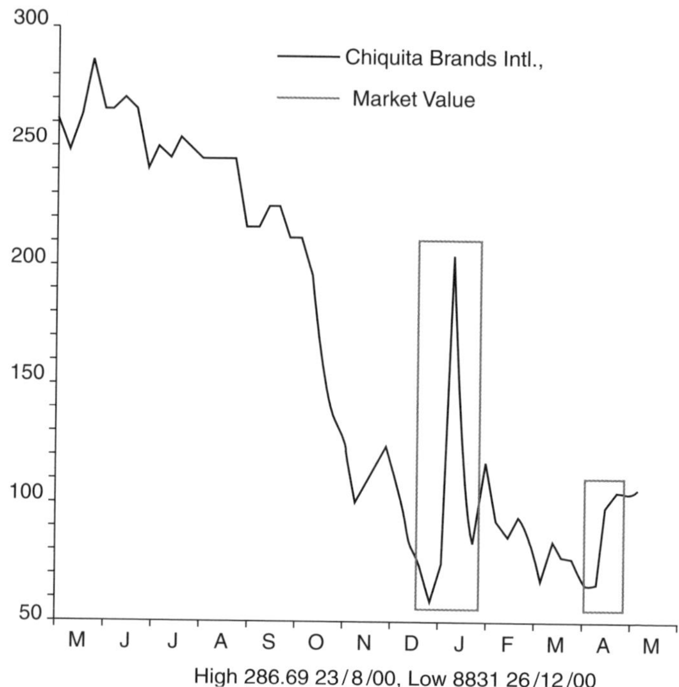

Figure 10.3   Chiquita's market value in 2000/2001
Source: Datastream.

In a joint statement, Commissioners Lamy and Fischler and Ecuador's Foreign Minister, Heinz Moeller, said the agreement was

> A fair balance between the competing interests. These interests include the main supplier of bananas to the EU, the ACP countries and of course the European consumers. It is also a clear victory for the WTO as it helped resolving a difficult dispute between developing and developed countries.[6]

Conclusions: lessons for public affairs

For the fruit companies, the Banana Trade Regime was a 'survival' issue, where legislation and regulation go straight to the 'bottom line' that reflects profit. The market value trend of all the principal players shows (1) the weight that traders gave the issue, and (2) how price movements were correlated with key decisions by the EU and the WTO.

The market value of Geest surged following its 'win' in the 1992/93 phase of the struggle, then declined due to the company's strategic management errors, later to recover dramatically in 1995, when Geest sold its banana business (Figure 10.2). Chiquita clearly suffered so long as its market share in Europe was reduced by the BTR. On 12 April 2001, the day following the Lamy–Zoellick settlement, 'Chiquita shares rose 50%, on news of the agreement to $1.55'(*Financial Times*, 12 April 2001) (Figure 10.3).

Figure 10.3 shows the reaction of the market, first to the belief that Chiquita's 'Caribbean' strategy would triumph in December 2000, the sharp disappointment when this proved not to be the case, resulting in near collapse, and then the uplift of gaining a result that favoured the company.

The swings in the value of the company players meant that Public Affairs had to be fully integrated into corporate strategy. No strategic approach would survive without it. On the other hand, public affairs alone was not enough. Geest 'won' the first round of the war (1988–93) but then their business collapsed because of a series of strategic errors. Chiquita, with its vigorous efforts, 'drove' the second round (1994–2001), but in both rounds placed perhaps too much reliance on achieving a 'dream' outcome by lobbying alone and was inflexible in its strategy. The company has achieved much of what it sought in the 2001 settlement, but the sourcing strategies it has pursued in the meantime have delivered strong negative value to shareholders.

How is access to Washington by a US company relevant to lobbying the EU? The Banana Trade Regime is clearly a European issue, by declaration integrated into the Common Agricultural Policy (CAP). Like many other of the CAP's regimes, however, it has external trade implications. (And not a few of those regimes are at the root of trans-Atlantic trade disputes.) A trade issue, by its nature, interests governments outside the EU and their weight may well be brought to bear to influence EU policy. As soon as the matter becomes a WTO issue, indeed, this is bound to be the case, because governments are contracting parties to the WTO and can bring complaints; commercial companies cannot.

Third-party governments were heavily involved in both rounds of the banana trade war. In the first round Geest built on its close connections with the governments of the Caribbean producer islands. They promoted the foundation of the Caribbean Banana Producers' Association and supported its operation and the strong lobby it developed. For reasons explored above, the US government was not able to support its companies in that round, but as soon as the situation changed, Chiquita, as an American company, used its own lobbying abilities to forge a strong and durable alliance with a powerful player.

Chiquita sporadically followed the rule that successful lobbying depends on *ad hoc* alliances. The alliance that it constructed within the USA was strong enough to trigger the application of Section 301, but did not include substantial players in the EU banana market. As the crucial moment of decision approached, however, they were able to set up a brief but telling alliance with the principal 'European' player, Fyffes, to move the debate ahead with the 1999 Caribbean Initiative.

A second principle of successful EU lobbying is to study the legal base. In this case, the period 1988–92 saw a vigorous debate within the Commission between the three services concerned – External Trade, Development and Agriculture. Agriculture emerged as the lead DG, so the legal base is Article 37 (then 43). This means that the key decisions are taken in the Agriculture Council. It is quite likely that had they been addressed essentially as trade matters in the General Affairs Council, results would have been different. The author's interviews and researches led him to the belief that the American companies that played in the first round did not fully take into account the importance of this difference. The other result of basing the proposition in Article 37 is that the role of the European Parliament is consultative. While it has to give an opinion and holds a strong one, this means that lobbying is more concentrated on the member state governments that make up the council.

The campaign throughout was a reflection of the force of the internal market idea. As in many other areas, the precise form of the internal market was the focus of vigorous lobbying by the commercial interests concerned. Like a number of other internal market issues, it is taking a very long time to resolve. One might compare it with the Chocolate Directive, debated from 1972 until its final resolution in 1999 and heavily lobbied throughout, and with the couriers' drive to liberalize the EU's postal markets. That campaign began in 1982 and is still not resolved. The three campaigns address three different aspects, but all are concerned with the full implementation of the internal market. Thus bananas addresses one of the very few cases where the internal market did lead to the construction of the 'Fortress Europe' that the Americans claimed to fear. Chocolate was about the fundamental principle that goods legally sold in one member state circulate freely; and couriers are attacking one of the few instances of enduring national monopolies.

Throughout the two rounds of the battle, the companies based on either side of the Atlantic have adopted very different approaches in forming their opinions and alliances. The American companies, not only Chiquita, have tended to adopt a much more focused and frequently legalistic approach, while the Europeans have been able to play 'emotion' on their side and to form alliances with NGOs.

Legal and legalistic: the WTO and the ECJ

The case has involved litigation at two levels. The first is the series of complaints to the GATT/WTO and the second the cases that were brought before the European Court of Justice (ECJ). In the context of a public affairs case, one might ask whether litigation represents a failure to influence the process by active and directed representation or whether, to misquote Bismark, it is 'the pursuit of influence by other means'? The practical and financial results of Chiquita suggest that it might well have been more effective to use the WTO procedure as part of a thought-through influencing strategy.

It is clear, however, that they decided to advance their case against what was to them a 'foreign' system by enlisting the support of their own US government by the Section 301 procedure, and then to test the recently-established WTO complaints procedure. It is also clear that this proved far more effective in producing action within the EU than had the previous attempts under the GATT system, even though the changes produced were not quite as favourable as those sought by Chiquita.

In the ECJ, as we have seen, the German government case failed and a case before the Court of the First Instance by a small German importer succeeded, though only to a limited degree. It might have been possible for the EU to amend its licensing system to cope with the result of the T.Port case, but the fact that the decision (November 1997) came just as the WTO appeals procedure confirmed the condemnation of the EU licensing system gave it added weight.

Public affairs: opening doors and contributing funds

The case is classic in that success depends on setting clear objectives and forming effective *ad hoc* alliances. It also illustrates a characteristic of the changing arena that is becoming ever clearer: that issues, while they may be debated and resolved in an EU context, are global. This case concerns a trans-Atlantic issue. Just as it is important for US companies to understand the process of EU decision-making and the political forces at work, it is important for European players in this issue to understand the dynamics of US government relations. One of the greatest differences is the large sums of money that openly flow around Washington. There is no suggestion that the payments made by Chiquita were illegal in the US context; cases in a whole series of EU member states suggest that there are similar payments made in Europe, where they are usually illegal.

Notes

The author would especially like to thank Bernard O'Connor, trade lawyer, for his ongoing willingness to be interviewed as the issue developed, for the information provided and for the structure he gave to a complicated scene. Johan Weick contributed valuable research, especially on the tactics of the company players and on the 1994 Framework Agreement. Others who kindly contributed by interview or on the telephone and whose assistance is gratefully acknowledged were Alex Mason of the UK Ministry of Agriculture, Fisheries and Food, Håkon Björklund of the Swedish Foreign Ministry, Robert Madelin and Dirk Lange of the European Commission, and Vincent van Dijk and Martha Zuluaga of Edelman World Wide.

1. Robin Pedler, 'The Fruit Companies and the Banana Trade Regime', in R. Pedler and M.P.C.M. van Schendelen (eds), *Lobbying the EU*, Dartmouth: Aldershot, 1994.

2. Christopher Stevens, 'EU Policy for the Banana Market: The External Impact of Internal Policies', in H. Wallace and W. Wallace (eds), *Policy Making in the European Union*, Oxford: Oxford University, Press, 1996.
3. Geest Plc annual report 1995.
4. Section 301–310 of the Trade Act of 1974 as amended (19 US Code 241–420).
5. USTR press release, 29 April 1997. <www.ustr.gov>
6. Banana Trade News Bulletin, May 2001.

11
CASTer: Creating the Future in Steel Regions

Ineke van der Storm

Introduction: the organization and the policy playing field

CASTer is the network of regional and local authorities representing the interests of steel towns (past and present), cities and regions across Europe. The network was established in 1995, in partnership with the European Commission's Directorate General for Regional Policy. CASTer's membership now covers the entire continent of Europe, including countries of Central and Eastern Europe.

The steel industry in Europe has undergone radical change over the past two decades, and this process is still going on. The particular issues arising within the steel industry that will result from the enlargement of the European Union are now being appreciated. The European steel industry also needs to find new answers on new instabilities in world markets. There is structural overproduction. Thyssen Krupp, for example, therefore aims for a 'forward integration with automotive industries', and wants to sell its steel division and specialize in automotive supply; while CORUS aims for a multi-metal strategy with high added value. Voest Alpine is moving beyond steel manufacturing into engineering services, and others, like Mannesmann, have shifted to high-profile electronics products and left the steel markets. Mannesmann survived (until acquired by Vodafone) but with a complete shift to new products and new markets. However, this product shift forced the company, due to strong competition, to relocate parts of its production first to Hungary, then to China.

At the same time, Central and Eastern European (CEEC) steel industries are in a desperate situation, facing bankruptcy. European steel industries *say* that they cannot bear responsibility for social costs that are necessary before they can start industrial restructuring. There is, however, one example of a US steel company that embarked in 2000 on a 10-year investment project and made agreements at the outset with the Slovak government on how to avoid social collapse.

Employment in the steel industry across Europe has reduced from 768 000 in 1975 to 290 000 in 1998. These are direct steel jobs. The importance for regional economies, however, is much higher, due to outsourcing and subcontractors. The key-question for CASTer is to understand, anticipate and influence this process of steel industry change in a globally interdependent world and assess its impact on people and workforces in regions, dealing with:

- global and/or European decision-making by producers and consumers;
- global and/or European investments and shareholders; and
- an increasing process of mergers, with questionable results.

The need for an active role of regions is increasingly important because globalization trends are pressing, while regions want to find adequate answers in their local economic structures. CASTer regions are therefore also lobbying for EU funds for social and regional adaptation processes.

CASTer regions also feel the need to influence this process of change in the steel industry from their positions; they want a strong voice for local and regional authorities in EU ditscussions. Questions that need answering include:

- Will the steel industry be concentrated in a limited number of European areas, with geographical assets, a highly skilled labour force or low wages?
- What will be the impact of enlargement, if the current dramatic situation of steel industries in the CEEC is not solved quickly?
- Will the rationalization of the steel industry result in a monopoly such as Microsoft's? Does Europe want only a few steel players left?
- What is a viable economic concept and at what geographical level, looking to the pyramid of steel activities (innovation and modernization, information and knowledge flows, the size of production volumes; and distribution and storage)?
- Or will steel disappear anyhow and are we facing the last days of a large EU industrial sector? Is it a sustainable sector as such? Or will new materials brush steel aside?
- Is it still an interesting sector for our regional economies and employment?
- If it does NOT disappear from a number of regions, then it is important to know what kind of business and regional development will help steel companies to create a more sustainable picture for the future and to create mutual benefits between regions.
- If it DOES disappear from a number of regions, then regions would like to define their future economic strengths, separate from steel. In that case steel becomes part of a region's history while the region wants to look to the future.

Furthermore the expiry in 2002 of the European Coal and Steel Community (ECSC) Treaty could mean the end of financial assistance towards the costs of future restructuring and redundancy within the industry.

There is, however, a recognition that no individual agency or body can work in isolation to confront and manage steel regional restructuring, in order to promote a viable European steel industry. CASTer aims to be inclusive and work on the basis of shared problems, solutions and experience. Lobbying mainly happens in three areas:

1. EU funding for social and regional restructuring (Structural Funds, RESIDER, ECSC and new Community Initiatives). Due to the large-scale adaptation processes in regions when steel companies close down or carry out industrial restructuring, funds are needed to help the workforce adapt, find alternative jobs and to reclaim derelict land and find new sectors with economic growth potential, both in EU15 and in CEEC regions.
2. Influencing EU policies (industrial policies, ECSC and enlargement) that might affect regions and cities dealing with steel industrial change. CASTer wants to understand, anticipate and influence this process because of its impact in the regions and cities where steel companies are located. CASTer feels it is increasingly urgent to lobby for an integrated EU approach, instead of separate sectoral policies for this industry in Europe.
3. Special Interest Groups. Due to the globalization/'Europeanization' of steel companies, the problem for the regions is that the boards of these companies have left the regions. Against this background, it is logical that CASTer-member authorities seek to share information and expertise. It is also logical to use this network of special interest groups as a platform from which to seek Europe-wide liaison and information-sharing arrangements with steel companies and others affected by the fate of steel.

The European Integration process started from the top down, with the European Coal and Steel Community in the 1950s. That Treaty expires in 2002. CASTer is working to initiate the integration from the bottom up by the local and regional communities in Europe who deal or have dealt with coal and steel companies. CASTer wants to work towards win–win strategies between regions. The focus is on the steel industry, but other industries are facing similar processes. The following example demonstrates that European regions cannot easily rely on international service sectors or telecom markets, the fruits of 'globalization'. Mannesmann moved parts of their production first to Hungary, only to close again and move to China. Forrester Research Institute and KPMG both predict a global battle resulting in four or five global players for mobile-phone markets. The virtual hype and global company structures seem to become a risky scenario for local and regional development.

Exchange of the political and practical work should therefore take place. European steel regions would like to analyse the balance and the expected shifts of locations in the future:

- Who will have the 'steel knowledge' in an increasingly open world of Internet and ICT?
- Who will be the organizers of steel production?
- Where will the production sites for steel be located?

- Will we face global management of know-how, brand and values of four or five steel companies and/or a shift towards regional steel plants?
- Which structure for the steel sector is the most sustainable and which one will enable us to maintain a European culture of diversification and *authenticity* for our regions and people?

Having posed these questions, one could say that in its next transition phase CASTer is moving from 'understanding, anticipating and influencing steel industry change' towards the phase of design and creation of the future perspective. Not from a steel industry point of view but from an (inter-)regional one. This gives the network the chance and the position to discuss the issues in real partnership with the steel companies. We could therefore say that CASTer is a pioneer, dealing with the changing steel industry and exploring the potential for new sustainable economic structures that are accepted by the local communities and the workforce.

On the other hand, CASTer works on the basis of shared problems, solutions and experiences, within and between regions, when steel companies have reduced their production capacity or when they disappear. A number of regions have defined joint proactive strategies or projects, and the network therefore aims to:

- Promote the exchange of experience and know-how between member areas.
- Sieve out and publicize examples of best-practice in regeneration techniques.
- Instigate/coordinate interregional cooperation among European steel regions.

Actual situation in the steel industry

Before we continue the CASTer case, it would be helpful to give an overview of the change process affecting the steel industry at the European and at the world level (Table 11.1 and 11.2). At the world level around 20 steel producers are still operating, each with a market share of 3–5 per cent. The steel industry in Europe is more or less regionally oriented, but at the same time expanding its markets to other parts of the world. It is seen as more competitive than the US steel industry, which is performing rather weakly and is not in its best

Table 11.1 Structural overproduction in world markets (million tonnes)

	1998	1999	2000
Global steel production (million tonnes)	777	788	840
Global steel consumption	692	710	752

Sources: International Iron and Steel Institute.

condition. The biggest phenomenon influencing the steel industry and its longer-term plans is the globalization of its customer-base, although this might shift back again towards regional markets (regions = Europe, Asia, USA). Industries are 'moving' in order to be strategically located to serve their markets most cost-effectively.

Steel is still a relatively fragmented industry, with the top 20 companies accounting for only 37 per cent of worldwide steel production (production for the top 10 companies is shown in Table 11.3), compared to 70 per cent covered by the six largest car producers.[1]

Table 11.2   Supply and demand for crude steel[1] EUR 15 (million tonnes)

	Out-turn				Estimate	Forecast
	1996	*1997*	*1998*	*1999*[R1]	*2000*[R2]	*2001*
Apparent user consumption[a]	139.5	149.8	158	154.4	162.0	163.5
Change in merchant stocks[b]	−4.0	1.0	2.0	1.0	1.5	−0.5
Apparent consumption	135.5	150.8	160.0	155.4	163.5	163.0
Imports EUR 15	12.2	14.4	21.4	20.7	24.0	22.5
Exports EUR 15	27.9	24.0	20.0	19.3	22.0	22.5
Changes in producer stocks	−4.0	−1.0	1.0	1.0	1.0	−1.0
Production	*147.2*	*159.4*	*159.6*	*155.0*	*162.5*	*162*

Source: *European Report*, 8 January 2001, 346/13,4–7.1.

Notes: [1] Factor for converting finished products to crude steel: 1.11.
  [R1] Figures revised on the basis of out-turn.
  [R2] Partially revised.
  [a] This aggregate is close to actual consumption. It includes changes in merchant stocks in all countries except Germany, France, the UK and Benelux, and changes in users' steel stocks.
  [b] Changes in merchant stocks in Germany, France, the UK and Benelux.

Table 11.3   The world's leading ten steel producers

Company	*Production (million tonnes) 1999*[2]
1. Pohang Iron and Steel (South Korea)	26.5
2. Nippon Steel (Japan)	25.2
3. Usinor (France)	22.2
4. Arbed (Luxemburg)	22.2
5. Corus (GB/NL)	21.3
6. LNM Group/Ispat (GB)	20.0
7. Shanghai Bao Steel (China)	16.7
8. Thyssen Krupp Steel (Germany)	16.1
9. Riva (Italy)	14.1
10. NKK (Japan)	12.8

European steel producers Usinor, Arbed and Aceralia announced a merger in February 2001, '*Newco*', and since then have become the world's largest steel producer with 44.4 million tonnes and an annual turnover of 30 billion euro. But they still do not enjoy more than 5 per cent market share. This initiative is considered a big step forward in the rationalization and concentration of the European steel industry, Although it is still subject to the approval of the European Commission. Strikes started immediately after the new company announced rationalization at '*Newco*' and probable closure in the medium term of Cockerill Sambre in Charleroi, Belgium.

Newco must achieve cost efficiencies by shutting plants that perform poorly, but big job cuts will create political problems in France and Spain. CORUS announced, in December 2000, 6000 lay-offs, coupled with a 20 per cent cut in capacity at its British plants.

Voest Alpine, the Austrian steel industry, producing 4.7 million tonnes crude steel in 1999, is one of the most profitable players, but the Austrian government has a stake of 39 per cent, which makes it a highly illiquid stock, probably safe from predators. So this raises questions about the appropriate level for productive plants. May be small is beautiful and flexible, in an environment of national commitment and partnerships?

Although European steel industries have a better market position than US steel makers, US Steel's take-over of Slovak steel-maker VSZ (end 2000) marks a turning point for the Central European steel industry. It is the first time in more than a decade that a US steel investor has entered Europe. This might change the arena for Central Europe's other steel makers, who all need to fight for survival.

The Americans have demonstrated to the Slovak government a long-term commitment, pledging investments of $700 million over the next ten years. They have also agreed to work to avoid social collapse, together with the Slovak government. If this business strategy turns out to be successful, the new company might become the major player in high value-added flat steel products, with a capacity of 4 million tonnes. It might quite rapidly affect Austria's Voest Alpine and Germany's Thyssen Krupp.

Is globalization unavoidable, and will national governments no longer be able to liaise with national companies?

This would have great impact and result in less opportunities for Central Europe. It implies that, if foreign investments fail, there will be no chance to compete in high-value added flat steel products.

The key problem with CEEC countries is the financing of social costs that is required before investors can start industrial restructuring. Poland tried to sell Huta Katowice and Huta Sendzimira to new investors, but UK/Dutch steel maker CORUS pulled out at the last minute due to the social costs expected and the political uncertainty over future restructuring. Bankruptcy then seemed to be the only scenario left for Huta Katowice.

Table 11.4   Central Europe's largest steel-makers[2]

Company	Country	World rank (99)	Status
Huta Katowice	Poland	49	Looking for buyers
VSZ Kosice	Slovakia	55	Bought by US Steel
Sidex	Romania	61	Bids due by year-end
Nova Hut'	Czech Repub.	76	Looking for buyers
Huta Sendzimira	Poland	n/a	Looking for buyers
Vitkovice	Czech Repub.	n/a	Sale in 2001
Dunaferr	Hungary	n/a	Sale in 2001

In this environment, when both Austrian and Italian steel makers try to build new plants in Poland, it obviously creates a risky economic and social scenario for all.

Will US Steel act as a breakthrough for the issue of social costs, in more countries of Central and Eastern Europe?

The European Commission is warning countries negotiating accession to the EU that state aid to their steel industries should stop.

EU rules on state aid to the steel sector only allow subsidies for research and development, for environmental purposes and for the social measures that accompany plant closures.

The Commission has given the candidate countries a last opportunity for state aid, in order to ensure a proper restructuring process. But under clear conditions and criteria, with a viable sector as result. Job redundancies and reduction of production were part of the bilateral 'Europe agreements'.

But the EC now has to face the fact that candidate countries have major problems in following these rules. Up until the beginning of 2001 no restructuring programme had been approved by the European Commission. Despite the low capacity utilization rate of around 67 per cent, and insufficient demand, it is obviously not an easy process to close or sell plants in Central and Eastern Europe.

The CASTer organization

We return now to the CASTer network, the organization, the stakeholders and the lobbies. The CASTer network operates through a series of meetings of its members, both on a political and an administrative level, facilitated by an international management team. The network currently has 13 members in the EU and Central and Eastern Europe, and is steadily growing. Current members are Amberg Sulzbach, Central Sweden, Krakow, Miskolc in Hungary, Nordrhein Westfalen, Nord Pas de Calais, North Holland, North Lanarkshire in Scotland, Riesa, South Yorkshire, Tees Valley, Terni in Italy, and Wales.

Common projects, bilateral cooperation agreements or active participation in CASTer conferences involve further regions and cities: Lorraine (Fr);

Kemi Tornio (Finland); Upper Austria; Katowice (Poland); Silezia (Czech Republic); The Basque Country (Spain); Genua (Italy); Kvemi Kartli (Georgia); and steel regions in Rumania.

At the political level the network is managed by a Troika of the President (South Yorkshire), Vice-President (Nordrhein Westfalen) and Treasurer (North Holland). The political members meet in a steering group at least twice a year, to direct the network. These meetings are prepared in close cooperation between the management team and the civil servants from member regions.

Stakeholders

CASTer has increasing influence through its Brussels network. This has been consolidated in the Committee of the Regions, the European Parliament and the European Commission by involving CASTer's steering-group members more in politically influential partnerships. Regular meetings take place with Eurofer, the ECSC Consultative Committee and the EU Metalworkers Federation. The regional CASTer politicians have regular discussions with separate steel companies and regional trade unions.

The following information gives a brief list of highlights in previous and present contacts with these stakeholders and their impact.

European Commission

Here portfolios include Regional Policy, ECSC, industry and enlargement.

1995/96	CASTer successfully got funding for RESIDER extended to 1999.
1996	Eneko Landaburu (Director General of DG XVI) calls for more exchange of experience and networking between steel regions during CASTer's conference in North Holland.
Oct. 1997	Commissioner Wulf Mathies announces creation of post-ECSC coal and steel research body at CASTer's Duisburg Conference.
1997/98	CASTer steering group and management meet Commissioner Wulf Mathies and DG XVI managers to discuss possible East–West cooperation.
1999	Several meetings with DG XVI and the Cabinet of Commissioner Wulf Mathies on the future Interreg programme, and CASTer submits its position paper.
1999	European Commission (DG V) invites CASTer to participate in a seminar on 'dealing with the social consequences of large-scale restructuring of enterprises'.
1999	European Commission (DG III) involved in CASTer Strategic Forum on the steel industry crisis following a number of bilateral meetings with this DG.

2000   CASTer President, together with the presidents of RETI and EURA-COM, meets Commissioner Liikanen about the ECSC phasing out.
2001   Restart of lobby for EU/ECSC support, due to a new rationalization process of EU steel companies, and the desperate state of CEEC steel companies. Such an EU fund should give local communities support for a rapid and flexible response to closures, relocations and mass redundancy both in the EU and in the CEEC.

European Parliament

Here the players include rapporteurs and members dealing with steel, ECSC and regional policy issues.

1995/96   Strong support from MEPs from the UK, Germany and Holland in lobbying for RESIDER.
June 1996   French MEP Gerard Caudron invites CASTer to contribute to his report on a 'Fresh impetus for restructuring the Community steel industry'.
Oct. 1996   CASTer contributes to a report by Spanish MEP Joan Colom I Naval on the incorporation of the ECSC into the EU budget (phasing in).
1997   Study carried out on the RESIDER programme and long-term support for steel regions, sent to and discussed with several MEPs.
1998/99   Strong support from MEPs from the UK, Germany and Holland for CASTer's position paper on Interreg, and joint lobbying by CASTer and RETI for a separate Community Initiative for Industrial Change: RESTRUCT.
2000   Participation of German MEP in CASTer meeting with Commissioner Liikanen.
2001   Restart of lobby for EU/ECSC support, due to the new rationalization process of Corus and Newco.
           Invitation to MEPs to join CASTer's debate about globalization and the need for local/regional political action.

Committee of the Regions (CoR)

Political members of CASTer's steering group are involved in influencing the CoR discussions.

1997   CoR Commission 1 invites CASTer to give a presentation on its activities and objectives.
1998   Ongoing networking between CASTer and RETI members of the CoR on the future of the Structural Funds policy 2000–06.
1999   Ongoing lobby for Structural Funds in several CoR commissions and plenary session. Rapporteur: RETI President.

2000   CoR unanimously adopts a report on the expiry of the ECSC Treaty co-written by CASTer Vice-President. CASTer formally submits its position paper on the issue and helps in the preparation of the report.
CASTer President invited to speak at a CoR forum on the future for Europe's coal and steel regions. CASTer also takes part in a CoR exhibition of coal and steel regions along with several of its members.

The position of the Committee of the Regions in European lobby-networks needs some more explanation; a number of critics underestimate its influence. The Committee is an interesting player for the European Commission, which is looking for partnerships in the implementation of European policies. It is therefore a useful instrument for the launch of new policies, for the creation of commitment between the Commission and the regions, and even for the preparation of new actions. When the Commission has got the support of the Committee of the Regions, it will be easier to convince member states.

On the other hand, one could say that regional and local authorities need the Commission and the European Parliament as players, and not only for regional policies but for a number of sectoral policies as well. What regions and cities are learning is to organize themselves in European-wide networks in order to increase the importance of their voice. They are creating systems for network-governance among local and regional authorities who are increasingly becoming the natural counterpart for the globalized economic players who are no longer dependent on national borders and regulations.

Within the structure and agendas of the Committee of the Regions, the members find the appropriate place for networking, building contacts all over Europe and organizing themselves into specific lobbies, such as CASTer.

Eurofer

The main activities here involve network contacts and partnership building.

1995   Eurofer Director General's presentation during inaugural conference in Brussels.

1996   Jasper Heusdens, Hoogovens Managing Director, together with Jacques Peries, Usinor Sacilor, President Director General of SODIE, involved in CASTer North Holland conference.

1997   Ekkehard Schulz, Krupp Thyssen CEO, in Plenary Debate of CASTer Duisburg conference.

1998/99   Bilateral meetings at management level between CASTer and Eurofer.

2000   Meeting between CASTer President and Eurofer Director General about interests in ECSC phasing out and future potentials for partnership.

2001   Meetings at management level between CASTer and Eurofer about new CASTer priorities (public–private partnerships (PPPs) at Pan European level with common interest for EU funds/ECSC support)

ECSC Consultative Committee

Again the main activities are in network contacts together with partnership building.

1995   Conference on the future of the ECSC Treaty, European Parliament Brussels. Resolution called for ECSC Consultative Committee to be retained, for ECSC social provisions to be protected when phased into the EU Treaty, and for funding for RESIDER to be extended.
1996   Bilateral meetings at management level between CASTer and ECSC committee.
2000   ECSC Consultative Committee Vice-President and Secretary and CASTer President call for a follow-up to the Committee during a CoR Coal and Steel Forum.
   ECSC Consultative Committee invites CASTer to comment on its declaration on the future of structured dialogue after the expiry of the ECSC Treaty.

Trade unions

Here we refer to activities at the EU and at the regional level.

1996   International Metalworkers' Federation's Director for Steel speaks at CASTer conference in Wales on Structural Change in the Economies of Steel Producing Regions.
1998   CASTer President invited to speak at the European Metalworker's Federation conference on the role of European Works Councils in the European Coal and Steel Industry.
2000   CASTer supports EMF as it lobbies to ensure a follow-up body to the ECSC Consultative Committee.
2001   Active networking between CASTer members and trade unions about job cuts in Corus and Newco.

Competitors or cooperative contacts

The CASTer network as such has no specific problems with competition. It is a body of local and regional authorities, and the intention is therefore to find partners, to cooperate and to build alliances when mutual benefits are obvious.

CASTer has regular and increasing contacts with RETI and Euracom and, depending on the progress and state of CASTer's strategy, partnerships could increase.

RETI: network of industrial regions

RETI is a network of 24 EU and non-EU industrial regions, including several CASTer members. It concentrates its efforts on regional policies and Structural

Funds lobbying for a wide variety of regions all working on regional economic changes and in a great number of industrial sectors. The main topics for this network at the moment are regional policy and interregional cooperation, innovation, research and enterprise, and EU enlargement.

One could say that while RETI is working on a broadening regional economic change process, CASTer is focused on the issue of steel industrial change and is working on an integrated EU policy for steel. The final objective is to work in public–private partnership *with its stakeholders, steel companies and trade unions*, both at regional and EU level. CASTer deals with interregional cooperation and EU enlargement in the same way: linked with steel industrial change.

It will therefore not be surprising that regular contacts between the two networks take place, both at political and management levels. Lobbying is coordinated, if appropriate, and there are discussions about future closer cooperation in 2001. Provided CASTer continues to succeed in providing a voice for steel regions in global changes in the steel industry, it will be a challenge to widen the discussions about economic and industrial evolutions in Europe by introducing RETI as a stronger voice for industrial regions. Is the model of global mergers and concentration of large companies one that will survive, and how does this respond to regions' and people's needs? Highlights in previous and present contacts between CASTer and RETI are:

1995	CASTer Vice-President invited to speak at RETI conference on the future of the Structural Funds.
1998/99	Reports on Structural Funds in the CoR, coordinated by RETI and CASTer members of the CoR.
2000	Coordinated meeting of RETI/Euracom/CASTer Presidents with Commissioner Liikanen about the ECSC. President of RETI invited to CASTer seminar with CEEC representatives to discuss future closer cooperation.
2000/01	Common meetings at political and management level to work on closer cooperation.

EURACOM: regions dealing with the coal industry

Since the start of CASTer, representatives have had regular contacts with this network of mining regions. The Euracom President is a Member of the European Parliament and CASTer's main contacts have been and still are with this network. Highlights have been:

1995	Spanish MEP, Euracom President, speaks at CASTer conference on the future of the ECSC Treaty.
2000	Coordinated meeting of Euracom/RETI/CASTer Presidents with Commissioner Liikanen about the ECSC.

Member states in Europe

It is important to mention the almost complete absence of member states in CASTer's networks and stakeholders. The local and regional authorities have not, so far, the impression that member states are able or willing to influence the globalization process in the way that local and regional authorities in CASTer want. Member states are mostly strong supporters of global markets and rationalization, for macro-economic reasons. Regions and local actors observe the process from a micro-economic point of view, looking for the regional balance between economic, social and environmental policies.

The impression is that the position of member states might probably change, now that even some of the national governments have experienced the failure of the global CEOs of steel companies to exchange information with national prime ministers ahead of restructuring processes. Which level of government is still able to act as the counterpart of global industry decision-makers? Transnational companies (TNCs) and international capital have become the *de facto* new world government.

Regions need to raise their voice. In this context, members of the national parliaments are less important. One member of the Dutch parliament recognized in March 2001 that it is very probably that the company that was formerly Hoogovens will probably be the victim of international finance agreements between CORUS, of which it now forms part, and large banks. If the UK arm of CORUS face losses, the Dutch may well have to bear the cost.

Size of the sector

How much is being played for? CASTer has lobbied on a number of occasions for EU funding. Due to the large-scale adaptation processes in regions when steel companies close down or implement their next restructuring, funds are needed to help the workforce adapt and find alternative jobs, to reclaim derelict land and find new economic potential growth sectors. Highlights in the lobbies of the last six years have been the following:

Resider: €500 m, 1994–99

Several individual regional lobbies with national MEPs started to flow into a concerted effort for steel regions' interests. MEPs put in a great effort to get amendments adopted by the European Parliament's Plenary Session, with the result that the problem of steel restructuring was the key focus and that regions that were NOT eligible for Objectives 1 or 2 would still be eligible for RESIDER. At the same time this was the kick-off for CASTer's network.

New community initiatives, 2000–06

Together with RETI, CASTer lobbied for a separate Community initiative which both organizations considered necessary as the next step for the four old Community Initiatives: RECHAR, KONVER, RESIDER and RETEX. This initiative should deal with closures, relocations and mass redundancies of globalizing industrial companies, and should enable local authorities to respond rapidly. They therefore designed a draft text for RESTRUCT and put great effort into lobbying DGs, Commissioners and MEPs.

However, the Commission and the Parliament had already committed themselves to a rationalization process for the Community Initiatives and wanted to reduce them from 13 to 3. Therefore the RESTRUCT lobby resulted in joint lobbying with Eurocities (the network of cities in Europe) and the final result was the acceptance of a fourth Community Initiative called URBAN.

In 2001 CASTer restarted the lobby for European financial support, due to the next phase of steel companies' rationalization (Corus and Newco) and the desperate state of CEEC steel companies. Funds are to be allocated from the ECSC's outstanding assets/general budget.

Interreg IIIC

Neither CASTer nor RETI were happy with the Commission's proposal to integrate all the interregional activities into the geographical areas of INTERREG IIIB, which would mean that there was no independent programme left for EU-wide networks. Both organizations work with EU-wide partnerships that are NOT the same as the geographical areas of IIIB.

The EC has decided to accept these comments, and there will now be one set of criteria at the EU level, one call for proposals for the whole EU, and partners will be allowed to cooperate across the whole EU (Interreg IIIC budget = 6 per cent of total INTERREG budget). This can be seen as a success for the CASTer and RETI lobby.

Phasing-out of ECSC

Outstanding assets of ECSC stood at €1.25 bn, with separate funds for R&D of €2 m. CASTer defined its position paper in 1999 after a number of discussions with the actors involved (EC, EP, ECSC Committee, Eurofer), with key points being:

- *Research*: CASTer believes that the work carried out under the ECSC Treaty Reserved and Technology Development (RTD) Programme has been of vital and valuable importance to the EU steel industry over the last four decades. It is therefore of strategic importance that the phasing in of the RTD Programme to the overall 5th Framework Programme does not lead to any devaluation of this.
- *Statistics*: CASTer supports the continuation of the ECSC statistical framework as a specific information system addressing the needs of the steel industry.
- *Regeneration funding*: CASTer is concerned about possible future restructuring in the steel industry and the potential effect of this on remaining steel regions, given the lack of specific assistance available in the future to alleviate this.

- *Enlargement*: enlargement will increase the need for restructuring in the CEEC steel industry and there will be a need to assist this process along the lines of what happened in the EU under the ECSC. In particular for CASTer, the new INTERREG Community Initiative presents an opportunity for increased interregional cooperation. It is important that exchange of experience and good practice is facilitated with non-member states.
- *European dialogue*: CASTer believes that the ECSC can be seen as a model for a multisectoral, multifaceted approach to restructuring. CASTer is therefore concerned that the expiry of the ECSC Treaty does not result in less-focused and less-coherent EU policies towards steel regions. There is a need and a value in retaining elements of sectoral dialogue. CASTer believes that the tripartite membership of the ECSC Consultative Committee should be augmented by the inclusion of regional and local government in order to continue this overall dialogue and focus within a successor body.

In April 2000, the Committee of the Regions unanimously adopted a report on the expiry of the ECSC Treaty, co-written by the CASTer Vice-President. After this success, CASTer started to lobby EU Commissioner Liikanen, in close partnership with RETI and Euracom, in order to raise CASTer interests. This is still going on. New redundancies and rationalizations in Corus, Usinor, Arbed and Aceralia will need more support than foreseen, both by the EU and by the regions.

Managing change: CASTer members' projects

CASTer member regions draw up common projects for the implementation of their agreed political strategy, with the support of EU funds. One could say that CASTer works at all four levels of a policy life-cycle:

- why = problem definition
- what = political strategy of the network
- how = management of political lobbies + network projects
- when = action plan and time frame

Here we can see the interrelated approach that will be explained in more depth below. Partnerships have been built up at two levels: through common projects and through political networking. Those cities or regions who start with a project network have later become more involved in the political networking, whilst those who started with the political networking have taken a next step with joint projects; two examples follow:

El Duende project, 1997–2001

This €4.5 m project defines an interregional strategy, methodology and a number of actions for business intermediaries and small and medium-sized enterprises on the issues of internationalization. At the same time, the project also has a conceptual focus: regions want to understand and anticipate the changes in international trends of knowledge-based economies. The six partner regions of North Holland, South Yorkshire, North Rhine Westphalia, Riesa-Saxony, Kemi Tornio and South Dublin have defined common SWOT models (Strengths Weaknesses Opportunities and Threats) on six sectors of their economies and are building interregional networks of business intermediaries, business clusters and networks of excellence between universities and product innovation centres (sectors: ICT, metal, transport, medical technologies, wood and tourism).

The project is funded by RECITE, European Regional Development Fund. The El Duende process (Figure 11.1) should help to develop assets in the 'new economy' within and between the regions. Five of the El Duende partner regions are also politically involved in CASTer.

The wheel of Figure 11.1 illustrates the process of the El Duende partnership. The axle stands for the international team, coordinated by ECONcept. The innermost wheel is the interregional network of the six partner regions; the second wheel demonstrates the widening of the network with business intermediaries from all six regions; and the outermost wheel represents the

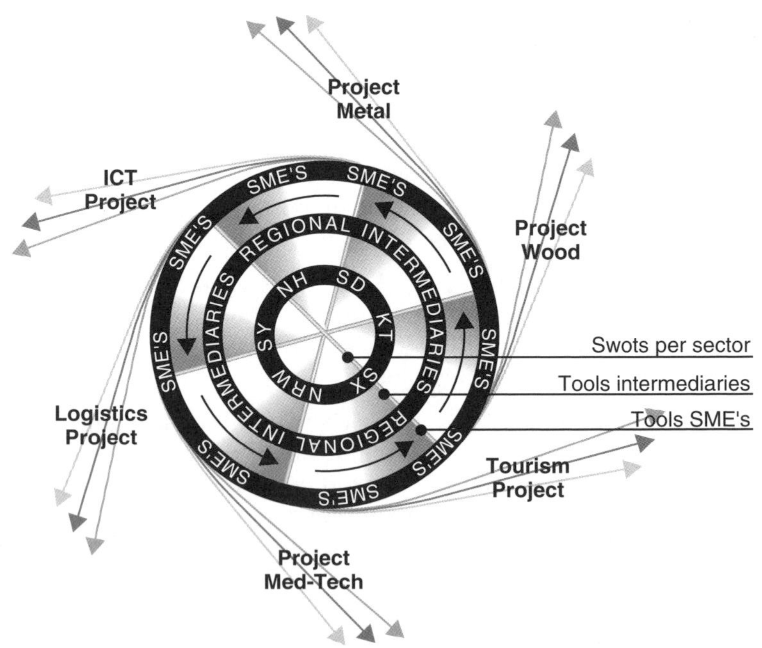

Figure 11.1   The El Duende partnership wheel

350 small and medium-sized enterprises (SMEs) that have been introduced in the network and the build-up of contacts with SMEs from other EU-regions.

The spokes indicate how the network has built the common actions needed to support networking between regions (SWOTs per sector), business intermediaries (tools for intermediaries) and SMEs (tools for intermediaries). The construction of the whole 'wheel' is based upon common strategies, planning and actions, allowing the definition of projects in six economic sectors.

CASTer projects, 2001–07

In 2001, member regions will have defined various projects that support CASTer's strategy. The overall aims for projects are now defined, at the time of this publication (June 2001), as:

- A CASTer-wide network project for the *strategic* monitoring and desk research of global changes in the steel industry. Decision-makers in cities and regions should build a pan-European public–private partnership (PPP) together with steel industries and trade unions, to exchange information. They should be able to define a number of common objectives for steel industries and for steel regions. CEEC partners should be invited to participate, and the network should be supported by sub-networks of PPPs around specific steel industrial groups such as Corus, Newco and Thyssen Krupp.
- Projects for coordinating measures to cope with steel restructuring between regions that deal with the same global steel industry. This is expected to take place more quickly due to decisions in companies such as Corus, Newco and others. Actions could include building clusters of SMEs at the interregional level, encouraging e-business, the adaptation of international skills in regions, and so forth. Partners will be able to use the El Duende experience, networks and methodology to move forward fast, and CEEC partners will be invited to participate.
- Knowledge and innovation, working on post-steel economic strategies, NOT related to steel industrial change anymore. This also shows the process in the network: those member regions that have lost steel industries, are working on a wider basis on diversification of regional economies.
- Projects that concentrate on quality of life within regions and communities, again NOT related to changes in the steel industry. Local actors want to regain possession of the local environment, and 'home-grown economies' is a key phrase for these projects.

The case

It is interesting to describe not just a lobby case as such, because that would only highlight a small part of CASTer's work and it does not demonstrate the essential difference between CASTer and other lobby groups. The words 'interest group' might better fit this network of local and regional actors in Europe.

We describe the CASTer case from different angles, first analysing the fundamentals for CASTer's existence and its forecast life-cycle. We then analyse the ambitions and actions of the past, present and future, and finally describe the core attitude and method used in lobbying and other actions.

The ground for CASTer's existence

We see the network's existence based upon the following elements:

- CASTer has a clear political agenda that is reviewed and updated every six months in the political steering group.
- CASTer wants not only to understand and anticipate, but also to influence the steel industry process, because the network's partners have built up a good knowledge base and have a clear overall strategy at the EU level, while the members have their local roots at the same time. From this standpoint they see the impact of international steel companies far away from people and local communities. CASTer wants to support steel companies in their transformation process, but for that it needs to be accepted by the steel companies as the 'voice of the regions'.
- CASTer wants to exchange views on the different perceptions of steel industry change, in order to get a common understanding between steel companies and regions, to anticipate and influence changes and even to design and create, in partnership, a more sustainable future, both for the local areas and for the international steel companies.

Figure 11.2 illustrates the policy life-cycle of CASTer. The life-cycle for the EU regions is from 1990 upto 2010, with the next life-cycle starting in 2001. The expected life cycle for the CEEC regions is from 2000 upto 2020.

Phase 1: understand steel industry changes and redevelop local areas, 1990–99

Since the mid-1980s, when large plants were closed down overnight in France and the UK, Europe has had to prepare itself for continent-wide restructuring. RESIDER was the Community Initiative created for EU support for steel areas, and most of the present CASTer members used RESIDER funds for this process between 1993–99. Local and regional public and private partnerships (PPPs) were built, some with and some without steel companies, and thousands of jobs disappeared over a short time.

Regions understood that this process was happening all over Europe and that cooperation between the regions would be an advantage. CASTer was created and regions lobbied for RESIDER funding.

Phase 2: anticipate steel industry global changes and develop a proactive regional economy 1997–2000

All CASTer regions had to reduce their dependency on the steel sector and find other sources of employment. Diversification took place but it appeared

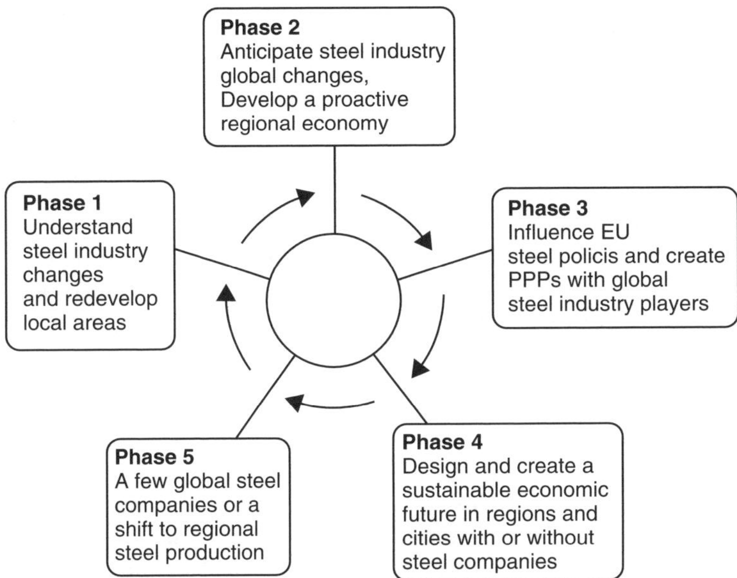

Figure 11.2   CASTer's life-cycle

to be a difficult, long-term process in mono-industrial areas like Wales and the UK Midlands, Lorraine (France) and the Ruhr area (Germany). Regional Innovation strategies were defined; regions redefined their Strengths, Weaknesses, Opportunities and Threats (SWOT); and regional clusters were built in different sectors of economies, mostly with small and medium-sized enterprises (SMEs).

Four CASTer members (North Holland, South Yorkshire, North Rhine Westphalia, Saxony Riesa) took a step further; together with Kemi Tornio (Finland) they Dublin (Ireland) they started a large cooperation network in the project El Duende (RECITE) described earlier. They defined a common interregional strategy and built a number of pilots for business intermediaries and small and medium-sized enterprises.

Three of the six El Duende projects are significance in CASTer is political discussions. Business clusters can support the transformation process of the steel companies in these regions and help to raise the cooperation between economic actors of the regions involved in the internationalization processes of the steel companies.

However, there are other stories to tell as well. A mono-industrial region such as South Yorkshire includes some parts of the region that feel 'victims' of industrial change. They face an ongoing process of change, from global, hard industries towards global, soft industries, and the workforce has lost its confidence in global decision-making. They had to change from jobs as steelworkers to call-centre workers, but a few years later those call centres have disappeared as well, even sooner than the steel industry, due to the Asian crisis.

In 2000, the Corus and Avesta steel companies were forced to announce 6000 further job losses, and went on to merge with Outokompu in Northern Finland. This has repercussions for a number of CASTer regions (South Yorkshire, Wales, Central Sweden, Kemi Tornio and North Holland). In South Yorkshire parts of the communities have decided to return to local economic concepts (capacity-building), whilst in North Holland the former Hoogovens workforce strongly protested against decisions made by the board in London. They disagreed with the results of the merger between Hoogovens and British Steel (Corus) and feared for their own survival. Corus then decided to make a new split between the Dutch plant and the UK part of the company in order to prevent the Dutch from suffering from UK rationalizations. This, however, was overruled by the big banks in March 2001, in the recent credit agreement with Corus London. The Dutch will pay for the UK losses. In the meantime the workforce in Kemi Tornio is growing due to the very profitable and expanding plants of Outokompu; new investments are being made.

Italian local authorities like that of Terni have defined new priorities, and dependency on large international companies is increasingly perceived as uncertain. The ownership of the local steel plant, for example, is in the hands of the German steel company Thyssen Krupp, and in the summer of 2000 the city read in the press about Thyssen Krupp's plans to sell its steelworks to Usinor Sacilor (France). This however, did not occur.

CASTer has the impression that people want to regain possession of the local environment and will have increasing problems if they cannot influence the decisions of global or European business players that impact on the economies of their regions.

Upper Austria, however did not see steel industrial change as a problem because Voest Alpine has so far been rather profitable and stable. It has customers within 500 km of the plant and the regional economy is booming; and it is important to mention the Austrian government's 39 per cent stake. However, the latest information about US Steel's take-over of Slovak steelmaker VSZ will bring a new and competitive next-door neighbour for Voest Alpine.

CASTer has learnt from its networks with CEEC players that local and regional societies have lost confidence in the leaders of both private companies and governments. There is a lack of trust which will be a major problem for restructuring. There is also a lack of funds to ensure a responsible process of social restructuring. Will the enlargement policies of Europe fail in the steel industry sector? Who will be able to get a breakthrough – US Steel? If steel companies want to invest in these countries and build up markets, networks with CASTer might help to build relationships of trust with CEEC players. RESIDER teams from Western Europe could support this process. However steel industries and EU regions need to have a common perception of their mutual futures.

The conclusion of the majority of CASTer regions is as follows:

- Regional economic planning is difficult when international decisions can suddenly reduce local jobs by thousands. Moreover, the issue of non-geographically located shareholders and the global development of footloose service sectors such as banking and information technology have dramatically influenced regional planning. This affects South Yorkshire, North Holland, Terni, Kemi Tornio, Central Sweden, and North Rhine Westphalia.
- A number of changes in local initiatives demonstrate that micro answers seem to appear when macro development is no longer understandable for citizens and workers (South Yorkshire and Terni).
- Local communities feel the need to define their own future vision (South Yorkshire and Terni).
- Investments and mergers in CEEC countries are a problem if steel companies and EU regions cannot build bridges with the local people in the CEEC. CEEC communities have no trust in large private company leaders or national politicians. Interregional networks of CASTer regions could support this process of trust building, adaptation and restructuring, but CASTer needs to have an open mind since the restructuring process might result in solutions other than those found by regions in the EU. Central and Eastern Europe has a different history and cultural background which influences decision-making at all levels.

Phase 3: influence EU steel policies and create public–private partnerships with global steel industry players, 1998–2004

CASTer regions are forced to lobby for a strong voice in EU discussions. They want to influence future economic processes related to global investments, companies, information technologies and individual decision-making of consumers on global markets. CASTer regions therefore feel the need to search for answers to the questions we raised in the introduction to this chapter. CASTer seeks to influence the steel industry process. It can see the impact of international steel companies, too far away from people and local communities. If European steel companies continue with this process in the current way, they will have abandoned partnerships at local level.

CASTer has therefore arrived at the third phase of its life-cycle in 2000 and is working on the following issues:

- Move from regional Public Private Partnerships towards organized interregional partnerships for regular contacts and open communication with the boards of multinational steel companies.

- Influence EU discussions in EC and EP about steel industry issues, ECSC policies, enlargement and regional policies, as far as they concern the steel sector.
- Take the ECSC as a model for a multisectoral, multifaceted approach to restructuring, with a tripartite membership augmented by the inclusion of regions and local authorities.
- Build political networks with colleagues from CEEC steel regions.
- Invite steel companies/Eurofer to work together with CASTer and trade unions. A pan-European public–private partnership is likely to emerge for the exchange of information and to define common objectives.

The main questions in these areas as they affect CASTer regions are:

- Could we expect and do we want in Europe a steel industry scenario similar to the 'microsoft monopoly'?
- Is there enough social, economic and environmental benefit for regions to keep the steel industry in their regions?

Phase 4: design and create a sustainable economic future in regions and cities, with or without steel companies, 2000–06

CASTer members have developed a proactive attitude to finding answers to steel industrial restructuring, although this is not always easy and there are large differences. The less diversified a region's economy is, the more problems have to be solved.

Together, the CASTer members have defined the focus for the coming six years, 2000–06. In this we can see the shift in the members' network: some regions no longer need to focus on steel industrial change because they see that as a problem of the past. We also see that local interests are shifting away from globalization. One could say that if macro development is too footloose, then people start to find their own answers in a safe local environment – micro development.

Some CASTer members are now interested in working on quality of life within regions and communities. They want to regain possession of the local environment, work on sustainable concepts and integrate home-grown economies. Craftsmen's skills are more highly valued than in past decades, and capacity-building in the social community is seen as important. The focus has changed from the steel industry towards the local needs of humans in their own environment.

However, other CASTer member regions are fully involved with steel industrial change and face globalization. They want to build projects for redevelopment, closely linked with steel companies. They expect the steel industry to be sufficiently viable and therefore part of their cultural DNA in an open competitive world market. Key words for these projects are: how to find a win–win situation for regions; what are the core competences of the regions and their workforce involved in an open international economy; and what needs to be improved?

Interregional cluster-building should take place in the metal and transport sector, supported by Information and Communication Technology (ICT) clusters in order to anticipate changes between production sites and the organization of production and logistics. CASTer members are fully aware of the international economic changes that are taking place in the steel industry and they are not only influencing the political discussions in Europe, but also managing the changes within and between regions to anticipate the future. The management of these actions is mostly done within EU projects under INTERREG and Equal Community Initiatives.

Phase 5: a few global steel companies or a shift to regional steel production?, 2006–10

This phase represents a prognosis and personal view of the author. Making prognosis for the longer term is risky; 2010 is far away and a lot can happen in an open global market for steel.

First, sustainable steelworks should be located in a number of EU regions. Steel is the world's dominant material; highly recycled and relatively easy to recycle, it is well-aligned with today's sustainability requirements.[3] The objective should therefore be to keep a viable steel industry in Europe. However, a number of developments demand rapid responses both from steel industries and from steel regions:

- Transport costs and environmental taxes on transport will increase, which makes long-distance transport difficult.
- Information technologies and the Internet facilitate a process of building networks of knowledge and therefore make the system of 'global brands' easy to connect with regional production plants everywhere. However, the physical neighbourhood of innovative clusters is still 'the diamond of competitiveness' (Porter). Each steelworks needs constant on-site innovation and modernization, in its own region. At the same time it can tap off the knowledge from virtual networks with steelworks all over the world.
- Shareholders and big banks are having a dramatic influence on the tornado restructuring of steel companies. They have no direct relation with one company, but want to see efficiency, profitability and proactive performance. Steel companies are therefore facing a life and death battle and seem to be unable to choose any course but 'moving forward and eat or be eaten by competitors'. Could Europe *still* change global shareholder positions towards national/regional stakeholder structures? And how could Europe increase its influence and involvement of public authorities?
- Global decision-making by producers and consumers seems to be an increasing threat to local and regional actors. Which level of authority will be able to counterbalance global private companies?

- An increasing process of mergers gives questionable results. Could there not be other models such as international cooperation among groupings of smaller steel industries to share their knowledge and expertise?
- The workforce and natural resources are the future scarcities in economics. If steel companies have to compete with other employers to attract more and more independent knowledge workers, they need to take into account that workers are increasingly interested in quality of life, especially in Europe. This includes a healthy and safe environment and solid local communities as well. Steel production in balance with natural resources will probably become a must within a very short time due to the local, national and global need to live and produce in a sustainable way.

CASTer regions must prepare themselves for the future through:

- building innovation structures and systems in each region with steel plants, supported by knowledge networks of highly innovative research and know-how; and
- supportive business clusters for ICT, metal and transport in each steel region, cooperating with each other through intranet facilities (universities, chambers of commerce, regional development agencies and small and medium-sized enterprises related to the steel production chain).

Regional and local authorities can only maintain commitment with their people if they can explain the steel industry life-cycle as well.

Why should Europe not be able to create sustainable systems for steel production, storage, distribution and transport in a large group of EU regions? This would create and maintain support of the people and workers in the regions, where people want to improve their quality of life Steel companies and CASTer members might use the assets of a culturally diversified Europe both in the EU and in the CEEC to help to define this future. This will have a major impact on steel industries' strategies. Europe should try to raise the debate about *decentralization* of steel production, in order to help the European steel industry to survive and enjoy a sustainable future. The question is, can steel industries stop the cut-throat competition process?

CASTer's attitude and methods

Interactive approach: strategic reflection + practical action

The process and organization of CASTer have been designed as an interactive model, working at the political level and the practical level at the same time. This ensures that the work planning of the two different disciplines is interrelated at the European level. This is still not common at the EU level between regions. Political networks need to be built up and local politicians still face a lot of scepticism in their own local councils if they deal with European networks.

A multidimensional scope

At the start of 1995, CASTer decided to bring the political and practical disciplines together and, as local and regional authorities, to work from several dimensions at the same time on this process of steel industrial change. The reason for this is that CASTer has a strong drive to understand the process at the political level; to anticipate within and between the regions by means of action plans and regional strategies at the practical level; and to politically influence EU debates based upon practical experience and CASTer's own political analysis of changes in the global steel industry.

CASTer has therefore mobilized a large number of actors, and in most of the member regions contacts have been built up on several levels: political, public authority management, political advisors, operational project workers and business intermediary organizations.

An open mind and open for partnership

The CASTer network has shown it operates with an open mind. What does this mean? CASTer tries to invite others to exchange ideas and perceptions and to try to get a better common understanding of the process by which the steel industry changes. The network believes in common solutions with its partners, and is therefore working on a partnership basis and intensive discussions are held in seminars and at strategic fora, together with European steel companies, trade unions, Members of the European Parliament and the European Commission.

A flexible lobby agenda in an ongoing process, to find a voice for the regions

CASTer lobbying activity does not follow a fixed agenda or aim for quantified targets. It can be described more as an ongoing flow in a process of industrial change. Subjects need to be adopted and updated permanently, and EU dossiers from different DGs are therefore followed. The key phrase is 'a voice for the regions'. CASTer strongly believes that unless this is found, Europe will lose its credibility with EU citizens.

Conclusions and lessons

1. In general one could say that CASTer is a frontrunner in Europe, gaining a strong voice for local and regional authorities in EU discussions. The increasing globalization of markets and companies requires answers and partnerships between public and private players at both the EU level and within regions. International industrial development is too often felt as a threat; regions represent citizens much better than national authorities can.

So: *global steel development needs a new balance with cities and regions, and lobbying for a voice for the regions is therefore worthwhile. CASTer is needed in the EU arena. The potential for decentralized steel production should be investigated.*

2. CASTer has now created a successful network of political members who have increasingly powerful positions in discussion with the European Commission and Parliament. Lobbying at the highest level, CASTer has no hesitation in working in partnership with RETI and EURACOM and engaging in joint lobbying (as with the ECSC).

   At the same time, CASTer has worked with its members to get a better understanding of economic and industrial changes, through research, monitoring and discussions. Also by building networks of key players within and between regions, members work together on proactive changes in the European and regional economies. Some examples are: regional and international cluster-building; finding answers to internationalization; defining new methodologies for SME intermediaries; and carrying out SWOT analyses of regional economies with sufficient awareness of international economic threats and potentials.

So: *regions have dealt with and managed steel restructuring within and between regions and are contributing successfully to a more competitive Europe. However, is competition policy in its final days, when only a few players are left?*

3. CASTer supports product innovation and the development of new materials, even when this might influence the location of steel production. But steel companies will increasingly see that they need local and regional partnerships in order to have a common understanding of future potential production processes.

   This is even more important and urgent in the EU enlargement process. Steel companies will need local and regional players from West European regions in order to carry out the restructuring in CEEC regions.

So: *CASTer has accepted the disappearance of steel plants in a number of regions. The key question is whether the global steel industry will accept participation in a pan-European public–private partnership with local and regional players, for its own sustainability in the future?*

Notes

1. Source: Steel Information Agency (SIA) (www.steelprofiles.com).
2. Source: International Iron and Steel Institute IISI (www.worldsteel.org/iisi) and BCE Business Central Europe (www.bcemag.com).
3. Source: International Iron and Steel Institute IISI and UK Steel Association: *Performance and Perspectives, The UK Steel Industry in 2000.*

Part V
Single Market Cases

12

Making the Single Market in Financial Services a Reality

Wim Mijs and Asunción Caparrós Puebla[*]

Introduction

ABN AMRO Bank is one of the three largest banks in the Netherlands and is present in all 15 member states of the European Union and more than 100 other countries worldwide. Aware of its relatively small home market in the Netherlands, ABN AMRO has always striven to enhance its presence in other countries and distribute its services cross-border. The European Union, having as one of its main pillars the four freedoms of movement (services, goods, capital and workers), presents an obvious opportunity for any European establishment. Consequently, ABN AMRO has a crucial interest in the further development of an internal market for services.

This is the reason why the ABN AMRO EU Liaison Office was established in September 1996, as the Bank's official link with the European Institutions. Our main task is to be in continual contact with these Institutions, to ensure that the Bank's interests are heard and secured. In the execution of these tasks the EU Liaison Office has three main objectives: (1) warning the bank's strategists and product developers in a very early stage of European policy developments, (2) offering the financial services expertise of the bank to support the EU legislators and (3) following legislation on financial services to ensure that the interests of our bank are secured.

The proactive monitoring of and continuous participation in developments in the EU legislative front is an integral part of our work. This goes hand in hand with coalition-building with other financial services providers and associations. Building our contacts within the EU institutions and reinforcing our coalitions with other providers not only ensures that the Bank's – and its customers' – interests are represented at the hub of the European Union, but it also makes our office a trusted, authoritative and prominent voice for the EU Institutions.

---

[*] All views expressed by the authors are personal.

In 1997 our office realized that the advent of the euro and swift technological developments, that is the internet and e-commerce, would lead to a cumulative effect in the integration of financial markets. At the time there was wide belief that the transparency and ease of use brought about by the euro would lead to almost overnight integration of financial markets in Europe. This was in the bank's view no more than a dream. From the reports of our network and of the product developers in Amsterdam, it was clear enough that there was still a myriad of rules in the European Union that would prevent almost every product from being sold in a Single Market even if the euro will be alive.

It was decided that there was an urgent need to get the completion of the Single Market for financial services high on the Agenda of the European Commission. With the support of the ABN AMRO Legal Department in Amsterdam and in consultation with various commercial departments (in order to give practical examples), it was decided to produce an authoritative study on the regulatory and legislative measures that still needed to be eliminated to achieve a truly single market for financial services. In other words, this study would serve as the main instrument for ABN AMRO to try to set the financial services agenda of the Commission for future years.

In this chapter we will describe how our study 'Single Market Review' was set up and how it was translated politically by the Commission in the 'Financial Services Action Plan'. We will also analyse who were the stakeholders and how we built coalitions. Finally, two case studies will be discussed to illustrate the work on the Financial Services Action Plan.

From single market review to financial services action plan

The single market review

With the introduction of the euro looming over the horizon in 1998, ABN AMRO Bank was (and is) in the process of developing highly efficient euro products and services and – where possible – cross-border service provision. The Bank found, however, that these products are difficult to deliver, even in the new euro environment. Clearly, unless a Single Market for financial services is created, doing large-scale cross-border business in Europe will remain an illusion.

The Single Market Review was drafted to research a single market in which the EURO had arrived and the internet had developed as an important distribution channel. Starting from that scenario, ABN AMRO tried to describe the additional measures that would have to be taken in order to bring the full benefits of the euro to Europe's businesses and citizens alike. The Single Market Review was drafted by a bank committed to the European Union and to European integration. The regulatory framework for credit institutions has been shaped by those Articles in the EU Treaty which allow for the free movement of goods, services and capital. In this regard the principles of home-country supervision of the Second Banking Directive and the

Investment Services Directive have assisted in the creation of a Single Market for financial services. However, the Single Market Review concluded that much of the regulatory framework at that time was created before the Single Market was an established principle. More importantly, it was established before the prospect of economic and monetary union became real.

The first and most basic conclusion of the Single Market Review was that it should ensure that member states properly implement existing EU legislation. For financial services companies operating in Europe, unclear and inconsistent implementation of EU measures can lead to fundamental legal uncertainty.

Furthermore, the Single Market Review study found additional barriers to the completion of the Single Market: Different national rules applicable to current accounts. For a customer to open an account in an EU country a wide range of official documents are needed. With every other EU country in which the client wants to open an account, the amount of documents increases exponentially because every country has different requirements. This is principally due to historical reasons arising from local banking laws and regulations, but also sometimes due to EU Directives that have been implemented differently in various member states. Thus, for every customer in every country, a bank must check what requirements it is legally obligated to fulfil – a most time-consuming task.

In May 1998, the Single Market Review was finally finished and ready for presentation. Whereas its main objective was to unearth the obstacles to the Single Market for financial services, the secondary objective was certainly to establish the ABN AMRO EU Liaison Office as an authoritative office in Brussels, able to provide expert input where needed in the legislative process and committed to European integration.

One member of our managing board and the Head of the Liaison Office presented the Single Market Review to Commissioner Mario Monti, responsible at the time for the Single Market and financial services, and subsequently to all levels within the Commission. The reaction of the Commission was very positive and we were invited to work together with the Commission in the High Level Strategy Review Group composed of 20 senior market experts, to further outline the source of some Single Market barriers. This group was mandated to identify the most urgent Single Market barriers still in place, following the introduction of the single currency. We had therefore succeeded in our basic objective of establishing the ABN AMRO EU Liaison Office as a supportive and authoritative stakeholder. The Single Market for financial services, however, was still far from complete.

The commission communication on financial services: 'Framework for Action'[1]

The final Conclusions of the High Level Review Group were widely accepted, and in June 1998 the European Council meeting at Cardiff issued an invitation to the Commission to prepare a Framework for Action for financial services: 'to improve the single market for financial services' by, in particular, examining the effectiveness of implementation of current legislation and to identify where amending legislation might be necessary. This led to the communication, 'Financial services: Building a Framework for Action'. In its final form, the Communication essentially sets out a revised Single Market programme for financial services recognizing the urgent need for legislation in view of market developments. It also addressed the question of a speedier legislative process in order to adapt to evolving market conditions. This is of course a recurring issue that was also addressed in February 2001 in the report on the integration of European Securities Markets by the group of Wise Men headed by Baron Alexandre Lamfalussy.[2] This proves to be a very difficult issue as it regards the balance of legislative power between the EU institutions. A swifter legislative procedure is certainly necessary, especially regarding detailed and complex financial regulation. It would, however, be detrimental to the EU if such a process were to lack transparency or the scrutiny of the European Parliament.

All in all, this Communication was important because it recognized the need for speed (of legislation). It was also the prelude to the Financial Services Action Plan.

The financial services action plan[3]

The Framework for Action Communication was followed by the Financial Services Action Plan that sets out a clear timetable (1999–2004) for action towards creating a Single Market for financial services, by prioritizing various regulatory issues. Along with the several new legislative and policy initiatives, this work programme will take at least the full present European Commission and European Parliament terms to complete; that is, from 1999 to 2004.

In the Action Plan, again, the main message is the recognition that the full benefits of the euro will not be realized for Europe's consumers and businesses unless the Single Market in financial services is completed. To this end, the remaining obstacles should be removed. What distinguishes the Action Plan from previous policy papers is the recognition of the work still to be done to allow consumers and industry throughout Europe to really enjoy the benefits of the euro. The inclusion of priorities and timeframes, some of them with a relatively short horizon, makes it possible to monitor the progress made. For the banking industry this is a unique opportunity to work together with the European Commission and to take part in the shaping of a truly European market for financial services.

The Action Plan measures are divided into three main sections as follows:

1. **Wholesale Financial Markets** (inter-professional services and services for institutional clients and corporations). An integrated pan-European wholesale financial services market is needed to ensure that EU businesses

get the capital financing to provide an engine for job growth. The measures in the sector include, among others:

- Removal of outstanding barriers to raising capital on an EU-wide basis: an effective European passport for prospectuses, in the event of an initial public offering (IPO);
- Upgrading the legal architecture for the securities and derivatives markets, European passport and 'country of origin' for investment services and definition of professional investor in order to establish different graduated rules depending on the type of the client;
- Allowing the effective use of cross-border collateral.

2. **Retail Financial Markets** (services for consumers). Consumers wishing to shop around for basic financial services, particularly with the spread of electronic commerce and other methods of distance selling, are likely to be frustrated by an array of legal, administrative and private law obstacles. The Action Plan addresses a number of these obstacles:

- Promotion of enhanced information, transparency and security to the consumer wanting to purchase cross-border retail financial services (e-commerce and proposed Distance Selling for Financial Services Directives);
- The creation of an EU-wide system for the resolution of consumer disputes (FIN-NET[4]).

3. **Prudential Rules and Supervision**. In the light of the increased cross-border financial activity and to keep pace with changing market realities national supervisors (National banks and securities supervisors) need to adapt the way they supervise while at the same time being able to guarantee a stable a safe framework for financial services. The Action Plan sets out the following measures:

- Update prudential legislation up to the highest standards, building on the work of the Basle Committee on capital requirements for financial institutions;
- Proposal for a directive on the prudential supervision of financial conglomerates.

The forum groups

An essential tool for carrying out the 'Action Plan' objectives has been the creation by the Commission of the so-called 'Forum Groups', comprised of industry experts. With the Forum Groups the Commission wanted to consult on technical issues with both financial service providers and consumers of financial services.

The original five Forum Groups which held their deliberations from late 1999 to the first half of 2000 addressed: Upgrading the Investment Services

Directive; Market Manipulation; Collateral; Consumer information; and (Retail) Market obstacles.

Although without any official status and just serving as a sounding board for the Commission, the forum groups proved to be the first opportunity for the ABN AMRO EU Liaison Office to pursue its strategy of contributing and supporting the Commission. ABN AMRO managed to get experts nominated in four of the five initial forum groups. We believe this relatively high participation was an excellent result as nomination ran through the European and national federations. Looking back at the results of the first five forum groups it is clear that the success was mixed. We concluded that the forum groups only work if they tackle a well-defined issue of a highly technical nature that has little political controversy. Only in this way will the experts be able to contribute their expertise without trailing or getting tangled in a political web. With this in mind, ABN AMRO set out to lobby for the installation of a new forum group which is the subject of one of our case studies.

Players and coalitions, an overview of the lobbying arena

Traditionally the financial services industry was, with a few exceptions, a relatively domestically-oriented industry, closely linked to the national governments and, of course, a sector that is heavily regulated. 'Lobbying' was a word that did not appear naturally in most bankers' vocabulary. In this world, only 15 to 20 years ago, the national federations represented the sector and the accumulated view was presented to the European institutions by the European federations: for commercial banks (Banking Federation of the EU, FBE[5]), savings banks (the European Savings Bank Group), and co-operative banks (European Association of Cooperative Banks). This was a very formal situation that worked well when the pace of integration in Europe was slightly more relaxed and the environment less competitive. All this has changed today. Domestic mergers in the late 1980s and early 1990s created a number of large banks in Europe (including ABN AMRO, the result of a merger in 1991). In the 1990s these banks became more and more ambitious to set up operations outside and throughout Europe. At this same time these large banks started to realize the direct impact European legislation had on their business. Today most of the large banks in Europe are represented, either by an office in Brussels or by a specialized department.

North American Banks are also very active in Brussels although, as most American corporations, they let their views be heard through European associations and the American Chamber of Commerce, which has an active financial services working group.

At Council level, the main stakeholder are the Finance Ministries represented at the ECOFIN Council and the respective council working groups. It is essential for any successful lobbying to have a continuous relationship with the Financial Attachés of the Permanent Representations of the Member States, which are participating in the Council working groups and will be preparing the different COREPER and ECOFIN meetings. Contacts with Economic Affairs and Justice Ministries are also important for e-commerce-related aspects.

At the level of the Commission, the main player is DG Internal Market, in particular two Directorates, Financial Markets and Financial Institutions. Interactions with DG Consumer Protection are also relevant for retail financial services.

In the financial services arena, as with the telecommunications sector, lobbying with national regulators is essential. The picture is quite complex since except for some countries like the UK, banking, insurance and securities products are supervised by different regulators. At the European level, the national securities regulators of the EEA have formed a European group, Forum of European Securities Commissions (FESCO[6]) to intensify cooperation and respond to the challenges of creating the European single market in financial services. FESCO is playing a crucial role in shaping the EU regulatory landscape for securities regulation by consulting with industry and issuing recommendations for legislation.

Within the European Parliament, the powerful Economic and Monetary Affairs Committee is responsible for the drafting of the European Parliament's Opinion on financial services legislation. This Committee, composed of 45 members, has several extremely active and interested members in financial services developments, from all nationalities. In order to stimulate interest in financial services, ABN AMRO Bank set up in 1998 an informal parliamentary Intergroup which meets monthly to discuss developments and regulatory proposals. This informal Intergroup is composed of several MEPs and several banks and financial services associations. Meetings are public and the Commission, Financial Attachés and consumer groups, where relevant, participate in the discussions.

For retail financial services, relationships with the Bureau Européen des Unions de Consommateurs (BEUC), the main European consumer group, are also essential. The cooperation of financial services institutions with consumer groups has not always been easy, but in March 2001, after years of negotiation, a European Code on information for mortgage loans was agreed among the mortgage-lending industry and consumer groups. This is a good example of cooperation among main stakeholders in the financial services arena.

Two case studies: lobbying for forum group '6' and defining europe's 'professional' investors

Having explained the main thrust of the lobbying activities in the financial services sector and the different stakeholders in the paragraphs above, we would like to illustrate current developments by giving two examples.

Forum group '6'

We have already described the set-up of the forum groups of market experts as a consultative group to the Commission after the Financial Services

Action Plan had been adopted. We concluded that the forum groups only work if they tackle a well-defined issue of a highly technical nature with little political controversy. ABN AMRO believed it had the right issue for a new forum group. The question of course was how to convince the Commission and the European federations of the need for its creation.

The bank's customers include many multinational corporations, and accommodate their demands in the euro zone the bank was developing cash management products. Cash-pooling is one of the classic products used in cash management set-ups, in order to enable a company to earn, or avoid, interest on a total balance of multiple accounts. Within national borders it is a well-established instrument. Cross-border cash-pooling would enable a customer to receive interest payments on the combined balance of their current accounts in different EU countries. A wider use of cross-border cash-pooling, for instance, would lead to a much more efficient asset use by European companies, and thus, lead to lower costs and higher competitiveness. For us it was clear that our multinational clients simply demanded that these cash management structures were set up. It would be logical to assume that within the Euro area, this would be easy to achieve across borders. However, this is not the case. There are still numerous legal, regulatory and fiscal barriers which will either make this an impossibility or a very difficult task.

At present there is an absence of common reporting requirements between the central banks of the Member States. This makes the offset of any notionally pooled amounts in different countries against a bank's consolidated balance sheets costly in case of overlap or duplication. Rules relating to the revocation of transfer orders, as well as the formal steps (if any) which might prevent this, differ from country to country. There are different rules relating to the payment of stamp duties in connection with these arrangements; these rules govern the circumstances, calculation, liabilities and consequences of non-payment of duty. Laws relating to the operation of bank accounts also differ between the Member States. There are vast differences in the operation of bank accounts with regards to the opening documents, the treatment of residents and non-residents, different interpretation of the EU money laundering requirements.

From the above description it would seem a typical and interesting topic for a Forum Group. Fairly technical and not very politically sensitive. We started our lobbying exercise by gaining the support of our national industry and the Dutch Ministry of Finance. We wrote a high level letter explaining the problems to our colleagues in the Dutch banking industry. Furthermore we wrote to the Dutch Ministry of Finance gaining their support. We also wrote to the Director of the Dutch Banking Association (NVB). The support of the Dutch association was instrumental for ensuring support of the FBE. These letters were followed up by presentations from experts to explain further the problem. The Dutch industry including the Dutch Banking Association supported the case.

The next step was to convince the European industry and the FBE. The support of the FBE was crucial since the Commission had been very formal in their approach to the Forum Groups: all formal communication had to run via the European federations and we believed only a request from the FBE would eventually lead to the installation of Forum Group '6'.

After several meetings and contacts with other European banks, the FBE requested the set up of this new forum group to the Director General of DG MARKT. At the same time, we had raised this problem with the European Parliament in their discussions on their Opinion on the Financial Services Action Plan. An amendment highlighting this problem and requesting the Commission to act was introduced in the final Opinion of the European Parliament on the Action Plan. This obviously helped to get the Commission's support. The Commission finally agreed on the necessity to look into these matters and installed a sixth forum group in June 2000.

We were successful in convincing the European Commission to install a forum group to look into the problems of our multinational clients. However, we will only be able to measure our full success once specific measures to enable efficient cross-border cash management are taken by the Commission.

Defining a 'professional' investor

Another challenging experience of our office has been to try to amend a definition already agreed by FESCO, the Forum of European Securities Regulators. In the framework of the provision of cross-border investment services – for example selling and buying securities – under the 1993 Investment Services Directive a provision was made as to the need for the member states to take into account the experience of the investor in implementing the Directive. Few countries had, however, taken into account the need to distinguish between pure consumer investors and other investors, such as banks, corporations or pension funds. This had led to a burdensome situation where relationships between investment firms and, for example, corporations were regulated as if they were relationships with consumers. Therefore, the transaction was overprotected.

FESCO, aware of these problems, had decided to issue their own definition of professional investor and to commit to try to implement this type of classification of investors at the national level. The problem was that FESCO had got the classification wrong. In short, FESCO had considered that even large multinationals should be considered as retail investors unless they would request not to be treated as professionals. Our office decided that the best way forward to convince FESCO to change its definition would be to propose an alternative. Most of the comments to FESCO from other active lobbying organizations such as ISDA and LIBA had concentrated on providing very sensitive and detailed comments to the definition, but they had not proposed an alternative classification.

In order to prepare our classification, we set up a working group within ABN AMRO including colleagues from the Legal Department, Compliance and different business units including Equities and Asset Management. We managed to agree internally in a couple of months on a detailed classification that we presented to the Commission and to FESCO. The challenge was now not only to convince FESCO to change its classification in the way worked out by ABN AMRO, but also to persuade other banks and associations to accept our proposal. Only by pressure from a broad alliance could FESCO be convinced that their agreement needed to be withdrawn.

Our proposal was therefore presented to ISDA, LIBA and the FBE as associations active in the field of investment services and to our colleagues in other European banks. We have to admit that the task had become more difficult than anticipated. Even if our proposal had tried to incorporate business practices of the main financial trading centres, not everybody was obviously in agreement with every single detail. But at the same time, for some of the associations consulted, it was also difficult to come up with specific alternatives.

Even if our primary goal was to obtain broad support of our alternative, even in an amended version, from associations, time was running fast and further pressure on FESCO was needed. We therefore decided to engage, parallel to our discussions with associations, in negotiations with other European banks where decisions could be made in a speedier way. If we managed to convince leading European banks to sign a joint paper with an alternative classification of investors, it would become easier to get agreement from associations.

The process to get agreement from the other European banks was not as quick as anticipated mainly because it was the first time that a paper with such detail was presented for joint signature. Other lobbying exercises that our office had undertaken involved letters to finance ministers on high level principles on the need to accelerate the creation of a Single Market for financial services. Signing a paper with a great level of detail, that could be accepted by FESCO and the European Commission, meant that each bank had to consult internally with different business units to anticipate whether the bank could work under the terms proposed. It also meant that the paper had to reflect not only different businesses' cultures, but also different investment services regulatory regimes.

In July 2001, eight leading European banks agreed a joint paper proposing to FESCO and to the European Commission an alternative classification. The classification presented in the joint paper was obviously not exactly the same as that originally prepared by ABN AMRO, since it reflected practices and regulatory differences from eight countries. However, our original classification could be easily accommodated in this joint proposal.

At the same time, the FBE had successfully convinced all its national associations of the merits of proposing an alternative definition of professional investor and was discussing in detail our joint paper. The FBE finally agreed to send the joint proposal, agreed by eight leading banks and its national associations, to the European Commission and to FESCO in July 2001. A partial victory had been achieved, the banking industry in Europe had managed to get an agreement on a detailed definition of professional investor. It will be difficult for the Commission and FESCO not to take due consideration of this agreement.

This cooperation had taken more than three months but it is a good example of the essential features of any successful lobbying effort: the need to build a broad consensus, continuous dialogue, understanding and accommodating each other's proposals and a lot of patience. At the time of writing, we know already that our efforts have been at least partially successful. We understand that the Commission has agreed that at least large corporations should be considered as professionals. FESCO seems also to have made some concessions in this direction. Only after an amended ISD Directive, in a couple of years, is finally adopted will we be able to evaluate how our initial efforts have been compensated.

Conclusion

New challenging experiences are about to start in the EU financial services decision-making process. On 17 June 2000, the Council of Ministers of Finance assigned a group of Wise Men, headed by Baron Alexandre Lamfalussy, to examine the lack of integration of European securities markets and to suggest improvements to the legislative framework. The final report of this group came out in February 2001. The basic idea is to speed up securities legislation and to make it more open, transparent and efficient. Achieving these objectives involves the creation of two separate committees, a Securities Committee composed of member states' representatives and a Committee of Securities Regulators (basically mirroring FESCO). While proposals for Directives in the field of securities legislation will be subject to the normal co-decision procedure, the content of Directives will be limited to main political decisions and the necessary technical measures will be adopted by the Securities Committee (comitology). This type of second-level legislation will be initiated by an advice to the Commission from the Committee of Securities Regulators that will have consulted extensively with industry.

Baron Lamfalussy's fresh ideas on speeding up the EU legislation process in the securities markets and making it more transparent and open should have, without doubt, fruitful results if all stakeholders in Europe are really committed to creating a Single Market for financial services. This in turn creates an essential need to adapt lobbying traditions in the financial services arena.

Internal consultation processes within our bank will need to be speedier and technical expertise will be needed more than ever. It is expected that implementing legislation by the Securities Committee will be enacted three months after a Directive has been passed. This means that as lobbyists our office will need to adapt to these new deadlines. At the same time, contacts at national level on a technical basis will need to be improved. Our office is already designing a detailed plan of action within the Bank to identify more business experts who will be committed to provide speedy expertise input at any stage of the EU decision-making process for the forthcoming review of the Investment Services Directive, a major piece of legislation which should considerably improve the way capital markets are regulated. At the same time, we are enhancing all our national contacts to ensure that we have efficient access to information on developments in the future Securities Committee.

A new dimension has also been introduced by officially incorporating national regulators in the form of the CESR in the EU decision-making process. It will therefore also be necessary to enhance the relationships with securities regulators not only at the European level but also at the national level in our main markets.

The Electronic Commerce Directive has also given new impetus to the integration of financial markets. The application of the country-of-origin principle of this Directive to financial services legislation has created the need to establish a clear plan – Communication on Electronic Commerce and Financial Services – for dismantling remaining obstacles in order to create a level playing field for offline services. This has added an extra timing pressure for harmonization of conditions at the national level. FESCO has taken this challenge with an extensive consultation with interested parties on harmonization of rules in relation to the provision of investment services to professional and non-professional investors.

In the coming three years our EU Liaison Office has an extremely challenging role to play in the shaping of the final design of the truly Internal Market for financial services. Our results so far have been satisfactory since we have successfully managed to assist in the creation of the necessary conditions (speedier, transparent and open legislative process and full application of the country-of-origin principle) for an Internal Market for financial services. However, legislation has still to be passed and agreed among the different EU Institutions and results, as always in lobbying, can never be 100% guaranteed.

Notes

1. COM (1998) 625, 28 October 1998. <www.europa.eu.int/comm/internal_market/en/finances/actionplan/index.htm>
2. <www.europa.eu.int/comm/internal_market/en/finances/general/lamfalussy.htm>
3. COM (1999), 232, 11 May 1999.
4. <www.europa.eu.int/comm/internal_market/en/finances/consumer/adr.htm>
5. <www.fbe.be>
6. <www.europefesco.org>

13
Electricity Liberalization

Justin Greenwood

Electricity was an obvious candidate in the renewed drive to complete a European Single Market in the Delors years. Despite the energy sector being the first candidate for European integration in 1951, electricity consumption remained, in the mid-1980s, tied to a regional monopoly supplier, resulting in the opinion of the Commission in inflated prices and a lack of innovation. As a key factor in production costs in manufacturing industry, and a contributory factor to every household bill, the electricity supply industry, wholly untouched by market logic, presented a ripe apple for a (then) confident European Commission keen to progress the frontiers of project Europe, and to demonstrate tangible results in European integration by the promise of lower prices arising from the introduction of competition.

Today, less than 13 years since the Commission started the ball of electricity liberalization rolling, a considerable degree of the European electricity supply industry is subject to competition, resulting in some degree of price reduction for consumers, with the prospect of complete market opening within the next five years. All of this has come about despite the opposition, at the outset at least, of most member states, and some of the largest producer organizations in Europe. How can this stark outcome be explained? What role did producer, consumer and public interests play in this outcome, and which factors explain this pattern? What lessons can be learnt about the role of private interests in European integration from this case?

The first part of the story of electricity liberalization, accounting for events up to a 1996 Directive leading to partial market opening, has been extensively undertaken elsewhere (Conant, 1999; Eberlein, 2000; Eising, 1999; Eising and Jabko, 1999; Schmidt, 1997, 1998), and is summarized in the section that follows. Some of the analysis is, however, contestable, and here some rival explanations are offered. Some analysis is also provided of events up to a second Directive, in draft form in January 2001, for acceleration of the process of liberalization providing a quicker route to full market opening than the 1996 Directive had envisaged. The second question – the role of producer, consumer and public interests in EU electricity liberalization – has never been comprehensively undertaken, despite the presence of some partial accounts included within analysis of a number of sectors (Bartle, 1999; Sietses, 2000). The third endeavour, the generalizability requirement of any case study, leads to analysis of the circumstances under which private interests are not in the forefront of European integration in particular policy sectors. This latter task remains under-theorized (Grande, 1996), notwithstanding well-recognized foci in the established 'interest-group' literature upon private interest division and disorganization. Despite the recent explosion of institutional analysis in political science, relatively little of this has been directed at understanding the conditions under which political institutions remain relatively insulated from private and public interest pressures.

The story of electricity liberalization

Ironically, one of the triggers to EU electricity liberalization was initiated by the organization which has since been the largest obstacle to it – Electricité de France (EdF), responsible for 95 per cent of French electricity generation and distribution, and virtually all the transmission grid (Klom, 1997). EdF's production capacity of electricity is around 250 per cent that of its nearest counterpart in another member state (Electrabel, 1999), and in 1994 was the largest exporter of electricity in Europe (Klom, 1997). Initially (1986–88), it saw the single European market as an opportunity to intensify existing systems of inter-utility cooperation (Bartle, 2001) to use its excess capacity to export to other markets in Europe. Alongside this, it filed a state-aid complaint with the Commission against the German Government subsidization of its coal industry (Schmidt, 1998). It had also been frustrated by Spain's refusal to allow it to use the Spanish grid to transport excess capacity in response to the request of a Portuguese consumer, which had been a contributory factor to a Council resolution of 1986 calling the Commission to action (Eising and Jabko, 1999). Later, EdF had cause to regret that its actions helped open the Pandora's box of electricity liberalization, and by 1989 it had come to appreciate the threat to its position that requirements to liberalize its home market might bring.

It would, however, be mistaken to see EdF as the principal trigger to EU electricity liberalization. The industry was always a likely candidate for liberalization, and the main thrust was provided by the broader climate of Single Market completion generated by the Delors years, and a Commission on the march. The window of opportunity was widened by the UK experiment in privatization, which was about to demonstrate (1989) the feasibility of devising a system of competition whilst still using a single transmission infrastructure. That is, the activities involved in delivering electricity to the factory or domestic doorstep could be segregated into the activities of generation, transmission to major centres for subsequent distribution, and traded supply to individual points of consumption. The combination of ideas, circumstances, bandwagon, and policy entrepreneur selling a solution, foretold by Kingdon's insightful analysis of the creation of policy agendas, was there. A potential support constituency interested in cheaper electricity prices could be mobilized. With a choice of legislative instruments to achieve its goal, the prospects seemed good. Based on resolutions dating from the Energy Council in 1986 and 1987 (EURELECTRIC and Lyons, 2000), the Commission issued its consultative Green Paper in 1988 with substantive plans to liberalize the sector (Commission, 1998), followed by separate, first-step Directives in 1990 on transit (90/547/EEC) and an uncontroversial set of measures on price transparency (91/296/EEC).

The Commission initially favoured use of an Article 90 procedure to achieve liberalization, granting it the independent competence to address directives to member states in order to ensure application of the Treaty rules for European competition law to state enterprises. This controversial procedure had already been used in another public-sector monopoly area, telecommunications, with some success in the form of a 1988 Directive. When Article 90 was proposed as the preferred instrument in conjunction with infringement procedures under competition law, a bullish path to liberalization seemed possible, and until the Autumn of 1991 was the chosen path of the Commission. In July 1991, the Commission circulated a draft Article 90 Directive, and initiated infringement procedures against import and export monopolies in electricity in nine member states (Conant, 1999). Yet by October 1991, the Commission had decided to abandon its use of an Article 90 Directive in favour of a more consensual approach, an Article 100a Directive (published in 1992) requiring a qualified majority and enabling the input of the Parliament with its newly-strengthened powers under co-decision. In fact, so contentious was the concept of liberalization in electricity proving that it required *de facto* unanimity in the Council, in that a Franco-German summit on the matter, with longer-term considerations for their relationship in mind, had ended with agreement not to leave each other isolated on the matter. The path was set for a highly compromised directive with somewhat watered down proposals for liberalization.

The opposition to the liberalization proposals was mainly member state-led. At the outset, only the UK (in the process of delivering its own liberalization), Ireland (with liberalization under consideration, although later to switch sides) and Portugal (with inadequate production capacity) supported it among the then member states. A number were implacably opposed, including France, and at the outset Germany. With these most basic of calculations, the Commission would have been unwise to press ahead with an Article 90 Directive. This opposition was also expressed in debates and public hearings in the European Parliament, and in the decision of national electricity utilities to establish a European-wide trade association, EURELECTRIC, to oppose the initiatives – although the ability of the latter to do so effectively would always be restrained by differing views.

Certainly, the Commission would have needed more time and nerve to press ahead with the use of Article 90 in 1991. Whilst the government of the Netherlands was soon to join the coalition in favour, it was not until the German presidency of 1995 that the German position had switched to being fully supportive of electricity liberalization, following incremental adjustment from 1993. Undoubtedly, Germany's conversion proved a major landmark in finally delivering liberalization, and has been explained by Eising and Jakbo (1999) as a gradual switch based on 'policy learning' by the German government, both from the UK experience and from acclimatization to the liberalization proposals within the Council of Ministers. Commission activism, the inevitability that some kind of agreement was likely to emerge, and some wish for damage limitation as to the type of liberalization scheme that might emerge may also have been a factor in acclimatization (Bartle, 2001). However, these considerations may underplay the role of other factors in the German *volte-face* to support EU electricity liberalization. Most of the German utilities had converted to the idea by 1994 (*ibid.*), while for German industrial consumer interests electricity prices were at that time the highest in Europe, and 50 per cent higher than those in the USA (*Financial Times*, 1996). As is evident later, most of the firms active in pursuing electricity liberalization at the EU level in the 'ENERG8' coalition were German. Of all countries, German industry has also been among the loudest voices seeking, recently, an accelerated programme of liberalization.

Just as crucial to the final achievement of a Directive was the final decision of the French to compromise. The 1992 draft Directive was a direct threat to the French public service tradition, causing a strike amongst EdF workers in 1992 organized by the Communist CGT (Confédération Général du Travail) Union. Three years later, a wave of more strikes among public-sector workers in general about issues of public-sector job security crippled the French economy. Whilst the use of an Article 100a procedure only required a qualified majority, there was never a question of a vote being used because the basic principle of vital national interest was at stake (EURELECTRIC and Lyons, 2000). In this context, the French willingness to compromise seems remarkable. The EU Electricity Liberalization Directive (96/92/EC) finally approved at the end of 1996 took intensive efforts from four presidencies involving significant compromises and trading of drafts, a Franco-German intergovernmental summit, and some fast footwork from the Commission to achieve. Among the latter, one strategy involved the maintenance of pressure by the use of infringement proceedings, leading to French fears of an outcome from European Court of Justice decisions (expected in 1998) which might be worse than a liberalization Directive. In short, French interests faced the classic dilemma of whether they would be better off on the inside trying to limit the damage, or outright opposition. They chose the former strategy.

Whilst French anxieties over ECJ decisions had been partly relieved by some surprisingly favourable 1994 decisions (the Corbeau and Almelo cases;

see Conant, 1999), some senior French civil servants were already finding the progressive loss of support (particularly Germany) in the Council uncomfortable, and had started to seek a solution. Almost as an exercise in damage limitation, France proposed an alternative ('Single Buyer' model, below) to the model proposed in the Commission's draft Directive, under the rhetoric of 'liberalization', yet in reality aimed at watering it down as much as possible. The Commission's skill in adapting and extending this to include it within the embrace of a compromise redrafted Directive helped achieve the outcome they wanted, not least because the Commission were also uncertain of where future ECJ decisions would leave the project.

The Commission also showed itself adept at responding to the concerns of the Parliament and environmental NGOs by changing the detail of those proposals which could be conceded without too much difficulty, and to trade unions by rhetoric to take initiatives to mitigate the effects on employ-ment of liberalization. These factors apart, a number of other events proved favourable to the Commission's cause, including the accession of Sweden and Finland, both enthusiastic to the electricity liberalization dossier, and the increasing warmth of Spain and Italy to the idea.

The initial 1992 draft Directive had proposed a system of 'regulated third-party access' (rTPA) as a key mechanism to achieve competition in electricity supply. This was part of a broader set of principles involving the separation of the process of electricity supply into generation, transmission, distribution and supply to the consumer using principles first adopted in the UK. Third-party access (TPA) involves the ability of the user to choose the supplier, while any supplier has a right of access to the grid at a regulated, or negotiated, tariff (Bartle, 2001). It is the quickest route to liberalization, because it does not require new market entrants to make long-term investments in capital-intensive equipment, such as generating stations or transmission wires/pylons. Indeed, until now electricity liberalization has left alone the monopoly positions of the national grid transmission networks, while in theory allow-ing complete competition in generation without expecting this to yield significant new market entrants as a result of the capital-intensive nature involved in market entry.

The solution to France's dilemma (outright opposition, or damage limita-tion on the inside) was to propose a rival system, the 'Single-Buyer' model, on which a very limited model of liberalization could be based. In this, the gen-erator/producer (such as EdF) could also act as the 'buyer' of all the electricity purchased by its consumers from other sources, using published tariffs, with the purchaser pocketing any profit between the price it paid to source the electricity, and the sell-on price to the single buyer. The initial version of this was sent for scrutiny by the Commission to an independent team of analysts in Germany, who concluded that whilst the initial proposal was inconsistent with internal market rules, it could be adapted to be consistent and for use in the Directive. Once the model had been proposed as a route to liberalization,

France could hardly revert to outright opposition, and the adapted version was used as a compromise. Hence, the final 1996 Directive enabled member states to choose between regulatory schemes – a negotiated third-party access (nTPA) system favoured by Germany and the European Parliament, a regulated third-party access favoured by other countries supportive of liberalization, and a single-buyer model then favoured by France and allied countries with liberalization concerns (Greece; Belgium). The menu of choice was extended by enabling member states to choose between a system of legal, management or accountancy separation of generation, transmission, distribution and supply systems. A further important feature was that the Directive was based upon an incremental system of market opening, starting with a requirement to subject 25 per cent of electricity demand to competition from the time the Directive came into force in February 1999 (Belgium and Ireland were given one-year extensions, Greece two), to 33 per cent by 2003. Consistent with the menu-choice nature of the Directive, those member states who wished to open their markets further were free to do so at any time.

In practice, by the time the Directive came into force, most of northern Europe had already fully opened up their electricity markets to competition, while some others (most notably Spain) have exceeded the requirements laid out by the 1996 Directive. The single-buyer model, designed to forestall liberalization, was eroding into disuse everywhere including its country of origin, France (Commission, 2000). Most countries have made the choice, from the menu available in the 1996 Directive, of the scheme most consistent with liberalization; that is, regulated third-party access together with a licensing procedure for generation, and most countries had liberalized at a faster pace than the Directive timescale. Market forces have matured, with most of the UK regional electricity companies by now bought up by American firms. American firms such as Enron have become aggressive market entrants to electricity trading, and very active at the European level in pursuing further liberalization. Spanish utilities have enthusiastically sought opportunities to raid capacities in the French market, while the once-reluctant Belgians did not use the full extension they were given to put the Directive into effect. Some of the original reluctants in the south of Europe have identified electricity liberalization as a means of pursuing lower inflation targets, and in gaining access to the grid for renewable sources. There are even stories circulating that the top executives of EdF, whilst avoiding public differences from their government, are now looking forward to some of the opportunities liberalization brings.

The principle of liberalization had clearly been conceded, the liberalizing tide had turned, and European industry had started to reap the benefits of some reduction in electricity prices. As the Commission had correctly predicted at the conclusion of the 1996 Directive, 'this deal partially opens the door. We hope the partially opened door will be kicked open by market forces' (*Financial Times*, 1996, p. 23). Electricity prices did fall in response to liberalization, and more so in those countries opting for complete market opening

(Commission, 2000). At a time when electricity consumption is forecast to increase by 40 per cent over the next 20 years (Matthes and Timpe, 2000), there seemed no turning back, and the logical thing to do was to extend the benefits to all Europe's consumers, domestic and industrial. Whilst pressures for more liberalization emerged from national governments, customers and electricity companies, it is the European Commission that has taken the driving seat, with President Prodi proposing to the March 2000 Lisbon summit that a new programme should be put in place which would produce 100 per cent liberalization by 2004. Whilst this was not adopted, it was decided that an acceleration of liberalization should be launched so as to create a fully operational internal energy market, and that the Commission should bring forward proposals to accelerate liberalization. At the public hearings on the detail of the new Directive, hosted in September 2000 by DG TREN (Transport and Energy) of the European Commission, EdF opposition to the pace and quantity of liberalization was somewhat isolated. Indeed, such has been the pace and momentum of liberalization that the French position has shifted to supporting the rhetoric of liberalization but opposing the detail.

Electricity liberalization: the role of producer and public interests

The story told above indicates the role of producer interests in informing the positions of national governments in preference formation, and the subsequent transfer of these to intergovernmental negotiations. German industrial consumers of electricity, subject to the highest prices in Europe, played some role in turning the position of their government towards electricity liberalization to a favourable one. The actions of the French government, on the other hand, were largely explicable by reference to their position as owner-shareholder of Electricité de France. But what of the role of producer, and other types of interests, organized at the European level?

Given the somewhat patchy coverage of this question in public literature, additional methods used in answering this question range from 'grey' literature available from a range of interest organizations, to the use of focused, semi-structured interviews. Where an assessment has been made of the impact of any one type of interest or organization, each assessment has involved conducting interviews with multiple sources. These span the producer industry, consumer industrial interests, public interest groups, and policy officials, as well as sources from the literature in conjunction with established tools of analysis. In total, some 18 interviews were conducted in this way, supported by wide distribution of draft text.

European-level organized interests have not been decisive to any of the outcomes described above. Taken together, differences among key producer utilities mean they have played a reactive role, following rather than driving agreements reached in the political institutions. EURELECTRIC had been formed to oppose the proposals for liberalization, and did so consistently until 1995, including a somewhat aggressively hostile approach in the early 1990s. This approach yielded changes to details, but not to the core principle of liberalization. The electricity supply industry, through EURELECTRIC and its regular dialogue with the Commission, had managed to tone down some of the more radical ambitions of the Commission in 1991, and had a major input into an influential European Parliament Opinion of November 1993, which prompted the Commission to publish revised proposals including, *inter alia*, the introduction of the concept of negotiated third-party access (EURELECTRIC and Lyons, 2000). A key turning point in the approach of EURELECTRIC towards liberalization was the accession of Scandinavian members into full membership in 1995, which changed the balance of internal opinion, causing the organization to publicly admit that different views existed within its membership on the internal electricity market debate (*ibid.*). EURELECTRIC's most positive role was finally to support the final draft of the Commission's 1996 Directive, and to call upon the Parliament (whose Energy Committee had been seeking to use its new co-decision powers to issue amendments) and Council to do so without amendment. Indeed, this was the outcome. EURELECTRIC's role in the years following the Directive shifted to one of behind-the-scenes technical cooperation with the Commission (including a move from Paris to Brussels), whilst the electricity supply industry in national contexts focused attention to the requirements for transposing the Directive. It is presently seeking to adopt a position on accelerated liberalization, although the realities of member differences, centred around EdF, mean that it is difficult for it to do so in detail, other than a position that it 'firmly believes that it is realistic to aim for a faster opening of the market' (EURELECTRIC and Lyons, 2000, p. 98).

European-level trade unions, whilst active throughout the debate in opposing liberalization on the grounds of its anticipated impact on employment, had little to fight with and seemingly no impact upon the outcome. Public interest groups, including consumers (with interests in lower electricity prices) and environmental NGOs, have supported the historic process to differing degrees, and both sets of interests broadly support the acceleration of liberalization, with some significant derogation of detail. Public consumer groups wanted the benefits to be delivered to domestic consumers much quicker than the 1996 Directive envisaged, though concerns about the universality, quality and safety could at that stage be reassured (BEUC, 1994, 1995a, b, c, 1996). For some environmental public interest groups, liberalization offered the prospect of more environmentally-friendly forms of generation, such as natural gas instead of coal and nuclear, as a result of pressures for cheaper and more energy-efficient forms of generation. In this, they found allies in a growing though still small segment of the producer sector, where recent technologies enable the production of combined heat and power simultaneously (co-generation), often using gas, resulting in a new sector association (Cogen Europe) representing equipment manufacturers and industrial users. The Commission has been receptive to these inputs, though not to the extent that environmental NGOs, and Cogen Europe would have wished. Other environmental groups, such as Greenpeace, have been more critical, drawing attention to the way in which electricity liberalization produces certain trends detrimental to the environment, such as increased consumption arising from downward pressure on costs (Greenpeace, 2000).

Environmental public-interest groups may have influenced some of the detail accompanying the debate (Table 13.1, below), sometimes through separate policy initiatives (such as transparency pricing to prevent hidden subsidies, or the present Renewables Directive), though these have not been central in delivering the outcome of liberalization. A recent report for the WorldWide Fund for Nature concluded that 'it can be expected that environmental considerations will play only a minor role in the [acceleration] process' (Matthes and Timpe, 2000, p. 8). Whilst EU environmental lobbies

Table 13.1   EU-level producer associations and collective fora

Organization	Description	Historic relationship to liberalization (+, −, active?)
EURELECTRIC – Union of the Electricity Industry	Members (national associations, or where absent, utilities) involved with the generation, transmission, distribution, and supply of electricity	Originally established to oppose liberalization, and did so through its continental members until mid-1990s. In regular dialogue with Commission throughout liberalization process. Now reflects the 1996 Directive position, and the activities and different views of internal active members (see below). Well-connected and involved with Commission, highly involved at a technical level, and acts to the limits of its member architecture. Presently working on a position on the extent and speed of liberalization (EURELECTRIC and Lyons, 2000), though articulates general support for accelerated liberalization. ECC industry member

Table 13.1 Continued

Organization	Description	Historic relationship to liberalization (+, −, active?)
'Northern Group'	Northern members of EURELECTRIC (minus Ireland), informal grouping, active from c.1995. Core members are, D, SF, NL, S, UK. Dk a background member; I and E late converts	First wave of liberalizers, still active in taking forward liberalization agenda. Now the dominant coalition within EURELECTRIC, the latter's positions are now pro-liberalization in rhetoric, though the detail and ability to be proactive of EURELECTRIC reflects the input of 'Reluctants' below
'Reluctants'	Edf plus Belgian, Irish (changed from pro during very early stages), Greek, Luxembourg members EURELECTRIC, France and Belgium are particularly reliant upon nuclear electricity generation.	Opposed. Original response to liberalization was the single-buyer model. Interests drawn from countries often last to implement directive. As the liberalization agenda has progressed, so the positions of this group have also progressed in public rhetoric – e.g. progression from single-buyer model to regulated TPA, and claims to support accelerated liberalization – though at a slower rate for % and timescale than 'Northern' group. EdF remains well-connected in EU high-politics arenas, and with some shareholdings in privatized companies, the potential (as yet, unrealized) to influence the positions of some actors in the 'pro' camp
European Association for Renewables	Now a grouping *inside* EURELECTRIC, once outside	Active to secure own position issues, e.g. with DG Environment interests on bio fuels, large combustion plant

Table 13.1   Continued

Organization	Description	Historic relationship to liberalization (+, −, active?)
		directive etc. though not a major liberalization player
EFET – Electricity and Gas Traders	Now a grouping established outside EURELECTRIC after a period (of dissatisfaction at their representation) within, though with membership for supply interest purposes. Encouraged by DG (then) XVII. The US firm Enron is a significant member, and voice for liberalization	Created at time of early Florence regulatory conferences, c.1998; *raison d'être* possible as a result of liberalization.
European Heat and Power Association	Overlapping membership with EURELECTRIC, plus municipal members. Formed 1994	Closely aligned with EURELECTRIC, though never anti-liberalization. Enjoys good Commission links. ECC industry member
CEDEC – European Federation of Local Public Energy Distribution Companies	Municipal Members from D, F, I, B, A, claiming a 20% market share of supply. Estab. 1992	Traditional, public-sector view of liberalization where focus is more on threats. Opposed 1992. Still active, broadly opposed, though never central. In 1999, issued a joint statement of opposition with the trade union organization EPSU (see below). Recent position paper (CEDEC, 2000) focuses on damaging employment effects of liberalization, seeking more gradual introduction (i.e. against accelerated liberalization), but to enable local distributors to compete with dominant producers. ECC industry member

Table 13.1   Continued

Organization	Description	Historic relationship to liberalization (+, −, active?)
Energie Cités	Wide network, formed c.1997, based around local and regional authorities in Western, Central and Eastern Europe, and representative organizations. 87 full (Western European) members. Producer (municipality as producer and distributor) and consumer interests	ECC industry member. Not significant in recent liberalization
Cogen Europe – European Association for the Promotion of co-generation	Co- (often, gas) generators & industrial users interested in their own generation needs, and equipment producers. Reflects some recent technological innovations whereby heat and power can be produced simultaneously. Established 1993	Pro-liberalization, and, consistent with its members business interests, promotes energy efficiency measures through co-generation with environmental NGOs such as WWF. ECC industry member
FORATOM – European Atomic Forum	Nuclear industry association. France and Belgium are most reliant on nuclear electricity generation, with 75% and 58% of electricity respectively in these countries generated by nuclear capacities (Matthes and Timpe, 2000)	State ownership meant never in forefront of political activity at any stage, though some large members pro and increasingly active since Directive
IFIEC – International Federation of Industrial Energy Consumers and **IFIEC Europe**	Association of Associations. IFIEC Europe has 13 federations representing 75–80% of industrial energy consumption in Europe – steel & alloys, chemicals, non-ferrous	IFIEC originally contained diverse views on liberalization (French members esp. satisfied with electricity prices), though has generally managed a supportive line. Rated by a number

Table 13.1   Continued

Organization	Description	Historic relationship to liberalization (+, −, active?)
	metals, cement, pulp & paper, food & packaging, automobile etc.	of players as central to the liberalization debate and for the Commission in building a consensus. Noted for delivering well-thought of responses to Commission consultation papers – which have stretched its limited resources. Seeking separation of responsibilities in supply chain (IFIEC Europe, 2000). ECC consumer section member
ENERG8	Formed 1992, partly in response to Commission prompting, though also in response to the difficulties of broad sector associations in reaching common positions. Large-scale user firms – Bayer, BASF, ICI, Dow Europe, Thyssen, Pilkington, DSM*, Akzo Nobel, Mercedes Benz, Ford (associate member)*, Enron*, KNP, BT*. Involves CEOs (* not founding member)	Pro, some impact on original liberalization debate leading to Directive, and on positions of Associations representing these members, e.g. CEFIC, UNICE (though see CEFIC below). Worked closely with 'Northern' group inside EURELECTRIC Inactive as a collective entity now, partly as a response to its growth in diversity, though original members individually remain active
CEFIC – European Chemicals Industry Federation **CEMBUREAU** – European Cement Association **UNICE** – Union of Industrial and Employers' Confederations of Europe **UEAPME** – European Association of Craft, Small and Medium-Sized Enterprises	Traditional EU sector or cross-industry associations	Members of consumer section of ECC. UNICE had no difficulty in being pro-liberalization prior to 1996 Directive as public sector utilities were not in its membership constituency. CEFIC became responsive over time to member demands (e.g. ENERG8 dual members) for liberalization as consumers, with some reports of early collective action

Table 13.1 Continued

Organization	Description	Historic relationship to liberalization (+, −, active?)
and **EUROFER** – European Confederation of Iron and Steel Industries		difficulties in member agreement
EUROPIA – European Petroleum Industry Association	EU downstream petroleum sector association	Member of industry section of ECC. Not historically active or significant in liberalization debate – no public positions
ERT – European Round Table of Industrialists	By invite only, chief executive officers (CEO) of Europe's largest companies; fluctuating over time around 45 members, more of an 'agenda-setting' think tank than an operational lobby organization	Active c.1991–93 in supporting the case for liberalization as part of wider agenda for competitiveness of European industry
EETC – European Energy and Telecom Consulting, and its conference format **EEMF** – European Energy Millennium Forum	Consultant-led forum group of producers formed December 1998. Brussels-based, now operated from offices of public affairs consultancy, Edelman	Pro, though not involved in detail of debate
UCTE, (formerly **UCPTE**) – Union for the Coordination of the Production and Transmission of Electricity	Grid operators formed 1951, then concerned with non-competitive Cross-border continental distribution, focusing Post-liberalization on switching and metering issues of exchange	Originally opposed to liberalization and then aligned with 'reluctants' group position. Not a significant player in political debate on liberalization. ECC industry member
ETSO – European Association of Transmission System Operators	Formed 1999 as a result of the liberalization Directive requirement for the independence of transmission system	Post-liberalization organization which, whilst technical in nature focusing on the regulatory issues of implementation

Table 13.1 Continued

Organization	Description	Historic relationship to liberalization (+, −, active?)
	operators. Network grid company users, whose formation encouraged by Commission. Aimed at solving problems such as congestion management, bottlenecks, transit costing of transmission – i.e. the technical requirements of Single Market creation	of the internl energy market, is company-driven
CIGRE – International Conference on Electrical Cabling	Cables specialist technical organization, with European and non-European members	Not significant in liberalization
CIRED – International Conference on Electricity Distribution	Formed 1971 for information exchange between parties active in electrical distribution, from utilities, low volume transmitters, to electrical engineers – knowledge, technical information, etc.	Not significant in liberalization
EUROGAS – European Union of the Natural Gas Industry	Gas generators. Possible future merger with EURELECTIC into mega energy-wide trade association. Already some overlapping membership, though competitive interests with electricity restrict extent	Broadly pro, though not central in electricity liberalization – mainly focused on gas liberalization, with significant member reservations on upstream gas liberaliza-tion. ECC industry member
EWEA – European Wind Energy Association	Formed 1982, focused on wind renewables	Not central in liberalization
GEODE – European Group of Enterprises and Organizations of Energy Distribution	Barcelona-based. Independent municipal distributors, e.g. Grenoble, Company-based	Very pro, differences in view as to how central a role they have played – well-connected with regulators. ECC industry member

Table 13.1   Continued

Organization	Description	Historic relationship to liberalization (+, −, active?)
Brussels Energy Round Table	Commissioner van Miert creation – network industry club formed c.1995 to assist with support for the liberalization agenda	Created to boost support for liberalization
CEEP – European Centre of Enterprises with Public Participation and of Enterprises of General Economic Interest	Public Sector Employers – though also active on wider public-sector issues	Originally anti-liberalization with employment-related concerns. An avenue for concerns of the 'reluctants' group. Member, consumer section of Energy Consultative Committee
EPSU – European Federation of Public Service Unions **EMCEF** – European Mine, Chemical and Energy Workers' Federation and **ETUC** – European Trade Union Confederation	EU-level trade unions most affected by liberalization	Anti-liberalization, based on concerns about job and membership losses. ESPU organized 'European Action Day' in May 1999 and a large protest demonstration (20 000 energy workers claimed) in Berlin, and issued joint statement of opposition to liberalization with CEDEC. Literature reflects that concerns to mitigate job losses have not been taken into account by any measures in EU legislation despite Commission statement to European Parliament in 1996 for specific measures (EPSU, 1999). EMCEF, EPSU and EURELECTRIC have recently (7 November 2000) concluded a joint declaration on the social implications of the Internal Electricity Market as part of their broader social dialogue,emphasizing consultation, retraining

Table 13.1   Continued

Organization	Description	Historic relationship to liberalization (+, −, active?)
		and structural employment adjustment, information dissemination (EPSU, 2000). Recent activities of trade unions have been based upon achieving such initiatives, and gaining consultative status in regulatory activities. EPSU, EMCEF and ETUC are all represented on the Energy Consultative Committee

benefit from coordination of campaigning (including the 'good-cop/bad-cop' team approach which embraces networks involving Greenpeace and WWF), liberalization in principle and practice can produce tensions within environmental movements. Firstly, in principle activists are not always persuaded by market principles. Secondly, in practice, market-induced downward pressures on costs can have positive environmental effects through the introduction of co-generation, and negative effects through increased consumption. Tensions can also arise in seeking to incorporate arguments that state aid be denied from one sector of industry (such as nuclear and fossil fuel production), and yet be granted to another (renewables), particularly in areas such as energy where there is no Treaty base other than through Internal Market measures.

A somewhat greater role has been played by industrial large-scale electricity consumers, although this should not be exaggerated. Their role has been a supporting one to the Commission, and even had they not been active at the European level, it is hard to imagine a different outcome to the one described above. The two most significant organizations in this limited contribution appear to have been the European section of the International Federation of Industrial Energy Consumers (IFIEC), an association of associations with 13 members representing 75–80 per cent of industrial energy consumption in Europe, and ENERG8, an issue network of large electricity consumption firms. IFIEC is highly regarded by the Commission, and is noted for delivering thoughtful responses to Commission consultation papers. A number of interview informants who have been on the inside of the process from industry have indicated that, of all producer interests, IFIEC played the greatest role. Despite these, there are a number of reasons to proceed with caution. Firstly, its work with the Commission has stretched its somewhat limited resources, and tends to have been reactive rather than proactive in nature. Secondly, some commentators have drawn attention to divisions within IFIEC, themselves not untypical for a federation-of-federations structure (Bartle, 1999; Sietses, 2000). Some of these are centred around French members (*ibid.*), who already benefited from some of the lowest electricity prices in Europe and saw no reason for change. A third factor is what Schmidt refers to as the ability of the industry to 'buy-off' its opposition. Everytime a consumer complained about its inability to access cheaper sources of electricity, industry could make arrangements to match the better bargain the consumer had found, and consequently only a trickle of cases reached the ECJ from producer interests (Schmidt, 1998).

Sietses links the formation of ENERG8 directly to the classic collective action problems of associations, and particularly to those of IFIEC, and to CEFIC, the European Chemical Industry Council (Sietses, 1988). In his analysis, the latter organization reportedly had problems until around 1995 in arriving at common positions because of the interests of oil and gas companies, themselves affected by attempts at gas liberalization, although how the blockage in CEFIC became lifted c.1995 is unclear. The downstream trade association of the oil industry, EUROPIA (European Petrochemicals Industry Association), has never had any position on electricity liberalization, despite its position on the producer section of the EU Energy Consultative Committee (ECC). Sietses also refers to the collective-action difficulties experienced by UNICE (Union of Industrial and Employers' Confederations of Europe), although this may be more a reference to its generally wide constituency and consequent tendency towards lowest-common-denominator positions than to the specific case of electricity liberalization. Its former General Secretary reports no difficulty at all throughout the process of electricity liberalization in UNICE taking a supportive role, because the public-sector monopoly utilities were not in membership of UNICE member organizations prior to the 1996 Directive. Nonetheless, Sietses is dismissive of the role of associations in the debate, and instead builds up a model of company interest representation at the EU level in electricity liberalization, starting with the European Round Table of Industrialists (ERT) c.1991.

Electricity liberalization represented the kind of high politics attractive to the ERT. It commented on the process in a number of reports between 1990–93, including some of its most famous commentaries on the climate for European business (e.g. *Rebuilding Confidence*, ERT, 1992; *Beating the Crisis*, ERT, 1993), pressing the case for liberalization on the basis of price comparisons with the USA. Once the issue had emerged fully onto the European agenda and was clearly heading for action, the ERT, true to its role as a 'big-issue' agenda-setter', withdrew from the issue. Some of its most affected members, as intensive energy users, took the issue on in the form of the ENERG8 coalition, so called because of the number of large firms involved at one time, including Bayer, BASF, ICI, Dow Europe, Thyssen, Pilkington, Akzo Nobel, and Mercedes Benz. Whilst the network followed the ERT format of invited direct membership and chief executive officer (CEO) representation in an attempt to avoid classic collective-action problems, it too became subject to lowest-common-denominator issues when membership grew in number and sectoral diversity. It first met in 1992, largely prompted by the European Commission in need of constituencies of support, who told large industrial consumers that 'no-one whistles your tune in the corridors of the Commission' (Sietses, 2000, p. 77). This helps explain its ability to get high-level access to the Commission, including Presidential level. ENERG8 sought to hasten the adoption of a liberalization Directive, and, once achieved, has withered to inactivity. One reason for exercising caution as to the role of ENERG8 is that a number of key figures in the debate have little recollection as to its role. It was a supporter of the process rather than a leader.

Table 13.1–13.5 provide an assessment of the role of all industrial interests and interest organizations with a role in the liberalization process; that is, private and public (non-state) interests in electricity liberalization.

Table 13.2   Firms very active at the EU level in electricity liberalization

Electricité de France (F)	Active in Brussels c.1989. Most reluctant party throughout, though some claims that there are more liberal pockets within EdF than the present public position of the French govt (see also 'Reluctants/EURELECTRIC' in Table 13.1)
Electrabel (B)	Always Brussels-based. Reluctants group, recently more detached
RWE (D)	Active in Brussels c.1989. Initially reluctant, later pro
Preussen Elektra (D)	Active in Brussels c.1989. Initially reluctant, later pro
Bayernwerke (D)	Active in Brussels c.1989. Initially reluctant, later pro
National Power (UK)	Active in Brussels c.1989. Pro from start
PowerGen (UK)	Active in Brussels c.1989. Pro from start
SydKraft (S)	Active in Brussels c.1989. Pro from start
Vattenfall (S)	Active in Brussels c.1989. Pro from start
Endessa (E)	Recently (c.1998) active in Brussels. Pro
Redelectrica (E)	Recently (c.1998) active in Brussels. Pro
Enron (US)	Electricity trader. Active in Brussels during liberalization. Pro, frustrated with progress of TPA, pursuing published price tariffs agenda
Enel (I)	Recently (c.1998) active in Brussels; positions not always historically clear
SEP (common Dutch generators organization)/TenneT (NL – joint grid ownership by state and largest producers)	Active in Brussels

Table 13.3 National business-interest associations historically very active at the EU level in electricity liberalization

Association of Electricity Producers (UK)	Founded 1997, yet to spread out beyond UK. Pro-liberalization, includes gas generators
Electricity Association (UK)	Brussels-based since c.1993
VDEW (Germany)	Brussels-based
EnergieNed (NL)	Brussels-based

Table 13.4 Public interest groups

Consumer Organizations	BEUC (Bureau Européen des Unions de Consommateurs), COFACE (Confederation of Family Organizations in the EC), EUROCOOP, IEIC (Institut Européen Interégional de la Consommateur) were supportive of liberalization, though to differing degrees. Some had concerns about the pedestrian speed at which price reductions were likely to come to domestic consumers, and about public-service obligations (safety; quality; universality) in the early stages of debate prior to the 1996 Directive (BEUC, *op. cit.*). Not all consumer organizations were active campaigners and none were central, though BEUC, COFACE and EUROCOOP are members of the consumer section of the Energy Consultative Committee
Environmental Non-Governmental Organizations (NGOs)	Four of the environmental 'G8'[1] EU public-interest environmental organizations have been active on EU Electricity Liberalization. Climate Network Europe (CNE; lead organization); WorldWide Fund for Nature (WWF); Greenpeace; and Friends of the Earth (FoE), have issued joint statements on the subject, though do not claim to have been influential. Whilst recognizing at an early stage in the (pre-1996) process the opportunities which liberalization might bring for environmental improvement (such as the development of natural gas combined heat and power stations rather than fossil fuels or nuclear, an outcome of liberalization in the UK), these organizations have pressed the case with the Commission for specific actions. Whilst environmental

Table 13.4   Continued

| | considerations are not expected by play a significant role in the Acceleration Directive draft,[2] many have found outlets in other policy initiatives, such as the May 2000 Directive on Renewables, transparency pricing, carbon tax, and emission trading. Some alliances with industry have emerged, e.g. joint statements from WWF with COGEN Europe (Matthes and Timpe, 2000; WWF and GOCGEN Europe, 2000). Some Greenpeace personnel are well-linked with the Commission as former employees. CNE is represented on the Energy Consultative Committee |
| Others | Never a central campaign issue for the European Citizens' Action Service (ECAS) or other NGOs |

Notes: 1. A network comprising European Environmental Bureau (EEB); WorldWide Fund for Nature (WWF); Transport & Environment (T&E); Birdlife International; Greenpeace; Friends of the Earth; Climate Network Europe; World Conservation Union (IUCN).
2. Representations have been made by environmental NGOs on measures to address state aid and subsidies; provision of information on source of provision; sources of funding for connection charges for renewable energy sources; and targets for co-generation supply.

Table 13.5   Other EU formally-constituted (non-industry) organizations

ECC – Electricity Consultative Committee	Formed 1998 post-liberalization, with sections for representation of producer (industry, trade union) and consumer (industry, household consumers). Has not been significant in liberalization debate
Council of European Energy Regulators	No EU regulator or uniform national model of regulation, hence a forum for regulators from national environments; 'acceleration directive' places pressures for harmonization of national systems of regulation, so likely to expand scope – though a 'European Regulator' not formally part of the agenda, most countries have positions on the concept
Florence Regulatory Forum	Council of Regulators, plus other central players in regulatory discussion & information-exchange forum. Established in 1998, two meetings per year, focused on the problems of cross-border trade, such as tariffs, and congestion management

Conclusion: what does electricity liberalization tell us about EU interest representation?

Interest intermediation is not in the forefront of the story of EU electricity liberalization. EU-level interest representation played nothing more than a supporting role for events that would have happened anyway, and does not appear to have influenced the main character of legislation that emerged. Only certain, largely non-central, details have been influenced by public and private interest actors. The key factors which explain the outcomes of electricity liberalization concern:

- the role of the Commission in driving the Single Market agenda forward;
- the presence of a recent model in the UK demonstrating its technical feasibility;
- the Commission's skilful use of competition policy powers to bring France/EdF to work within the scope of a Directive which interests in that country might otherwise not want;
- the Commission's fleetness of foot in turning the 'single-buyer' model to its advantage, and willingness to compromise with a 'menu of choice' Directive, and to accommodate a variety of outside inputs to achieve a foot in the door, which other forces would later throw open; and
- the march of the liberalization tide, and the accession of 'pro' countries.

Interest intermediation therefore played a role mainly at the domestic level, and through France's position as owner-shareholder of EdF, in shaping the character of the first Directive. The interesting task is to try to identify the conditions under which interest intermediation is likely to take a back seat in European integration. Grande (1996) rightly draws attention to the ways in which the multi-level architecture of the EU limits the role of outside interests in the EU political systems, generating pressures for pluralistic outcomes because of the ways in which multiple entry points create a 'lobbying free-for-all'. Political systems can help insulate themselves from outside interest pressures through this multiple architecture, knowing that bargains struck in one setting cannot be made for other arenas, and by playing 'two-level games'. Tendencies over time to disperse power between and within political institutions, through procedures such as QMV and co-decision, provide for greater levels of insulation through complexity. Yet these are largely factors that do not vary across Single Market policy arenas. Integration in some sectors has been driven by outside interests, whereas in others such interests have taken a back seat. What features about the electricity sector, which may well be present in other sectors, predict the latter outcome?

The first contributory factor concerns the nature of the debate under question. The issue of electricity liberalization was high politics, because it involved the delivering of an essential commodity to every enterprise and household in Europe, national systems of essential commodity delivery, and challenges to national champions. It also involved challenging national principles, such as the French tradition of public service, through the alternative system of liberalization. This is quite different from technical issues of widget harmonization which might safely be left to trade associations to undertake. No matter how fuzzy the formulation appears in concept, the original distinction of Hoffman (1966) between 'High' and 'Low' politics retains considerable utility of a rough and ready character in practice. High politics are dominated by member states and political institutions, whereas low politics are dominated by largely private interests and their representative organizations, in conjunction with political institutions.

The second contributory set of factors concerns the nature of the product and the characteristics of the industry sector. Where the interest concerned is already involved in substantial trading on a transnational basis, colonized by firms used to operating in different national environments, so there is likely to be a prior history of transnational organization. Unlike telecommunications, electricity has yet to become a global market because of the difficulties involved in transporting, trading and exchanging electricity on a global basis. At best, it can only be a product exchanged within a regional basis in the globe (e.g. Europe), because it is limited by the distance it is possible to construct physical infrastructure for transporting electricity across high-voltage wires. Telecommunications, on the other hand, can become a global industry because of satellite technology. These realities, together with the absence of liberalization and the presence of regional and national monopoly suppliers, meant that transnational organization has historically been weak, and, where it has existed, tends to have been focused on technical issues of exchanges rather than political representation (Bartle, 1999). Interest organization within the industry varied across Europe in national settings because of differences in the way the industry was constructed, making transnational interest organization difficult. In France, for instance, the presence of monopoly suppliers owned by the state meant that there was no need for significant political organization. In Germany, on the other hand, the industry has historically been populated by a large number of distributors, including a number of dominant regional monopoly utilities, which has meant that there has been an interest organization (VDEW) of long standing for the industry. Such a mixed ownership pattern across Europe, ranging from large monopolies to small municipal suppliers, is not conducive to transnational interest organization. Indeed, today, at the European level the electricity supply industry includes separate associations for large utilities (EURELECTRIC), and smaller municipal suppliers who are themselves differentiated in interest organization (CEDEC, GEODE).

A third set of explanations for the lack of interest dynamics concern the lack of regulation, the absence of a 'common enemy', and the ways in which differences in interests to regulation condition associational capacities. Where there is a history of regulatory competencies invested in transnational authorities, so the industry is likely to have some degree of transnational organization. None of these factors were present in the electricity sector prior to the 1988 Green Paper. Until the Commission proposed liberalization, interest organization of the business sector at the European level was either non-existent, or at the margins and focused on technical exchanges of electricity and know-how. The Commission Green Paper changed these dynamics, and prompted the electricity supply industry to create a European level organization to oppose the proposals (EURELECTRIC). Yet once organizations that were favourable to liberalization participated, so the capacity of the industry to deliver common positions was completely undermined. There was no 'common enemy' in regulation, nor in the position of industry consumers whose organization required the assistance of Commission stimulation and which lacked substance where electricity prices could be kept low. These are not favourable conditions for trade associations to operate in. For trade associations to be effective, they need as a basis to exist in a climate of trust between members, which enables a high degree of autonomy to be provided to the association secretariat to engage with political institutions. Without these factors, and in the circumstances of fundamentally opposed member interests, interest representation is likely to be channelled through national routes.

A final factor that took the arena beyond private interest politics at the EU level was the strong position of the Commission from which to take liberalization forward. They did so as part of the wider drive to complete the single market, which in the wake of the passage of the Single European Act and 'project 1992' had unstoppable momentum and widespread support among big business interests as whole. Historically, the Commission of the late 1980s was a confident one on the march, led by a visionary. Even when the Commission ran into the turbulence of the early 1990s, it could still rely upon a choice of regulatory instruments, including the opportunity to apply pressure through the European Court of Justice. The competent units within DG XVII/DG TREN were of sufficient size, while the issues were large enough to attract patronage within the Commission at the highest level throughout. From 1989, a working model for the scheme was provided by the UK, regulatory and scientific expertise was always available, while the prospect of Nordic accession always promised to enlarge the constituency of support. Large firms could be mobilized and stimulated to collective action in support by the prospect of cheaper electricity (EFET, ENERG8), and the utilities themselves were divided. Amongst non-business interests, only trade unions, hardly equipped to stop the process at the European level, expressed outright opposition to the proposals, whilst consumer and environmental organizations were broadly supportive on the thrust, if not always the detail. In these circumstances, it seems, the Commission had little to fear from taking the agenda forward, and adapting to accommodate the diversions it met en route.

Taken together, a combination of circumstances made the issue unlikely to be one in which private and public interests were able to take a front seat. These were: a 'high politics' issue and the intergovernmental nature of the politics which underlay these; a climate driven by ideas; the unfavourable circumstances for transnational collective action provided by the characteristics of the industry, the structure of private business producer interests, and the nature of regulation; the factors disabling concerted industrial consumer pressures; the plurality of interests within private, and among private and public interests; and the favourable circumstances for the Commission to drive the issue forward independently. Ideas, and institutions, it seems, triumph over private-interest intermediation as explanations for EU electricity liberalization.

References

Bartle, I. (1999) 'Transnational Interests in the European Union: Globalization and Changing Organization in Telecommunications and Electricity', *Journal of Common Market Studies*, 37(3), September pp. 363–83.

Bartle, I. (2001) private communication.

BEUC (Bureau Européen des Unions de Consommateurs) (1994) *BEUC in BRIEF*, no. 9, April, p. 4 (Brussels).

—(1995a) *Annual Report 1994*, p. 26 (Brussels).

—(1995b) *BEUC in BRIEF*, no.13, April, p. 3 (Brussels).

—(1995c) *BEUC in BRIEF*, no. 14, July, p. 3 (Brussels).

—(1996) *BEUC in BRIEF*, no. 18, July, p. 2 (Brussels).

CEDEC (European Federation of Local Public Utilities) (2000) Submission to Public 'Hearing on the Completion of the Internal Energy Market', 14 September 2000, <http://www.cedec.com/index-en.html>

Commission of the European Communities (1988) *The Internal Energy Market*, COM(88) 238 final of 2 May 1988 (Luxembourg: Office for Official Publications of the European Communities).

—(2000) *Second Report on the State of Liberalization of the Energy Markets*, COM (2000) 297 final (Luxembourg: Office for Official Publications of the European Communities).

Conant, L. (1999) 'Law and Politics in the European Union: The Europeanization of Market Regulation and its Discontents', paper prepared for the Biennial Conference of the European Community Studies Association, Pittsburgh, 2–6 June 1999.

Eberlein, B. (2000) 'Configurations of Economic Regulation in the European Union: The Case of Electricity in Comparative Perspective', *Current Politics and Economics of Europe*, 9(4), pp. 407–26.

Eising, R. (1999) 'Reshuffling Power: The liberalization of the EU Electricity Markets and its Impact on the German Governance Regime', in B. Kohler-Koch and R. Eising, *The Transformation of Governance in the European Union* (London: Routledge).

Eising, R. and Jabko, N. (1999) 'Moving Targets: Institutional Embeddedness and Domestic Politics in the Liberalization of EU Electricity Markets' (European University Institute Working Paper, Robert Scherman Centre 2000/6, European Forum Series, Florence).

Electrabel (1999) *Annual Report 1998* (Brussels: Electrabel).

EURELECTRIC and Lyons, P. (2000) *75 Years of Cooperation in the Electricity Industry*, (London: Atalink).

European Federation of Public Services Unions (EPSU) (1999) 'Internal Market for Electricity in Europe; "A New Era or a Dark Age"?' <www.epsu.org/Campaigns/sumstudyen.efm>

European Federation of Public Services Unions (EPSU) (2000) 'Joint Declaration of EURELECTRIC, EMCEF and EPSU on the Social Implications of the Internal Electricity Market' <http://www.epsu.org/structures/StandingCommittees/Public Utilities/socdialog/Eurelectric/JointstatEN.cfm>

European Round Table of Industrialists (ERT) (1992) *Rebuilding Confidence: An Action Plan for Europe*, (Brussels: ERT).

—(1992) *Beating the Crisis*, (Brussels: ERT).

Financial Times (1996) 'Comment and Analysis: Plug for the Generation Gap: Power Generators Fear the New EU Agreement on Energy Liberalization Unduly Favours the Monopolies', London, 26 June, p. 23.

Grande, E. (1996) 'The State and Interest Groups in a Framework of Multi-Level Decision Making: The Case of the European Union', *Journal of European Public Policy*, 3(3), September, pp. 318–38.

Greenpeace (2000) 'The Liberalization of Europe's Electricity Markets – is the Environment Paying the Price for Cheap Power?' <http://www.greenpeace.org/search.shtml>

Hoffman, S. (1966) 'Obstinate or Obsolete? The Fate of the Nation-State and the Case of Western Europe', *Daedelus*, 95, pp. 862–915.

International Federation of Industrial Energy Consumers (IFIEC-Europe) (2000) 'Public Hearing on the Completion of the Internal Energy Market' <www.ifiec-europe.be/Elec5.htm>

Kingdon, J. (1984) *Agendas, Alternative and Public Policy* (Boston: Little, Brown).

Klom, A. (1997) 'Effects of Deregulation Policies on Electricity Competition in the EU', *Journal of Energy and Natural Resources Law*, 15, pp. 1–22.

Matthes, F. and Timpe, C. (2000) *Sustainability and the Future of European Electricity Policy* (Freiburg: Institute for Applied Ecology) – Report Commissioned by the Heinrich Böll Foundation and the WorldWide Fund for Nature (WWF)<http://panda.org/epo/publications/cepub.cfm>

Schmidt, S. (1997) 'Sterile Debates and Dubious Generalizations: European Integration Theory Tested by Telecommunications and Electricity', *Journal of Public Policy*, 16(3), pp. 233–71.

Schmidt, S. (1998) 'Commission Activism: Subsuming Telecommunications and Electricity under European Competition Law', *Journal of European Public Policy*, 5(1), March, pp. 169–84.

Siestses, H. (2000) 'The Interest Representation of Big Dutch Business at the European Union: An Inquiry into the Logic of EU Business Interest Representation', MA thesis, Erasmus University, Rotterdam.

WorldWide Fund for Nature (WWF) and COGEN EUROPE (2000) 'Electricity Liberalization – A Disaster for Clean Energy' <http://panda.org/epo/publications/cepub.cfm>

Part VI

Corporate Social Responsibility

14
Corporate Social Responsibility: A New Approach to EU Policy-making

Laurentien van Oranje-Nassau and Sonia Casino-Diaz

Introduction

This is a case about how EU policy-makers, corporations and non-governmental organizations are finding new ways to tackle a theme that goes across business sectors, countries and issues. This is not a case study in the classic sense, whereby one organization has mounted an extensive lobby campaign to change a particular piece of EU legislation. Rather, it is an example of the evolving role of the European Institutions and that of other players, who do not only address specific legislation, but are also leading actors in broader policy areas that affect all European societies in the widest sense. The issue at stake is called 'corporate social responsibility'.

Corporate social responsibility is an example of the shift from a more confrontational model o a model of cooperation between the various stakeholders, including cooperation between businesses. This contrasts with the 'classic' situation where an industry sector merely tries to stop a piece of legislation or ensure that it is as little intrusive as possible.

It also applies for the relationship between industry and NGOs: the traditional scheme has evolved from a confrontational model to a more constructive and dynamic pattern. In some cases, this new pattern is reflected in the form of a partnership and in others in the contribution to companies' objectives through NGOs' specialised knowledge.

The backdrop to the issue of corporate social responsibility is multi-fold. For one, consumers have become a powerful voice of social responsibility, as they are becoming increasingly critical towards the products they buy.[1] The media has an important role with its intense scrutiny into actions – and non-actions – of governments and corporations in particular. In parallel, the influence of corporations is growing. Of the world's 100 largest economies, 50 are now corporations. The world's 500 largest industrial corporations, which employ only 0.05 per cent of the world's population, control some 25 per cent of the world's economic output.[2] Given this new societal dynamics, governments and the private sector – as well as NGOs and the media – are searching for new roles.

A European issue

Against this background, it is not surprising that the European Union, as one of the world's leading economic powers, takes a real interest in searching for answers on the role of corporations in society at large. At the European level, there have been various policy initiatives in the field of corporate social responsibility.

In December 1999, the European Commission published its Communication on Fair Trade, stating that: 'a prime EU objective is to pursue trade liberalization in a way that is compatible with the protection of social and environmental standards'. The European Commission has also held two joint symposia with the US Department of Labor in 1998 and the European Commission Directorate-General for Employment and Social Affairs organized a workshop on 'Monitoring Codes of Conduct and Social Labels' in November of the same year. In addition, there are several budget lines for the co-financing of joint activities on codes of conduct, labels and Social Rights,[3] and activities involved in Fair Trade.[4]

Various Members of the European Parliament have also taken an interest in the issue: there is the Howitt Report on EU Standards for European enterprises operating in developing countries;[5] the Sainjon Report on Trading Systems and international labour standards[6] and the Fassa Report on Fair Trade.[7]

The Conclusions of the 23–24 March 2001 European Council in Stockholm state that it welcomed initiatives taken by businesses to promote corporate social responsibility. The Commission announced its intention to present, in June 2001, a Green Paper on corporate social responsibility and to encourage a wide exchange of ideas with a view to promoting further initiatives in this area.

Stakeholders

In the area of corporate social responsibility, everyone is a stakeholder. Arguably, globalization has caused a shift of power from states and governments to markets and companies. European citizens have become primarily consumers; they are well-informed and therefore increasingly critical. In this context, industry is being held more and more accountable for all aspects of their activities: social, environmental and political as well as ethical. Business is well aware that in this context, corporate behaviour, and in particular the public's perception of such behaviour, is crucial. One could argue that industry has woken up to the importance of corporate social responsibility to a large extent because of the very public scrutiny of non-governmental organizations (NGOs). This is no doubt true to some extent. Interestingly, the issue of corporate social responsibility is traditionally one that is considered to belong to NGOs' field of competence and is now being incorporated into companies' own missions.

The media is a stakeholder in that it provides the backdrop to the issue. NGOs live by the media; businesses have been crucified by them, not least on the issue of corporate social responsibility over the last few years. The media will continue to play a driving role on this issue. However, as the issue is becoming increasingly sophisticated – that is, from pure confrontation to signs of cooperation – the media too has to adjust its reporting on the issue. And today, even media groups such as the *Financial Times* are becoming involved in the issue as businesses themselves.

A key stakeholder is, of course, industry. For industry, too, dealing with corporate social responsibility is a continuous learning process. Take the highly publicized case of Shell's joint venture in Nigeria (SPDC),[8] SPDC ran an active community development programme in education, medical and welfare services, youth training, agricultural support and infrastructure for a number of years aimed at poverty alleviation in the Niger Delta. In 1998, SPDC launched a new community support programme, a change of approach based on the realization that it needed to involve independent experts (that is developmental agencies and NGOs) and obtain input in the form of best practices. These elements were crucial in order to develop a long-term, part-nership-based approach to community support, with emphasis on direct involvement of communities in making the choice for their own develop-ment and future. In the context of this shift from a 'top-down' approach to a more participatory approach, the SPDC intensified its relationships with NGOs. SPDC has publicly recognized that: 'the relationship with NGOs has not been without its challenges', that it 'has learnt that it does not have all the answers to community development' and further, that it 'does not have all the means to solve all the developmental needs of the Delta'.[9] The situation regarding Shell in Nigeria continues to this day.

A mini case study of good practice: Levi Strauss in west Flanders

Corporate social responsibility initiatives do not necessarily have to be in developing countries – they can be much closer to home. The Community Foundation for West Flanders in Belgium is another example of a tangible initiative, taken by Levi Strauss that started in April 2001.

This community foundation is the first of its kind in Belgium, operating under the auspices of The King Baudouin Foundation. The aim is to provide leadership and support for addressing local economic and social issues in a region where Levi Strauss & Co. has recently closed plants. The Levi Strauss Foundation's intention is to encourage the development of a permanent charitable fund that would serve the entire population of the region. The total project budget provided by the Levi Strauss Foundation for three years is €790 000.

The three main objectives of the grant are to:

- Establish a community foundation in West Flanders that will reflect the dyn-amics, needs and conditions of the community and provide support for addressing local economic and social issues.
- Engage and empower citizens, organizations and institutions to improve the quality of life in West Flanders.

- Forge new partnerships among citizens, non-governmental organizations, corporations and local authorities to address community problems such as crime, drugs, homelessness, unemployment and youth development.

The rationale behind the initiative is that West Flanders, while a fairly prosperous region, has several social and economic issues that need to be addressed. These include a shortage of adequately skilled labour, lack of industrial sites for new entrepreneurs, and even lack of infrastructure such as running water and electricity in some places. The number of jobs created by multinational companies and agricultural industry is decreasing in the region, so there is an increasing need to develop alternative employment.

Possible projects to be supported include mentoring young entrepreneurs, organizing job-training and job-creation for low-skilled workers, providing companionship for senior citizens, and other initiatives designed to address the specific economic and social conditions in West Flanders.

A broadly representative board, comprised of citizens who enjoy a good reputation in the region and are known for their personal social commitment, has come together to start and govern the community foundation. The first order of business for this body is to define a two to three-year plan for growth and a strategic focus for initial projects. This board will set specific fundraising goals in the future, but The King Baudouin Foundation wants to prove to the local corporations and individuals that the community foundation can make a difference before undertaking a broad fundraising campaign.

The Community Foundation for West Flanders is created as a separate fund within The King Baudouin Foundation, which supports the foundation's initial operating costs. Over time, the community foundation's board will actively seek additional sponsors and raise funds to help the foundation increase its capacity. Levi Strauss has opted for the community foundation model – which helps people of all income levels develop habits of giving and provides a way for citizens to participate in improving their community – since it believes that it will provide a sustainable, long-term resource for citizens and local organizations to acquire support to address these economic and social problems effectively.

There are countless other examples of individual company initiatives such as the one involving Shell and Levi Strauss. Industry is showing leadership on the issue of corporate social responsibility. The case we describe in this chapter is about a joint industry initiative that focuses on the sharing of best practices.

The case

The issue

The examples quoted above show that corporate social responsibility is an extremely broad policy area. It can include anything ranging from actions aimed at improving human rights and combating child labour to fostering local development and diversity within the workforce to ways in which companies can improve their communication and reporting on their labour practices. This case study covers one angle of corporate social responsibility – that of an initiative by companies for companies, supported by the European Commission. It is about a platform that is today called CRS Europe. Although CRS Europe has evolved considerably during its five years of existence in terms of issues of focus, it has also had a common thread: the realization of the need for practical solutions.

The definition of what politicians and civil society believe corporate social responsibility to be is not a task for an individual company and certainly not only for business at large. In fact, the debate seems to have evolved into a situation where the different players are reaching some comfort level about what it entails. In any case, it implies an exercise that brings a lot of soul-searching and dialogue of companies with other stakeholders. This needs to be done individually at company level as well as in a group, within a framework that enables sharing of best practices

The idea was never to establish a traditional trade association, but rather to establish a vehicle that could foster dialogue between corporations, NGOs and EU policy-makers. Initially, the focus was 'social exclusion'; over time, the initiative addressed a much broader range of issues. The idea behind the business network was to learn from each other and then feed the knowledge back into the policy arena, through close cooperation with the European Commission.

Lead player's objectives

The initial objective of the business leaders of what is now called CSR Europe was to establish a fluid and open network:

> We do not want to be a lobby platform. On this issue, there is no one way of doing things. We do not want spend our time formulating positions, trying to find the lowest common denominator. We want to focus on action – whether it is individual, at company level or collectively.[10]

CSR Europe's stated mission is to help companies achieve profitability, sustainable growth and human progress by placing Corporate Social Responsibility (CSR) in the mainstream of business practice. The idea behind it is to 'initiate win–win partnerships'. It aims to achieve this objective by serving over 500 000 business people and partners through print and other publications and best practices, by offering business managers learning, benchmarking and tailored capacity-building programmes and by including CSR issues in stakeholder dialogue and focusing in particular on the European Institutions.

Although CSR Europe is essentially a business-to-business network, it envisages stakeholder dialogue as one of its key activities. The network identifies as its stakeholders: European institutions, National and International Governmental Bodies, NGOs and Civil Society, and Employers and Business Organizations.

The story behind CSR Europe

In January 1995, then President of the European Commission, Jacques Delors, launched a 'European Manifesto of Companies against Exclusion', which had been developed following the Copenhagen Summit of 1993. The manifesto aimed to make companies more aware of the issue of social exclusion. At this stage, about 20 representatives from major European companies were involved in the initiative.

In May the same year, about one hundred European business leaders came together in London to sign and adopt the Manifesto, the European Business Declaration against Social Exclusion. As signatories, the business leaders committed themselves to promote integration on the labour market. In other words, they committed themselves to trying to avoid dismissals or accompanying them by appropriate measures if dismissals are inevitable, focusing on the promotion of new jobs and vocational training. The Manifesto was accompanied by practical guidelines based in existing experiences of companies in this area. The broad acceptance of the principles outlined in the manifesto showed the willingness of the European business community to address in a more coordinated manner issues that most of them were tackling as individual companies.

However, it soon became apparent that 'social exclusion' was a negative approach and one that was far from timely for some companies that were in process of plant closures (such as Levi Strauss), and therefore were hardly in the position to talk about fighting unemployment. The Manifesto, which had played a critical catalyst role for the start of the network's activities, fell into disuse. It could even be argued that inevitably, the manifesto had a limited lifespan. The nature of the organization was turned into something considered more positive, namely 'social cohesion'. In addition, the approach changed from a French-style, more ideological manifesto to an Anglo-Saxon, more pragmatic model that focused on actions. The majority of the Anglo-Saxon companies were not ready to sign declarations (which, in some instances could even raise legal problems in the context of plant closures). They were, however, keen to share best business practices to foster social cohesion.

At the end of June 1996, the network became the European Business Network against Social Exclusion (EBNSC). As before, the focus was to share best practices across different European member states in the area of job creation through investment in training and community projects. Eight business enterprise agencies were also involved to ensure coordination across the participating countries.

In September 1997, as a contribution to the European Year Against Racism, the EBNSC organized a conference in Lyon. Then Commissioner for

Employment and Social Affairs, Padraig Flynn, applauded the work of the EBNSC and stressed the role in and commitment of the European Commission to the effort.[11] In the same year, the network published a study of some 100 case studies of projects across 10 European countries aimed at tackling social exclusion. It seemed that the sharing of best practices was successful in helping avoid making mistakes from one project to the next.

The business network continued to make its mark. In March 2000, the EBNSC was invited by the Portuguese Presidency of the EU to make an input into the Lisbon European Council Summit of 23–24 March 2000. They did so. The network submitted a letter and 12 proposals to the Summit, signed by 19 European business leaders.[12] The proposals were aimed at focusing on 'concrete areas where the synergy between business and government action can be most effective', such as the information society, education, reporting of social performance of companies and research into partnership models.[13]

In the context of the Lisbon Summit, the business network also launched the idea of a Europe-wide campaign for 2000–05 aimed at

> embracing and enacting core values of corporate social responsibility, trying to enlist half a million European businesses to share best practices in this area and establishing a European award for 'exemplary' business initiatives and partnerships',

as outlined in more detail below.

The result was that during the Lisbon Summit, European Heads of State and Government launched a 'New Strategic Plan for Europe 2010'. In this context, Europe's political leaders made a special appeal to businesses to 'combat social imbalance, invest in people and share practices that make Europe work'. While the European governments are working towards 2010, the EBNSC has set 2005 as a benchmarking date.

At the first European Business Convention on Corporate Social Responsibility, which took place in Brussels on 9–10 November 2000, the EBNSC changed its name to CSR Europe to reflect the shift of focus from social cohesion to corporate social responsibility. The main topics of discussion were socially responsible investment and consumer attitudes towards corporate social responsibility. During the Convention, a European survey conducted by CSR Europe was launched.

CSR Europe today

CSR Europe continues to campaign actively to place corporate social responsibility in the mainstream of business practice. It now consists of over 40 member companies and collaborates with over 15 organizations in 12 EU member states.[14] These are called National Partner Organizations (NPOs) and promote corporate social responsibility among businesses at national regional and local level. Different countries respond differently to the initiatives, with Denmark, the Netherlands and the UK having longstanding traditions in this area while other countries such as France and Italy have joined the debate at a later stage.

The response of industry to the Lisbon 'Special Appeal' has taken the form of 'The European Campaign 2005 for Sustainable Growth and Human Progress'. The stated objective of the campaign is to ensure that when enterprise, government and other stakeholders look for ways to realize their economic and social goals, they see corporate social responsibility as a 'powerful and refreshing tool' in this process. The 2005 campaign is centred around three main pillars. CSR Europe seeks to:

- mobilize half a million business people and partners in Europe to implement corporate social responsibility 'principles', practices and processes;
- improve stakeholder dialogue and foster new partnerships between business, government, investors and civil society;
- help companies and organizations to innovate in their strategies and management on key CSR-related issues, such as lifelong learning, diversity and entrepreneurship.

The objective of the 2005 campaign to focus on 'improving stakeholder dialogue and forging new partnerships' will be particularly important, given the fact that the campaign aims to 'show how the products, practices and principles developed within the framework of corporate social responsibility can bring Enterprise, Government and Civil Society closer to the envisioned Europe'. The response of non-governmental organizations to the initiative remains to be seen.

It needs to be emphasized that the 500 000 business people are not asked to sign up to any principles – as there are none, given the wide scope of definitions of corporate social responsibility that exist. The aim is precisely to get the businesses in one way or another involved in corporate social responsibility in a practical way. Although the precise nature of the activities is in process of being defined, it is intended that the campaign should culminate in a Special European year on Corporate Social Responsibility in 2005. CSR Europe hopes to be able to showcase the practical results of the campaign during this special year.

Programmes run by CSR Europe

CSR Europe runs several programmes designed to address key issues pertaining to corporate social responsibility in Europe. Although they have different themes, the programmes have some common elements. All programmes aim to:

- be business-led;
- contain a European as well as national element;
- include an element of benchmarking;

- have stakeholder involvement;
- include a bridge to EU policy.

The *Programme on Communications and Reporting* aims to 'create a real culture of social information and corporate communications on social practices by sharing expertise and benchmarking best practices.' The programme was developed in close cooperation with the European Commission and targets both multinationals and small and medium-sized enterprises (SMEs). Examples quoted include the 'BP Alive' triple bottom-line report that is available on-line; Volkswagen's environmental report, Levi Strauss' Sourcing and Operating Guidelines; Danone's Social Reponsibility Report; and the so called 'managed stakeholder dialogues' initiated by TXU Europe.

Launched in 1998, the programme initially developed the CSR Matrix, an on-line tool to encourage companies to share best practices, benchmark and evaluate their performance. Today, the matrix features 45 company cases on ways in which corporations use communication and reporting methods. It combines topics on which companies communicate (such as workplace climate, human rights, community involvement and environment) and communication channels (such as social reports, Codes of Conduct, stakeholder consultation, standards and labels, cause-related marketing). Companies can visit the website <www.csreurope.org/matrix> and learn from the case studies on how to establish or improve corporate communication and reporting on the range of topics.

Preparing Today's and Tomorrow's Managers on CSR is a programme developed jointly by CSR Europe and The Copenhagen Centre (TCC).[15] Launched in 1998, its main aim is to stimulate academics to introduce and diversify courses on corporate social responsibility, citizenship and business ethics at all levels of study. The two organizations conducted a survey to investigate the extent to which universities and business schools are integrating social and environmental responsibility subjects into their traditional curricula. The results of the survey are now available on-line; the database contains outlines of 90 courses offered by more than 60 universities throughout Europe. Following the survey and database, CSR Europe and TCC have established 'The On-line Guide to Teaching Business in Society'.

Responsible Investment is another example of CSR Europe's programmes. The rationale behind the initiative is the increasing trend towards Socially Responsible Investment in Europe; that is, investment in 'socially sound companies'.[16] CSR Europe launched the first-ever, close cooperation of nine Investment Research Groups to assess the performance of 46 European companies in seven different business sectors on social and employment issues. The assessment was done according to identical criteria. A set of qualitative and quantitative indicators were identified, based on four pillars of the 'European Employment Guidelines' – adaptability, employability, equal opportunities and entrepreneurship.

Political dialogue

Although the main focus of CSR Europe is to be a business-to-business network, the network's area of influence is also at the political level. CSR Europe is in continuous dialogue with authorities both EU and national. The European Commission publicly supports the work by the network and, today, a little under 50 per cent of CSR Europe's budget comes from the Commission.

The European Commission recognizes that there is no single definition of what corporate social responsibility is or should be in Europe. It sees its own role as one of facilitator, whereby initiatives have to come from within companies. The European Commission has indicated that it believes it to be premature to develop legislation in this area, since it believes that 'best practices' cannot be easily legislated; in its view, 'legislation reinforces standard practice'.[17] The European Commission has indicated that it intends to pursue a two-fold approach to the issue: by directly addressing companies' sense of corporate social responsibility and at the same time by putting pressure on companies through their stakeholders.

In a follow-up to the European Commission's Social Policy Agenda that was adopted in June 2000,[18] the Commission is currently preparing a communication (possibly in the form of a Green Paper) on corporate social responsibility. It will outline the core principles that businesses across Europe will have to respect in each of the areas covered under corporate social responsibility.

The role of 'civil society'

In the context of corporate social responsibility, it would be wrong to talk about 'civil society' as one coherent block. Within the NGO community, there are significant differences between the attitudes taken and techniques used towards furthering this cause. Some have been more critical about the work of CSR Europe, others have been more open to its objectives. For instance, the Business Group of Amnesty International has been invited to share its expert views at meetings of the network. In addition, CSR Europe is forging alliances with organizations such as The Prince of Wales Business Leaders Forum (PWBLF) and Business for Social Responsibility (BSR) in the USA.

The European NGO, the Anti-Poverty Network Europe (APNE), has played an important role in the creation of the original EBNSC network. It was a good fit: APNE's focus on poverty and social exclusion with the EBNSC addressing similar issues from a business perspective. However, today, the relationship appears to be more at arm's length.

NGOs have played, and continue to play, an important role in putting corporate social responsibility high on the political and public agenda. From those origins, and due to globalization of issues and problems and higher society demands on global companies especially, civil society first (Seattle) and the public sector afterwards have started to look at the issue of what social responsibility can be asked from companies. The precise relationship between NGOs and CSR Europe is not entirely clear at this stage. There seems to be a kind of consultant relationship with a number of selected NGOs whereby they provide insight into the 'other side's point of view'. NGOs are invited sporadically to meetings to do just that. But, still, the relationship remains somewhat uneasy. Thinking ahead, this relationship needs to be better defined – both by the member companies of CSR Europe as well as among NGOs themselves.

Media coverage and public interest

Apart from NGOs, the media has also played an extremely important role in putting corporate social responsibility on the political agenda. It has successfully used brand names to bring the issue to the attention to consumers. One could argue that media scrutiny has been vital in awakening companies to take the issue of corporate responsibility seriously.

Generally speaking, the media has responded well to the CSR Europe initiative, although media coverage has been fairly limited. Companies are faced with a certain difficulty when it comes to creating awareness of the issue through the media, as they are easily criticized – particularly (and understandably) by NGOs – for engaging in corporate social responsibility initiatives merely for public relations. At the same time, every stakeholder in this evolving issue, including the media and NGOs, must take a responsible stance in balancing the public debate. The issue has progressed too far to continue the negative reporting on company initiatives. There are issues – of which corporate social responsibility is one – that need to be driven from within companies. As stated above, this is even recognized by the European Commission.

The fear that reporting too positively about the business initiatives would result in a decrease in real commitment of companies to the issue, is of course a real one. However, the media would do justice to the debate by providing a balanced viewpoint, as it is in the interest of all to promote socially responsible business practices.

Conclusions and lessons learnt

Corporate social responsibility is an ongoing process; the issue is moving rapidly both at the political as well as at the business level. Therefore, there are no easy solutions to this and there is no precise timeframe. It is also clear that corporate social responsibility is perceived differently in different European countries. The Commission has indicated that it believes that 'dialogue, debate and raising awareness' in the individual companies are all necessary steps in the process.

CSR Europe is one of many approaches to try to include social responsibility into the mainstream of business practice of European corporate governance.

Whether or not the approach taken by CSR Europe will be successful remains to be seen. Going forward, all stakeholders need to find their place in the debate. A difficult challenge for CSR Europe is of an internal nature. CSR Europe will need to keep defining itself, by virtue of being a loose network that lives by the commitment of some very different companies. Exactly because the issue has so many facets, it has a different meaning for each company. Consequently, member companies have different expectations of CSR Europe, and so there is a continuously difficult job at hand to manage expectations of members.

CSR Europe was right specifically not to become a lobby platform – and it should stay that way. Should this change, it will become easy prey for NGOs and the media; it would become easy to criticize CSR Europe for using commitment to corporate social responsibility for public relations purposes. Thus, companies – and CSR Europe – should address the possible catch-22 situation: if they talk too much about their commitment to corporate social responsibility, their commitment is likely to be criticized for being 'a PR exercise'. And if they do not, they miss valuable – and much needed – opportunities for promoting the issue more widely!

The future of CSR Europe will be largely driven by external developments. In this political and economic context evolving continuously, the challenge will be to continue to respond to external needs and expectations, of which there are many – by the European Commission and European Parliament, NGOs, the media and businesses themselves. It will be a continuous challenge for CSR Europe to demonstrate its added value. That said, CSR Europe may well disappear in the medium term; it is very useful in helping to create initial awareness on corporate social responsibility issues now, but as such its lifespan will be limited. Thus, the more tangible projects CSR Europe develops, the higher its chances of surviving.

Notes

1. According to a MORI-CSR Europe poll, 44% of European consumers are willing to pay more for environmentally and socially responsible products.
2. *Source*: *Business Community*.
3. Budget line B3-4000.
4. Budget line B7-6000.
5. Richard Howitt, 'Resolution on EU Standards for European Enterprises Operating in Developing Countries Towards a European Code of Conduct', 15 January 1999 – calls on the Commission and Council to develop a European Code of Conduct and monitoring platform.
6. André Sainjon, 'Report on a Communication from the Commission to the Council on "The Trading System and internationally Recognized Labour Standards"', 13 January 1999 – calls on the Commission to propose a minimum code of conduct for EU multinationals.
7. Raimondo Fassa, 'Own-Initiative Report, "Fair Trade with the Developing Countries"', 2 July 1998 – calls on the Commission to promote fair trade in its Development and Trade policies.

8. The SCPD joint venture comprises the Nigeria National Petroleum Corporation, Shell, Elf and Agip.
9. Paper by Noble Pepple, Corporate Advisor, Shell International Ltd, presented at the EC/NGO Interim Steering Group on Nigeria (ISG) at the Nigeria Seminar on 'Good Governance and Poverty Alleviation in Nigeria', held in Brussels on 28–29 January 1999.
10. Interview on 11 December 2000 with Alan Christie, Vice-President Public Affairs at Levi Strauss Europe, Middle East and Africa and Chairman of the CSR Europe Board of Directors.
11. 'Gaining Diversity', conference by the EBNSC, Lyon 29–30 September 1997.
12. 'For an Entrepreneurial and Inclusive Europe – 12 Proposals for Action', March 2000.
13. Viscount Etienne Davignon, Chairman of the Advisory Board of the EBNSC, quotes in *Reuters*, 8 March 2000.
14. CSR Europe members today include: ABB, Accor, AerRianta, Banco Ambrosiano Veneto, BP, Bracco, BT, Caisse des Depots Consignations, Cariplo, Danone, Diageo, EDF, France Telecom, Generale, Glaverbel, Group 4 Falck, Groupe Casino, Group Cockerill Sabre, Honeywell, IBM, Johnson & Johnson, Kingfisher, KPMG, La Poste, Levi Strauss, L'Oreal, Merita-Nordbanken Group, Motorola, Nike, Nyforetagar Centrum, Portugal Telecom, Price Waterhouse Coopers, Randstad, Rabobank, Shell, Spar Nord Bank, Suez Lyonnaise des Eaux, Telecom Italia, Volkswagen AG.
15. TCC is an international organization established in 1998 by the Danish Government to promote new voluntary social partnerships between government, business and civil society.
16. In 2000, more than €2.3 million worth of investments in Europe were made based on ethical criteria. In the UK alone, Socially Responsible Investments accounted for 5% of all funds invested (*source: Tendances*).
17. Interview with Marie Donnelly, Head of Unit for Adaptation to Industrial Change, Work Organization and the Information Society, European Commission Directorate General for Employment and Social Affairs (*CSR Magazine*, October 2000).
18. Communication of 28 June 2000, COM (2000) 379 final. In Annex 1 of the Social Policy Agenda Communication, under the heading of 'Anticipating and Managing Change and Adapting to the New Working Environment', the European Commission commits itself to preparing a communication and conference on corporate social responsibility (triple bottom-line approach) in 2001.

15
Changes in the Arena: Lessons from Lobby Cases

Robin Pedler

The cases described prompt a series of questions. The experiences of the 'lead players' and the authors suggest answers with general application and future value. The questions are:

- Was it worthwhile? Do the cases show the lead players advancing their causes or improving their bottom line?
- How large is the arena? How has it changed in the past ten years and how will it change in the next decade?
- What do the cases tell us about significant changes in the institutions and processes of the EU?
- Who sets the agenda when an issue is contested and settled in the arena, and how can a player become involved in setting the agenda?
- How much more effective are the NGOs becoming, individually and in partnerships?
- Are industry trade associations still powerful players and is their power increasing or declining?
- What have been the alliances that have proved effective in their arenas?

Winning in the changed arena

Lobbying gets results, within limits. The most successful lobbyists are those who: 'appreciated the limits of what the lobbying process can achieve'.[1] Eleven of the lead players in these 14 cases achieved some degree of success. To the extent that their success was less than total, one may draw conclusions about the limits to what lobbying can achieve. In the other three cases, one sees the preparation and construction of a campaign, but the jury is still out on the results to be achieved.

The two cases with the greatest degree of success are both limited to a single issue and both are international, involving trade into and out of the EU: Slovenia and the EU, Chapter 7, and Safe Harbor, Chapter 1. In the first case, the Slovenian steel industry followed very precisely the EU procedures, as they knew they must, and avoided the imposition of anti-dumping duties. Their lobbying, though effective, was significantly limited to the Slovenian government and media – an interesting example of the use of third-country governments to influence the EU.

The second case moves a step further down the line. It is likely that the US companies involved would have preferred not to have had an EU Directive on Data Protection, but that was the legislative situation with which they had to deal. Therefore their lobbying objective was more limited. They created an alliance that found, by an imaginative approach, a *modus vivendi* that enabled companies to transfer data freely across the Atlantic. Tellingly, however, the key move in the game was 'a chance personal encounter [as so often in European public affairs?] that appears to have detonated serious US government attention'.

Two other companies that gained most of their lobbying objectives were Chiquita and Fyffes in Chiquita Declares War and Wins, Chapter 10. But it took them a very long time and they suffered great financial damage in the interim. Even at the end they had to be realistic enough to accept a solution that benefited their market share by allowing the principle of a 'reference period', but not the most beneficial reference period they had been seeking.

Another example of living with the EU system as it exists and finding solutions to mitigate the aspects that do not appeal to the lead player is to be found in Japanese Lobbying in Europe, Chapter 9. The Japanese auto industry would have preferred not to have had the quota system, but rather than fight it through the WTO, they adapted with a combination of the VRA and local 'transplant' factories. Achieving the VRA and enabling the transplant factories to survive nevertheless took substantial lobbying.

When the companies combined in trade associations, as in Clean Air and Car Emissions, Chapter 5, they were again successful to a limited degree. Both the oil and auto industries succeeded, by involving themselves in the underlying research process, in avoiding what might have been worse results. The auto industry, particularly, was satisfied by this aspect; the success of the oil industry was apparently limited to minimizing the expense of the outcome. But they both finished up with stringent and expensive regulations that they would probably have preferred to avoid. In the latter stages of the case they were joined by the NGOs who gained the tactical advantage of a seat at the table. The strategic result of this tactical gain remains to be seen.

Success in agenda-building is also the hallmark of WWF and Climate Policy, Chapter 4, and Getting Animal Welfare on to the World Trade Agenda, Chapter 8. The WWF already has substantial success to record. As the authors say:

The distinctiveness of the EU position in international climate negotiations over the past decade, especially with its focus on domestic policies and measures to reduce energy demand, is due in no small part to the activities of environmental organizations throughout this period.

Eurogroup for Animal Welfare has had up to now a more limited objective. As the title indicates, it has sought to get its issue onto the agenda, and it has succeeded, and it has also joined a group of NGOs in regular civil society consultation on EU trade policy. It will not be until there is a new trade round that the full effect of its work will become apparent.

Meanwhile, Lafarge and Global Warming, Chapter 3, describes a company that has taken its place in building the agenda, but also has some concrete achievements to record. These include, notably, the deferment of the carbon tax. It has achieved results firstly by building business alliances, more recently by forging a partnership with WWF.

ABNAmro gives its first objective in *Making the Single Market in Financial Services a Reality* as: 'to establish the ABNAmro EU liaison office as a supportive and collaborative stakeholder'. This they clearly achieved, building on their very substantial research input in 1998 that enabled them to present to the Commission their report *The Single Market Review*. Cooperating with The Netherlands government and with European banking associations, they were also able to secure a Declaration from the 1998 Cardiff summit, an interesting example of the European Summit setting the agenda. They achieved two further objectives by creating a sixth Forum Group on cross-border cash pooling with themselves as members and getting a satisfactory definition of a 'professional investor'. As they conclude, however, 'legislation has still to be passed … and results, as always in lobbying, cannot be guaranteed'.

In the one case in which the Commission is the lead player, Electricity Liberalization, Chapter 13, it has gone a long way to achieving its objectives. Its lobbying has included using the influence of member state governments and of an alliance of business interests.

There is also a tactical success for CBI and their partners in Promoting Consumer Confidence in e-Commerce, Chapter 2. They achieved the public hearing that they sought and have no doubt put some sound ideas into circulation and on record, but the text of the regulation, as it stands, does not reflect their concerns.

CASTer and Corporate Social Responsibility, Chapter 11, show two very different groups putting together robust alliances to meet strong challenges, but the results of their lobbying remain to be seen and evaluated.

The global arena

The cases were selected for their value in demonstrating the lobbying of the European Union. Yet a connecting thread that runs through them is that all the players, including the EU institutions, are in a global arena. This may be a feature of how the EU has developed over the past decade and how it has extended, not just geographically but also into new areas of competence that affect the lives of citizens, businesses and civil society.

It may equally arise because much-discussed globalization is real, and the same effect would appear in a series of cases focused on any one region. Japanese Lobbying in the EU, Chapter 9, addresses this question as it reviews actions and reactions in and between the world's three largest trading blocks. While it shows that each of them is active in lobbying the other two, it quite clearly demonstrates that Japanese business finds the culture and the process of influencing it differs greatly between the USA and the EU.

Safe Harbor, Chapter 1,shows how US business interests in Europe, organized through the American Chamber of Commerce EU Committee (AmCham) monitor developments in the EU, appreciate when they have trans-Atlantic reach, and use formal and informal channels to defuse potential problems. Global influence is not one-way. This case poses the question: 'Why was the US so agitated about EU legislation?'

Apparently the strongest example of the 'global arena' is provided in Chiquita Declares War and Wins, Chapter 10. The company, frustrated in its efforts to protect or even enhance market-share by lobbying within the EU, went on the achieve its ends by using US law to make the American government launch, pursue and win a WTO dispute. Getting Animal Welfare onto the WTO Agenda, Chapter 8, however, shows the EU institutions so sensitive to global, or at least trans-Atlantic, influences that the mere threat of a WTO dispute is sufficient to stay the implementation of decisions.

Global influence does not need the formal application of WTO rules to be felt in the EU. CASTer, Chapter 11, is all about how European steel industries and their regions adjust to cope with the effects of global overcapacity. One reaction, shown in Slovenia and the EU, Chapter 7, may, however, bring the debate back into the trade arena as the EU industry seeks to protect itself against one competitor through an anti-dumping action.

Clean Air and Car Emissions, Chapter 5, shows that the manufacturers (increasingly global companies) are conscious not only of the effect of exhaust emission regulations within the EU, but also how that impacts on global competitiveness. Hence they demand common global standards. Global standards, if achieved, would probably be declared not in the trade arena, but as a United Nations convention. The environment cases: Lafarge and Global Warming, Chapter 3, WWF European and Global Climate Policy, Chapter 4, and Clean Air and Car Emissions, Chapter 5, all show how UN conventions impact severely on EU businesses and underline the need to influence events in that arena as well as in the EU.

The most fundamental change in the EU lobbying arena is clearly shown to be that it has expanded to become global. The players who recognize that fact and use it to advance their case are those most likely to influence the EU process.

Setting the agenda

> [WWF recognized] that some of the most profound impacts on the environment came from other economic sectors lying outside the scope of more narrowly conceived environmental policy. This 'integrationist' approach of looking at environmental policy as an issue cutting across many different sectors was given formal expression in a European WWF strategic planning exercise conducted in 1995.

WWF and European and Global Climate Policy, Chapter 4, shows how a leading NGO set out, successfully, not only to influence but in significant ways to write the agenda for the development of the EU's environment policy.

Agenda-setting is a particularly strong tool in the hands of NGOs. Getting Animal Welfare onto the WTO Agenda, Chapter 8, as its very title suggests, shows how the Eurogroup for Animal Welfare took an issue in which it believed strongly, but which most of the other actors did not want to see on the world trade agenda and by persistent lobbying of all the EU institutions persuaded the EU that it should feature. It is significant that the Eurogroup decided not to join other NGOs at Seattle in protesting against the whole idea of a new trade round. '[Eurogroup] saw no inherent problem with international trade, only with the way in which it was currently organized' (Chapter 8, this volume). So they devoted themselves to getting it organized differently.

Business too recognizes the importance of writing the agenda and in several cases shows that it is effective. Clean Air and Car Emissions, Chapter 5, shows the automobile manufacturers moving from reaction to pro-action. The willingness of ACEA to accept the impositions of the 1998 Directive were due mainly to the fact that they had taken part in the EPEFE research programme and hence been closely associated with the Commission at the agenda-setting stage. They thus see the research basis as essential for developing the ongoing Auto Oil II programme and are devoting considerable efforts to directing it. Of course, from the start of Auto Oil II they have been joined in agenda-setting by the eight NGOs allied in Working for Environmental Sustainability.

Safe Harbor, Chapter 1, demonstrates the agenda-setting role of the Trans-Atlantic Business Dialogue:

> [In] late 1997, the concerns about the EU directive got onto the Trans-Atlantic Business Dialogue (TABD) agenda, where it was to remain until its resolution in mid-2000. Shortly afterwards, the transfer of data to third countries also appeared on the Trans-Atlantic Consumer Dialogue and the Trans-Atlantic Legislators Dialogue agendas. This was significant from a public affairs perspective because it ensured that the issue was regularly

on the bilateral six-monthly EU–US summits, in turn receiving top-level
political attention and maintaining pressure on the officials to produce
results. (p. 19, this volume)

CASTer, a regional alliance seeking its role in setting the agenda, empha-
sizes the (as Ineke van der Storm says) often underestimated importance of
the Committee of the Regions:

> It is therefore a useful instrument for the launch of new policies, for the
> creation of commitment between the Commission and the regions and
> even for the preparation of new actions.(p. 238, this volume)

That the moment of setting the agenda is the key time to influence process is
confirmed. The change in the arena is that there are new fora where ideas are
generated and matured before they influence the EU policy-making process.

The EU institutions in the new arena

The commission

'The Commission proposes.' These cases all concern issues in the EU's First
Pillar. For them, it is still true that nothing happens unless and until the
Commission does propose, and that the subsequent debate is directed by and
around that proposal. While several cases suggest that other institutions have
gained influence at the expense of the Commission, the right of initiative
remains a powerful tool, and hence influence ahead of the formal proposal is
particularly effective. Electricity Liberalization, Chapter 13, shows how 'the
Commission started the ball of electricity liberalization rolling'. It goes on to
detail: 'The electricity supply industry, through EURELECTRIC and its regular dialogue with the Commission, had managed to tone down some of the
more radical ambitions of the Commission'. pp. 270, 276 in this volume.
   Promoting Consumer Confidence in e-Commerce, Chapter 2, explains how

> At this relatively early stage – and with no formal proposal yet released by
> the Commission – our overriding concern was that despite knowing that
> the proposal was due to be released very imminently, there had been *no
> prior process of consultation* with interested parties … from the Commission
> departments concerned. The potential impact of this text had not, it
> seemed, either been noticed or properly assessed. (p. 39, this volume)

The case goes on to show how, when it proved impossible to achieve effective input at that stage, the players had to fight a strong rearguard action in
both European Parliament and Council.
   The Commission is also a vital player in the implementation of policies
once they have been determined. As Safe Harbor, Chapter 1, records: 'the

European Commission is the most consistently active player'. It may do this through its own Directorates General, as when it seeks to enforce anti-dumping policies in Slovenia and the EU, Chapter 7; or in managing policies it may also make use of committees, as further detailed in Safe Harbor:

> Comitology articles established two authorities to advise the Commission. The Article 29 working party consists of representatives from the 15 national data protection authorities and is responsible for the protection of individuals in relation to the processing of personal data. The Article 31 Committee is the authority that judges the adequacy of third countries.

While, as Julian Oliver says, the committees included representatives from the 15 member states and were sometimes critical of the Commission, earlier work by this author demonstrates that Committees very rarely come to the point of disagreeing with Commission proposals.[2]

The world of comitology is obscure and the proceedings of committees difficult to track, but these cases show both the direct effect on commercial interests of committee decisions and also some possibilities for access and influence.

Committees that are not formally constituted are particularly difficult to access but may have considerable effect. Promoting Consumer Confidence in e-Commerce, Chapter 2, finds that

> We were in serious danger, therefore, of the Regulation being rushed through the legislative process as just a formality…This risk was all the greater given that the *ad hoc* JHA working party of member-state representatives had already been established in December 1997 and was reaching informal agreement on an internal text…This text was therefore circulating in the Commission as the near final draft. (p. 39, this volume)

The European Parliament (EP)

The EP is often rated as the institution that has gained most power and influence from the process changes agreed at Maastricht and Amsterdam. So do the cases reflect this 'change in the arena'? It is clear that the increase in power is especially evident when the 'legal base' for an issue involves co-decision. In other areas, the EP's powers remain limited. In some cases power and influence is reflected in the concentration of lobbying effort expended on the EP. Perhaps the most striking example is in Promoting Consumer Confidence in e-Commerce, Chapter 2. As Pointer explains, the Commission's proposals to amend the Brussels Convention were based on Articles 65 and 67 of the Treaty, so the EP's role was limited to consultation. Nevertheless, sustained and well-directed lobbying ensured that the Parliament took the consultation very seriously and indeed voted amendments in language that suited the industry lobbyists. This showed, deduces Pointer, '[that Parliament] has gained in confidence and is maturing' p. 46. The limits to the EP's power under consultation were, however, clearly demonstrated when the Commission, in its revised text, ignored their amendments.

CASTer maintained a continuous lobby of the EP over a five-year period. As van der Storm says in Chapter 11:

> regional and local authorities need the Commission and the European Parliament as players and not only for regional policies but for a number of sectoral policies as well.

She believes that the views of the EP have clearly been favourable to putting across CASTer's case.

Clean Air and Car Emissions, Chapter 5, describes both the intensity of lobbying devoted to the EP and also the very high costs that may be inflicted on industries by EP amendments. The case, however, underlines the limits that the Plenary voting system imposes on parliamentary committees that may be tempted to vote extreme amendments. It also gives a practical example of the EP exercising its co-decision powers at the conciliation stage by 'trialogue'. The case shows the EP where its powers are greatest: on a 'First Pillar' issue subject to co-decision. In other areas, it is seen as less influential and less lobbying effort is invested. As Fisher says in Getting Animal Welfare on to the World Trade Agenda: '[Parliament's] role is limited because it has little influence over common commercial policy or agriculture policy. This fact affected Eurogroup's lobbying strategy and priorities,'(Chapter 8). The view is echoed in WWF and Climate Policy, Chapter 4: 'Parliament and Council secretariat are not major players in this debate. Although the Parliament will issue resolutions on climate issues these are rarely followed up and are not very influential in formulating Common EU positions.'

One interesting example of where the EP's powers *were* enhanced by Amsterdam and of the lobbying effort that industry devoted to the EP as a result is in *Safe Harbor*, Chapter 1. The 'exculsive' data-protection measures that industry opposed were, as we have seen, driven by the work of two committees. But

> The Parliament's opinion was required as part of the new comitology introduced as a result of the Amsterdam treaty in May 1999. Since the resignation of the Santer Commission in March 1999, the Commission had not over-ridden a negative opinion in the Parliament.

The Council of Ministers

The Council co-decides with the EP even on issues where the legal base imposes that process. On many other issues, the Council clearly takes the lead. This sends the lobbyists either to member-state capitals or at least to the permanent representations in Brussels. Promoting Consumer Confidence in e-Commerce, Chapter 2, shows the CBI taking both routes and also acting as a message carrier between ministries in the national capital:

> early drafting in the JHA *ad hoc* working group had only involved the UK's Lord Chancellor's Department, given the nature of the majority of the Convention's content (this was generally true in other member states also). It was important, therefore, that we alert other UK departments such as the Department of Trade and Industry (DTI) to the specific consequences in respect of e-commerce so that these concerns were reflected in the overall UK position in the EU's Council of Ministers. This was done through the latter part of 1998 and early 1999 by means of numerous meetings and letters. This effort was reinforced in Brussels through the UK's Permanent Representative to the EU (UKREP). (p. 48, this volume)

They recognized, however, as a national federation, the need to involve other member states:

> For the CBI and our allies, this meant daily – if not hourly – contact with the UK authorities during the preparation for the JHA Council, and also ensuring that our counterparts in other Member States were doing the same.

The outcome of this case provides an interesting example of the dynamics of the EU process and also of limits on the application of the national veto. Decision in Council was by unanimity and since the CBI had ensured that the UK was opposed to the Commission's proposal, it appeared in a strong position to defeat it. But: 'it was not an issue on which the UK particularly wanted to use the explosive veto option.' When, on the other hand an issue *is* one where a member state wants to insist, its ability to block the process is remarkable, as is the case for France in Electricity Liberalization (Chapter 13).

WWF and Climate Policy, Chapter 4, explains how the EU decides its position on international conventions and how the NGO puts its case to member state civil servants:

> The process: Member State civil servants and Commission staff negotiate internal common EU positions. These are agreed by Ministers at the Environment Council and then used as the basis for the ensuing international Convention discussions. The Presidency is responsible for co-ordination and is very influential.

The influence of the presidency is significant in lobbying the EU and would certainly appear to have increased since the previous series of cases. This may well be because European Councils of Heads of State and Government have become much more regular (now they occur four times a year). They are increasingly those who set the EU's agenda. Getting Animal Welfare onto the World Trade Agenda, Chapter 8, tells how the Eurogroup for Animal Welfare made specific and, so far as they were concerned, very beneficial approaches to the Finnish and Swedish presidencies. The author is aware from other sources that the EU Committee of the American Chamber of Commerce now conducts preparation briefing of presidencies well ahead of time. These lobbying initiatives would seem to reflect a significant change in the arena.

Member states feature in these cases not only as decision-makers but also as administrations that must implement (or not) the policies decided. Safe Harbor, Chapter 1, shows four member states prosecuted by the Commission for failure to implement data protection. Lafarge and Global Warming, Chapter 3, laments the difficulties faced by a Europe-wide company forced to deal with governments that have very different views and priorities on the issue. Clean Air and Car Emissions, Chapter 5, looks at the role of the member states both as champions of their car industries and in implementing the Exhaust Emissions Directive by a mixture of inspection techniques and tax incentives. Electricity Liberalization, Chapter 13, shows that while member states are bound to liberalize, they may choose between several ways of doing so.

The Council, especially its working parties and COREPER, remain the most opaque of the EU institutions and lobbying in several member states as one must to influence results remains difficult. These cases show, however that active lobbyists do deploy their energies at council level and that they have achieved measurable results, especially when they have targeted the presidency and sparked the interest and support of that country.

In the institutional arena the cases show a clear growth in the influence of the EP, both in cases that are now co-decided and in the EP's still very new degree of control over the comitology system. Within the council, the power of the presidency is growing and its importance is recognized. Both of these changes are reflected in the focus and effort of those whose lobbying to influence the process we have studied. The changes must not, however, be allowed to obscure a constant: that in nearly all the cases, the Commission is not only the initiator but also the developer of policy and its manager, so that lobbying effort must be and still is concentrated on that institution.

Non-governmental organizations (NGOs)

NGOs made their influence felt and not only in the two cases where they are the lead player. WWF describes how they established the agenda for climate policy and presented it to the other players in the EU. Their influence in the field is also recognized in Lafarge and Global Warming, Chapter 3. Lafarge has entered a formal partnership with WWF and Boyd says: 'Our objective is to find agreement with WWF in a way that satisfies their environmental objectives as well as our business objectives.' Clean Air and Car Emissions, Chapter 5, shows how WWF has also, as a member of Towards a

Sustainable Environment formally established a place at the table in developing emission control policy in Auto Oil II.

Getting Animal Welfare onto the World Trade Agenda, Chapter 8, charts how consultation with civil society has developed rapidly to become a formal part of the development of EU international trade policy. The same case, however, suggests frustration at the limits to NGO influence that were revealed earlier. Safe Harbor and Promoting Consumer Confidence in e-Commerce (Chapters 1 and 2) both show the effectiveness of consumer interests when they are organised into an NGO such as the European Consumers' Association (BEUC). The need to satisfy consumer interests was a significant limitation to the solutions available to the commercial interests.

Chapter 14, Corporate Social Responsibility, poses an interesting question as to whether companies are moving into parts of the arena that NGOs had come to assume were their territory. A significant change in the arena since the last series of lobbying cases is the increased influence of the NGOs, exercised both formally and informally.

There is a lively debate currently about whether the influence of *Trade Associations* is increasing or decreasing,[3] and there are two cases where industry federations are the 'lead players'. In the first of these, Promoting Consumer Confidence in e-Commerce (Chapter 2) the Confederation of British Industry (CBI) has the role. The case also shows the important role of UNICE in coordinating the views and activities of national industry federation members (CBI and their counterparts in other member states) when it became evident that the issue had to be lobbied at the level of the Council of Ministers. It also shows that while the CBI had a close working relationship with the Alliance for Electronic Business, it was able to go on and involve 13 other sectoral and advertising federations in giving it support at the public hearing. All of this suggests that federations organized nationally are significant players in the arena.

In Chapter 5, Clean Air and Car Emissions, the lead federations are very different in character. The case shows the federations that bring together the leading companies in two industries, motor manufacturers (ACEA) and oil producers and refiners (Europia), combining to cooperate closely with the Commission at the stage of research and agenda-setting and also dealing directly with member-state governments.

There are other cases in which federations are significant players. In Chapter 13, Electricity Liberalization, Justin Greenwood identifies nine federations specifically active on electricity generation matters as well as charting the role of 'general' bodies such as UNICE and ERT and federations from associated industries. He concludes, however, that the ability of these federations to divert the course of electricity liberalization was 'limited'. Thus:

> EURELECTRIC had been formed to oppose the proposals for liberalization, and did so consistently until 1995, including a somewhat aggressively

hostile approach in the early 1990s. This approach yielded changes to details, but not to the core principle of liberalization.

The case clearly shows that the influence of various federations was limited not just by the determination of the Commission to press ahead, but also by the representation of fundamentally opposing views by different federations.

Another grouping that is often cited as an effective player appears in that role in Safe Harbor, (Chapter 1): the EU Committee of the American Chamber of Commerce in Belgium (the EU Committee). In the case

> In November 1997, The EU Committee hosted a public workshop on 'The Impact of Data Protection on Global Trade'. Effectively a dialogue was conducted between the major industry associations and the major Commission officials concerned. Representation included the Secretary General of UNICE, and member companies from Eurobit (the then leading IT industry association), the European Banking Association, FEDMA and the EU Committee.

This showed the EU Committee bringing together sectoral federations and addressing the Commission at an important stage in the setting of the agenda. The American approach is in sharp contrast to that detailed in Chapter 9, Japanese Lobbying in Europe. Kewley finds that there is no corporate voice of 'Japan' in Brussels, though there is the Japanese Motor Manufacturers' Association (JAMA). It seems that Japanese approaches are still predominantly through member states.

One other leading association, the European Round Table of industrialists (ERT), is specifically mentioned as a player that is supportive to Lafarge in Lafarge and Global Warming (Chapter 3) and opposed to national electricity monopolies in Electricity Liberalization (Chapter 13). The latter case is perhaps the more significant, since of course Bertrand Collomb, Chairman of Lafarge, is himself a member of the ERT.

Industry associations appear in nearly all the cases and the conclusion to be drawn is that when they are focused and intervene at the appropriate time, they are effective. However, there are several cases in which they are clearly not effective. There is probably a very long-term change in the arena, in that the Commission does not appear to regard a 'European Federation of ...' as a privileged or even essential dialogue partner. Whether associations are becoming more or less effective is shown to be less relevant than whether their leaders are skilled and well-organized lobbyists.

All the cases show that the move from representing interests to influencing policy is made when the lead player forms an effective *alliance*. The author understands an alliance to be an arrangement that generates mutual effort but is not formalized to become an association or federation. The alliance may be broad and long-lasting or very focused and temporary. The two most striking short-term focused alliances are both trans-Atlantic. In Chiquita Goes to War and Wins (Chapter 10), the alliance is between Chiquita and Fyffes in 1999–2001. The two companies, hitherto apparently sworn enemies, identified common interests that enabled them to propose what came to be the peace formula for the long-running banana trade war. Their proposal was powerful precisely because it did come from leading players on both sides of the Atlantic. In Safe Harbor (Chapter 1) the alliance that unlocked the door that had seemed fast shut was that between a lobbyist – a manager in a major US corporation – and a senior official in the US Mission to the EU, who both decided that something must be done. They remained in contact as they each worked through their own networks to achieve the result.

There is a very different alliance at the heart of Electricity Liberalization (Chapter 13). It has a broad reach and is long-lasting. It brings together consumer and environmental NGOs, major electricity consumers, some major producers and some member-state governments. The alliance has held together for ten years and is still a driving force towards liberalization.

In both the NGO-led cases: WWF and Climate Policy (Chapter 4) and Getting Animal Welfare onto the World Trade Agenda (Chapter 8), the authors identify global and regional alliances of NGOs in their field, and go on to select those with whom they decide to work on the specific issue described. The major change in the arena from the previous cases, which also showed alliances as determinant, is the extent to which effective alliances now include NGO players, and indeed the willingness of many NGOs to step outside their own world and enter alliances where interests do not conflict and the chance of successfully driving and issue seems to be enhanced.

Regulation remains the most common stimulant to lobbying. It is the theme of 10 of these cases. In six of them, there is a 'classic' case of industry seeking to mitigate the impact of regulation, frequently in opposition to NGOs seeking to ensure its imposition.

In two cases, Making the Single Market in Financial Services a Reality (Chapter 12) and Corporate Social Responsibility (Chapter 14), commercial interests are volunteering self-regulation as the most effective solution to a problem identified by institutions and consumer representatives. The lead player in Promoting Consumer Confidence in e-Commerce (Chapter 2) seeks the same conclusion, but so far without success. Safe Harbor (Chapter 1) describes an alternative regulatory method; US companies that take part do so voluntarily, but their conformity is guaranteed by the Department of Commerce.

The change in the arena is the increased proposal of self-regulation as a solution in these cases. This is particularly true in cases that concern 'new business' (where one might include financial services together with e-commerce). It suggests that the processes followed by EU institutions would be too slow and cumbersome in the new world and also that the experts with the ability to understand what is required are still concentrated in the main economic players. The successful ones use their knowledge and skills to set up effective alliances and use them as a base for a parallel, voluntary system of regulation.

Outlook

The cases show changes in the arena that mean:

- A global dimension to the EU arena. Successful players recognize and exploit that change.
- New fora in which to set agendas. The ability to be in that part of the arena gives players the opportunity to contribute at the 'ideas' stage, even before policy-making begins.
- Rebalancing between the institutional players in the arena. The EP is powerful and effective in co-decisions, especially when these reach the stage of conciliation. It is also beginning to exercise power over comitology decisions. Lobbyists must and do recognize this. The presidency is emerging as a more significant player at the level of Council. The Commission, although it has formally lost a little power, remains the motor of the system and the priority for effective lobbyists.
- NGOs have more influence on the process. They exercise it both formally and informally.
- European Federations are no longer considered privileged partners for the Commission. Those that represent the industries of individual member states appear to be enhancing their influence. All federations, when well-directed, can be effective players and form part of winning alliances.
- Alliances are the key to achieving influence. They work when they give a new aspect to the case, by presenting a global front, or by combining commercial and civil society. They may be short-term or long-term.
- Self-regulation is increasingly a means of dealing with challenges from the institutions. This is especially true in cases that concern the 'new economy'.
- The winners are the players who recognize, indeed cause, these changes.

Lobbyists will over the next decade, be working in an EU that is itself becoming larger and more complex, as it grows from 15 to 27 members. Many of the new member states have a political background and culture very different from any of the countries that already belong. Lobbyists will face new challenges as the EU institutions, processes and systems adapt to take account of the new forces and the new opportunities of enlargement. The global forces that are already apparent will become even stronger, not least because the enlarged EU will be such a powerful player on the global stage. Among these forces will be the power of global NGOs and their ability to plan and execute campaigns using the new media of the Internet.

The cases show that the successful lobbyists of the future will be those who operate at the interface of the ever-faster-moving global economy and the still slow-moving processes of the EU. They will need to be creative to turn challenges into solutions.

Notes

1. Robert Hull, chapter in *Lobbying in the European Union*, Oxford: Oxford University Press, 1995.
2. R.H. Pedler and G.E. Schaeffer (eds), *Shaping European Law and Policy – the Role of Committees and Comitology in the Political Process*, Maastricht: EIPA, 1996.
3. J. Greenwood, *Inside the EU Business Associations*, London: Palgrave, 2001.

Index